L.F.C.

130 YEARS

L.F.C.

130 YEARS

THE ALTERNATIVE HISTORY

Reach Sport

L.F.C.
130 YEARS

First published in Great Britain in 2022

www.reachsport.com
@reach_sport

Reach Sport is a part of Reach PLC Ltd,
5 St Paul's Square, Liverpool, L3 9SJ
One Canada Square, Canary Wharf, London, E15 5AP

ISBN: 9781914197420

Photographic acknowledgements:
Liverpool FC Getty Images, Alamy.

Production Editor: Michael McGuinness
Writers: David Cottrell, William Hughes,
Chris McLoughlin, John Hynes
Jacket design: Colin Sumpter, Glen Hind

Printed and bound by CPI Group (UK) Ltd, Croydon, CR0 4YY.

Not your average history...

LIVERPOOL Football Club. Formed in 1892. Based at Anfield. Play in Red. Turned 130 in 2022.

What's new? LFC's history has been written about zillions of times and this book was first published in 2017 to mark the club's 125th anniversary. But it didn't include a Premier League title. Or winning the European Cup in Madrid. Or Virgil van Dijk, Alisson, Diogo Jota and Luis Diaz.

So to mark the 130th anniversary of Liverpool Football Club, we've updated our story. Split into 130 chapters, you won't find yourself journeying on a chronological trawl through the last 130 years. Nor is this a comprehensive compendium of everything that's ever happened at Anfield since 1892.

This is an alternative history of LFC. A collection of stories, memories and moments told from different angles and other perspectives by mixing star names, legendary managers and famous matches with lesser-known players, quirky occurrences and humorous happenings.

From John Houlding to Jürgen Klopp and the Team of all the Macs to Trent and Thiago, everybody you'd expect to find in a Liverpool FC history book is featured, but we also turn the spotlight onto less prominent Reds such as the striker who netted 18 goals in a youth team game, LFC's Wartime heroes and the stories behind everything from BOSS Nights and street art to tactical triumphs and the men who made the Shankly Gates. Those that we have lost are also remembered.

So what are you waiting for? Turn the page and indulge yourself in 130 years of LFC. We've got a hi**story** like no other...

About the authors

WILLIAM HUGHES

DESPITE colleagues claiming to the contrary, this William Hughes is not the man who played for Liverpool during the 1893/94 season. Rather, his greying locks are a tribute to Glenn Hysen. Bootle-born, his grandfather made several appearances for the club's Reserves in the 1930s. Having inherited his love of LFC, William was so keen to see Kenny Dalglish's side in action at Old Trafford in April 1987 that he stood on the Stretford End with a white 'Crown Paints' away top hidden under his coat. He had attended his first game in May 1980 – the testimonial of his first Reds' hero Ray Clemence – wearing a full LFC trackie. Hughes has worked on LFC publications for more than a decade and has included spending time at Melwood with a slipper-wearing Dalglish when helping write his manager's programme notes.

CHRIS McLOUGHLIN

THE son of an Evertonian who used to stand on the Kop during Merseyside derbies, McLoughlin thankfully listened to his granddad and supported Liverpool instead – a life-changing decision. A match-going Red since 1987, he edited The Kop Magazine for 15 years, has written for the LFC Magazine and the matchday programme for almost two decades and has penned a number of Liverpool FC books. A former Merseyside Junior Subbuteo Championship runner-up, McLoughlin has also been to a Polish BBQ with Jerzy Dudek, driven down the wrong ramp of a multi-storey car-park with Terry McDermott, had a night out in The Grafton with Didi Hamann and has been wearing the same Liverpool scarf since 1992, sparking claims that it was some kind of Premier League jinx until the Reds won the title in 2020.

DAVID COTTRELL

DAVE went to his first Liverpool game before he was born: his dad took along his mum, who was six months' pregnant with him, to the European Cup second-round second leg against Ajax at Anfield in December 1966. He was subsequently middle-named after one of the players on the pitch that night, but it wasn't Johan. He's enjoyed two stints editing the club's official matchday programme, and he can usually be found in Block 207 on the Kop on matchdays, just in front of Bobby and Eddie, a few rows down from Jim and Rob, half-a-dozen seats along from Steph, Bernie, John and Mick, and often gabbing with Frank the Flag at half-time.

JOHN HYNES

"WHERE were you in Istanbul?" was a chant directed towards LFC's rivals in the glorious aftermath of a fifth European Cup win. Hynes' answer to that query is 'Zanzibar' for it was there, despite a power-cut during the penalty shoot-out, that he watched the drama as a long-planned holiday coincided with 25 May 2005. Seeing such success up close as an Anfield regular had been decisive in John's move from Tipperary to Liverpool to attend university, and helped secure a dream job writing for the club in 2006. Only the pull of home eventually took him away from Merseyside in 2017. Still writing about LFC, his advice to his boys - Cormac loves Alisson and Charlie idolises Mo Salah - is to revel in the Klopp era and ensure holidays never clash with European fixtures!

1/130

In the beginning

THINK of Liverpool Football Club's founding fathers and the names John Houlding, John McKenna and William Barclay spring to mind.

But while those three men were undoubtedly powerhouses in helping to create the club we all love today, there would have been no LFC without the influence of Benjamin Swift Chambers.

He was the clergyman who changed the footballing landscape in Liverpool back in 1877 when he was appointed circuit superintendent and minister of St Domingo Chapel in the Everton district of the city.

After forming St Domingo Cricket Club for members of his congregation, Rev. Chambers established a football team to keep the cricket side fit during the winter months of 1878. The St Domingo Football Club soon attracted players from churches outside the parish too and so, in November 1879, it was felt appropriate that the football section of the cricket club be re-named Everton.

Of course, as we now know, if there had been no Everton Football Club, there would have been no Liverpool Football Club and so Chambers' role was pivotal in the foundation of both Merseyside's most successful clubs.

In Everton's last season before they joined the newly-created Football League in 1888, they paid Anfield landlord Houlding a rent of £100, but after finishing runners-up in their second league season the rent was set to be increased to £250 a year. Unhappy with this situation, the Everton committee met in May 1889 and decided to look for another ground. Some of them objected to having the club's affairs run from a licensed hotel, The Sandon, but others were reluctant to lose the money invested in the club's fixtures and fittings at Anfield.

A compromise rent of £180 was suggested to Houlding, who responded by offering Everton the whole plot for the then huge sum of £6,000.

When the club refused, Houlding served them notice to quit, and attempted to form his own Everton FC and Athletic Grounds Limited at Anfield (he succeeded, but the new club became known as Liverpool, with the league ruling that Everton could take their name with them).

Everton held a special meeting in January 1892, at which committee member George Mahon, an occasional organist at St Domingo, revealed that he had an option on a field on the north side of Stanley Park, called Mere Green.

On 15 March 1892 the formal parting of Everton from Anfield was announced and on 3 June, the Board of Trade sent a certificate to Houlding confirming that his club formally constituted a company and could now trade.

In the first decade of the 21st century, Ben Swift Chambers' grave at Shepley in Yorkshire was found in a dilapidated state by Wirral schoolteacher Peter Lupson, while researching his book on the church's early influence on the game, *Thank God For Football*.

Both Everton and Liverpool agreed to restore the grave in tribute to Chambers' influence on their respective histories and in 2008, the year that the city of Liverpool enjoyed Capital of Culture status, a special service took place at Shepley.

It was held on 2 July – exactly 131 years to the day that the Reverend Chambers took his first service at St Domingo.

Liverpool chief executive Rick Parry, Head of PR Brian Hall and club chaplain, the Rev. Bill Bygroves, represented the Reds, while Everton life president Sir Philip Carter joined former player Graeme Sharp and club chaplain, the Rev. Henry Corbett, on behalf of the Blues.

In a move to signify the unity of the clubs shown at the funeral of Anfield landlord Houlding when players from both clubs carried his coffin, Academy players from both sides were present with Cory Sinnott and Michael Jensen representing the Blues and Joe Kennedy and Shane O'Connor attending for the Reds.

Addressing the congregation inside the church, Rick Parry said: "It is right that Liverpool Football Club salutes a caring man, a committed man and a Christian man."

Sir Philip Carter added: "Ben Swift Chambers was a man of vision and real enthusiasm. Everyone involved in football on Merseyside owes him a tremendous debt of gratitude."

Both clubs contributed to the cost of restoring the grave. The stonework and engraved words on the headstone were cleaned up and undergrowth cleared around the plot.

It is now inscribed: "In Memory of the Rev Ben Swift Chambers. Born Aug 30 1845. Died: Nov 24 1901. Also his beloved wife Elizabeth who died 9 June 1925 aged 80 years."

The Latin words 'In Te Domine Speravi' are also engraved alongside one side of the grave which translates as: "In thee, O Lord, I have hoped."

A tablet was added at the bottom of the grave which reads: "In memory of the Reverend Ben Swift Chambers who set the ball rolling that led to the birth of Everton and Liverpool Football Clubs."

I name this club

IN many ways William Barclay is the forgotten man when people talk about significant figures in the early days of Liverpool Football Club.

There is no doubt that the two Johns, Houlding and McKenna, played a pivotal part in the club's formative days. But, after the split from Everton Football Club, it was Barclay who suggested to Houlding that the new club be named Liverpool Football Club.

Barclay was born in the Kilmainham Auxiliary of the South Dublin Workhouse on 14 June 1857, the eldest of five boys.

He married Emily Jane King on 5 June 1878 but the couple suffered personal tragedy in 1880 when they lost their first child, Harold David Grant Barclay before his first birthday. Understandably, the loss had a huge impact on their lives.

The Barclays lived in Everton Terrace after William took over as governor of the Liverpool Certified Industrial School. An Everton season ticket list of 1884/85 recorded Barclay as the club's vice-president. On 23 August 1888 he issued and signed the by-laws of Everton Football Club and was elected the club's vice-chairman on 9 June 1890.

Indeed it was Barclay who chaired the meeting at the Royal Street Hall on 15 September 1891 at which he proposed John Houlding's resolution to form Everton into a limited liability company. Four days after the Toffees decided not to accept Houlding's proposal, including the increased rent of Anfield, Barclay tendered his resignation from Everton Football Club.

He continued to work closely with Houlding in forming a new team to play at Anfield and proposed the name Liverpool Football Club in the belief that this name would attract supporters from all over the city.

Houlding then asked Barclay to run the new team along with local businessman McKenna. Barclay's role seemed to be the equivalent of a modern chief scout. A respected judge of a player, it also seems likely that he had an active role in team selection, effectively making him the first Liverpool FC manager.

An article in the *Liverpool Journal* published on 17 November 1894, recognised his attributes. It read: "Secretary of the Liverpool Football Club. A very great enthusiast in football management. Is a most successful organiser, a fine judge of the great game and knows everybody in the football world. Few men have travelled so much to football matches as he. One of Mr John Houlding's staunchest supporters. He is the successful headmaster of the Industrial Schools, Everton Crescent, and is, further, widely known and everywhere esteemed. An able man all round."

3/130

This was Annfield

MOST Liverpool FC fans are clued up on the history of the club's stadium: the plot of land was first used as a playing field as early as 1879 by original tenants Everton FC; the first stands for spectators were built along what used to be Kemlyn Road (later the Centenary Stand and now renamed the Sir Kenny Dalglish Stand) and Lake Street (today's Main Stand) as the area developed into a densely-populated suburb of the city.

But what about the ground's actual name? Does it have a more divine origin than people suspect? In fact is it even spelt correctly?

The name 'Anfield', so they say, comes from the 'Hangfields' or narrow strips of land which were there long before the famous football venue came along. Or does it? A closer look at some historic documents suggests another possible provenance.

One Ordnance Survey map from 1845, held by the city's Central Library Record Office, shows buildings in the district called Annfield House, Annfield Villa, Annfield Lodge and Annfield Cottage, none of which remain, plus Annfield Lane which eventually became Anfield Road.

There is also a St Ann's Hill House. St Ann or St Anne, by pure coincidence, was often depicted in a red robe and known as the patron saint of sailors and a protector from storms.

One hundred and seventy years ago the booming seaport of Liverpool was on the verge of a cholera epidemic, and its wealthier merchants had fled to leafy, healthier 'Annfield' and Breckfield to build the kind of grand houses your average professional footballer might live in today. On the 1845 map you can just make out Cabbage Hall Inn and Willow Bank House which survived as pubs, while the site of the modern stadium is a diamond-shaped field south of St Ann's Hill House between Annfield Lane and Walton Breck Road.

A later OS map of the area, this time from 1891, has more local landmarks: the Albert Hotel and Park Hotel, two much-loved matchday pubs today, plus the Royal Hotel, now the Arkles, named after a well-to-do Liverpool banker. But the stadium, with its distinct pairs of stands and pavilions, is clearly marked as Everton FC territory. Also shown is a 'Flagstaff' in one corner, home to the newly-installed top mast of the Great Eastern steamship.

This map was drawn up a matter of months before the great split which saw the Toffees move out and brewer and politician John Houlding found a new football club. Houlding's home, Stanley House, is also overlooking the park between the two grounds.

By 1928 LFC had been established for 36 years, having won four top-flight titles and reached its first FA Cup final in 1914, and an OS map shows the newly-roofed Spion Kop and a familiar step-ladder pattern of streets to the northwest and southeast, with the open spaces of Stanley Park (and a couple of nearby vicarages) to the north. By then that extra 'n' in the name had disappeared. This was, simply, Anfield.

4/130

Who's the Daddy?

FAST forward 25 years from now and can you imagine Mo Salah making tasty smoothies in a popular city juice bar?

It might seem far-fetched but the Reds did once pay a club record fee for a winger who later swapped his runs down the grassy flanks of Anfield for pulling pints at a favourite L4 watering hole.

Back in 1902, when LFC were not quite 10-years-old, the media was showing a keen interest in the man who became the club's record signing for the then princely sum of £460.

Arthur Goddard proved to be a fantastic servant to Liverpool and was a regular scorer from his position on the wing for nearly a decade-and-a-half.

After hanging up his reinforced toe-capped boots, he became a publican near the ground, running the Oakfield Hotel based at 47 to 49 Oakfield Road.

His footballing abilities came to the notice of Glossop when they played cup matches against Stockport County and they signed him during their only season in the Football League's top-flight in 1899. He continued to excel and joined Liverpool for that club record transfer fee in February 1902.

The *Manchester Evening News* reported at the time: "That Liverpool are seriously alarmed by their lowly and unfavourable position in the league is shown by the payment of one of the largest transfer fees on record for Arthur Goddard, the brilliant outside right of

Glossop. It is some weeks since negotiations were first opened up with [Liverpool manager] Mr Tom Watson, and both at that time and since it is no secret that at least four other prominent clubs made overtures to Mr Oliver and his fellow directors. It was thought at one time that it would end in Goddard going to Nottingham Forest, but the shrewd gentlemen who manage the Liverpool club clinched the matter."

Goddard was handed his debut at Wolves on 8 March, starting a run of 11 successive matches until the end of the season, in which he scored twice.

His exciting playing style was captured in a description by the *Lancashire Evening Post*: "Goddard is a clever dribbler, beats a half-back very smartly, and centres with excellent judgement. He is also a good shot, and plays the game most intelligently. At first he does not look fast, but his long strides take him over the ground quickly, and as an all-round player he has large possibilities."

In 1904/05 he won a Second Division championship medal and followed that by being part of the team that won the Reds' second First Division title a year later, doing so as the only ever-present in the side.

His popularity at Anfield was captured by a *Liverpool Echo* sketch which featured the following verse: "A marvel at playing the ball, His opponents he beats one and all; He's always so bright that as outside right, He is voted 'the Daddy of all.'"

Goddard was appointed captain ahead of the 1909/10 season and led by example as Liverpool finished runners-up in the league, their best placing since winning the championship in 1906.

Goddard contributed more to the goalscoring than in most recent years too – reaching double figures for the first time since 1903.

The 1913/14 season proved to be his final campaign at Anfield as he lost his place in the autumn and was given a free transfer to Cardiff City.

However, he returned to Liverpool as a wartime guest, making a further 49 appearances and scoring seven times.

In November 1915, Liverpool defeated Everton 4-1 in a Lancashire Section derby which attracted a crowd of 20,000 to Anfield. Fred Pagnam scored a hat-trick with Goddard also playing a starring role. In their match report, the *Liverpool Echo* stated: "The local 'derby' is now being talked over in the trenches. The Tommies will have some fierce arguments over the unexpected turn in events, and for the first time for sixteen years the Liverpool FC followers will be able to crow. It was a blow to all 'formulas.'

"Goddard's pertinacity and somewhat roving style brought him into the leading lights of the game. They call Goddard 'the old war horse'. But a man's as old as he feels, and Goddard can spend many a season yet as pivot of the team."

Goddard was nearly 40-years-old when he played – and scored – against Stockport County in a 4-2 win on 20 April 1918.

His status as one of the club's top players was further illustrated by the fact that he was granted two benefit matches – the league wins over Bolton Wanderers in January 1908 and Preston in March 1914.

In total, he made 414 appearances for Liverpool, scoring 77 goals before returning to the city in his capacity as pub landlord.

He is buried at Anfield Cemetery where a special commemorative plaque lies next to his resting place.

5/130

Oh when the Reds

LIVERPOOL Football Club. Red shirts. Red shorts. Red socks. Red all over.

You probably call them the Reds. Or the Redmen. Or even the Mighty Reds. The common theme is that three letter word. Red. Synonymous with all things LFC, the colour the club is renowned for wearing identifies the football club as much as, if not more than, anything else. Yet the famous all-red strip has been worn for less than half of the club's 130 year history.

Following Everton FC's departure to Mere Green Field – better known as Goodison Park – and the formation of Liverpool FC by John Houlding in 1892, Anfield's new tenants needed some clobber to wear.

Everton had left behind a set of Cambridge blue and white halved shirts with a buttoned collar – think Blackburn Rovers to picture it – before moving across Stanley Park, so when Liverpool FC took to the field for the first time in a friendly against Rotherham Town in September 1892 they did so in blue and white.

Ironically, Everton had started to wear cherry red following their move, only switching to an all-blue shirt in 1895, although it was 1901 before they adopted the royal blue they are now famed for.

With both Mersey clubs playing in a blue of some sort in 1895/96, Liverpool evidently decided to do something different and on 1 September 1896, for a Division One game against The

Wednesday at Olive Grove, they turned up in some noticeable new gear.

"Liverpool's new dress of red shirts and white knickers is striking," commented *The Cricket and Football Field*, "and a contrast to Everton's blue shirts and white knickers." Knickers, incidentally, referred to knickerbockers rather than frilly underwear as shorts weren't short enough to be called shorts back in the 1890s.

By 1904 Liverpool loved playing in red so much that the club, rather bizarrely, demanded that the Football League introduce a rule stating all clubs must wear a red shirt and white knickers for home games and a white shirt with dark knickers when playing away. Precisely why this was is unclear.

The men from the Football League, they said no, but in 1906 Liverpool again made the same demand and this time had the backing of Manchester United who themselves had adopted red shirts and white knickers after changing their name from Newton Heath in 1902. As you've probably guessed, both clubs were given the short shrift − or the knickerbocker shrift as it was maybe called back then − and didn't ask again.

At Anfield the red was here to stay until the summer of 1935 when the club introduced a burgundy shirt and, for the first time, red and white striped socks. The outbreak of World War II in 1939 resulted in the suspension of the Football League and when the action resumed in 1946 Liverpool were back in red shirts, now featuring numbers on the back following the introduction of new regulations.

Wartime shortages meant that Liverpool wore four different red shirts in 1946/47 including a tatty red one with a rounded neck and a red jersey with a white collar during a pre-season tour of the USA. They then began their league campaign in a red shirt with a red collar but later that season were photographed wearing a red shirt with a white rounded neck. Whatever they wore didn't harm the team's fortunes, however, with George Kay's men becoming the first post-war champions.

The first V-necked red jersey appeared in 1955 when optional short-sleeved shirts were also first introduced in response to the number of players, Billy Liddell being one of them, taking to the field with their sleeves rolled up. It was also the year when Liverpool started to wear the iconic Liver Bird upon their chests on the red shirt, having done so for the first time when wearing their change strip of white in the 1950 FA Cup final against Arsenal at Wembley.

Still, though, Liverpool's shorts remained white, something that only changed under the management of Bill Shankly.

After winning the First Division title in 1963/64, Liverpool had a first European Cup campaign to contend with and when the Reds drew champions of Belgium Royal Sporting Club Anderlecht in the second round, Shankly was a worried man.

The Belgians had more European experience, a team full of internationals – such as star forward Paul Van Himst – and Shankly had watched their key players in action for Belgium against England at Wembley.

"I had seen the Belgian team give England an exhibition at Wembley," he wrote in *Shankly: My Story*. "It was 2-2, but the score was a farce. Belgium had murdered England. When I came out of the ground I said to Joe Mercer 'Christ Almighty, how do we beat these?'"

The first leg was at Anfield so Shanks, fearing a tough task in Brussels, decided that his team had to not only win, but win well on Merseyside, to have a realistic chance of progressing. It was time for some of his famous psychology.

Real Madrid won the European Cup the first five times the competition was held, between 1955/56 and 1959/60, and Shankly liked the cut of their jib. He thought they looked smart in all-white – regal – and with Anderlecht playing in an almost identical strip it gave him an idea.

Captain Ron Yeats was pulled aside after a training session and asked to put on a pair of red shorts with his normal red shirt. "I had to run down the tunnel, up the stairs and then out," he recalled.

Shankly's eyes lit up. "Jesus Christ, son, you look about eight feet tall in that," he declared. "You'll scare the living daylights out of them."

Ian St John then suggested Yeats should wear red socks as well and that was it – Liverpool's now-trademark all-red strip was born. However, despite popular folklore to the contrary, pictorial evidence shows that Liverpool actually wore white socks with red tops below their red shirts and shorts against Anderlecht at Anfield, presumably because the club had been unable to source a set of red socks in time for the match.

They did, however, wear red socks during the second leg at Heysel Stadium in Brussels, meaning LFC's all-red strip was truly born in Belgium on 16 December 1964. Liverpool won that second leg 1-0 courtesy of a Roger Hunt goal having initially beaten Anderlecht 3-0 at Anfield on a night when Shankly gave 19-year-old Tommy Smith the number 10 shirt, but played alongside Yeats at centre-half, effectively inventing a new four-man defensive system.

The Liverpool manager subsequently decided to reserve the new all-red strip for 'special occasions' so there was surprise, therefore, when his side next took to the field in it: "Curiously enough Mr Shankly sent the team out equipped in their European Cup strip in which, of course, they are so far undefeated," reported the *Liverpool Daily Post* the morning after Liverpool won an FA Cup fourth round replay away to Stockport County, who had earned a shock Anfield draw the previous Saturday despite being bottom of the Fourth Division.

It remains unclear as to why Shankly picked Edgeley Park as the first domestic venue for Liverpool to play in all red at – perhaps it was a sign of how desperate he was to win the FA Cup – but with the *Daily Post's* Horace Yates commenting: "It may have been more than coincidence that Liverpool were more red-blooded in their efforts tonight than apparently they were on Saturday," and the Redmen winning 2-0, it further cemented the idea in Shankly's mind that the all-red strip gave his team an advantage.

For the rest of the 1964/65 campaign Liverpool continued to wear it in both the European Cup and FA Cup – which they won for the first time at Wembley – and on the opening day of the 1965/66 season they were dressed all in red for the first time in a league game, triumphing 3-1 away to Leicester City at Filbert Street.

Strangely, however, the Bill Shankly boys had white shorts back on again for the first Anfield game four days later against Sheffield United. The Blades won 1-0 – one of just two home defeats suffered in the league all season – and by the time Fulham arrived in L4 for Liverpool's next home match the white shorts had been discarded. Shankly's men won 2-1 and the all-red strip they wore that evening has remained a fixture ever since, bar for occasional kit clashes such as when white socks had to be worn in matches at Bolton Wanderers and Portsmouth.

The appearance of kit manufacturers' logos and shirt sponsors were the next major changes in the 1970s – the Reds became the first professional English club to feature a shirt sponsor in competitive games in 1979 – while a yellow Liver Bird had appeared on the shirt for the first time in 1976/77. It proved to be lucky as Bob Paisley's side won a league and European Cup double that season.

Pinstripes first appeared on the red jerseys in 1982 and since then all manner of different designs have been introduced – some more popular than others – while squad numbers and names on the back of shirts were introduced by the Premier League in 1993/94, a year after the division was formed. The strip that Liverpool wore during Brendan Rodgers' first season in charge in 2012/13 is also worthy of note as it was the first all-red strip featuring no white on it whatsoever that the club had ever played in.

To mark LFC's 125th anniversary in 2017, kit manufacturer New Balance created a special strip in a richer, darker red with a commemorative crest embroidered onto the breast and tonal pinstripes. The fundamentals, however, were still the same and have remained so since Nike took over as kit manufacturer in 2020.

Red shirt. Red shorts. Red socks. Red all over.

6/130

Big Macs

ONCE Liverpool Football Club was formed and given a licence to trade, they had to go about the business of finding players to build their first team.

It seemed appropriate that a man named John McKenna was handed responsibility for running the club, alongside William Barclay. As previously explained, secretary Barclay was effectively Liverpool manager from 1892, but McKenna was also heavily involved in team selection and recruitment before becoming club secretary himself in 1895.

McKenna was an Ulsterman who decided his best bet was to search Scotland in the hope of finding good quality players who would not cost a fortune.

Andrew Hannah, who left Everton to become Liverpool's first captain, was joined by his former team-mates Duncan McLean and Tom Wyllie in staying put at Anfield to help provide the backbone for the new team.

McLean became the first 'Mac' to register for LFC but such was the success of McKenna's recruitment policy north of the border, Liverpool were quickly dubbed as 'the Team of the Macs.'

Four 'Macs' were present in Liverpool's line-ups for the club's first games: a friendly against Rotherham on 1 September 1892 and the inaugural Lancashire League fixture versus Higher Walton a couple of days later. Joe McQue, Malcolm McVean and Jim McBride joined McLean in the starting elevens.

By the end of the club's first campaign, the number of Macs had doubled with eight featuring in the squad: Billy McOwen and John McCartney being joined by a pair of brothers who would be pivotal in the early history of LFC – Matt and Hugh McQueen.

Matt was already into his 30th year when he joined Liverpool, two months into the club's debut season. He featured regularly in his first four seasons at the club, making English football history as the only man to win two league medals, albeit in the Second Division, as both an outfield player and a goalkeeper.

Years later, in February 1923, he was offered the chance to take over as the team's manager when David Ashworth surprisingly left the defending champions to move to Oldham Athletic. McQueen duly saw the club safely through to their second successive league championship. However, a car accident in November 1923 changed his life as the joint Everton/Liverpool programme noted in March 1924. "Our opening note must be one of deep sympathy with the unfortunate and regrettable accident which occurred to Mr Matthew McQueen a little time ago, and which has led to the amputation of a limb. We are certain that all our readers will hope that the popular manager of the Liverpool club will speedily regain health and vigour and that his physical disability will not preclude him from enjoying many years of activity in the football world."

Sadly health issues led to McQueen resigning his position as manager in February 1928 but he continued to live just a stone's throw from Anfield at 32 Kemlyn Road. He was a regular and welcome visitor to the club from the day of his retirement until his death at the age of 81 on 28 September 1944.

Since that first LFC season of 1892/93, another 34 Macs have pulled on the Liverpool shirt, some to great effect.

Another Scot, Donald MacKinlay, played 433 times for the club and captained them to league titles in 1922 and 1923. His compatriots Jock McNab and Jimmy McDougall racked up 222 and 356 games respectively between 1920-1928 and 1928-1938. In the same era, inside-forward Archie McPherson scored 19 goals in 133 games.

During the 1970s and early 1980s, Englishman Terry McDermott became the club's most decorated Mac. Four league titles, three European Cups, two League Cups and one UEFA Cup were part of his roll of honour, along with the 1979/80 Football Writers' Association and Professional Footballers' Association Player of the Year awards.

Scotsman Kevin MacDonald was part of the Reds' league and FA Cup double-winning team of 1985/86 as was Englishman Steve McMahon, while another England international, Steve McManaman, starred in the 1992 FA Cup win over Sunderland and was also man of the match in another Wembley success, the 1995 League Cup final defeat of Bolton Wanderers.

Birkenhead-born Ireland international Jason McAteer was part of Roy Evans' Liverpool team of the mid to late 1990s and made 100 league appearances for the club, while it was another Scot, Gary McAllister, who made a telling contribution during the twilight of his career by helping the Reds claim a historic cup treble in the 2000/01 season.

The Scottish meaning of 'Mc' or 'Mac' in the prefix to a surname is 'son'. The contribution of these men to the story of LFC would have made the club's founding fathers extremely proud.

7/130

The leading of Liverpool

AS Liverpool Football Club celebrated its 130th birthday on 3 June 2022 it had amassed an astonishing 50 major trophies – the 2022 Carabao Cup and FA Cup wins completing the half-century – in domestic and continental competition.

Given the club's history, it was fitting that a Scotsman, Alex Raisbeck, captained LFC to a first top-flight title in 1901, following it with another in 1906. Another Scot, midfielder Graeme Souness, holds the honour of being Liverpool's joint-most successful skipper, lifting a magnificent seven major trophies: three league championships, three League Cups and a European Cup.

With Donald MacKinlay, Willie Fagan and Alan Hansen also lifting seven major trophies between them, Scottish players have captained LFC to 16 of those triumphs.

The responsibilities of a captain may have changed over the years but he has always been the leader on the field. The role has always existed as part of the laws of the game with the captain designated as the player who tosses up for choice of ends before kick-off.

For much of Liverpool's history, a winning call at Anfield has resulted in opting to kick towards the Anfield Road end in the first-half to enable the Reds to attack the Spion Kop as the game reaches its conclusion.

In Ragnhild Lund Ansnes' book *Liverpool Captains: A Journey of Leadership from the Pitch*, Souness said: "When I was starting off, maybe I wasn't at the races in the first-half and I'd be growled at by other players or Joe Fagan, Ronnie Moran and Bob Paisley. I like to think that when I became skipper, I did the same. Kenny [Dalglish] and I used to square up to each other, nearly had to be held apart at half-time. The young ones must have thought: 'what's going on here?' But we knew we'd win. Nobody spoke about it, nobody said anything. We knew.

"I was with the best club in the world at that time. We were winning everything. We looked like winning everything. We knew at the start of each season, when we were photographed along with the trophies, that there was a fair chance they were going to be in the same picture the following year."

As well as great Scots, there have been plenty of local lads who have worn the armband with pride, most recently Steven Gerrard, who captained LFC more times than anybody else [473]. Gerrard, widely considered one of the club's best ever players, led Liverpool to success in the European Cup, FA Cup and League Cup.

Speaking in *Steven Gerrard: My Captain's Book*, he explained: "I learned more from being Liverpool captain when things hadn't gone too well. You learn more in football from bad experiences. Obviously I had some tremendous highs as captain with the trophies I lifted – every time we won a football match and I was wearing that armband the feeling and the buzz was unbelievable – but going out of competitions, bad defeats or falling short in the league, you remember and learn from all of that too.

"In the Champions League final in Istanbul, everything was new for me and it took its toll. I wasted a lot of energy with nerves before the game, but I didn't make the same mistake again. When you're nervous you get tight, you don't make the right decisions and you don't play to the best of your ability. I think that probably showed in the first 45 minutes. The comeback was incredible, but we shouldn't have been in that position in the first place.

"As captain I felt more responsible, particularly when we got beat. I'm sure I speak for Jamie Carragher too. When we got on that bus after a defeat we knew there were hundreds of thousands of people around the world who were disappointed, but I'd argue to the death that there weren't two people who felt it more than me and Jamie. We were captain and vice-captain, the leaders in the pack."

Tommy Smith was the first Scouser to lead Liverpool to a major honour, inspiring the team to a fantastic double of league and UEFA Cup in 1972/73.

Phil Thompson was another local lad charged with leading the team, and a central defender who wore his heart on his sleeve. His two-year stint with the armband, starting in April 1979, brought further success to the club in the shape of a third European Cup, league titles number 11 and 12 and a first League Cup in 1981. Liverpool manager Bob Paisley once said: "I regard Phil as one of the best possible examples of a true professional."

'Thommo' said: "It is a great moment in your life when you get the nod to be captain of Liverpool Football Club. My nod came from Bob Paisley when we played Arsenal at Anfield in April 1979. It was an emotional day for me.

"An hour before kick-off, Bob gave me the captaincy. He never said to me that he saw me as a Liverpool captain, he just said: 'You're captain today, Phil.' I was enormously proud."

Robbie Fowler was another Scouser to lift a trophy, captaining Liverpool to League Cup glory in Cardiff in 2001, following in the footsteps of another great LFC centre-forward, Ian Rush, who had raised the same trophy aloft at Wembley six years earlier.

Emlyn Hughes and Alan Hansen were two fine players whose names go down in LFC folklore as inspirational leaders.

Emlyn, dubbed 'Crazy Horse', was originally an all-action midfielder but eventually moved back into defence. Soon after signing him from Blackpool in 1967, Liverpool manager Bill Shankly predicted that 'Crazy Horse' would captain England. He did and also became the first man to lift the European Cup for Liverpool, in 1977 and 1978. He also captained the team to two league titles, one FA Cup, a UEFA Cup and UEFA Super Cup, lifting seven trophies with the armband on.

Alan 'Jocky' Hansen took over the captaincy in the summer of 1985, promptly leading the team to a league and FA Cup double before lifting two further titles prior to a knee injury curtailing his glittering playing career in 1990. Bob Paisley described him as: "the defender with the pedigree of an international striker. He is quite simply the most skilful centre-half I have ever seen in the British game, a joy to watch."

Another Scottish centre-back to lead Liverpool was one of the most significant signings and skippers in the Reds' proud history. Ron Yeats was one of Bill Shankly's early signings, taking over the captain's armband from Dick White on Boxing Day 1961 and remaining as skipper until the end of the decade during which time he had led the team in 417 matches. He captained the team to promotion from the old Second Division and then to two top-flight titles. He was also the first Liverpool captain to lift the FA Cup in 1965 and led the Reds in their first European adventures.

Sami Hyypia was yet another centre-back who was enormously popular with Liverpudlians. The Finnish international had been brought to the club by Gerard Houllier in 1999 and two years later he was leading the Reds to two parts of their cup treble in the 2000/01 campaign: the FA Cup and UEFA Cup.

During the club's early years, full-back Donald MacKinlay had been a losing finalist in the 1914 FA Cup final but he recovered to skipper the side to successive league titles in 1922 and 1923. The long-serving Scot finally bowed out after 433 appearances.

In addition to the legion of leaders referred to above were men who led the Reds to single successes.

Scotsman Willie Fagan helped the side to the first post-war English league title, in 1946/47. A strong and skilful inside-forward who could also operate through the middle, flame-haired Fagan had cost the Reds £8,000 – then a record for a teenager – when he arrived from Preston North End. He was a frequent goalscorer and a popular choice to take the armband when Matt Busby departed in 1945; two years later came that championship medal.

Talented midfielder Ronnie Whelan became the only Irishman to lead Liverpool to a major trophy when he lifted the FA Cup following the Reds' 3-2 defeat of Everton at Wembley in 1989.

Three years later, England centre-half Mark Wright matched his feat as he led the Reds up the famous Wembley steps following a 2-0 victory over Sunderland. It was particularly poignant for Wright, who had broken his leg playing for Southampton against Liverpool back in the 1986 FA Cup semi-final. "My dad is Scouse and so are lots of my aunts, uncles and cousins," he explained. "There was only one place I wanted to go to and that was Liverpool. I lifted the FA Cup and thought: this is why I joined."

Jordan Henderson had become a Red in the summer of 2011 for similar reasons to Wright and replaced Steven Gerrard as captain in 2015. Yet, when the chance to collect his maiden trophy while wearing the armband came along after the 2-0 Champions League final victory over Spurs in Madrid in 2019, he wanted to share it rather than bask in the glory alone.

"That night was not about me lifting the trophy," he explained of the moment in the Wanda Metropolitano stadium. "I felt me, Millie [James Milner] and the gaffer should have lifted it together.

"The team photo would have meant the same if the manager was lifting the trophy and I was stood behind him. It was more about the team. When I look back and see the faces of the lads, that's what means more to me."

With both Milner and Jürgen Klopp politely declining the unbelievably generous invite, it was left to Henderson to joyously raise our sixth European Cup aloft – but not before he performed what has become known as the 'Hendo shuffle'.

Since then his fancy footwork has become a real symbol of success for the Reds. When they completed the job in competitions such as the Premier League, UEFA Super Cup, FIFA Club World Cup, Carabao Cup and FA Cup the eventual lifting of the hard-earned silverware was preceded by Henderson's joyful shuffle with the trophy in his hands before he thrust it into the sky.

It's a sight we all hope to see again on many occasions, perhaps in the not-too-distant future.

8/130

French connection

IF asked the question who scored Liverpool's first goal in Europe, you would presumably answer Gordon Wallace in Reykjavik. First goal in European competition at Anfield? Gerry Byrne.

However, that accepted wisdom could be challenged by a couple of fixtures that took place four years earlier.

Indeed some would argue that the Reds' first venture into European competition came during the 1960/61 season when they entered the Anglo-Franco-Scottish Cup, also known as the 'Friendship Cup'. A short-lived tournament, it was organised by the French Football Federation with French clubs competing against English and Scottish sides.

The original idea was to have four teams from Scotland and four from England competing together as one nation against eight teams from France. Due to an objection by the Scottish League, however, this proposed format was abandoned.

Two separate trophies were cast – one for Scottish clubs competing against French sides and another for English clubs taking on the chosen French representatives.

It was decided that individual clubs would not be able to win the competition, but instead a Ryder Cup-type system was introduced with respective countries being awarded points for aggregate victories.

Entry to the competition was based on a club's final league

position at the end of the previous season. With some sides guaranteed entry into official UEFA-endorsed European competitions such the European Cup and the Inter-Cities Fairs Cup (both of which started in 1955), the idea was that it would open up a chance for other clubs who finished lower down their domestic leagues to have a taste of Euro action.

Despite finishing third in the Second Division in 1959/60, the slightly random invitation process saw Liverpool asked to compete in the inaugural competition.

Before the English clubs got involved though, it was the turn of the Scots. Games were played home and away between August and December with Scotland emerging triumphant by three matches to one. Motherwell defeated Toulouse, Clyde saw off Lens and Dundee defeated Valenciennes.

Celtic would become the first British team to lift the European Cup in 1967 but their introduction to this competition was not so glorious as they were the only Scottish side to lose, going down 6-3 to Sedan on aggregate, following a 0-3 defeat in France with a draw at home. In fairness to Celtic they were third-choice representatives. Ayr United had initially been asked to compete but had to withdraw due to a lack of floodlights. They were replaced by Hibernian, who then pulled out due to a number of their players being involved in a match between an Edinburgh Select XI and Chelsea!

Newcastle United defeated Racing Club de Paris 3-2 in the opening match of the Anglo-French Friendship Cup in the French capital on 10 August 1960. The following day Liverpool took on Nantes at the Stade Marcel Saupin, nine days before Leeds United were due at Anfield for the opening Second Division fixture of the 1960/61 season. Roger Hunt scored the opening goal in a 2-0 victory six minutes before the break, with Kevin Lewis completing the scoring midway through the second half.

The Liverpool line-up that day was: Slater, Moran, Byrne, White, Leishman, Wheeler, A' Court, Melia, Lewis, Hickson, Hunt, but with a busy fixture schedule to negotiate, the second leg didn't take place until three-and-a-half months later!

It came three days after a 4-2 win over Sheffield United at Anfield with Liverpool running out 5-1 winners, Scottish midfielder Jimmy Harrower converting two penalties and Dave Hickson, Hunt and Johnny Wheeler also on the scoresheet.

Liverpool's 7-1 aggregate victory contributed to a 4-0 English clean sweep in the first Anglo-French Friendship Cup. Elsewhere, Newcastle completed a 5-3 aggregate win over Racing Club de Paris, Bolton Wanderers overcame Le Havre 5-1 across the two legs and Middlesbrough were 6-2 victors against Lille after winning home and away.

The competition didn't exactly capture the imagination of supporters however. Barely 72 hours after Anfield had accommodated just under 40,000 fans for the win over the Blades, a crowd of just over 10,500 turned up for the Nantes game.

It did take place again in 1961/62. France, represented by Le Havre, Rouen and Nimes, took on Aberdeen, Third Lanark and Motherwell respectively and won back the trophy with three aggregate victories to one.

England retained the Anglo-French version of the competition, winning 2-1 with one match tied. The second edition saw England represented by Southampton, Blackburn, Derby County and, curiously, Cardiff City!

With crowds still low and the concept of a Friendship Cup being undermined by a large number of bookings, the tournament was discontinued ahead of the 1962/63 campaign.

Liverpool however, had been given an early taste of continental cup competition which whetted the appetite for future glories in Europe.

9/130

Ship shape

A striking feature of Anfield that even pre-dates Liverpool Football Club's formation is the 50-foot flagpole that stands outside the Kop.

Most sources suggest the flagpole had once been the top mast of Isambard Kingdom Brunel's ship the SS Great Eastern before it was purchased by Everton FC from a shipyard in Rock Ferry in 1891. However, Kjell Hanssen, a respected historian with an interest in LFC-related newspaper cuttings, has found one article from 1906 which seems to challenge this perceived wisdom.

The paragraph in the *Sheffield Evening Telegraph* claims the flagpole may have been a part of the Royal yacht Alexandra though little other evidence exists to support this.

The Yorkshire newspaper stated: "Few among the thousands of habitues of the Liverpool Football Ground are aware of the fact that the enormous staff which bears the red flag of the club has historic associations. This flagstaff was formerly one of the masts of the old Royal yacht Alexandra, which was once much used by the Royal Family. It was the Alexandra which took the present King and Queen, then Prince and Princess of Wales, to Dublin on their first visit to Ireland so long ago as 1864. The Football Club acquired the mast through a captain now retired and living in the neighbourhood of the club's headquarters. The staff is a very high one, and a great deal of care had to be exercised in placing it in position. The flag it bears is of crimson colour, with a figure of the 'Liver Bird', so called."

However, the only yacht bearing the name Alexandra was completed in 1908, two years after the article was written. The only royal yacht that does fit the timeline is Her Majesty's Yacht Victoria and Albert II which was scrapped in 1904.

Virtually all other sources state the flagpole was taken from the Steam Ship Great Eastern in 1891 with reports explaining how it was floated across the Mersey and hauled up to Anfield by a team of horses before being positioned inside the corner of the Oakfield Road outer wall.

Flying from it later that year was the ground's first league championship flag as Everton won the First Division at only their third attempt.

The SS Great Eastern was an iron sailing steam ship built by J Scott Russell and Company at Millwall on the River Thames. At the time of her 1858 launch, she was by far the largest ship ever built at 292 feet and had the capacity to carry 4,000 passengers from England to Australia without refuelling.

Brunel knew her affectionately as the 'Great Babe'. He died in 1859 shortly after her ill-fated maiden voyage, during which she was damaged by an explosion. After repairs, she was used for several years as a passenger liner between Britain and North America before being converted to a cable-laying ship and laying the first lasting Trans-Atlantic telegraph cable in 1866.

She finished her life as a floating music hall and advertising hoarding for the city's famous Lewis's department store before being broken up in 1889.

The flagpole has remained a prominent feature of the ground throughout Liverpool's tenure of Anfield from 1892 and is a popular meeting point for fans at the corner of the ground where Walton Breck Road meets what used to be Kemlyn Road.

10/130

Lake Street Wall

IF you're a Red who has sat in the Main Stand lower tier, you'll know one of the first things you see after coming through the turnstiles is an unassuming gold line along the floor.

One of many nods to the past in the concourse, the line marks where the ground's boundary wall stood until late 2014 when demolition work began on the old car park wall as redevelopment work commenced to build a new Main Stand.

The wall might sound unremarkable in itself, but not when considered in the full context of the history of Anfield.

It had marked the original perimeter line of the stadium, and, prior to mass housing in the district, the boundary between the two fields owned and farmed by the Orrell brothers, Joseph and John. Everton had played on one side of the wall since 1884 and Liverpool after 1892, initially renting the field from John Houlding who had negotiated a deal with the Orrells and acted as representative tenant.

The wall has been seen in images from various decades and also marked the border of the Liverpool team's training area until their move to Melwood in the 1950s. The Main Stand's upgrade saw 500 bricks from the wall preserved for display in the club's museum.

LFC museum curator Stephen Done explained: "Although it was just a humble old wall, it was a very important part of everyone's matchday experience. People would come through the Shankly

Gates while the players used to park their cars there at one time...we were all familiar with it. There are pictures of Bob Paisley playing a game of football in the 1950s with the wall in the background.

"So from the public's point of view the most significant thing about Anfield changing was the wall coming down. It was almost a symbol that things are really moving forward.

"The wall could have been forgotten about but both the owners and the architects take the club's history very seriously and the idea is that the line that the wall took would be commemorated in the fantastic new building. So that wall will always be remembered as a symbol of football on Merseyside being played in that space."

A cast-iron sign for Lake Street was also salvaged from one elevation of adjacent terraced housing along with the bricks of the wall.

Renowned architect Archibald Leitch had unveiled ambitious plans for a revamp of Anfield in 1906, and his project included an impressive Main Stand which was better-known at the time as the Lake Street Stand, giving the sign a rich significance to the history of the club, just like that old perimeter wall.

11/130

Who shot Alf West?

LIVERPOOL had high hopes for talented full-back Alf West who made a solid start to his Anfield career after signing from Barnsley in November 1903. However, he would miss the first half of the 1904/05 season – after being shot by his athletics trainer.

As well as playing football, West was a keen sprinter and regularly took part in various athletics meetings during the summer break. It was while practising for an event in Cumbria that he was hospitalised.

According to the club's matchday programme: "West had been training for a 120-yards handicap and finished his preparation with a week at Lytham. Everything was complete, and he, accompanied by his trainer, William Norman, went to take the final spin before leaving for Keswick where he was due to run the following day.

"Not having had much practice at starting with the pistol, it was decided to adopt this method. Whilst the trainer was handling the weapon, it accidentally went off and West received a bullet under his right shoulder.

"He walked away some 200-yards, and then, staggering, fell into his trainer's arms. Fortunately the bullet did not penetrate the lungs, but spent itself by travelling along the outside of the ribs to the front part of the chest."

A gifted defender, the 21-year-old had been coveted by many clubs before he joined Tom Watson's charges at Anfield. It was widely thought that Small Heath (Birmingham City) had won the race for his signature but they failed to come up with an acceptable fee. It was later reported that Liverpool had stumped up £500 for his services, then a record fee for both selling club Barnsley and the Reds. In a *Sheffield Daily Telegraph* report of his move, the Nottingham native was deliciously described as being "a tee-toller *(sic)* and practically a non-smoker." Practically!

However, West was left in a critical condition after he was shot with two bullets just above the heart by Norman who was naturally said to have been "much upset."

It was only on Christmas Eve 1904 that West made his first appearance of that campaign before being given a warm welcome by Liverpudlians for the Boxing Day win over former club Barnsley.

His story made him something of an early cult hero at Anfield but his high skill levels quickly cemented a place as a regular in the Liverpool line-up.

An article in the club programme in March 1905 said: "West is an ideal full-back, reliable in tackling, and always cool and collected under the severest pressure. His methods are such as to commend themselves to all who desire to see football played with a maximum of skill and a minimum of physical force. West does not rely upon the latter quality; he calmly awaits the oncoming forward and judges the precise moment for intervention with admirable facility."

When Liverpool hosted Bury towards the end of his debut season with the club, fans clamoured for him to take a penalty after defender Jimmy Lindsay had tripped Reds forward Sam Raybould.

Raybould usually took on the penalty duties for Liverpool, but his record was mixed – he had missed four of the 10 spot-kicks he had taken. He was spotting the ball up for this one when the crowd bayed for the popular West to step forward and take on the responsibilities. The defender had not scored for Liverpool at that stage but it was reported that he struck the penalty with such force down the middle that Bury goalkeeper Hugh Monteith ducked out of the way!

He wasn't always so successful from the spot, however. When the Reds hosted Leicester Fosse in an FA Cup first round tie in January 1906, he missed two spot-kicks, one in each half, with both efforts saved by Leicester keeper Walter Smith who, presumably, was not quite as accommodating as Monteith. Thankfully for Alf and Liverpool, the visitors' Billy Bannister also failed with a penalty against Sam Hardy and Liverpool won the tie 2-1.

West made 16 appearances as the Reds won the Second Division in 1904/05 and he then missed just one game the following season as the club won its second First Division championship.

Following a brief stint with Reading towards the end of the decade, the full-back returned to Anfield in 1910 but only made four more league appearances for Liverpool before being transferred to Notts County.

He served in the First World War as part of the Footballers' Battalion and was wounded in action in 1916 but went on to recover and later earn a good reputation as a talented golfer.

There is no doubt that West was always a popular figure among the Anfield faithful and few Liverpool careers began in such strange circumstances.

12/130

He was just seventeen

NOVEMBER 2016. The Anfield scoreboard clock illustrates 80 minutes of the League Cup tie with Leeds United have elapsed when Gini Wijnaldum takes a pass from Divock Origi in the penalty area and then intelligently squares the ball towards the back post where a colleague is waiting in space. That happens to be Ben Woodburn, aged 17 years and 45 days, who with little fuss dispatches a first time finish high into the Kop net.

As he wheels away in euphoric celebration the teenager has little idea that he has just become LFC's youngest ever goalscorer, a record that was previously held by Michael Owen.

Owen was 98 days older when he came off the bench away at Wimbledon in 1997 to calmly slot the ball away after running on to a Stig Inge Bjornebye through pass, a sight that would become familiar over the years that followed.

Sandwiching Woodburn and Owen in the Reds' all-time top three list is winger Kaide Gordon who became Liverpool's youngest FA Cup goalscorer when he opened his account for the club in January 2022. Gordon was aged 17 years and 96 days when he latched onto a pass from fellow teenager Conor Bradley before calmly dispatching a clever finish at the Kop End during Liverpool's 4-1 third-round win over League One opponents Shrewsbury Town.

Woodburn, meanwhile, had also been part of the youngest ever starting line-up in LFC history in 2017 when Jürgen Klopp selected a team with an average age of just 21 years and 296 days at home to Plymouth Argyle in the FA Cup with captain Lucas Leiva being the oldest player a day before his 30th birthday. We say 'had' because during the 2019/20 campaign, the Reds twice named even younger starting elevens due to unusual circumstances.

In December 2019, Liverpool's senior squad were in Qatar to contest the FIFA World Club Championship given their status as European champions. However, the team had also progressed to the quarter-finals of the League Cup against Aston Villa in a game which was scheduled for the same midweek as the Reds' semi-final against Club de Futbol Monterrey in Doha.

Therefore Liverpool were left with no choice other than to field an Under-23s team for the fixture at Villa Park. The Reds, managed by U23s coach Neil Critchley, handed out a record eight senior debuts in a game which saw them beaten 5-0. The average age of the starting line-up was 19.48 years.

However, even that was eclipsed less than two months later when Critchley took on the role of manager again for an FA Cup fourth-round replay against Shrewsbury Town. After being held to a 2-2 draw in the initial clash at the New Meadow, the date for the replay fell at the same time as the Premier League's first ever winter break.

Klopp was adamant that his senior side needed that break as they aimed to follow their triumph in Qatar by maintaining their pursuit of a first Premier League title. So Critchley took the reins again and named a team with an average age of just 19 years and 102 days for the game at Anfield. Liverpool won too, emerging as 1-0 victors thanks to an own goal by Shrewsbury defender Ro-Shaun Williams from a Neco Williams pass.

Prior to 2017, the youngest team in the history of the club had been chosen by Bill Shankly for a league fixture with Wolves just ahead of the 1965 FA Cup final. Clearly with the Wembley meeting with Leeds United on his mind, the Scot selected a team that had an average age of 22 years and 83 days. Included amongst the XI who won 3-1 at Molineux that Monday evening were debutants Alan Hignett, Thomas Lowry, Billy Molyneux and John Sealey.

When it comes to the youngest player in the Reds' history the Midlands also features as it was at West Brom in a 2012 League Cup outing that Jerome Sinclair – aged just 16 years and six days – came off the bench to help Brendan Rodgers' men triumph 2-1. The Jürgen Klopp era has seen another three names enter the top five list of the Reds' all-time youngest debutants with Harvey Elliott, James Norris and Kaide Gordon also playing before their 17th birthdays.

At the completely opposite end of his career was goalkeeper Ned Doig, who featured in his final LFC outing against Newcastle in April 1908, aged 41. A £150 purchase from Sunderland who had started out as a winger in amateur football, his record as Liverpool's oldest player is unlikely to be beaten, even by James Milner!

Amongst the many feats the legendary Billy Liddell accomplished during his time at Anfield was to become our oldest ever goalscorer. He did so by finding the net as a 38-year-old in a 5-1 rout of Stoke City in March 1960.

Nowadays, of course, anyone who reaches such an age, or older, has the opportunity to play for the LFC Legends XI with Steven Gerrard, Jamie Carragher, Luis Garcia, Dirk Kuyt, Vladimir Smicer and Patrik Berger amongst those who enjoy a run-around to raise funds for the LFC Foundation – and the chance to display that they've still got it!

13/130

The hard road back

AS annoying as a poor performance or result can be and as frustrated as you might feel if an attempted transfer target fails to walk through the Shankly Gates, perspective is something that no Liverpool supporter should ever lose sight of. Nothing should be taken for granted. There is no divine right to success. Everything achieved here had to be earned.

As hard as it might be to comprehend now, Liverpool endured eight seasons, between 1954 and 1962, in the Second Division. The previous two years were spent battling against relegation – a fight that was depressingly lost – and things weren't much better in the FA Cup with ignominious defeats at Division Three South Southend United (1957) and non-league Worcester City (1959) serious low points that we've thankfully never experienced again since.

The appointment of Bill Shankly in December 1959 was the biggest turning point in the history of our football club and by 1962 he had led Liverpool back into the First Division. But are you aware of how he did it?

Shanks revealed all in a 14-week series of articles published in the *Football Echo* in the summer of 1962 (that were rediscovered and subsequently republished as *Shankly: The Lost Diary* in 2013 to mark the 100th anniversary of his birth). Written in his own indomitable style, in unprecedented detail spanning over almost 25,000 words, an unusually candid Shankly provided a quite remarkable insight into how he transformed Liverpool Football Club, starting with introducing a new training regime.

"I was most fortunate in having a really first class team in Reuben Bennett, Bob Paisley and Joe Fagan, and no praise can be too high for their efforts. Between us, we set about preparing a plan for improving the training routine and the facilities which at the time existed at Melwood. We reorganised the whole training system."

One specific change Shankly made was to split his players into groups and give them different training programmes whereas previously the entire squad had followed the same routine irrespective of their physical condition. He also took a new approach to player involvement in tactics.

"Another aspect of training in which I believe in implicitly is that of tactical talks. A tactical session is more like a good discussion in the Forces with me as the officer leading it. I start the ball rolling, but anybody who has anything to say knows that he is expected to say it. When necessary I become chairman and call the meeting to order, but I have found this method gets results because everyone has his chance of voicing his opinion."

Shankly also set up what he called "a first class nursery," – effectively the first Liverpool FC Academy – to plan ahead for the future and, to get the best out of the players he had at his disposal, introduced a new 3-3-4 formation, the like of which had never been seen before. However, in 1960/61, his first full season as Reds boss, promotion was missed by one place and with the play-offs still 30 years away from being invented another season in the doldrums beckoned.

That summer, with substantial transfer funds finally made available to him by the Anfield board, Shankly was able to make the team-transforming signings of fellow-Scots Ian St John and Ron Yeats. They became the spine of his team, yet quite incredibly

The Saint only became a Red because Shankly had spotted a paragraph in a Sunday paper stating that he had indicated a desire to leave Motherwell. The following day, Shanks drove straight up to Scotland with Liverpool chairman TV Williams and didn't leave until he had thrashed out a deal.

"The tug-o-war dragged on until well past midnight, and eventually agreement was reached. We had the most delicate part still to do and that was to persuade this great little player and his wife that it would be in their interests to come to Liverpool. St John was introduced to members of the board and then whisked away by car with Mrs St John to view the particular house we had in mind for them. My male readers will understand my relief when they returned with the news that Bette St John was extremely pleased with what was to be her future home."

Despite his star billing, St John was paid exactly the same as every other Liverpool player – Shankly's socialist views made him a vocal opponent of the abolishment of the maximum wage – and with Yeats also on board, plus the established Dick White appointed as captain, the Reds were ready to push for promotion from day one, beginning with a 2-0 win at Bristol Rovers.

"My study of the fixture list gave me the impression that the early matches were the difficult ones. I wanted a good start to the season for both practical and psychological reasons."

Shankly's attention to detail was also coming to the fore and was best exemplified before an August midweek match at promotion rivals Sunderland's Roker Park.

"It was a bright sunny evening and this fact presented a tactical problem which I found difficult to solve; in fact I never solved it. The sun was commencing to set behind one of the goals and it was obvious that until it dipped below the levels of the stand, defenders would find it almost impossible to 'find' a ball against a backdrop of blinding light.

"I made enquiries from the locals about the time it took for the sun to fall below the top of the stand, but I was not able to get any information. I even tried timing its rate of settling, but this turned out to be quite futile. After all this, Dick White lost the toss and I could scarcely believe my eyes when I saw that Sunderland had chosen to play into the sun!"

The Reds won 4-1 and Sunderland eventually missed promotion by a point.

Liverpool's other opening away games also saw them visit Norwich, Brighton and Newcastle – about 1,800 miles in total for the five fixtures – but rather than simply travel by train to each venue, as was conventional at the time, Shankly instead opted to go by road to some as it meant his team could return home immediately after Saturday games instead of wasting a Sunday recovery day on a return train.

Things didn't always go to plan when travelling by rail or road. A connecting train from London to Norwich became stranded in Colchester during a heatwave on Shanks' birthday, meaning Liverpool only arrived at Carrow Road half an hour before kick-off and, after they won 2-1, the bus taking them back to the station failed to turn up.

The result was that Shankly and as many of his players as possible piled into Norwich keeper Sandy Kenyon's car for a lift to Norwich Station while the rest of the squad faced a brisk mile-and-a-half-walk in 80 degree heat to ensure they didn't miss the train!

There were far fewer issues on the pitch.

Shankly's side kept winning, scored 99 goals in total, were never lower than joint-top of the table and had promotion back to the First Division secured on 21 April, after a 2-0 Anfield win against Southampton, with five league games still to play.

"Quite truthfully, our promotion marks the proudest moment of my life," he wrote before turning his attention to the Anfield crowd.

"It is difficult to generalise when writing of so many thousands, but I have the feeling that they and I have one thing in common. They hate to be beaten and so do I."

So the next time you feel frustrated if the Reds haven't won or didn't get a transfer target, remind yourself that you support a club that spent eight consecutive seasons in the second division.

It quickly puts things into perspective.

14/130

Gone to Iceland

"WE were close enough to see lava spilling everywhere. It's not every day you see an erupting volcano when you're on the way to a game."

If Liverpool FC thought European football was to be a trip into the unknown, the words of midfielder Willie Stevenson confirmed such.

The Scot was part of the Liverpool party that flew from Prestwick Airport near Glasgow to Iceland in August 1964 to contest the club's first match in the European Cup against Knattspyrnufelag Reykjavikur (or KR Reykjavik!)

Before boarding the flight, Stevenson and company had taken a six-hour bus ride from Liverpool to their overnight headquarters. As the team coach pulled up outside their accommodation, there followed a famous exchange involving team manager Bill Shankly.

At his behest the Reds' base for the evening was Butlin's holiday camp in Ayrshire.

Stevenson recalled: "From the front of the bus, Bill stepped forward and informed the security guard: 'We are Liverpool Football Club and we are on our way to Europe...'

'Then I think you're on the wrong road,' replied the guard."

Playing in the European Cup was the Reds' reward for winning the league in 1963/64 and Shankly's men had undergone a testing preparation with a gruelling pre-season tour of the USA.

Forwards Ian St John and Alf Arrowsmith missed out on the club's first European adventure due to injury. Even so, the home side's chairman, Einar Saemundsson, was still anticipating a Liverpool victory. "We expect to receive a lesson but with such opponents it will have been worthwhile," he told the local press on the eve of the game. "Only one thing is certain – this is the end of the road for us in Europe."

A noisy crowd of more than 10,000 were full of hope as they welcomed their heroes onto the pitch. KR were decked out in black-and-white stripes, a kit that dated back to 1912 when the club won the inaugural Icelandic title and the club's board decided that they would henceforth wear the same colours of the English champions of that year: Newcastle United.

Gordon Wallace, who had recovered from a broken leg inside a matter of months, was selected to fill one of the forward berths and he calmed any nerves by putting Liverpool in front in the third minute. The Reds went on to record a comfortable 5-0 victory with Wallace and Roger Hunt scoring twice each and Phil Chisnall netting his first goal for the club.

A month later, Reykjavik, who were the first Icelandic team to play in Europe, made the return trip to Anfield with Liverpool winning 6-1 to complete an 11-1 aggregate victory. They made the most of it after the game with a couple of nights out in a city centre which was fast becoming the continent's capital of culture.

Stevenson recalls: "The Kop took pity on Reykjavik and by the time we'd reached double figures on aggregate, the fans started booing us whenever we attacked! It was typical Scouse humour."

On that occasion Gerry Byrne scored an early opener – the Reds' first European goal at Anfield – before the returning St John scored twice, his goals sandwiched either side of efforts from Hunt, Bobby Graham and Stevenson.

Victories over Anderlecht and Cologne set-up a semi-final with Inter Milan which saw the Reds controversially eliminated 4-3 on aggregate following some more than questionable refereeing decisions during the second leg played in Italy. It cost Shankly's side a place in the final against Benfica and the chance to end their first season in Europe as champions.

Liverpool's trip to the world's northernmost capital city was a humble beginning to an explosive history in European competition and one that left a lasting impression on all those involved.

15/130

Big Al

TALL, rangy, elegant, classy… All adjectives associated with the best kind of Liverpool centre-halves in the last four decades or so, most recently embodied by Joel Matip and before him Sami Hyypia, and most certainly originating with Alan Hansen.

One piece of vintage game footage epitomises what made Hansen special, even if it's hardly Kenny Dalglish's best moment in a Liverpool shirt. It's Old Trafford, April 1980, and it's one apiece between Manchester United and Liverpool in the first half after goals from Dalglish and Jimmy Greenhoff. In the centre-circle Hansen has the ball at his feet as the entire United outfield team charges forward to catch the visitors offside. Without hesitation he chips it over all of them and surges onto his own pass, suddenly and sensationally alone in the United half, bearing down on goalkeeper Gary Bailey with referee Pat Partridge correctly waving him on.

Kenny sprints to Hansen's left with not a single United player in sight. They're inside the six-yard box now, Bailey bolt-upright, resigned to being beaten. If you've never seen it, Google: 'Dalglish miss Old Trafford'. The build-up is sublime but the last bit should be viewed from behind the sofa.

"He was onside, but I was offside," Dalglish recalled. "They tried to push up and Big Al's cleared the lot of them and ran after it. In my stupidity, and I must have got a good start, I was the first one up to support him, and Gary Bailey started running backwards towards goal. Big Al's run in and I'm going: 'Hit it! Hit it!'

"He doesn't really want to hit. Sometimes if Big Al couldn't get rid of it, he'd get a wee bit of fright when he got up in the opposition half. So he takes another touch, and I get up beside him. And he looks at me, and he just dips his shoulder. Sells the goalie a dummy, sells me a dummy too. And I'm waiting for the pass. He's knocked it in front of me and I must be a yard out in front of the Stretford End…and I missed it. That wasn't a very pleasant moment…"

A rare one, too, when the duo got their wires crossed.

It's now almost four decades since Hansen, Dalglish and fellow countryman Graeme Souness played together in a Liverpool XI. Kenny turned 71 in March 2022, Souness 69 in May, Hansen turned 67 in June.

For Liverpool fans that remember his earliest appearances in the red shirt as a youthful centre-half with a touch of unquestionable class, it's hard to believe. So too is a myth peddled by some of a similar age down the East Lancs Road that in those same days when Liverpool reigned supreme – most of the 1970s and 80s – Manchester United were better to watch.

United were always the 'glamour team', of that there is no doubt. They also had players like Gordon McQueen and Kevin Moran in central defence. They didn't have anyone like Hansen.

In his first season with the Reds, aged 22, he'd won the European Cup. The final was his 26th appearance of the campaign, having replaced the injured Tommy Smith (who'd contrived to drop a pick-axe on his foot in a bizarre accident at home) for the three league games leading up to the final.

As a youth international Hansen had represented Scotland in three other sports – golf, volleyball and squash – before joining elder brother John at Partick Thistle where he played as a winger then centre-half. When he moved to Liverpool for £100,000 in May 1977 his arrival was noted in one brief paragraph on page 32 of the matchday programme for a title-clinching match against West Ham United. "I have high hopes for him," was the simple appraisal from manager Bob Paisley.

A dozen years later Tom Saunders, the club's youth-development officer, revealed in the programme that Hansen had been rejected by Liverpool as a 15-year-old following a four-day trial: "We've never claimed to be infallible and Alan is one of the youngsters whom we allowed to leave after a very brief period of time. He came down to Anfield with three or four other lads from Scotland, but we didn't take matters any further and he returned home.

"There are so many things to consider when it comes to signing a lad of that age," continued Saunders, "and obviously we couldn't have been sufficiently convinced. Alan admits that until he left school at 18 he enjoyed his golf more than playing football, yet he never felt he was good enough to become a professional golfer. He had no thoughts of becoming a professional footballer either – but after ten weeks of working in an insurance office he realised that wasn't for him.

"Newcastle and Bolton both had ideas about signing him, but with Partick battling to avoid relegation they wanted to keep him. That was when we appeared on the scene again – and so Alan returned to Anfield, this time to sign on the dotted line as a fully-fledged professional. We'd been keeping an eye on him for the best part of two years, and even when we signed him he was 'one for the future'.

"Geoff Twentyman, our chief scout, watched Alan play various roles: as a sweeper, in defence, and as a midfielder. He was a good reader of the game, possessed good control, and passed the ball well. Geoff remarked that because he made everything look so easy, Alan was not an easy player to assess."

Dalglish joined Liverpool three months after Hansen. They became pals but tended to avoid each other before a game in the dressing room. Kenny recalled: "I'd be in the shower room, trying to get a feel for the ball, booting it against the wall, because we'd never go out for warm-ups then. Big Al would sit reading the programme. I don't know whether he was relaxed, but he'd be reading it."

He wasn't, far from it. Perhaps finding strength in numbers as one of the team's dapper Scottish contingent, Hansen steadily became one of the big beasts in the dressing room jungle and a notorious practical joker. But in the early days of his Anfield career he's since admitted he felt "totally inadequate and out of my depth.

"In 1977 they thought I was the coolest character. I never warmed up and I'd sit in the dressing room holding the programme singing the Billy Joel song *Don't Go Changing*. They'd look at me and go: 'That's unreal for a kid'. But underneath I was scared."

On the pitch though it was a different story, with Hansen explaining: "To have someone like Kenny up front, to hold your passes and turn them into golden goalscoring opportunities, was manna from heaven. When possible we'd give each other a little hand signal – mine to let him know I wanted to pass to him and his told me which side he wanted it. He could always be relied upon to turn a bad ball into a good one. This did wonders for my confidence."

Hansen's languid gait belied excellent anticipation and a refusal to hoof the ball upfield. Like a young Franz Beckenbauer, with whom he was compared, he always seemed to have time on the ball. Most thrillingly he could stride out of defence and straight into the heart of enemy territory to set up attacks, the way he did at Old Trafford.

Against Bruges at Wembley two years earlier his accomplished display at the back epitomised a new, improved Liverpool that refused to panic when presented with stubborn opposition – particularly in Europe – and remained patient in its approach. Incredibly, Hansen was back in the reserves at the start of the following season, 1978/79, but when Emlyn Hughes got injured he regained his place and never relinquished it.

Hansen won two more European Cups with Liverpool, in 1981 and 1984, and was the last man to lift the old Football League championship trophy for Liverpool – his eighth in a red shirt – in 1990. By then he was club captain, and at the end of that season he retired with 620 appearances to his name.

Over two decades as the voice of football punditry on BBC's *Match of the Day* were about to begin.

16/130

Billy Liddell's cocktail cabinet

CHANCES are that at some stage you've received a Christmas present that isn't particularly useful.

Whether you're a vegetarian who was given an Atkins Diet cookbook, the owner of a 10th floor flat who found a garden gnome in your Christmas stocking or your nan got you a set of fluffy dice for your moped, you'll understand how Billy Liddell felt at Christmas 1957.

Our legendary Scottish forward was teetotal – he once refused to even sip from a glass of wine offered to him by the Liverpool-supporting crew of a ship he was on, instead insisting on orangeade – so when the Anfield board decided to honour Billy for becoming the Reds' all-time leading league appearance maker in 1957 they chose a rather bizarre gift: a cocktail cabinet.

He may have left opposition full-backs shaken and stirred through a heady cocktail of sublime skill and sheer power, but the most Cosmopolitan thing about 'King Billy' was that he was a Scot from the mining town of Townhill playing 'fitbae' in England. Fortunately Liverpool chairman TV Williams also presented Liddell with the more useful gifts of a radiogram and a china cabinet, but it wasn't the only occasion when the club didn't quite get things right regarding one of our all-time greats.

Billy was such an unknown when he first joined Liverpool as an amateur from Scottish junior club Lochgelly Violet in 1938 that nobody was quite sure how his surname was spelt. "Believe it or not," wrote esteemed *Liverpool Echo* reporter 'Ranger', "Liverpool club officials did not spell his name correctly and for several weeks gave it out as 'Liddle'."

By the time he made his club record-equalling appearance at home to Notts County on 9 November 1957 everyone knew who Billy Liddell was, although a statistical miscount at the time meant it was believed he was passing Elisha Scott's tally of 430 that afternoon when in reality he did so away to Ipswich Town the following weekend. Even so, there was plenty of press coverage, all the Notts County players lined up in the centre-circle before kick-off to shake hands with him and the Liverpool skipper marked the occasion with one of his 228 goals for the club in a 4-0 win. Not that he enjoyed the limelight.

"I am not overkeen about records," wrote the 35-year-old in his *Football Echo* column, "this afternoon's game will just be another match to me. There are far too many more important things to think about in life than the goals I've scored. The goals to come, for instance." He later admitted: "The press made so much of this milestone in my career that, for the first time in my life, I felt self-conscious as I ran onto the field before the match to great applause from the crowd."

Despite his dislike at being the centre of attention, there can be no denying it was richly deserved. To some Liverpool supporters in the 1950s, William Beveridge Liddell was THE reason to go to Anfield every other Saturday when the Redmen were languishing in the second division. Billy was our first post-war superstar – if such a thing existed back then – yet playing football for a living wasn't always on the cards.

"As a youngster, just leaving school, it was a toss-up which way fortune led me," he wrote in the *Football Echo*. "I had no particular preference for anything. The minister of the church, which I and my parents attend, suggested that I might go into his profession, or failing that try for a job in the Civil Service. It was the late Mr George Kay, then manager of Liverpool, who tipped the scales in favour of football."

Kay, Liverpool boss from 1936 to 1951, had been tipped off about Liddell's ability by his captain, Matt Busby.

"As a Liverpool player I still retained many connections with Manchester City and my playing colleagues at Maine Road," wrote Sir Matt in *Matt Busby, My Story*. "Alex Herd and I, as playing colleagues, used to play a lot of golf together in Scotland during the close season and I saw no reason why my move to Merseyside should interfere with such enjoyable summertime activities.

"One day Alex did not turn up for his round of the bunkers and when I went in search of him I was told that he had taken Willie McAndrew, the Hamilton Accies manager, in his car to see a 15-year-old boy called Liddell playing football for Lochgelly Violet. No business was done with Hamilton because Billy Liddell's parents wanted some assurances about their son's future in the game and Willie McAndrew's club were not really in a prosperous enough state to make lavish promises in that line.

"When Alex Herd told me the story, I immediately telephoned George Kay at Anfield and suggested he might succeed where Hamilton Academical had failed. He did, and Billy Liddell became a Liverpool player, a very fortunate day for Liverpool."

That was in July 1938, but it was nine months later before Liddell signed a professional contract and even then his parents weren't quite convinced football was the right career for him so they had it written into his contract that he would also work at Liverpool accountancy firm Simon Jude & West. So, while the rest of his Anfield team-mates trained full-time, Liddell joined them for just two mornings a week (Tuesday and Thursday) then played on a Saturday, although he had to wait until January 1946 to make his full Liverpool debut due to World War II, during which he served as a RAF navigator having travelled to Canada to learn the job.

He did, however, score 82 goals in 152 wartime appearances for the Reds so when Billy netted twice in an epic 7-4 Anfield victory over Chelsea on his league debut in September 46, Kopites already had an inkling that the 24-year-old was a special talent. Liverpool went on to be the first post-war champions in 1946/47, but that was Liddell's only honour in a red shirt with the kicking he received from Arsenal's players in our 1950 FA Cup final defeat, something he had to get used to. Second Division football, after the Reds' relegation in 1954, was even harder to accept.

Liddell's ability to strike the ball – and the old leather footballs they used back in the day got a lot heavier when it rained – was his calling card. Reports suggest he took a White Hart Lane net off some of its crossbar hooks when scoring a hat-trick there in 1951 and had a unique method of striking free-kicks 'straight on' with his body-shape reminiscent of the technique now adopted by Cristiano Ronaldo and Gareth Bale. Indeed, he struck one such free-kick so hard in a 5-2 win against Nottingham Forest at Anfield in 1955 that visiting keeper Harry Nicholson fractured his arm when tipping the ball over the bar.

Billy also proved his loyalty to Liverpool in 1950 when the Bogota-based club Santa Fe twice tried to persuade him to move to South America to play in El Dorado – a rebellious Colombian Football League that broke away from FIFA – but he turned down the opportunity to cash in, saying he was happy living in Liverpool with wife Phyllis, whom he married in 1946. "I think it was estimated to be worth a total of £12,000 which was a huge sum in those days," recalled Phyllis in *Billy Liddell – The Legend Who Carried The Kop*. To put his decision into perspective, the maximum wage a footballer could earn at the time was £12-per-week. It would've been some pay rise.

A father of twins, David and Malcolm, Billy's devotion to his family was perhaps best emphasised when his father died in 1951, leaving his mother looking after three young children. He immediately invited them all to live in his home on Westfield Avenue in Knotty Ash before moving Phyllis and the kids to a new property.

He also became a Justice of the Peace in 1958, was heavily involved in the church, a treasurer at Huyton Sunday School and gave his time up for various charitable projects, including Dj-ing for young patients at Alder Hey on the hospital radio. Every Liddell helps.

Aged 39 when he made his final Liverpool appearance in 1960 at the beginning of the Bill Shankly era, Liddell hung up his boots after netting 228 goals in 534 games for the club. Add his wartime statistics on and his tally rises to 310 goals in 687 appearances, a figure only Ian Rush can better.

No wonder Kopites raised plenty of glasses to 'King Billy' during his outstanding Liverpool career, even if he wouldn't have done so himself.

17/130

Reds on tour

SINCE the summer of 2014, the Reds' pre-season tours have taken them to America, Thailand, Australia, Malaysia and Hong Kong.

The COVID-19 pandemic intervened, preventing summer tours in 2020 and 2021, but tours will resume in 2022 and such is the club's global appeal there is often pandemonium wherever the players go. In many places they are greeted by local fans amidst chaotic scenes reminiscent of Beatlemania.

It was a very different situation when LFC embarked on their second overseas tour in 1914. The players set sail for Sweden and Denmark 11 days after completing their 1913/14 league programme with a 2-1 win over Sheffield United at Anfield, which had helped them finish 16th in the 20-strong Division One table.

The travelling party arrived virtually unnoticed with the players slipping into Gothenburg the picture of working-class men with their waxed haircuts and centre-partings.

Rather than emerging from a first-class flight which had soared through the sky, they stepped off the boat following a gruelling three-day journey which had taken the Reds to the Swedish port via Harwich, Holland and Hamburg.

Despite the effects of the travel, the Liverpool squad led by manager Tom Watson were excited at the prospect of embarking on the club's first foreign tour. One of the players, Thomas Fairfoul, kept a diary of the trip which took in seven games in 17 days in

Gothenburg, Stockholm and Copenhagen. Lining up alongside players such as Elisha Scott, Don MacKinlay and Ephraim Longworth, the right-half recorded events as they unfolded in Scandinavia.

On the evening of the Reds' first fixture, a 4-1 victory over local side Orgryte, Fairfoul wrote from his room at the Hotel Eggers in Gothenburg: "We arrived here on Saturday after travelling for three days. We had an inspection of the ground previous to turning out. It is really a skating pond, but they run water off in the summer.

"The surface is covered with gravel and rolled as hard as our toll roads. I may say the look of the pitch caused serious misgivings amongst our boys, especially the wing players, as a cement cycle track runs right along the touchline, and it is much closer than Aston Villa's used to be.

"I won't attempt to give the Swedish team, but had the players been as formidable on the field as their names appeared on paper we would have stood a very slight chance of winning."

Next on the agenda were three games in the Swedish capital. Liverpool won the first of them, 6-2 against Djurgarden, and Bill Lacey struck a hat-trick; however, the opposition still managed to suitably impress Fairfoul and his team-mates.

"These people seem to have a thorough knowledge of the game, and are a fine sporting race. Overall the Swedish team played good, sound football," he wrote. There was also a sign of things to come on the journey back to the hotel. Fairfoul explained: "We had another great reception when coming home, the road being lined for over a mile with spectators, who kept up a continual cheer. It was very flattering to our team, who, needless to say, felt rather proud."

The summer heat continued to beat down on the Swedish capital as the Liverpool squad spent their recreational time by boarding a steamer which took them out into the Baltic Sea. Their next two clashes came against AIK Stockholm and a Swedish XI, games which the Reds won comfortably 3-0 and 8-0.

From Stockholm, Watson and his squad moved on towards their final destination, Copenhagen.

The next leg of the trip took them 13 hours and upon arrival, the reception was lukewarm. The few locals who did come to welcome their guests from England arrived with a warning that Liverpool's next opponents, Kjobenhavns Boldklub, had not lost a game in two years.

"This record they intended keeping intact, and it was no secret, in fact, they were very boastful of Liverpool being included in their list of victims," wrote Fairfoul.

"When the boys heard of this it gave them the needle, and they were determined to show the Copenhagen public their team had still to learn something of the art of football." Liverpool thrashed Boldklub 5-2 with the prolific Lacey on target twice.

"The Danes gave a very half-hearted cheer at the finish, and it was plain they didn't relish the idea of their record being broken," said Fairfoul. "One of their best players came up to me at the finish and remarked that we would get a harder match on Sunday against the 'selected'."

The player in question had a point – Liverpool drew after playing out a thrilling 3-3 tie with the Copenhagen XI – before rounding off their tour of Scandinavia with an emphatic 7-1 win over a Denmark XI.

The Reds' party then set off on the journey back to England, but within months World War One would begin to wreak widespread destruction. Come the autumn, many of the Liverpool side who were beaten in that year's FA Cup final by Burnley would trade the Anfield turf for the muddy, blood-soaked trenches of Europe.

Fairfoul was implicated in a match-fixing scandal in 1915, found guilty along with six others after suspicions were aroused by a 2-0 Manchester United win at Old Trafford.

He and his cohorts had been concerned at their lack of income as league football was suspended. He received a lifetime ban, but that was later lifted in recognition of brave service for his country in the course of the conflict.

The Reds had first toured in 1910, but the 1914 tour blazed a trail for future trips, including the 1946/47 tour to America that helped the players gain weight in the post-war age of rationing in the UK. It could well have been an important factor in Liverpool's unlikely league title triumph in the season that followed.

This, and the annual pre-season globetrotting that was put on hold due to COVID-19 until the summer of 2022, are a far cry from the few thousand fans who witnessed the Reds on tour in Gothenburg, Stockholm and Copenhagen over a century earlier.

18/130

You'll Never Walk Alone

WHEN Richard Rodgers and Oscar Hammerstein sat down to write their second musical, little did they know the lasting impact one of the show's tunes would have on Merseyside's footballing fraternity.

Rodgers and Hammerstein's 1945 Broadway hit *Carousel* was described by the *New York Press* as "beautiful and beguiling, a fable of love, death and redemption."

It tells the story of a love affair between Billy Bigelow, a travelling carnival worker, and Julie Jordan, a local factory girl. Desperate to support Julie and their unborn daughter when he loses his job, Billy is killed during an attempted robbery but is turned away at heaven's gate until he redeems himself on earth. In the second act, Nettie Fowler – Julie's cousin – sings *You'll Never Walk Alone* to comfort and encourage her. It is reprised during the finale.

In 1963 Gerry and the Pacemakers recorded their version of *YNWA*, the song which would become part of the fabric of Liverpool Football Club. It has since been adopted by numerous football clubs and recorded by more than 100 artists from Elvis Presley and Tom Jones to Kiri Te Kanawa and Katherine Jenkins.

Liverpool was the cultural capital of Britain at the time of Gerry and the Pacemakers' release of the tune. Huyton MP Harold Wilson was less than 12 months away from heading a new Government, Everton were league champions and Bill Shankly was determined to knock them from the summit with his exciting team. Musically, the city dominated the landscape too.

On 3 October 1963 the BBC screened a documentary called *The Mersey Sound*. During the period from April 1963 to May 1964, the number one single was recorded by a Liverpool artist for a staggering 51 weeks. One of those chart-toppers, of course, was *YNWA*.

Gerry Marsden, who sadly passed away in 2021 with a tribute to him unveiled by his family on the Kop in 2022, recalled: "We were performing it around the clubs in Liverpool for more than a year before we recorded it because we loved the song so much. The audience would just stop, stand there and listen. I just loved the words and melody.

"We recorded it and I wanted it released. We came in the day after putting it down and then I first heard George Martin's string score. That was it. The strings did it for me, it just gave it another bit of magic."

65

The band changed the lyrics slightly from 'keep your chin up high' to 'hold your head up high' and added more tempo and energy.

Gerry wanted to release the song as the third single from their debut album *How Do You Like It?*

Their first two singles *How Do You Do It?* and *I Like It* had both gone to number one but legendary music producer Martin and Brian Epstein (the Pacemakers' manager) were not as convinced about *YNWA* as they felt it had been slow to catch on. Gerry was told it would be on his head if the song didn't get to number one.

On 2 November 1963 however, *YNWA* replaced *Do You Love Me* by London band Brian Poole and the Tremeloes at the top of the hit parade and stayed there for four weeks.

For a number of years Anfield disc jockey Stuart Bateman had played a rundown of the top 10 singles to entertain the crowd prior to kick off.

That November, the Reds hosted Fulham and Burnley in Division One fixtures. As *YNWA* was no1 it was played closest to kick off and it inspired the Reds to 2-0 wins in both games as Shankly's side took further steps towards winning the championship.

Kopites took to the song immediately and have embraced it ever since as a unifying anthem in times of joy and times of sorrow. When it fell out of the top 10, Liverpool supporters requested that it continue to be played.

Liverpudlians have always been pioneers of fan culture. They have also been credited as being among the first to adapt the old spiritual song 'Jesus is my captain, I shall not be moved' to the well-known refrain 'We shall not be moved.' And the famous 'clap, clap, clap, clap, clap, clap, clap, clap, clap St John,' chant in appreciation of great forwards was said to have started on the terraces around the same time as *YNWA*, based on the 1962 hit *Let's Go* by The Routers (sometimes played ahead of the second half at Anfield). It has since been dedicated by Kopites to Kenny Dalglish, Robbie Fowler, Fernando Torres, Luis Suarez, Daniel Sturridge and, after he scored against Leeds United in February 2022, Joel Matip. Kopites have always had a sense of humour!

In the last 20 years Johnny Cash's *Ring of Fire* and Bob Marley's *Three Little Birds* have been adopted by Liverpudlians. But it is *You'll Never Walk Alone* that has endured as the Reds' soundtrack.

In 1965, when Gerry's wedding was announced over the PA system, the Kop responded by serenading him and his wife with the song.

Gerry's favourite memory was during the early 60s when he performed the song with the team on *The Ed Sullivan Show* when the Reds were in America on tour. A television audience of 60 million saw it. He recalled: "Afterwards Bill Shankly came over to me and said: 'Gerry son, I've given Liverpool a team – you've given us a song.'"

YNWA has also been a comforting anthem in times of tragedy. A new recording in 1985 raised funds for the families who lost loved ones in Bradford City's Valley Parade fire disaster. It again reached number one.

In 1989, on the Wednesday following the Hillsborough tragedy, the European Cup semi-final between AC Milan and Real Madrid in the San Siro was stopped after six minutes and fans of both clubs sang a moving rendition. Then, during that year's FA Cup final against Everton, the national anthem was famously drowned out by a 100,000-strong Mersey choir.

More recently, ex-Reds captain Steven Gerrard said the incredible comeback at the 2005 Champions League final in Istanbul was inspired by the players hearing Liverpool supporters singing *YNWA* while they were in the dressing room at half-time, contemplating their 0-3 deficit.

In the summer of 2013, many were moved by the raucous

version at Australia's Melbourne Cricket Ground during the Reds' pre-season tour while in April 2016, there were emotional versions sung by fans of LFC and Borussia Dortmund ahead of both legs of the Europa League quarter-final just weeks before the jury at the Hillsborough inquests found that the 97 supporters were unlawfully killed.

And who will ever forget Jürgen Klopp and his players, standing arm in arm, singing YNWA in tandem with the Kop after Liverpool's remarkable 4-0 Champions League semi-final win against Barcelona in 2019? Mo Salah, ruled out of the game with concussion, aptly wore a t-shirt with 'Never Give Up' on the front that night.

Liverpool FC legend Sir Kenny Dalglish summed up perfectly what the song represents to Reds when he said in his book *My Liverpool Home*: "The important thing for everyone at Liverpool Football Club is to work together for the same cause. That has always been The Liverpool Way, going back to Shanks. It's what *You'll Never Walk Alone* means."

19/130

Steve naïve

THE undisputed king of the Anfield fall guys, in the nicest possible sense, was Steve Nicol, who was the butt of practical jokes inflicted upon him by merciless Liverpool FC team-mates in the 1980s.

The funny thing was, though, the Scottish international relished it and often gave as good as he got. "The banter was constant," he recalled in his autobiography *5 League Titles And A Packet Of Crisps*. "I couldn't wait to get into training of a morning, not to train but to get started on all the joking and winding each other up. I'd actually be driving in thinking: what's going to happen today, who'll be on the end of it all?

"Going into the dressing room as a young lad was a test of character, but the important thing was that none of the jokes were ever done to belittle anybody. It was done to have a laugh, but there was never any malice behind it.

"That said, when you're constantly on the receiving end then naturally you begin to think: when am I gonna get a break here?!"

The worst culprits were fellow Scots Alan Hansen, Graeme Souness and Kenny Dalglish, with one prank taking even their black humour to another level...

"We're in Israel preparing for the '84 European Cup final and I've done my hamstring so I think I'm going to miss the game," recounted Hansen. "We're out having a drink and I'm sat there, down in the dumps. Kenny isn't there, he's not drinking. Nicol turns to me and says: 'Alan, is there something wrong wi' Kenny?' Off the top of my head I say: 'He's got six months to live – he's dying'.

Nicol goes like this [hands on head] and says: 'Nooo – you're kidding?' I say: 'It's true. He's in his room. But don't tell anybody'.

"Nicol goes to the toilet. Graeme Souness has clocked this and says to me: 'What did you tell him?' I say: 'Kenny's dying – incurable disease'. So Graeme says: 'Take him back to see Kenny. I'll phone and tell him you're coming'. So Nicol comes back and we get in the taxi. He's looking out of one window, I'm looking out of the other. He turns to me and says: 'See when we get there? Show him no pity – the worst thing you can do is show him any pity'.

"We get back to the hotel and take up two beers and a Martini-

and-lemonade for Kenny. We get in, sit down and Nicol's going: 'I just can't believe this'. Kenny says: 'Alan, I thought I told you not to tell anybody'. I say: 'Well he was upset and wondering what was wrong so I had to'.

"Nicol's sat there shaking his head. Then suddenly he turns to Kenny and says: 'Here, I was wondering why you were playing so badly'…"

But it was another, less celebrated Anfield Scot who was on the receiving end of arguably the best wind-up of the lot, and this tale is retold by Danish midfielder Jan Molby…

"We were playing Luton Town at home in a midweek cup replay. We went to the hotel in the afternoon and Kenny Dalglish was the manager at the time, so the routine was we'd have a sleep then Roy Evans would wake us up at 5pm for everyone to be on the coach for 6pm ready to go to Anfield.

"But Roy woke us up with the news that the game was off – Luton couldn't get up to Liverpool because of snow in the Midlands.

"We'd just signed a young lad called Alan Irvine, but he was in another part of the hotel and hadn't heard the news. So when we walked out to the coach he was sitting there none the wiser that the game was off. Which is when Alan Hansen decides to have some fun. He has a word with Kenny who calls Irvine up to the front and tells him he'll be dropping Ronnie Whelan and that he'll make his debut instead.

"We get up to the dressing room and all sit round as Kenny drops the bombshell that Ronnie's dropped and Irvine's in. Ronnie throws a fake tantrum and we all shuffle about pretending to get changed. We heard Irvine on the phone telling his wife to drop everything because he's making his debut, and with that he goes off to the toilet. That's the cue for us to turn out the light, run for the coach and bugger off home.

"Ten minutes later Irvine collars a steward demanding to know where everyone is, still protesting that he's playing. But the steward, not recognising him, tells him to take the kit off and throws him out of the ground with a warning that next time he'd call the police.

"Half-an-hour later his missus arrives at a deserted ground and gives him an ear-bashing. I'm telling you, that one kept us going for the rest of the season…"

Top that? Ian Rush tried his best in April 1989 when he played a practical joke – on practically everyone – by appearing on the front cover of the football magazine *Shoot!* wearing an Everton shirt with a headline proclaiming he'd signed for our neighbours.

It was no secret that the Welshman had been a boyhood Blue, but thousands of Reds were left rubbing their eyes in disbelief when they looked inside to find an article entitled 'Why I'm Leaving Liverpool'. When they were asked to turn the page again, it said: "April Fool! Rush For Everton Never-ton! Liverpool fans can heave a sigh of relief. Everton fans can dream on. Ian Rush has fooled you all…he's not going anywhere."

Rushie recalled: "I was a columnist for *Shoot!* and a couple of weeks before they'd asked if I fancied doing something a bit different. It was good-humoured fun although I got a few calls from people asking me what I was doing!"

Another taken in by the prank was a young Evertonian who became another LFC legend. In *Carra: My Autobiography* Jamie Carragher wrote: "If I wasn't a footballer I'd have gone on *Mastermind*, my specialist subject *Shoot!* magazine during the 1980s. One edition still traumatises me. I was convinced Everton had signed Ian Rush because he was on the cover of *Shoot!* wearing the blue kit. I ran home shouting to everyone, 'We've signed Ian Rush!' only to discover it was an April Fool joke."

And Reds fans had the last laugh as Rush ended that season by repeating his feat of 1986 – scoring twice against Everton in an all-Merseyside FA Cup final.

20/130

Testing times

DURING the first 100 years or so of LFC's existence, playing in benefit or testimonial matches was a relatively regular occurrence.

Clubs would often reward individuals for long service or those who had fallen into times of particular need.

Testimonial matches down the years have seen the Reds take on all manner of teams, from Bootle Boys Brigade and Newton Heath back in the 1890s to more exotic opposition such as Bayern Munich, Anderlecht and Real Sociedad. They have been the stage for some unlikely happenings: Bobby Charlton with a Liver Bird upon his chest, a Ray Clemence hat-trick, an 8-8 draw in a snowstorm and a man missing his own benefit game!

The first testimonial played at Anfield saw Liverpool take on Bootle Boys Brigade in a match for Dan Kirkwood in March 1893.

Kirkwood was a great Evertonian representing the club as a player, director and manager for a period extending over 40 years, but he remains a little known figure in the club's history. A right-half, he also played for the Liverpool Caledonians team who were briefly based at Woodcroft Park before becoming defunct.

You would think testimonial matches would live long in the memory of the recipients. But that was not the case for Carlisle United's Billy Hogan who was awarded such a fixture against the Reds in March 1954...because he missed it!

A crowd favourite at Carlisle, the inside-forward starred for the club under the management of Bill Shankly and was granted a benefit game against Liverpool after seeing his career stall after he suffered serious knee damage in a league game against Crewe in 1952. When the *Carlisle Evening News* conducted a poll in 1982, he was voted as the club's greatest-ever player.

His testimonial at Brunton Park attracted a crowd of 6,500 for a fixture that ended in a 3-3 draw but Hogan wasn't among them – having missed the train to the game!

Hogan's transport issues meant he was stranded at home on the Tuesday night that the match was being played in his honour, but he could still be proud of his career with the Cumbrian side that saw him score 27 goals between September 1949 and May 1956.

One of the greatest arrays of footballing talent seen at Anfield turned out in September 1960 for a benefit match for the great Billy Liddell. A crowd of almost 39,000 saw Liverpool defeat an International XI 4-2 with the opposition including Bert Trautmann, Jimmy Armfield, Don Revie, Jimmy McIlroy, Stanley Matthews, Nat Lofthouse and Tom Finney in their line-up.

There was plenty of entertainment for the 41,000 at Anfield when Liverpool took on an All-Star XI in a benefit fixture for crowd favourite Gerry Byrne in April 1970. The spectators were rewarded with 16 goals and a snowstorm as the match finished all-square. Ian St John scored twice for the Reds – as did goalkeeper Tommy Lawrence – adding a sensational solo effort to an earlier penalty! To add to the spectacle, Shankly had led a team of Liverpool training staff against a Jimmy Tarbuck side in a seven-a-side match during the half-time interval.

That game for Byrne also saw the first Anfield outing for a Warwick University undergraduate who Shankly had wanted to see play for the All-Star XI. It would not be the young winger's last. In years to come, Kopites would have dreams to dream and songs to sing – with Stevie Heighway on the wing.

The biggest attendance for an Anfield testimonial came in April 1972 when 55,214 saw Liverpool defeat an England XI 8-6 in a match played for front man Roger Hunt. The Reds managed to field their 1965 FA Cup-winning team and Hunt netted a hat-trick in a fixture which also saw Martin Peters score for Liverpool after putting through his own goal!

A more unlikely hat-trick hero came in April 1976 when Ray Clemence scored a treble at Prenton Park in a benefit game for Tranmere stalwart Ray Matthias. The goalkeeper netted a treble in a 6-5 Rovers win with two coming from the penalty spot.

Clem was also on target twice when Tommy Smith's testimonial saw the Reds take on a Bobby Charlton Select XI in a game which was also memorable for the fact it briefly saw Manchester United legend Charlton wearing a Liverpool shirt. The game ended in an astonishing 9-9 draw with Emlyn Hughes taking a spell in goal and a substitute appearance from delivery driver Lol Cotterell. An amateur footballer with the Wheatsheaf team in the Crosby and District League, Cotterell won the chance to play as part of a BBC television show *The Big Time* hosted by Esther Rantzen. The 'Anfield Iron' left the Liverpool scene after the game and the *Liverpool Echo* featured a photograph of him literally hanging up his boots!

A couple of games in the late seventies also saw a few instances of players swapping sides. It may seem hard to comprehend nowadays but three Everton players guested for the Reds when they took on Bolton in May 1978 in a tribute match for ex-Liverpool and Wanderers winger Peter Thompson.

Goalkeeper George Wood, defender Terry Darracott and forward Duncan McKenzie were the guests in a 5-5 draw which saw David Fairclough score a hat-trick for Liverpool with the other two goals coming from…Darracott and McKenzie!

21/130

Men at work

WHEN the first edition of this book was published, back in 2017, plans to combine Liverpool FC's first-team training and Academy operations and move to a brand new complex in Kirkby had just been announced. But Melwood was still very much home.

Five years on, there's no place like the AXA Training Centre, so smooth has been the transition and such is its inclusive, welcoming atmosphere in state-of-the-art surroundings. Melwood, though, will always have a special place in LFC hearts.

The story began in 1950 when it was originally acquired as a 13-acre site, having previously belonged to St Francis Xavier School – two of whose sports teachers, Father Melling and Father Woodlock, lent their names to its new incarnation with the football club.

But when Bill Shankly was appointed Reds boss in December 1959 he was far from impressed by what he found, describing Melwood as "a sorry wilderness" years later in his autobiography. "One pitch looked as if a couple of bombs had been dropped on it [and there were] trees, hills, hollows and grass long enough to hide in standing up! But I said to [my wife] Ness: 'It's big and it can be developed, at least there is space here'."

Shankly installed a gym, all-weather pitch and outdoor 'target-boards' to improve shooting and passing accuracy, plus a much-improved pavilion later in the Sixties. In those days the players trained at Melwood before being bussed back to Anfield to wash and change.

As Liverpool proceeded to dominate football at home and abroad, things remained largely unchanged until the return of former skipper Graeme Souness as manager in 1991; he introduced baths, a canteen and a lounge area. Modernisation continued under subsequent boss Roy Evans then Gerard Houllier, who was involved in the design of what was dubbed 'the Millennium Pavilion'.

He promised "new changing areas, a gymnasium, swimming pools, saunas, a hydrotherapy pool and rehabilitation rooms – more in tune with what a club of this standard wants to achieve." Houllier also had his new office built on the upper floor, looking out over the main training pitch.

In subsequent years further improvements and additions were made, including an indoor astroturf pitch, to ensure that as the game continued to evolve, so did Melwood. But 12 months after Jürgen Klopp's appointment, it was clear that it could no longer accommodate the club's longer-term ambitions.

"I really love Melwood, but football changes," said Klopp when plans for a new combined facility was announced. "We can't stay like we were and hope we can compete with the other clubs. It's really good that our owners give us the opportunity to make this big step in the future.

"Bringing the Academy and the first team together is one point, but it's also about improving a lot of things that we can't improve here. It will only be good for the future of the club."

At the end of 2019 the first images of the new complex were released, with work ongoing and on course for completion by the following summer. Meanwhile the club handed over the ownership and operation of the newly-redeveloped Eddie McArdle pitches (located at the north end of the site) to the local community.

In March 2020 a video was posted on LFC's official website updating fans on progress in Kirkby and it was confirmed that three pitches measuring 32,000 square metres would be made to mirror Anfield's hallowed turf as closely as possible, complete with under-soil heating and floodlighting.

Meanwhile, the design of the main building would provide a clean, modern and warm environment with lots of natural daylight and simple but crisp detailing celebrating the club's history. There would be two gyms, a full-size sports hall, pool, hydrotherapy complex and specialist sports rehabilitation suites; dedicated TV studios, press-conference facilities and office accommodation.

The eco-friendly complex would boast a newly-installed borehole to extract groundwater to irrigate the pitches and tend to the landscaping on site, along with a biological vehicle wash-system, allowing groundstaff to wash equipment, vehicles or parts and reclaim the water used.

The pandemic may have delayed the AXA Training Centre's official opening until Tuesday 17 November 2020 – 722 days since construction began – but it was worth the wait and the occasion was commemorated by the installation of a steel time-capsule which would be opened in 50 years' time.

Inside it was a USB stick with video messages from, among others, manager Klopp, captain Jordan Henderson and Reds legend Sir Kenny Dalglish. Also included: a letter from club owners Fenway Sports Group; a pair of Klopp's glasses, signed boots from Virgil van Dijk and signed goalkeeping gloves from Alisson Becker; a 2020/21 season Nike home shirt and AXA training shirt; the Liverpool v Chelsea matchday programme from 22 July 2020 when the Reds were crowned Premier League Champions; a 2019 UEFA Champions League final shirt signed by the Reds squad; a tribute to those who lost their lives at Hillsborough; and a mini feature-film on Melwood's history.

Liverpool FC had finally left the training base where so many titles and cup triumphs had been plotted down the decades, and so much joy and happiness and occasionally sadness had been shared – and they'd done so as champions.

In the meantime, Melwood was officially handed over to a new, socially-responsible owner and in February 2021 fans had the opportunity to bid for memorabilia – everything from the red desk-lamp in the manager's old office to a wooden chair from the canteen to a car-parking space nameplate – in an online auction to raise funds for LFC Foundation's COVID-19 community response work.

Klopp took one last look back, describing Melwood as "an important place in my life. I think my most vivid memory is the first day. In Germany only the players, coaches, groundstaff and kit men are at the training ground, so it was completely new to me having so many people here on a daily basis – I loved this kind of environment.

"I will miss it, but that's how it should be. Melwood was really good, but Kirkby will be great."

The final word went to long-serving gateman Kenny Grimes: "I was opening the back gates [at Melwood] about 40 or 50 times a day – so multiply that by how many years I was there. It was a job I loved doing. When you first walked in, especially when the lads had been cutting the grass, you could smell the turf and it was lovely.

"It was a waste of time trying to stop fans standing on the purple bins looking over the fence – you'd tell them to get down and then the next minute they'd just move further up!"

At least that isn't a problem in Kirkby…the bins are maroon, grey and blue!

22/130

It's a toss-up!

THINK of penalty shoot-outs in relation to Liverpool FC and Rome 1984, Istanbul 2005 and Wembley 2022 instantly come to mind.

But back in the 1960s, the idea of sudden death from the spot had not been conceived. Nor had the away goals rule.

So when the Reds came up against FC Cologne in their debut season in continental competition and three games and five hours of football failed to separate the sides, a toss of the coin was deemed necessary to settle the outcome of the quarter-final clash.

Both home and away fixtures ended goalless and after a third draw, a 2-2 split in Rotterdam described by Bill Shankly as: "the most bruising game of football I have ever seen," the Reds' fate lay in the lap of the gods.

Even then, there was a further twist as Liverpool's hopes of booking a place in the last four against Inter Milan got stuck in the mud. Literally!

The *Liverpool Echo* explained the following day: "The great all-or-nothing decision was delayed and the suspense was stretched. The counter stuck upright in the soft turf. Centre-forward Ian St John and other players held their heads as though in despair as the referee tossed a second time. It landed to end the nerve-wracking moments and St John and Ron Yeats led the Liverpool players in a victory dance that would have done credit to Maori tribesmen."

Liverpool captain Yeats, who had lost both tosses for choice of ends before the start of the game and ahead of extra-time – is alleged to have later recalled: "I got in first to the referee and said: 'I'll have tails.' Lucky for me the referee said ok. Liverpool tails, Cologne heads. Up it went and didn't it stick in a divot! I said to the referee: 'Ref, you're going to have to re-toss the coin.' And he went: 'You're right, Mr Yeats'.

"The German captain was going berserk because it was falling over towards the heads. He picked it up, up it went again and came down tails.

"We were coming off the pitch and who is standing there but Bill Shankly. I was first off and he went: 'Well done, big man. I am proud of you. What did you pick?' I said: 'I picked tails, boss'. I was waiting for the adulation but he just went: 'I would have picked tails myself' and just walked away!"

However, according to the *Liverpool Echo* an orthodox coin wasn't used at all with a wooden counter, painted red for Liverpool and white for Cologne, flipped by Belgian referee Robert Schaut.

Either way, delighted as he was at Liverpool's progress, Shankly was unimpressed at the method used for deciding the winners.

"It's a ridiculous way to decide any football match or, indeed, any sporting event," he said after the game. "Surely there must be a way to relate victory to the game itself. If, for example, it had been decided on corners in the last 30 minutes that would have been more satisfactory – and I'm not just saying that because we had more corners."

Three years later a similar situation cropped up when the Reds were paired against Spanish side Athletic Bilbao in the opening round of the European Fairs Cup.

Following a 2-1 defeat at San Mames, late goals from Chris Lawler and Emlyn Hughes saw Shankly's side reverse the scoreline at Anfield. With the aggregate scores locked at 3-3, the coin toss was again used to decide the victors. This time, Yeats' luck was out.

He recalled: "I guessed wrong and when I told Shanks I had chosen tails, he said: 'You should have said heads! I don't know why you picked that – never call tails!'"

There was generally little sympathy for Liverpool, however, with most sources feeling they should have put the tie to bed across the three hours of football against the Basques. Nonetheless, the general feeling was that the coin toss had been a victory for defence over attack.

In the book *Liverpool in Europe*, author Ivan Ponting wrote: "Splitting these two teams by the toss of a coin was nothing short of a travesty. Liverpool had surged forward skillfully and relentlessly while Athletic had resisted with astute defensive tactics and considerable fortitude, and an outcome based on football rather than fortune was the least they deserved."

The away goals rule came into force for the European Cup Winners' Cup in 1965/66. As luck would have it, not a single tie during the entire season had to be settled on away goals and Liverpool, who had qualified as FA Cup winners, went all the way to the final where they lost to Borussia Dortmund at Hampden Park.

The following season, in the European Cup Winners' Cup second round, Belgium's Standard Liege became the first club to progress on away goals against the now-defunct BSG Chemie Leipzig, but the rule hadn't been introduced into other competitions.

Liverpool beat Petrolul Ploiești 2-0 at Anfield in the European Cup that year, but after a 3-1 second leg defeat in Romania the tie was settled by a play-off in Brussels - the Reds winning 2-0 - instead of on away goals.

In 1967/68 the away goals rule was introduced in the European Cup but, rather strangely, only for the first round and with extra-time goals scored by the away team not counting double. So no wonder there was confusion on the Anfield terraces when late goals by Alun Evans and Roger Hunt gave Liverpool a dramatic 3-2 win over Vitoria Setubal in a European Fairs Cup tie in 1969. Liverpool supporters stayed in their places expecting extra-time and it took a PA system announcement to confirm that the two away goals had been enough to see the Portuguese through to the third round after their 1-0 victory in the first leg!

Liverpool later reached the 1973 UEFA Cup final and 1981 European Cup final with away goal wins against Tottenham Hotspur and Bayern Munich respectively, but such days are now gone after UEFA scrapped the away goals rule ahead of season 2021/22.

It's also worth noting that in April 1895 a meeting of the executive committee of the Liverpool and District Association was held at the Neptune Hotel to arrange a date and ground for the Liverpool Senior Cup final between Everton and Liverpool. After a lengthy discussion it was decided to allow the clubs to toss a coin for choice of grounds, providing their respective committees agreed. They didn't! The game took place at the Police Athletic Ground with a crowd of around 4,000 seeing Everton win 3-0.

23/130

Match pint

YOU can barely move upstairs in The Twelfth Man on matchdays, but it's worth the squeeze not just for the friendly welcome and Kop-like atmosphere of this historic public house – just a goal-kick from the stadium on Walton Breck Road – but for the LFC memorabilia that adorns its walls: from a giant Hillsborough justice mural, to vintage photos of the likes of Bill Shankly and Billy Liddell, to rare matchday programme and magazine covers.

The Twelfth Man was originally called The Salisbury, the same title as another pub slightly further away from the stadium. Both were named after one Robert Gascoyne-Cecil, 3rd Marquess of Salisbury and Conservative Prime Minister for three terms between 1885 and 1902. His family owned a series of fields stretching from Walton Breck Road to Breckfield Road North.

Roughly south-east from there, onto Oakfield Road on the other side of the football ground, is the famous Sandon Hotel. It's been claimed that this was where the players changed in the very early days of Liverpool FC, although respected Reds historian Kjell Hanssen has since unearthed a small note from July 1892 stating that the new club rented a house at 27 Kemlyn Road to act as dressing rooms.

"Everton's players used The Sandon when they played at Anfield," says Hanssen, "but never Liverpool, although it was LFC's headquarters for many a year after 1892."

Indeed it was here that the club celebrated its promotion to England's top flight for the very first time, in May 1894 after a play-off victory over Newton Heath (now Manchester United) at Blackburn's Ewood Park. *The Liverpool Review* newspaper reported: "Needless to say there were great rejoicings among the Liverpool contingent after the victory, and on arriving at Tithebarn Street Station, the team was met by an enormously big and correspondingly enthusiastic crowd.

"Different players were carried shoulder-high to their special conveyance, and after lubrication at the Alexandra Hotel [on Dale Street, where the club's founding fathers conducted much of their business], the men drove off to The Sandon where another tremendous reception awaited them. Altogether it was a big match, a big win, and a big day for the Liverpool club and Liverpool football."

The Sandon, like The Twelfth Man, The Albert, The Park and The Arkles, is one of a wealth of charismatic pubs in the area – most still thriving, a few sadly closed – and virtually all built in the second half of the 19th century. In fact their presence helps explain the history and development of the neighbourhood's landscape.

The following is taken from the English Heritage book *Ordinary Landscapes, Special Places: Anfield, Breckfield and the Growth of Liverpool's Suburbs*: "Prominent street corners, so attractive for the siting of churches, were also seized upon by brewers whose ministry to corporeal needs assumed very different architectural forms, some revelling in the challenge of using a triangular plot effectively.

"The larger public houses of the late 19th century temptingly offered a home from home – a heightened version of the domestic ideal. They are substantial, ostentatious and frequently gaudy, their exteriors – often brightly coloured with glazed brick or terracotta, and incorporating fanciful embellishments – promising instant gratification for the senses rather than rewards in the hereafter.

"Typically containing two or more bars and a separate area for off-sales as well as function rooms, letting rooms and accommodation for the publican's family, they required careful planning and preferably multiple entrances – one factor in the popularity of corner sites.

"Besides serving refreshments, the larger establishments, like The Arkles (formerly The Royal Hotel) and The King Harry Hotel, both on Anfield Road, provided meeting places for a range of purposes, and since they were eye-catching they became natural reference points for residents and visitors alike."

Cheers to that!

24/130

Captivating comebacks

BURNLEY FC, 12th in the Premier League on Boxing Day 2019, crowned as champions? Ridiculous.

Leeds United winning the title in 2020/21 having been 12th the day after Boxing Day? Ludicrous.

So when it comes to footballing fightbacks, surely little can compare to Liverpool FC's achievements in 1981/82.

Topping the table having been 12th on 26 December? Fact.

Christmas cheer was in little supply among Liverpool fans as they trudged out of Anfield that Boxing Day in 1981 having just seen their side slump to a disappointing 3-1 defeat by Manchester City.

Bob Paisley's team sat in the bottom half of the table with just 24 points from 17 matches, nine points behind surprise leaders

Swansea City and eight adrift of second-placed Manchester United. However, that City setback sparked an astonishing response which saw the Reds win 20 out of their next 24 matches to claim the championship. Liverpool even secured their league title success with a game to spare!

Another stirring comeback came in 1985/86 and was the catalyst to Liverpool winning the club's only league and FA Cup double to date.

When Everton won the Merseyside derby at Anfield towards the end of February, the Blues looked odds-on to retain their title.

Liverpool centre-half Alan Hansen recalled: "It was Kenny Dalglish's first season as player-manager and on 22 February we were beaten 2-0 at Anfield by Everton, leaving us in third position and Everton eight points clear of us at the top. I went for dinner with Kenny after that game and I remember saying to him that this was the worst Liverpool side I had ever played in."

Following that derby, the Reds were on a run of two wins, four draws and four defeats in 10 league matches. Few then were prepared for what happened next.

As history records, Liverpool produced an incredible sequence which saw them notch 11 wins and one draw from their final dozen league games. A win at Chelsea in the final fixture was enough to secure the title.

Left-back Jim Beglin created the winning goal for Dalglish. Speaking to the *LFC Weekly* magazine in 2011, he recalled: "I knew Kenny was to my right so I just had to help it on. He took it on his chest and stuck it away. I'll never forget that ball hitting the net. It's nice to know that I played a little part in it. I'm sure it was one of Kenny's greatest moments, and he had dozens to choose from.

"It's a victory and a memory all of the players who were involved in are rightly proud of. Winning the title is the ultimate achievement."

Football managers often talk about spirit and character, but few clubs have demonstrated those characteristics as often as Liverpool Football Club.

The thrilling UEFA Europa League quarter-final fightback against Borussia Dortmund in April 2016 was one of many examples of the Reds not knowing when they were beaten.

A good comeback is one of the most captivating parts of football and the Reds' 'bouncebackability' has captured the imagination of Kopites and the wider footballing fraternity on numerous occasions.

It is doubtful if any fightback will ever cap that which saw Liverpool win the 2005 Champions League on a never-to-be forgotten night in Istanbul.

Had the script been taken from the pages of a comic-strip, it would have been dismissed as far-fetched.

Three goals down at half-time, to a crack AC Milan team, many Reds supporters were more concerned with damage limitation than the possibility of winning the trophy. Stirred by a rousing rendition of *You'll Never Walk Alone* that could be heard from the dressing room, Rafael Benitez's men came back from a seemingly impossible position.

As we all know, captain Steven Gerrard gave Liverpool hope before Vladimir Smicer and Xabi Alonso levelled the score during a remarkable six-minute spell. Goalkeeper Jerzy Dudek then produced a wonder-saver from Andriy Shevchenko in extra-time before saving spot-kicks by Andrea Pirlo and Shevchenko in the penalty shoot-out to clinch a stunning victory.

The Reds' fifth European Cup was all the more remarkable for the fact that earlier in their run, it had looked doubtful that they would progress beyond the group stages.

Benitez's side went into the home game against Greek side Olympiacos in December 2004 knowing they had to win either 1-0 or by two clear goals to advance to the knockout stages. Rivaldo's 27th minute free-kick left them facing an uphill struggle.

Florent Sinama-Pongolle put the Reds back on terms after the break, before Neil Mellor edged Liverpool into a 2-1 lead with nine minutes to play. Then up popped Gerrard, rifling home a 20-yarder into the Kop net with just four minutes remaining to give the team the required margin of victory.

The blueprint (shouldn't that be redprint?) for great European comebacks at Anfield had been written in March 1977 when the Reds went into a European Cup third round second leg tie trailing 1-0 to French champions St Etienne following the first leg in France.

Kevin Keegan handed the Reds hope with a second-minute effort, only for Dominique Bathenay to draw the visitors level with a precious away goal, meaning Liverpool had to score twice more without reply to reach the semi-finals. Ray Kennedy struck just before the hour mark to offer some hope, before substitute David Fairclough went scampering away towards the Kop before firing home one of the ground's greatest goals with just six minutes to play.

In December 1991, the Reds produced a similarly memorable fightback to earn another 3-2 aggregate victory over French opposition. In the club's first season back in Europe following a six-season ban, Graeme Souness's team lost 2-0 at Auxerre in the first leg of their UEFA Cup second round tie. Only 23,094 were in attendance for the second leg but it felt like a lot more as goals inside the first half-hour from Jan Molby and Mike Marsh levelled the aggregate scores. With seven minutes remaining Mark Walters made it 3-0 on the night to the delight of every Liverpudlian inside Anfield.

Fast forward to 2016 and that night against Borussia Dortmund. Jürgen Klopp's Reds had drawn the first leg 1-1 in Germany and anticipation was high ahead of the game against his former club, played on the eve of the 27th anniversary of the Hillsborough tragedy.

However, goals from Henrikh Mkhitaryan and Pierre-Emerick Aubameyang inside the opening nine minutes put the visitors firmly in control.

Attacking the Kop after the break, Divock Origi quickly halved the Reds' arrears but Marco Reus restored Dortmund's two-goal advantage with a third away goal before the hour mark.

Philippe Coutinho handed Liverpool hope midway through the second-half before Mamadou Sakho's goal meant Dortmund's lead was on away goals only.

With the game in added time, James Milner sent a cross back into the Dortmund box after a neat exchange with Daniel Sturridge. Dejan Lovren rose to meet the ball and his header flew past goalkeeper Roman Weidenfeller to send the ground shaking and book Liverpool's place in the semi-finals.

Then came the Barcelona game in 2019. Beaten 3-0 at Camp Nou in the first leg, Lionel Messi scoring twice, the Reds had to try to achieve the improbable without Mo Salah and Roberto Firmino, Origi and Xherdan Shaqiri coming into the team.

Origi pulled an early goal back, but Liverpool needed three more in the second half and lost Andy Robertson to injury at the interval. On came Gini Wijnaldum and everything changed. The Dutch midfielder converted Trent Alexander-Arnold's low cross in the 54th minute and with Barca still reeling amidst a scarf-twirling, raucous Anfield, Wijnaldum popped up again less than two minutes later to head Shaqiri's cross home.

Barcelona, with ex-Reds Luis Suarez and Coutinho in their team looked stunned, and in the 79th minute they switched off. When Alexander-Arnold forced a corner off Jordi Alba, 14-year-old ballboy and Academy starlet Oakley Cannonier threw a different ball to the right-back. Spotting Barca had lost their concentration,

Alexander-Arnold whipped a corner taken quickly to Origi, eight yards from goal, and by the time the visiting players had realised what was happening the ball was in the Kop-end net. 4-0, and Liverpool were heading to the final in Madrid.

"This is Liverpool's gift," wrote Jonathan Liew in *The Independent*. "To rip up what you thought you knew about football and footballers, to take you - mentally and physically - to a place you didn't know and never wanted to go. To make your eardrums ring and your sinuses twang and your heart thump to the point where it's all you can think about.

"To the point where you start to question yourself. To the point where you don't realise you've left a massive gap in your left channel until it's just a fraction of a second too late."

Suarez certainly felt it. "The days after, back in Barcelona, were the worst moments of my life and my career. I wanted to disappear from the world."

In 2022 it was Villarreal on the end of a Liverpool comeback in a Champions League semi-final. Two goals down from the first leg at Anfield, the 'Yellow Submarine' got the aggregate score back to 2-2 during the first half at El Madrigal.

Unai Emery's men had the momentum, but then Luis Diaz came on at half-time and changed the game. Fabinho got a goal back, Diaz quickly made it 2-2 and Sadio Mane completed a 3-2 win to seal Liverpool's spot in the final after another comeback.

In terms of domestic football, the Reds claimed another penalty shoot-out success a year after the Miracle of Istanbul, despite looking to be down-and-out in the FA Cup final against West Ham United.

Jamie Carragher's own goal and Dean Ashton's finish had put the Hammers in command in the Cardiff final, before Djibril Cisse cut the deficit on the half-hour. Gerrard levelled the tie at 2-2 before Paul Konchesky edged the Londoners back into the lead. With just seconds remaining, Gerrard produced an incredible long-range strike to take the game into extra-time. Liverpool prevailed on penalties, winning 3-1, with only Teddy Sheringham finding the net from West Ham's four attempts. Didi Hamann repeated his Istanbul trick, while Gerrard and John Arne Riise (who missed at the Ataturk) slotted home before Pepe Reina's successive saves.

Another FA Cup final comeback triumph at the Millennium Stadium came in 2001. A strong Arsenal side who would complete the league and FA Cup double the following year, had taken a second-half lead through Freddie Ljungberg. It was a dominant display against Gerard Houllier's young Liverpool side that would have been over but for a series of goal-line clearances. Michael Owen then came to the fore, equalising with seven minutes to play before an angled drive across keeper David Seaman on 88 minutes helped the Reds to the second part of their cup treble that season.

In terms of great fightbacks in league football, it is hard to look beyond the match in April 1996 that has since been voted as the Premier League's greatest game.

Liverpool's visitors to Anfield that evening were title-chasing Newcastle United, managed by ex-Red Kevin Keegan.

Robbie Fowler struck for Liverpool after just two minutes, but Les Ferdinand and David Ginola had Newcastle leading 2-1 inside the quarter-hour. Fowler equalised after the break, only for Faustino Asprilla to put the Magpies 3-2 ahead before the hour-mark. Stan Collymore grabbed his first goal of the night with little more than 20 minutes to play to tie the game at 3-3. Newcastle thought they could claim a point but the end-to-end encounter's last action saw Collymore close in and slot home Liverpool's winner late on.

Footage of Keegan slumped over the advertising hoarding in front of the dugout still helps to encapsulate that breathless night and the raw emotion that goes with a captivating comeback.

25/130

The field of praise

TWITTER. Facebook. YouTube. Instagram. Snapchat. Tik-Tok. And all the rest. The social media generation have grown up in a world where video sharing of football fans belting out songs and chants in their seats, in stadium concourses, on planes, trains, buses, pubs, town squares and even walking down the street is commonplace. Taken for granted.

Call us big-headed, but it's all thanks to the Kop.

"You got yer education from the Kop," might not get many airings these days, but that particular barb, directed at rival supporters, rang true.

Liverpool was a boom city in the early 1960s. Business was brisk at the docks, the Mersey Sound – led by four fab lads called The Beatles – was resonating around the world and at Anfield, after almost a decade in the Second Division doldrums, Liverpool had been galvanised by Bill Shankly.

In 1963/64, just their second season in the top flight after winning promotion, the Redmen were chasing the championship, but it wasn't just the football on the pitch that was capturing the attention.

The scenes on the Kop during Anfield matches had never before been witnessed in English football.

"Released from the grievous restraints of war that had dogged preceding generations and fuelled by the increasing sixties affluence that offered a diversion away from the drudgery of the workplace, the natural wit and exuberance of the Scouser suddenly found itself all manner of platforms on which to express that latent talent," wrote author Alan Edge in Chris McLoughlin's *Oh I Am A Liverpudlian and I Come From The Spion Kop*. "As it so happened – with the exception of the Fab Four's unique worldwide arena – the Anfield Spion Kop became the biggest stage of them all. Certainly it was the loudest.

"As the Mersey Sound resonated around the world, the full throttle of 28,000 of its own kind promptly amplified it. Cocooned and isolated in a way you could never get today, the patrons of the Kop simply did what came naturally to them and – amongst other more base tendencies – swayed and sang along heartily with the pre-match Tannoy.

"Here the Liverpool-Irish pub sing-song culture was clearly to play a significant role. Not many of the Kopites at the time were exactly strangers to belting out a communal tune from the comfort of their own ale-house on a Saturday night.

"The Kop simply became a giant extension of that concept."

That spontaneous singing, creative chanting and rhythmic swaying became such a phenomenon that the BBC dispatched a reporter and cameraman to Anfield on 18 April 1964 – the day the Reds could clinch the title with a victory against Arsenal – to see what all the fuss was about.

This, remember, was four months before *Match of the Day* was introduced, ironically for another Liverpool versus Arsenal game at Anfield, at a time when nationwide coverage of any kind of football match was rarer than a dodo with a set of hen's teeth riding Haley's Comet. The mesmerising scenes captured the attention. The footage accelerated a football culture revolution. Fans all over the land thought to themselves 'if the Scousers can have so much fun going to the match then why can't we?'

To what extent the footage seeped into the consciousness of the nation will always be debated by our detractors, but with 17 million TV sets being in homes across the land in 1964 (compared to 27m in 2020) it would appear that where the Kop led, others followed.

Before long, singing and chanting became prominent at football grounds all over the country. It caught on. Kopycats were everywhere. And all because a plummy-voiced *Panorama* reporter, who looked genuinely awestruck as 28,000 Reds sang and swayed behind him at half-time of Liverpool's title-clinching 5-0 win, gave the Kop a whole new stage to showcase their vocal talents upon...

"The gladiators enter the arena, the field of praise. Saturday's weather perfect for an historic Scouse occasion."

[The Kop] *"And it's, Li-ver-pool! And it's, Li-ver-pool! And it's, Li-ver-pool! Li-ver-pool! Li-ver-pool! Li-ver-pool! Li-ver-pool! Li-ver-pool!"*

"Liverpool, in red shirts, were playing before their own spectators for the last time this season. The desire to win was an agonised one. They would be the champions of England and they wanted their own people to see them become so. They care so much about football. This season over two million people on Merseyside have watched Liverpool or their neighbours Everton, last year's champions. But they don't behave like any other football crowd, especially not at one end of Anfield ground – on the Kop."

[The Kop] *"And she loves you, and you know you should be glad – woooo! She loves you yeah, yeah, yeah, she loves you, yeah, yeah, yeah, and with a love like that, you know you should be glad."*

"The music the crowd sings is the music that Liverpool has sent echoing around the world."

[The Kop] *"You know it's up to you, I think it's only fair. Pride can hurt you too, apologise to her. Because she loves you, and you know that can't be bad. She loves you, and you know you should be glad – woooo! She loves you yeah, yeah, yeah, she loves you yeah, yeah, yeah, and with a love like that you know you should be glad."*

[With Cilla Black's *Anyone Who Had a Heart* now ringing out behind him] *"It used to be thought that Welsh international rugby crowds were the most musical and passionate in the world. But I've never seen anything like this Liverpool crowd. On the field here the gay and inventive ferocity they show is quite stunning. The Duke of Wellington, before the battle of Waterloo, said of his own troops 'I don't know what they do to the enemy but by God they frighten me'. And I'm sure some of the players here in this match this afternoon must be feeling the same way."*

[The Kop] *"Knowing I love you so! Anyone who had a heart would take me in his arms and love me, too, you couldn't really have a heart and hurt me..."*

"An anthropologist studying this Kop crowd would be introduced into as rich and mystifying a popular culture as in any South Sea island. Their rhythmic swaying is an elaborate and organised ritual. The 28,000 people on the Kop itself begin singing together. They seem to know, intuitively, when to begin. Throughout the match they invent new words, usually within the framework of old Liverpool songs, to express adulatory, cruel or bawdy comments about the players or the police. But even then they begin singing these new words with one immediate, huge voice. They seem, mysteriously, to be in touch with one another, with Wacker, the spirit of Scouse."

[The Kop] *"I wanna be in that number, oh when the Reds go marching in."*

"The spirit is good humoured and generous when they're winning, but not necessarily when they're losing. On Saturday they were certainly winning..."

[huge cheers erupt as Kop-end goals by Ian St John and Alf Arrowsmith go in]

"In an hour Liverpool scored five goals and could have scored more. Their poor, sacrificial victims were Arsenal. Southerners."

[more cheers and applause as Peter Thompson (two) and Roger Hunt score at the Annie Road end]

"On Merseyside, football is the consuming passion. It's hard to persuade people to talk about anything else, except perhaps the beat groups which the Kop crowd do a lot to explain."

[The Kop] *"We won the league, we won the league, ee-aye-addio we won the league! We won the league, we won the league, ee-aye-addio we won the league. Liverpool (clap-clap-clap)! Liverpool (clap-clap-clap)! Liverpool (clap-clap-clap)! Liverpool (clap-clap-clap)! Liverpool (clap-clap-clap)! Liverpool (clap-clap-clap)! Liverpool (clap-clap-clap)! Liverpool (clap-clap-clap)!"*

Times have changed. Could you imagine 12,500 Kopites singing along to current chart hits at half-time now? Probably not. Ed Sheeran and Adele just aren't The Beatles and Cilla, although maybe Jamie Webster would have half a chance as events in Basel and Kiev suggest it can still happen.

During half-time of the Reds' 2016 Europa League final against Sevilla in Basel, The La's *There She Goes* was played over the St Jakob-Park PA system, prompting thousands of travelling Kopites to sing along in unison, just like their dads and granddads used to. And before the 2018 Champions League final in Kiev a live performance of *One Kiss* by Dua Lipa had the travelling Kop singing along and adopting it as a new anthem that became a song of celebration amongst Liverpool supporters when the Reds beat Chelsea on penalties in both the 2022 Carabao Cup and FA Cup finals at Wembley.

Panorama wasn't there, but you can still see the footage on Twitter. And Facebook. And YouTube...

26/130

Let the brawl do the work

THE elevators of Tel Aviv's swankiest hotel were never built to withstand the synchronised bouncing of 12 grown men, nor to be soundproof. Two conclusions quickly drawn by room-mates Graeme Souness and Kenny Dalglish in the early hours of a May morning in 1984.

"We were in our beds," recalled Souness, "and Alan Hansen's come banging on the door. 'Get up! Get up!' he's shouting. 'Why?' 'They're all fighting each other down there!'

"So Kenny and I got up and got in the lift. Coming up the lift shaft, for about ten feet, was a chorus of *Suicide Is Painless* and *I Don't Know What It Is But I Love It*. What they'd done, a dozen or so of them, they'd got stuck in the lift and jumped up and down and it'd got stuck.

"Call it team spirit. Call it madness. Call it drink. But that was how we were back then. Great times."

Everyone knows the on-pitch story of LFC's fourth European Cup win: how the Reds beat AS Roma in their own backyard thanks to goalkeeper Bruce Grobbelaar's 'spaghetti-legs' routine in the penalty shoot-out and Alan Kennedy's winning spot-kick, earning Joe Fagan a trophy treble in his first season as manager.

But there was a story behind the story, too, which took place at LFC's training camp (the Reds had actually been invited to play a friendly against Israel's national side eight days before the final) and broken lifts were only a part of it.

Striker David Hodgson, who was an unused substitute that night in Rome's Stadio Olimpico, remembered "playing 'fizz-buzz', one of those drinking games. There was Hansen, Kenny, Brucie, Stevie Nicol, myself, Ronnie Whelan, Ian Rush, Sammy Lee, all drinking in this square in Tel Aviv.

"Things got said between us all and a fight started. Me and Rushie were quite close, we travelled in together [to training back at Melwood]. So it's us, back-to-back, against everybody else. Unbelievable. Somehow it calmed down and I went back to the hotel with Rushie and Alan Kennedy, who fell on the ground and couldn't get up.

"You remember the old Liverpool director, Mr Moss? Always away with the team on the big trips, the big cup finals. Well, he was coming out of the hotel just at that moment. So I've got down to pick up Alan Kennedy and I couldn't get up either. And Mr Moss is stood above us, frowning. He says: 'Gentlemen, this is Liverpool Football Club'.

"So I grabbed hold of his trousers and pulled myself up his body. As I'm pulling myself up, I'm pulling his trousers down. And I put my arm round him and said, 'Mossy, you old bugger, you might be a director but I think you're a great fella!'

"So the next morning, Bob Paisley [there as a member of LFC's travelling party] collars us when we come down for breakfast. He knew what had gone on and there were three empty chairs next to him at the front of the table. I come down first and he says: 'You, sit there'. Then Rushie comes down. 'You, sit there'. Then Alan

Kennedy. 'And you, sit there'. Bob turns to me and Rushie and says: 'So you think you're hard, youse two, fighting?'

"Then after breakfast they call this big meeting upstairs and around the table there's Bob, Joe Fagan, Ronnie Moran, Roy Evans…and Mr Moss, who stands up. 'I've been at this football club for over twenty years', he says, 'and I have never, ever witnessed anything like last night in my life. I've had many accolades passed on to me, but never have I received one so touching as that from David Hodgson'. Then they lift up the tablecloth – and underneath it's piled high with beer!"

After a punishing domestic season in which the Reds had clinched another league title and League Cup, and ahead of a daunting appearance in a modern Roman amphitheatre, it was simply a way of letting off steam before the utmost professionalism kicked in again – and it worked.

In his autobiography, Paul Walsh, then a new signing who'd been invited to join up with the squad but watch the European Cup final from the sidelines, described the pre-match build-up and post-match celebrations. "There were no airs and graces about the Liverpool lads at all – they weren't 'big time Charlies', even if they had every right to be.

"There were holes in the training kit, everything was pretty basic and they were happy to play football wherever they were asked to. On the morning of the final we all trained on a gravel pitch near the hotel, which was no more than Sunday League standard. It was quite refreshing considering they were about to play the biggest club game in the world…

"The game itself was tense but [after] Liverpool beat Roma on penalties it began to sink in that I was now playing for the champions of Europe. There was a party that night at a hilltop villa in Rome where a reception was held. Later we went back to the Holiday Inn hotel in the city where there were loads of

Liverpool fans staying. As you might imagine, they were delirious, in high spirits and mostly p****d.

"The lads just casually chatted and mixed with the supporters in the bar and the European Cup was passed around by everyone – it was ridiculous on some levels and fantastic in other ways. It was great to see how the players and fans had a genuine relationship. That was something I learned pretty quickly. Liverpool fans and the players had a real connection and that bond was a big part of the club's success over such a sustained period."

27/130

Voice of Anfield

"AND now, introducing your home team at Anfield for tonight's game against Arsenal. In goal, number one Alex Stepney. Number two, Tommy O'Neil...at nine, Bobby Charlton, 10, Denis Law and 11, George Best."

That may sound bizarre but words along those lines were uttered by George Sephton in August 1971 in only his third match as public address announcer at Anfield.

Following acts of hooliganism the previous season, the FA had insisted on Manchester United playing their opening two 'home' games of the 1971/72 campaign outside Manchester.

And so on a Friday night in late August, there was the strange sight of a team other than Liverpool wearing red-and-white and being cheered on from the Kop for a First Division fixture.

United won the game 3-1 in front of a crowd of 27,649 and

Sephton told the *Guardian* in 2010 that his memory of the game was a little sketchy: "It was spooky. I had just started, it was an extra match, it was Friday night so a bit of peace and quiet, I thought.

"Did I play *You'll Never Walk Alone*? I couldn't swear on the Bible but I'm pretty certain I didn't. It's been 'our' song since 1963. It was weird because Anfield felt like a neutral ground but from my perspective I was just happy that I had an extra couple of quid in my pocket because I was young, just married and was saving up for a house.

"The enmity with United wasn't as bad in those days as it is now so it was nice to turn up and watch a game which you weren't bothered about in terms of the result. If it happened nowadays of course, I'd be cheering Arsenal on!"

Less than a fortnight earlier, George had made his bow as the club's PA announcer on a day that will be remembered for another notable Anfield debut. Kevin Keegan stole the show as Liverpool defeated Nottingham Forest 3-1. In 2021, George celebrated 50 years in the role – an incredible achievement that has seen him christened the 'Voice of Anfield.'

He explained: "Alan Jackson took over from Stuart Bateman who was famous for first playing *You'll Never Walk Alone* in October 1963. However, Alan was desperate to get his foot on the ladder in radio. He finally got his lucky break and a six-month contract for Manchester Radio. He went to talk to Peter Robinson, the club secretary at the time, explaining it was his big break and that he would leave his brother in charge. But he used to play the vinyls at the wrong speed and struggled to pronounce the English names, never mind the foreign ones!

"Anyway, I was there at Anfield for a midweek game in April 1971 and Alan's brother made a massive mistake. I said to my wife: 'I bet I can do better than this fella', and that very night I wrote to Peter Robinson putting my case forward. To my delight I got a reply from him asking to come and see him.

"To cut a long story short I think I made him realise that I could do a better job. I had no trial run or anything which I thought was strange. Anyway, the next thing I know I was upstairs in the Main Stand gantry as it was then known."

George believes the number of first-team home games he has missed in 50-plus years is in single figures. In addition to his duties at senior side fixtures, he has also taken control of the microphone at youth team and Liverpool FC Women matches. Naturally, the playing of *YNWA* has been a big part of his role.

"Over the years I've worn through a few copies of the record! The original seven inch vinyl copy is now in the museum at FC Twente in Holland. They invited me over a couple times a few years ago as they also sing *YNWA* before games. When I moved over to CD, I thought it would be a nice gesture to give them the record. The last I heard it was still on the wall in the museum there.

"Using CDs is considered old-fashioned these days but I still use a CD version of the song. I also have one back-up copy on mini-disc. I'm paranoid about it now because there was one occasion in the early 80s when I turned up to Anfield without *YNWA*. We were still using the vinyl versions back then. I unpacked my case and realised I'd left it at home. There was nothing I could do, so I just held my hands up and 'fessed up to the crowd! I said: 'I'm sorry, I've come without the record, you'll have to carry on.' And, of course, they did. That was the one and only time it's happened but from that day on, I always have a couple of copies."

Hearing George's dulcet tones has become a part of the matchday experience at Anfield but he is also known for championing the sounds of others, particularly when it comes to promoting Liverpool bands.

He told the LFC matchday programme: "I consider Liverpool to be the birthplace of rock or pop – however you define it – because of what happened in the sixties and for the fact that the Kop would always sing songs by local artists. That's one of the reasons why I like to play records by so many local bands at Anfield.

"I've become renowned for it now but I am old enough to remember when The Beatles were playing around Liverpool for £10 a night and having seen what's happened to those guys, I'm a great believer in encouraging talent in whatever shape or form it takes.

"I have a lot of CDs and MP3 files sent to me. Some of it is not good, a lot of it is, yet completely unsuitable for a football stadium. But it's amazing how often you play something and you think: 'Wow, where did that come from?' There are a couple of bands who have said that the first recognition they had was being played at Anfield. A lot of people have also phoned and emailed me and said they've had such a reaction because I've played one of their songs at Anfield. It's a pleasure to hear but that's the magic of the Liverpool Football Club name."

28/130

Forgotten fixtures

LIVERPOOL FC's rich history features many memorable matches but there are also a few 'hidden gems' – games that have perhaps been overtaken by others given the magnitude of some of the Reds' successes during the past 130 years.

For one of the first, we have to trawl back more than a century to the home game against Tottenham Hotspur in October 1914. The teams' rivalry was in its infancy back then with this fixture just the 11th between the sides. A crowd of 20,000 saw Tom Watson's Reds run riot in the closing stages to notch an emphatic 7-2 win – a fair feat considering they only led 3-2 going into the 78th minute! Forward Fred Pagnam helped himself to four goals, including a 10-minute hat-trick between minutes 70 and 80 before winger Jackie Sheldon completed the rout with goals in the 86th and 88th minutes. Pagnam's Liverpool career was stalled by the First World War and it would have been interesting to see his stats had the conflict not occurred. As it was he netted 30 goals in 39 games for the club following a £75 move from Blackpool earlier in 1914.

Another game which saw the Reds put seven goals past London opponents at Anfield came against Chelsea in September 1946 at the beginning of a season which would see Liverpool claim an unlikely title in the first full season of league football following World War Two.

Two of the biggest legends in Liverpool FC's history, Bob Paisley and Billy Liddell, finally made their league debuts seven years after signing professional forms for the club.

George Kay's side led 4-0 at half-time and 6-0 after 50 minutes with Liddell and Bill Jones scoring twice but nerves started jangling among most of the 49,995 spectators inside the ground when Chelsea reduced the arrears to 6-4 with 18 minutes still remaining. However, Willie Fagan's second of the match eventually secured a 7-4 triumph and inspired hopes among the home faithful of a promising campaign to come.

From the heights of that season's successes to the disappointments of April 1954 and a home game against Middlesbrough. Little did any Liverpool fan know it at the time but the final Anfield fixture of that 1953/54 campaign would be the last top-flight fixture the stadium would host for eight years and would also mark

Liddell's final goal in English football's top division. For what it was worth, already-relegated Liverpool won the game 4-1 against the also-relegated Teessiders but a 0-3 defeat at Blackpool five days later saw the Reds drop into the Second Division for the first time in 50 years. Despite finishing bottom, they scored 68 goals in their 42-game league campaign. However they also shipped 97 – the most in all four divisions.

By the 1970s, Liverpool were firmly established back in the top-flight having won the championship in 1964 and 1966, either side of a first FA Cup triumph. The rivalry with Everton, dubbed the Mersey Millionaires, remained fierce and when the clubs met at Anfield in November 1970, Harry Catterick's side were the reigning league champions.

It is a game that is sometimes overlooked, but remains Liverpool's greatest derby comeback victory at Anfield and will be hard to top whatever the years ahead may conjure up.

Goalless at half-time, the Blues took control with goals from forwards Alan Whittle and Joe Royle a few minutes either side of the hour mark.

But then Tommy Smith sent Steve Heighway away down the left flank and the winger glided past defenders John Hurst and Tommy Wright before sliding the ball beyond Toffees keeper Andy Rankin. Game on.

Seven minutes later Heighway went racing down the wing again before sending a cross into the penalty area. John Toshack, the Reds' recently recruited 21-year-old centre-forward, powered home a header and Liverpool were all-square.

The momentum was suddenly all with Liverpool and they swarmed forward in search of a winner. Alec Lindsay's ball was nodded down by Toshack into the path of the on-running Chris Lawler and Liverpool's 'silent knight' sent Anfield into raptures of delight by firing the ball home.

Liverpool Echo journalist Horace Yates later recalled the crowd not wanting to leave at the final whistle. On enquiring why, Shankly was told that perhaps fans were waiting to hear scores of the other fixtures. "Why?" retorted Shanks. "Was there any other game today?"

Liverpool's road to a third European Cup triumph in 1980/81 continued with a second round tie against Aberdeen. In the programme notes for the first leg clash at Pittodrie, Dons boss Alex Ferguson had described Liverpool as 'a great club'. Bob Paisley's men won 1-0 that evening but when the teams reconvened at Anfield on Bonfire Night, the Reds hammered Fergie's side 4-0 with Scottish duo Kenny Dalglish and Alan Hansen among their marksmen along with an own goal from Aberdeen centre-back Willie Miller, leaving Ferguson inwardly seething.

Liverpool recorded an 18th top-flight championship in 1990. Strangely, however, the game on the day the Reds clinched the title – QPR at Anfield – remains largely forgotten.

Perhaps that was partly down to the fact that the team went into that fixture needing four points from their last three games to win the championship and some felt it would have come down to the game at home to Derby County a few days later, or even at Coventry City's Highfield Road in the season's finale. The fact that it wasn't televised may also be a factor.

QPR, managed by Don Howe, were out to spoil Liverpool's party plans and took an early lead through Roy Wegerle. Soon afterwards, fellow front man Colin Clarke left the Reds' crossbar shaking after crashing a shot at goal. However, five minutes before the break Ian Rush took down a Steve Nicol centre and steered his 25th goal of the season past David Seaman to set up an intriguing second-half.

Liverpool's main rivals for the title were Aston Villa but they were in the midst of drawing 3-3 with Norwich City and, though the Reds did not know it at the time, it meant a winning goal would be enough to see them crowned as champions.

Almost 20 minutes into the second-half, QPR defender Danny Maddix fouled Nicol on the edge of the area and referee Robbie Hart pointed to the spot despite protests from the visitors. Footballer of the Year John Barnes stepped up and converted via the foot of the right-hand post.

News then spread that Villa had blown a 3-1 lead against Norwich, sparking chants of 'champions, champions' before the final whistle and Reds boss Kenny Dalglish was naturally delighted when it was confirmed that Liverpool had won title number 18. "We won the title because we have been the best team this season," he told reporters afterwards, "and not because Norwich held Aston Villa to a draw. If someone wants to help along the way we are grateful, but we don't expect it."

Fast forward another decade and a Premier League game against Leeds United in February 2000 may have been a routine home win as the Reds ran out 3-1 victors – but referee Mike Reed seemed every bit as delighted as the staunchest Kopite.

The Birmingham official was seen pumping his fist after Patrik Berger scored at the Kop end to put the Reds 2-1 up before Danny Murphy struck a late third. Reed later claimed that he was pleased because he had allowed play to go on instead of blowing for a foul on Vladimir Smicer in the build-up, and was happy that his own free-flowing refereeing had resulted in a goal.

"I clenched a fist in front of my shorts in celebration of the fact that I had played an advantage to Liverpool," he later told *BBC Radio 5 Live*. "There's no better feeling for referees than playing an advantage and the ball ending in the net. I've been accused of being a fan of quite a few teams in the past, but Aston Villa are my only team," added Reed, who was not permitted to take charge of games involving teams from the Birmingham area.

Liverpool supporters of a certain vintage will also remember referee Norman Burtenshaw seeming to celebrate at Wembley following Arsenal's 1971 FA Cup final triumph over the Reds which clinched the Gunners the league and cup double. Check out the YouTube footage of the scenes at the final whistle!

Kopites had plenty to celebrate on a chilly Wednesday night in December 2013 when Luis Suarez came up against his favourite opponents, Norwich City.

By the end of the night the Uruguayan ace had become the first Liverpool player to score three hat-tricks against the same club and also the first player in the history of the Premier League to achieve this feat. He helped himself to four goals in a 5-1 victory, leaving Canaries keeper John Ruddy sick of the sight of him. 'Done Four – King Luis now a record breaker', screamed the *Daily Mirror* back page the following morning.

Reds skipper Steven Gerrard said afterwards: "You have seen a world-class performance, probably one of the best individual performances I've seen at Anfield – and I've been playing here a long time. Having worked with him every single day, it's probably less of a surprise to me as it is to the supporters.

"I've been pushing his corner for a long time that he is up there with the best in the world. I think he's getting so close to the main two, Ronaldo and Messi. If he keeps going, I think he can catch them. His fourth goal was average and it was a 30-yard free-kick, so I think that sums his performance up."

The Boot Room boy

IN the grand scheme of things, the day when Joe Fagan lugged three or four crates of Guinness Export into the famous Anfield Boot Room seems somehow insignificant.

The crates had been given to Fagan, then Liverpool FC trainer, in the early 1960s by local councillor Paul Orr as a 'thank you' gift during Bill Shankly's reign as manager.

Orr, who in 1977 became Lord Mayor of Liverpool, was manager of local amateur side Guiness *(sic)* Export (who played in the Lancashire Combination between 1964 and 1968) and Fagan had allowed the players to use the Anfield treatment room to be treated by Bob Paisley.

Guinness Export was higher in alcohol content than the draught Guinness available at the time so made a good gift, but it was the crates the bottles were stored in that proved to be the unlikeliest of catalysts for a significant part in Liverpool's history.

The Anfield Boot Room was, in reality, nothing more than an over-sized cupboard situated off a long corridor inside the old Main Stand which had the players' boots hung up on pegs. But, because Fagan and his fellow backroom team members – which included men like Paisley, Reuben Bennett, Ronnie Moran, Tom Saunders, Roy Evans and John Bennison over the years – wanted somewhere inside the ground where they could sit and discuss matters or invite opposition coaches in for a quick drink after a match, they turned the room into a social meeting place. It was inside that room where Moran wrote his Boot Room Bibles, a daily diary of everything that was going on at LFC, used by the backroom staff as reference points and a knowledge base.

Liverpool's coaching staff didn't have desks then, never mind offices, so Fagan had to be creative and it was he who tipped those crates of Guinness Export onto their sides to use as makeshift seats.

With that simple action the Anfield Boot Room – the mystical, magical cubby-hole that has gone down in folklore as the secret behind three decades of Liverpool success – was created.

Fagan wasn't just an original member of that Boot Room. He was the man who set it up.

"If the door is closed you stay out," recalled Graeme Souness, who was wrongly accused of having the Boot Room demolished in the 1990s. It was actually the board's decision to create bigger press facilities, as required by UEFA for Euro 96, at a time when the players had started to report directly to Melwood each day for training whereas they'd been bussed in from Anfield in the past.

"It is the place where all the playing decisions are made and where the big pow-wow takes place after every home game when it is simply out of bounds to us mere players. When that door is locked and bolted you can only imagine what goes on inside."

Fagan would eventually go on to manage Liverpool Football Club between 1983 and 1985 having first arrived at Anfield in 1958.

Born in Liverpool's Walton Hospital on 12 March 1921, he was a strapping centre-half who spent his playing career with Manchester City – after serving aboard a minesweeper off the Egyptian coast during World War II – before becoming player-manager of non-league Nelson FC in 1951. He helped to make ends meet by inspecting gas meters for leaks in local factories, but it was the explosion of goals his team scored in the 1951/52 season which caught the eye.

Nelson won the Lancashire Combination First Division title, scoring 139 goals in 42 matches. The following season they finished fifth (Wigan Athletic won the league!) but Fagan's managerial capabilities had been noted and in 1953, aged 32, he moved to Rochdale, via a three-game spell as a player at Bradford Park Avenue, to work as trainer under the management of Harry Catterick, a former team-mate at City.

It was May 1958, shortly after Liverpool had missed out on promotion to the First Division for the fourth consecutive season, when Fagan got his Anfield opportunity. Four months earlier, ex-Motherwell assistant trainer Bennett had been appointed as head coach to help out manager Phil Taylor with former player Paisley working as physio.

Liverpool's frustrating failure to go up resulted in a further backroom reshuffle and, ironically, it was Catterick, who later went on to manage Everton, that recommended Fagan to Taylor after receiving a call from him. Taylor liked what he heard and so Fagan was appointed as LFC's assistant trainer, replacing Dickie Dorsett.

Bill Shankly, of course, arrived from Huddersfield Town as manager 18 months later and the sleeping giant that was Liverpool FC awoke from its slumber with the Boot Room that Fagan subsequently created underpinning the success that followed.

Inside it, all men were equal. Everyone's input was expected and respected. It was a room where ideas and opinions were pooled, a sanctuary away from the manager and players, but also an interrogation room that visiting managers were invited into for a post-match drink and shrewdly tapped for information without evening realising it.

"When visiting managers and coaches were invited in for a drink, they usually accepted gratefully, aware of the honour," recalled Kenny Dalglish in *My Liverpool Home*. "They'd perch on a skip, sipping whisky from an old glass, totally unaware they had walked into an ambush. 'You're building a good team there. Got any kids coming through?' Joe asked. Responding to such flattery, the visiting manager would talk about some promising teenager on the books of his club. Within days Liverpool scouts would be checking him out."

It wasn't just rival managers that were weighed up in the Boot Room. One of the most famous visitors, after seeing his side beaten 3-1 at Anfield in December 1982, was Watford chairman Elton John, as former *Daily Express* journalist John Keith recalled.

"He emerged full of the experience to tell me: 'I've just played a live concert in America to thousands, but I was much more nervous stepping into this world famous holy of holies. When I was asked what I'd like to drink I said a pink gin. Joe said to me: 'Sorry, lad. You can have a Guinness, a brown ale or a Scotch – and that's yer lot'. I had a beer. It was just fantastic being in there."

Fagan was a hard man – he earned extra money from bare-knuckle fighting during the War – and while he would be an approachable confidante for players who came to regard him as 'Uncle Joe', he also wasn't shy of dishing out rollickings when he thought they were needed.

"I can give anyone the mother and father of a hiding, verbally," he once admitted. "You can't let the players think you are a soft touch, not here or at any club."

Also known as 'Smokin Joe' for his constant dragging on cigarettes, Fagan rose through the ranks at Anfield, taking over as first team coach from Bennett in 1974 following Shankly's shock departure, before becoming assistant manager in 1979 following Bennett's retirement.

Continuity was a huge part of Liverpool's success. A structure was in place that ensured when the top man stepped down, the next man stepped up, but when Paisley announced at the start of 1982/83 that he would be retiring from his position as manager at the end of the season, Fagan didn't initially want to step into his shoes, particularly as he hated the public gaze that came with the job.

"When Bob decided to retire, it frightened me that they might ask me to take over," he said. "I thought that I might be too old for it. My first reaction at that time was that I wouldn't take it, but I thought about it carefully and realised that someone else might come in and upset the whole rhythm. I finally decided to take it and keep the continuity going for a little longer. I know the drill, what goes on and experience comes into it."

Even when Joe got the manager's job – he agreed to take it in December 1982 but the official announcement was only made in May 1983 – his down-to-earth attitude remained and he and wife Lil stayed in their modest home on Lynholme Road, just five minutes walk away from Anfield. He also made it clear that even though he was 62, his appointment was no 'old pal's act' and that he wouldn't simply follow what Paisley had been doing.

"I must start afresh," he said. "I am my own man. I will do the job the way I think is right. That's not to say there will be drastic changes – just little ones.

"We are up with the game here. There are no fuddy duddies. I am starting with a clean slate because just thinking about following Bob would be mad. That's the secret of our success here. We never look back, always forward."

And forward Liverpool went to an unprecedented and still unmatched treble of league title, League Cup and European Cup in Joe's first season in charge, a marathon campaign spanning 67 games that ended with Alan Kennedy's winning penalty kick against AS Roma in Rome and Fagan becoming the first Englishman to be named as Manager of the Year in his debut season.

Fagan took Liverpool to the European Cup final again in 1985, the Reds' 1-0 defeat to Juventus being overshadowed by the tragedy of Heysel when 39 Juve fans lost their lives after a wall collapsed following fighting between the two sets of fans, but by then he had already decided that he wished to step down.

His decision was made in February 1985 after a meeting with chairman Sir John Smith, although the press only got wind of it before the European Cup final in Brussels three months later.

"There are two reasons for me deciding to go," he stated. "In the first place I now think I am too old to carry on any longer as manager. Secondly, I am starting to feel a bit tired.

"It is time for a younger man to take over, and to supervise any team building that may be necessary next season. I have enjoyed the chance to manage Liverpool very much indeed, but since February have begun to think it was time I called it a day.

"When I first took over I said that I thought two years would be about enough, and that is how it has proved. At heart I'm still one of the backroom boys."

Fagan passed away at the age of 80 in 2001. He'll be eternally remembered for leading the Reds to that famous treble in 1984, but his true legacy is the Anfield Boot Room. Where would LFC have been without him and that mystical, magical room?

30/130

The kid who would be King

FEW Liverpool FC supporters would disagree with the statement that Kenny Dalglish was, and is, the club's best ever signing.

The Scot was snapped up from Celtic for a then British record fee of £440,000 in the summer of 1977 as a replacement for Kevin Keegan. Bob Paisley had been chipping away at the Parkhead club that summer and finally received the breakthrough he desired when, following a bid of £400,000, he was told by Bhoys' boss Jock Stein to 'add another 10% and you may have a deal.' And so Dalglish joined Liverpool and the rest is history.

However, not so many Liverpool supporters are familiar with the story of how a lad called Jimmy Bowman scuppered Kenny's bid to making a scoring start in a Liverpool shirt or how his LFC story could have panned out very differently indeed.

The conventional wisdom is that Kenneth Mathieson's first game in a Liverpool shirt was in the Charity Shield of 1977. However that was not the case as a teenage Dalglish came to the club on trial when Bill Shankly was manager in the 1960s.

Shanks wanted to sign the talented teenager but Kenny's parents felt it was too early for him to leave his Glasgow home.

Norwegian statistician Jonny Stokkeland has spent countless hours researching the club's fixtures, not only at first-team level but also reserve and junior matches. His findings led to him setting up a statistical database called the *Liverpool Official Archives*.

And Jonny's efforts also established that when Dalglish first pulled on a Liverpool shirt, it was not the no7 jersey with which he would become synonymous. Instead, he played his first 90 minutes with a Liver Bird upon his chest in the no8 shirt then associated with Roger Hunt and more recently with Steven Gerrard. He was just 15-years-old.

Jonny explained: "I went through some of the old *KOP* newspapers from the 1960s and came across the very game in question. It was a 'B' team match played on 20 August 1966 and despite having Kenny in the team, Liverpool were beaten one-nil by Southport."

In his 2010 book *My Liverpool Home*, Kenny recalled the game: "I was just me, desperate to win as always. When we were losing 1-0, I had a chance to equalise but as I was about to roll the ball into the Southport net with my left foot, a wee guy called Jimmy Bowman nicked it off my toes and missed. I would have scored. Afterwards I trudged off the Melwood pitch, still seething at the incident and losing."

After also impressing during an Under-16s trial game, Kenny was accompanied by Shanks back to the YMCA near Lime Street station where he was staying. Bill informed the youngster that he wanted to sign him and would send representatives to see his parents in Glasgow.

However, Kenny's father decided he was too young, and although he would later have a trial with Ron Greenwood's West Ham, Kenny would go on to start his professional career in his home city of Glasgow with Celtic, emerging from the club's reserve team of several future Scottish internationals known as the famous Quality Street Gang.

Eleven years later he finally made his senior debut for Liverpool in that Charity Shield against Manchester United at Wembley, this time in the no7 shirt he would wear with distinction for most of the other 514 occasions apart from when player-manager Dalglish started naming himself as substitute!

It was the beginning of a mutual love affair between Dalglish and the club, albeit one that could have started eleven years earlier.

Of course he went on to inspire the Reds to numerous successes both as a player and during two spells as manager, during which his Liverpool teams added another six trophies to the Anfield roll of honour.

Jonny adds: "It is interesting to think what might have happened had Kenny signed more than a decade before he actually did! It also seems significant that his 'debut' outing was against Southport – the town where he would eventually set up home. Either way, that 'B' team game is certainly an interesting part of his overall Liverpool story."

31/130

Scouting for goals

TALENT-SPOTTERS are present at almost every football match played up and down the country.

Former Reds Tom Bush, Geoff Twentyman and Ron Yeats worked tirelessly for many years in their efforts to spot unpolished gems.

Less is known, however, about Harry Mooney, a man whose opinion was valued by all three.

Along with Twentyman, he played a part in unearthing a couple of players who became Liverpool FC's top-two goalscorers of all-time with 631 between them!

"I was a referee in the Mid Cheshire League and had never done any official scouting until I happened to see a good player one day," Mooney told *LFC Weekly* magazine just months before his death in 2011, aged 91. "Tom Bush, Liverpool's centre-half before the war, was the club's head scout and I knew him very well. He lived near the ground off Anfield Road and I used to go out with his wife's younger sister.

"He asked me if I ever saw any good lads when I refereed and I replied that I often saw lads who would do well. He asked me to pass them on but I explained that I wasn't allowed to affiliate myself with any club. He said: 'This is my private address and private number. If you see anybody, telephone me and I'll do the rest'."

Not long after that discussion, Harry spotted one such player he thought was worth contacting Bush about.

"I was refereeing Stockton Heath in a match against ICI," he recalled. "They had this big lad up front, who was very strong, and he broke through the defence and scored two similar goals before half-time. I thought he looked a very good player. He was unselfish and had plenty of speed.

"I went into the dressing room at half-time and said: 'What's your name, son?' He said: 'Roger Hunt.' I asked him how come no-one had picked him up and he told me his dad was a haulage contractor and that he regularly drove a wagon for him.

"I told him I thought he was a good player and asked whether he would like to join Liverpool. 'Oh, I'm a Liverpudlian,' he said. 'That's my team!' I rang up Tom Bush and he said he would send Bill Jones [another ex-Reds centre-half and scout] to watch him the following week.

"Roger played centre-forward and after a while he banged one in. 'Goodness me, you've found one there,' said Bill. "By half-time he'd seen enough. He went into the dressing room, called Roger to one side and said: 'How would you like to join Liverpool?' Roger replied: 'Oh, that would be my heart's desire but I have never been approached.' He said: 'Well you've been approached now. I'm Bill Jones on behalf of the club.'"

Liverpool made sure that Stockton Heath didn't suffer. The club received £500 – a very healthy sum in those days.

Harry added: "At the time, Stockton Heath Football Club had a small hut for the teams to change in, a small room for the referee and linesmen to change in and no social club at all. With the money they got, they built a new clubhouse with a games room, put up new changing rooms and had Roger's photograph over the bar. He was made president of the club."

Over the next 11 years, Hunt scored 285 goals in 492 matches, overtaking Gordon Hodgson's club record.

"It turned out alright!," says Harry. "What would you pay for someone like that nowadays? After the World Cup in 1966, Alf Ramsey said that without Roger Hunt England wouldn't have won the World Cup because he broke up the Germany defence to make room for Geoff Hurst and Martin Peters to score the goals."

Mooney was also present when the Reds recruited the man who would in turn overhaul Hunt's goalscoring record.

"Geoff [Twentyman] and I went to see Ian Rush at Chester and he scored three goals. We came back and we were told they wanted a small fee for him. I said: 'Pay it!' It was probably one of the best signings we ever made."

Another example of scouting judgement being key was illustrated one night in the early 1970s when Mooney accompanied Twentyman on a particular mission.

"One day Geoff told me: 'I'm going to Scunthorpe to see a lad called Keegan. Do you want to come with me?' Once at the ground, Geoff said: 'That's Keegan – the outside right. He was found by the same fellow as Ray Clemence, who had joined Liverpool a few years earlier. Anyway, he was running inside for the ball and picking it up. In the end he scored a goal. The bloke who was sitting next to me said: 'Who's Geoff Twentyman watching?' I said: 'I can't tell you.' He said: 'I bet it's that blimmin' Keegan. They want £30,000 for him. I wouldn't give them 30 blimmin' pence.'

"I said: 'Oh. And who are you?' He said: 'I'm a scout for Arsenal.' What a find he missed. Geoff had wanted me to give him the once over because he trusted my judgement and we knew enough to understand that he was what the Liverpool team wanted."

32/130

Watch the birdie

AT the AXA Training Centre it is the first thing that visitors, not least new signings, see when they arrive: designed into the shiny panelling behind the main reception desk is a red bird as big and imposing as the pair perched on the twin peaks of the Royal Liver Building in Liverpool city centre.

At Anfield it stands majestic, wings elevated, outside the stadium in two large metallic-grey Liverpool FC crests at either end of the expanded Main Stand. It is depicted in red on a white crest upon the Shankly Gates at the corner of the Sir Kenny Dalglish Stand and Anfield Road, along with a saltire and thistle below the club anthem You'll Never Walk Alone. On the other side of the ground, facing Walton Breck Road, it adorns the Paisley Gates that honour Bill's managerial successor.

The Liver Bird of Liverpool Football Club. It made its first elegant bow upon the club's crest in 1901, nine years after the dispute between LFC founder John Houlding and the ground's original occupants, Everton FC. Interestingly, Liver Birds appear on very early Evertonian memorabilia.

Today our fabulous feathered friend is on the scarves, replica shirts, hats and flags of LFC supporters and of course the chests of all those legendary players who have run out onto the hallowed turf since the 1950s – when the Liver Bird first appeared on the kit. As early as 1901, though, it was inscribed upon medals awarded for Liverpool FC's first league title triumph, and it was also stitched gloriously upon the club's official 'Championship flag' for 1921/22. It began to feature regularly in the official matchday programme from the Second World War onwards.

Upon the shirt down the decades it has variously stood inside a simple oval, within a shield that has evolved into today's club crest bordered by eternal flames, and currently in white embroidery upon official kit sponsor Nike's jersey for the 2021/22 campaign. In 2017/18, to mark the club's 125th anniversary, it was positioned between the dates 1892 and 2017, standing above 'LFC' and '125 YEARS'.

Just like its various incarnations on the red shirt, the creature can be found in every style, shape and size all over the city of Liverpool – upon everything from old banks and hotels, museums and libraries, schools and hospitals, pubs and fire stations, cemeteries and bridges, and even lamp posts and bollards.

But why a Liver Bird? This particular ornithological specimen never flies the nest to compete with gulls and pigeons for the day's scraps, and you won't find it in any conventional guidebook. On the seal granted by King John to the small town of Liverpool 800 years ago it resembles an eagle. Alongside Neptune on the heraldic coat of arms ratified in 1797 it's officially a cormorant, 'the wings elevated, in the beak a branch of seaweed called Laver; the motto 'Deus Nobis Haec Otia Fecit' – which comes from a poem by the Roman writer Virgil and means 'These gifts God has bestowed upon us'.

Ancient stuffed specimens of young and adult cormorants were once displayed in the Town Hall and today they're held at World Museum Liverpool. The authoritative *Birds Britannica* book calls the species a "powerfully heraldic bird" which can be "remarkably handsome."

Another recent school of thought contends that the original Liver Bird was indeed a white-tailed sea-eagle – a large, fish-eating species that was a common sight in the Mersey estuary until the early 20th century. But today in sculptures and statues around the city it's pretty much every species in-between, nesting in shields and shells alongside fabulous creatures of the deep, majestic crowns and Latin mottos celebrating Liverpool's heritage as a great port. And as a rule it faces to the left, although it can be found facing forward and even depicted overhead.

No two Liver Birds are quite the same: one for instance might have the hefty chest of an ostrich, sprouting an osprey's powerful wings with legs ending in a duck's dainty webbed feet; another, the looped neck of a swan, slender bill of a heron and fanciful crest of a grebe paired with a peacock's flamboyant tail.

The National Museums Liverpool Maritime Archives & Library insists that the Liver Bird "is part of Liverpool's modern, rather than ancient, folklore" and that the copper creatures crowning the Liver Building "helped to fix in the popular mind the myth that the Liver was a fabulous bird that once haunted the Pool inlet." William Enfield's *History of Liverpool*, published in 1774, corroborates this view, declaring that the bird existed only "in fabulous tradition and the Herald's office."

But the truth is, no one is ever quite sure where the bird came from, or what exact species it is – which is all part of its mystique. Next time you've got a little time to kill on matchday at Anfield or you're just wandering the historic streets of the city centre, take a closer look – and make your mind up for yourself.

33/130

Mr Liverpool

TRYING to put the achievement of spending 49 years at Liverpool Football Club into some sort of context is difficult, but perhaps our club's 130th anniversary is the perfect opportunity to re-remind every Kopite of a truly remarkable career.

For more than a third of LFC's existence, Ronnie Moran worked for the club. He dedicated nearly half-a-century of his working life – and when you're a player, captain, trainer, coach or acting manager at a football club then first-and-foremost it is a job – to Liverpool FC. Truly phenomenal.

No wonder he became known as Mr Liverpool.

Could you imagine working where you are now, in different roles, as Ronnie did at Anfield and Melwood from the age of 15 in 1949 until he was 64 in 1998? It almost seems too far-fetched to be true. Yet it isn't. There are jobs and dream jobs, but Ronnie's career is perhaps the greatest boy's own fairytale in Liverpool history.

Following his sad passing at the age of 83 in March 2017, after a five-year battle with the memory-stealing demon that is dementia and a subsequent short illness, it felt like the world of football had finally realised just how big a pillar 'Bugsy' was in propping up the unmatched success that the Redmen enjoyed during his time here. Everybody's life story is unique, but few have been as remarkable as Ronnie Moran's.

Ronnie was born on 28 February 1934 and grew up in Crosby, firstly on Coronation Road and then Alexandra Road. The youngest of nine, he had four brothers and four sisters and, being a Scouser, his first love was football, closely followed by football and football. Like so many kids from that era he watched Liverpool on Saturdays when they played at Anfield and Everton the following weekend when in action at Goodison Park. A life in the game beckoned.

A Merseyside Championship Cup winner with Bootle Boys in 1948, his big footballing break came in 1949 when a local postman, who had seen Ronnie play, mentioned his name to Liverpool director TV Williams – who eventually became chairman in 1956 – while delivering letters to his house.

Shortly afterwards, Williams and Liverpool manager George Kay arrived at Ronnie's home and offered him amateur terms. They acted just in time as a week later Everton manager Cliff Britton told Ronnie he'd like to sign him, but by then it was too late. He was a Red.

As 'sliding doors' moments go in the history of football on Merseyside, they don't get much bigger.

Because of what Ronnie and Liverpool achieved during his coaching career his playing days are often overlooked, something that does an injustice to a man who made 379 appearances for the club between his debut in November 1952 at Derby County in the First Division and his final match away to Inter Milan in the European Cup semi-final in 1965. Those 379 games put Moran 32nd on LFC's all-time appearance list, ahead of fellow greats like Gordon Hodgson, Robbie Fowler, Graeme Souness and Kevin Keegan.

Moran spent most of his career at full-back, both on the left and right, and was the only member of the Liverpool team relegated in 1953/54 (a season he played in just once) to still be at the club when the Reds won the Division One title a decade later in 1963/64 (a season he made 39 appearances in) under the management of Bill Shankly.

During that time he scored 17 goals including what looked like an 89th minute winner against Manchester United at Old Trafford in 1962, only for Johnny Giles to make it 3-3 in 'Busby time', and a famous 119th minute FA Cup 4th round penalty winner against Burnley in front of almost 58,000 inside Anfield. One Kopite there on that night in 1963, celebrated screenwriter Jimmy McGovern, regards that 2-1 win as the "first biggie" of his match-going days.

Ronnie also captained Liverpool 47 times, having been handed the job at the start of the 1959/60 campaign, by when he was both married – to Joyce in 1957 – and a father with daughter Janet born on Christmas Day of that year. Son Paul followed in 1962.

Shankly had kept Ronnie in his side after taking charge, but appointed Dick White as his new captain in the summer of 1960, suggesting that Moran's long-term future probably lay away from Anfield. Little did anybody know that Shanks had bigger plans for him.

After spending 1965/66 in the reserves and with no new contract offer on the table at the age of 32, Ronnie was understandably nervous when Shankly called him into his office that summer.

"I thought 'this is it,' he's going to tell me another club have come in for me," he recalled in his 2017-published life story *Ronnie Moran: Mr Liverpool*. But instead, Shanks offered him a job on his Anfield backroom staff, working initially with the youth team. He took it, marking the start of a truly remarkable Liverpool coaching career that stretched for 32 years.

Ronnie was youth team coach from 1966 to 1971, reserve team

manager from 1971 to 1974, first team trainer from 1974 to 1979 and first team coach from 1979 until his retirement in 1998. During that time he was acting manager for 10 games in 1990/91 – following Kenny Dalglish's shock resignation – and caretaker manager for eight games in 1991/92 while Graeme Souness was recovering from triple heart bypass surgery.

Indeed, he could've even become permanent manager following Dalglish's departure in 1991. Moran was the obvious candidate to replace Kenny at a club that had so successfully appointed from within for three decades, but he told chairman Noel White that he didn't want the job only to later have a change of heart. It was too late. Souness had already been offered the position.

So while he may never have ended up with the top job on a permanent basis, it in no way diminishes what he did for Liverpool.

The stats don't lie. The Reds won 23 of the club's 49 major honours with Ronnie Moran on the coaching staff. 10 league titles, four European Cups, three FA Cups, one UEFA Cup and five League Cups. Add to that a Second Division and First Division title he won as a player, the Reds winning an FA Cup (1965) and another title (1966) when he was out of the team, 13 Charity Shields and a European Super Cups (plus the fact he only missed one first team match between 1974 and 1998 – Arsenal away in 1997 due to a family illness) and it is absolutely no coincidence that LFC was so successful when Ronnie was an employee.

Talk of 'The Liverpool Way' has become a cliche in the eyes of some. Critics and rivals dismiss it as a soundbite without meaning. They're wrong. It was anything but, and Ronnie underpinned it.

Pass and move. Keep it simple. Never stay still. Remain humble. Work for one another. Listen. Respect those in charge. Understand your own mistakes. Learn from them. Keep your feet on the ground. Adopt a winning mentality. And do it again. And again. And next year.

That was The Liverpool Way. That was what Ronnie preached; what he believed in. And he put his points across in his own indomitable style that earned him the reputation of the 'bad cop' on the Melwood training pitch, a sergeant major style coach who would hand out rollickings but in a manner that made the most astute 'bigheads' – the term he used for first-team players – listen and positively react to the golden nuggets of advice he was passing on.

There's no better example of the influence he had than Kevin Keegan's transformation in 1971.

Signed from Scunthorpe United at the age of 20 in May 71, Keegan was a midfielder who was trying to model his game on Trevor Brooking. When the Reds jetted off on their pre-season tour that summer, Shankly left him behind to work with Moran in the reserves and following a practice match against Tranmere Rovers at Prenton Park he found himself on the end of Ronnie's wrath: "What do you think you're doing? You're not playing like a Liverpool player. You're just charging about midfield. You've got responsibilities defensively as well." And so on.

Despite his vociferous annoyance, Ronnie had seen enough during that game to believe Keegan would make a better forward so when Shankly, who had never seen Keegan play before, returned, Moran told him to start the youngster up front in a friendly against Southport. He scored both goals in a 2-1 win. Four days later Keegan scored a hat-trick, while playing up front again, as the first team beat the reserves 7-1 in one of the annual pre-season friendlies that used to take place.

Shanks now knew what he had signed. He fast-tracked Keegan into the first team, handed him the number seven shirt and 12 minutes into his Anfield debut watched him score the opening goal as Nottingham Forest were beaten 3-1. The Kop had a new hero and Keegan later admitted: "One of the reasons I played so well [in pre-season] was that I wanted to make Ronnie Moran eat his words. I wanted to show him that I could play, because I did not think he rated me."

Has there ever been a finer example – tangible proof – of just how important and influential backroom staff can be for both a manager and in the career of a player?

Following Shankly's retirement in 1974, Ronnie was promoted to the role of first-team trainer by Bob Paisley and became a member of the Anfield Boot Room. It was there where he began to write the Boot Room Bibles, a collection of books that document the secrets behind Liverpool's success.

Every day, Ronnie would keep a diary. He noted down everything – in BLOCK CAPITALS – from what the players had done in training, who was injured and what treatment they'd received to the starting XIs for first and reserve team games. He even kept spread-sheet-style game-by-game appearance records before anyone knew what a spreadsheet was!

Paisley, Joe Fagan, Ronnie and Roy Evans would then sit in the Boot Room and use those historical records to analyse what had worked well in the past – and what hadn't – when planning future training sessions and tactical approaches. On such attention to detail, an empire was built.

And that is how Mr Liverpool should be remembered. He was a team player. A loyal one-club man. A crucial cog that kept the relentless Anfield trophy machine turning. A truly influential figure. A backbone of Liverpool Football Club and all that was achieved.

34/130

Keep Flags Scouse

THEY'VE been proudly unfurled and hung from countless vantage points all over the world. They've been held aloft in stadiums wherever Liverpool FC has played. They've been attached to poles, hoisted high and waved upon the Kop for decades.

Heroes have been hailed, rivals have been mocked, songs and poetry adapted. From the philosophical to the funny, from protests to proclamations, banners and flags are part of the unique DNA of a Kopite.

They've become synonymous with supporters of Liverpool Football Club for over half a century and been a huge factor in making the Kop the most famous, vibrant and colourful stand in English football.

Every club's supporters have flags and banners, but none can boast such a vast array as those belonging to – and made by – Liverpudlians. Nowhere else will you find the same ingenuity, creativity, inventiveness, humour, philosophy and messages of support or defiance.

Take a look at the Kop before kick-off the next time you're inside Anfield or watching as *You'll Never Walk Alone* rings out on your TV screen. How many St George's Crosses bearing the name of a town you've never heard of do you see? How many Union Jacks can you spot hung over the advertising boards? None.

Why? Because We Are Liverpool. We do things differently. Our banners and flags are our unique identity. And Kopites want to keep it that way.

Kop banners largely consist of white text on red fabric. Sometimes Kopites flip the colours, but it's always red and white and, to ensure this proud tradition has remained with the Reds' global support growing during the Premier League era, the Keep Flags Scouse campaign was initiated by a secretive group of supporters.

Started in 2000/01 under the Boss Wednesday Agreement – a mysterious, mythical treaty laying out the rules of Scouse flags that exists in folklore, but not on paper – the campaign's aim is to ensure that Liverpool banners remain true to those that came before; to insist that every banner-making Red, no matter where in the world they are from, adheres to the proud traditions and history that have for so long made Kopites stand out from the crowd.

It's a campaign that has proved to be successful, proven by the vast array of brilliant banners and flags that have greeted LFC on pre-season trips to Asia, Australasia, America, Scandinavia and Ireland. You don't have to be Scouse to be a Kopite, but you need to know the score.

While the Redmen have wowed people on the pitch, Liverpool supporters have done so off it. Our banners and flags have become an integral part of every big match the club plays both at home and abroad.

There are too many to mention, and you'll no doubt have your personal favourites that remind of certain nights and places, but two from our most famous European Cup victories – Rome 77 and Istanbul 05 – deserve to be flagged up.

'JOEY ATE THE FROGS LEGS, MADE THE SWISS ROLL, NOW HE'S MUNCHING GLADBACH' read a giant banner that travelling Kopites took all the way to AS Roma's Stadio Olimpico in 1977. It was made in tribute to Welsh left-back Joey Jones and referenced the fact that France's St Etienne and Switzerland's FC

Zurich had been beaten by Bob Paisley's Reds en-route to the final where Liverpool had Germany's Borussia Moenchengladbach on their plate.

Twenty-eight years later, on the day that Rafa Benitez's side won the Champions League in Istanbul's Ataturk Stadium against AC Milan – clinching a British record-extending fifth European Cup for keeps – there were scores of LFC flags draped all over Taksim Square, but one captured the mood, and the essence of Liverpool banners, better than any other.

'THEM SCOUSERS AGAIN'.

Without such identity affirming calling cards, Kopites simply wouldn't be Kopites.

35/130

Clem's research

MAY 1973 saw Liverpool blaze a trail which would become well established by the end of that decade. Winning European trophies.

There had been near misses before. First was the controversial European Cup semi-final against Inter Milan in the Reds' maiden campaign in continental competition. A year later there was heartbreak at Hampden as Liverpool lost the European Cup Winners' Cup final to Borussia Dortmund in extra-time. And the seventies themselves had started with Bill Shankly's men being edged out by Leeds United in the semi-final of the Fairs Cup as Billy Bremner's goal at Anfield proved to be the only goal of the two legs.

So by the time Liverpool had reached the final of the 1973 UEFA Cup they were hungry for some Euro silverware.

Their opponents in the two-legged showpiece were German side Borussia Moenchengladbach, who had just finished fifth in the Bundesliga and whose route to the final had started with a 9-5 aggregate win over Aberdeen.

Liverpool's road to the last two had already seen them see off three German sides in Eintracht Frankfurt, Dynamo Berlin and Dynamo Dresden as well as Tottenham Hotspur in another semi-final inevitably dubbed as a 'Battle of Britain' in the press.

The Moenchengladbach side included some star names such as Berti Vogts, Gunter Netzer, Rainer Bonhoff and Jupp Heynckes, a man better known to younger generations of fans for his later exploits as a Champions League-winning manager of Real Madrid and Bayern Munich.

The first leg at Anfield proved vital – when it eventually went ahead. There had been heavy rain in Liverpool in the week before the fixture but Austrian referee Erich Linemayr decided the game would go ahead. But minutes into the match it became apparent that conditions were unplayable as the rain had intensified following the kick-off and the players were unable to pass the ball. The game was abandoned after 27 minutes and scheduled to be replayed the next evening.

However, that had been long enough for Shankly to realise that Gladbach defender Netzer was suspect in the air and so named John Toshack in his team for the re-run instead of Brian Hall.

Toshack's recall proved vital though most people will recall the part of his strike partner Kevin Keegan in Liverpool's 3-0 victory that night. A mixed first-half for the no7 saw him open the scoring with a diving header (from Toshack's knock-down) which has since featured on many club history highlights reels. He then missed a penalty in front of the Kop before bundling home his second of the evening (from another Toshack assist). In the second-half, it was Keegan's corner which picked out an unmarked Larry Lloyd to head home the third.

However, two minutes after the centre-back's goal came what proved to be a pivotal moment in Liverpool lifting a European trophy for the first time.

Gladbach winger Henning Jensen cut in from the right flank and made his way into the Reds' penalty area. The backtracking Steve Heighway tackled and seemed to win the ball cleanly with his left foot. Astonishingly, referee Linemayr deemed it a foul and pointed to the penalty spot.

Heynckes was given the penalty duties and Anfield held its collective breath, knowing an away goal would give the Germans a crucial way back into the tie.

As the striker placed the ball on the spot – which was just about visible in a muddy 18-yard box – Liverpool keeper Ray Clemence composed himself. Behind him lay sheets of toilet paper which had been flung onto the pitch.

Heynckes' run-up was straight and he placed his shot to Clemence's right. The fans' favourite read the forward's intentions and flung himself to that side of his goal to claw the ball to safety. The Kop let out an almighty roar.

The England goalkeeper later admitted: "I watched Heynckes take a penalty in the semi-final [against FC Twente] on television and decided to dive the same way. The save was a reward for my homework."

Shankly added: "It was an international-class game. Really tremendous. I am not making predictions about the second-leg, but we have a distinct advantage because we did not give away a goal."

The boss couldn't have been more accurate.

Liverpool had to avoid losing by three clear goals in the Bökelbergstadion to win the competition. A crowd of 34,905 watched Borussia take the lead in the 29th minute courtesy of a Heynckes goal and when he curled in a second to double Borussia's lead 11 minutes later, the Reds' nerves were jangling.

However, a Heynckes header which flashed narrowly wide five minutes into the second-half was as close as they came to breaching Clemence's goal again and so Liverpool were able to celebrate an inaugural Euro triumph as Tommy Smith lifted the trophy.

Of course, had Heynckes scored his penalty at Anfield it would have been his side celebrating courtesy of an away goals victory, leaving Liverpool with a huge debt of gratitude to Clemence and his pre-match research.

36/130

Allez les Rouges

MANY young Liverpool FC supporters dream of making the transition from a watching brief in the stands to stepping out at Anfield with a Liver Bird upon their chests.

But there is another route to shaping the Reds' destiny as Gerard Houllier discovered.

In September 1969, the Frenchman stood on the Kop for a European night, little realising that three decades later he would be overseeing an LFC Euro triumph from the dugout in the capacity of team manager.

Houllier's love affair with the club commenced on that evening out, which came soon after he had started a year as a teaching assistant at Alsop Comprehensive School – part of his English degree.

Houllier, who had just turned 22, attended the game with his friend Patrice Bergues – his future Anfield first team coach – and the pair saw the Reds put 10 goals past Irish side Dundalk in the old European Fairs Cup, with Bill Shankly's team boasting seven different scorers as they fired home five goals in each half.

Left-back Alec Lindsay had a debut to remember as he found the net, while Alun Evans, Tommy Smith and Bobby Graham all scored twice with Ian Callaghan, Chris Lawler and Peter Thompson completing the scoring.

Recalling the night with the website *lfchistory.net*, Houllier said: "I suppose going to the game with Patrice that day was a touch of destiny. Patrice had come over to spend a few days with me because I was here on my own, and so we decided to go and see Liverpool play Dundalk.

"What impressed me first of all was the atmosphere inside the stadium. We were on the Kop, and it was fantastic to see the unconditional support of the fans.

"I was also impressed by the energy which was shown in the game, and the stamina of the players. I think 15 minutes before the end of the match the score was 8-0 and still Liverpool went looking for goals. In fact the score at half-time was 5-0. In France, if you are 5-0 up at half-time the game is over in the sense that you don't bother trying to increase your score. It's not like that in England."

Houllier also played as a midfielder for amateur side Liverpool Alsop during his year in the city before embarking on a teaching career back in France and working his way up to deputy head before the lure of football came calling.

In 1973 he began his full-time managerial career as player-manager of Le Touquet. Following spells as manager of Noeux-les-Mines and Lens, he was appointed manager of Paris St Germain in 1985 and won the league title in his first season in charge. His efforts impressed the French Football Federation and in 1988 he was appointed as assistant to national team manager Michel Platini before briefly replacing him ahead of Aime Jacquet's appointment in 1994. He continued to work with the national team's age group sides and his efforts did not go unnoticed in the Anfield boardroom.

In the summer of 1998, it was felt that the acquisition of Houllier to help manager Roy Evans could propel Liverpool to the league title.

However, the joint-managers experiment failed with neither man comfortable with the arrangement and in the November, Evans decided to step down following a 3-1 League Cup defeat at home to Tottenham.

Ultimately, 1998/99 proved to be a season of transition for the Reds as they finished seventh, leaving Houllier with the challenge of building a new squad capable of challenging for honours.

An overhaul of the playing staff was carried out quickly with newcomers such as Sami Hyypia, Stephane Henchoz and Didi Hamann providing extra backbone to the new-look team. The Reds just missed out on qualification for the Champions League in 1999/2000 with the team finishing fourth.

But 2000/01 would prove to be the defining season of the Houllier era at the helm as his Liverpool team won a unique treble of League Cup, FA Cup and the UEFA Cup.

Those triumphs restored Liverpool FC's reputation as one of the best sides in Europe, but with that came raised expectations ahead of the 2001/02 campaign.

Houllier was determined to oversee further successes but the exertions were taking their toll and on 13 October 2001 he fell ill during a 1-1 draw with Leeds United at Anfield.

His illness would have dramatic repercussions for the rest of the season as Phil Thompson took temporary charge of team affairs while Houllier recovered from life saving heart surgery.

Thompson ran a steady ship and although the return of Houllier could not inspire Liverpool to league or Champions League glory, a second-placed Premier League finish would again show progress.

Houllier remained determined to continue, saying: "When people told me I had to stop being a manager, I told them I would rather stop breathing than give up football."

But in 2002/03, LFC's upwards curve started to level out, then dip. The League Cup was secured but the Reds finished in a disappointing fifth position, while in 2003/04 a top-four berth was secured, but the team was unable to sustain a title challenge.

Despite his reluctance to leave the club, Houllier departed in the summer of 2004 after Liverpool's board had come to the conclusion that a change was in order.

His legacy included revamped training facilities at Melwood and a restored reputation for LFC among the leading lights of the game. "Everyone knows that Liverpool is deep in my heart and always will be," he said of a relationship that had commenced with that Tuesday night on the Kop back in the late sixties.

Gerard Houllier sadly passed away in December 2020 at the age of 73. RIP.

37/130

Cult heroes

EVERY now and again, a player comes along who becomes a cult hero with supporters.

LFC has had its share of such players throughout its rich history, men whose various quirks and foibles made them firm favourites on the Kop.

Perhaps the first such figure was goalkeeper Billy McOwen. He helped the team win promotion from the Second Division in 1893/94 before opting for a change in career path to practise as a dentist, a profession in which he would be able to command far more money.

As a goalkeeper, he was known for his cunning on the pitch. It was reported in the *Blackburn Standard* in December 1893 that: "McOwen, the Liverpool Football Club goalkeeper, jumps up and pulls the crossbar down when the ball appears likely to hit it. It makes the crowd laugh, but it doesn't look fair."

Having said that, he was also a good shot-stopper in his own right. During a playing career that also saw him play for Blackburn and Blackpool, McOwen faced 13 penalty kicks and saved 12 of them!

Of all the nuances and superstitions that footballers have, that which was carried out by 1890s forward Abraham Hartley would be frowned upon by the Reds' modern day sports science department.

To the amusement of supporters, Hartley, who made a dozen appearances for the club in 1897/98, placed a rolled-up cigarette behind one ear prior to kick-off, somehow managing to keep it tucked there for the 45 minutes before smoking it during the half-time interval!

During the 1920s, left-winger Fred Hopkin became the epitome of a cult hero with supporters. An ever-present during Liverpool's 1921/22 championship season, he helped the Reds retain the title a year later when he missed just two matches. He literally sent sparks flying when he bagged his first goal for the club in a 3-0 win over Bolton Wanderers in March 1923. His strike was followed by a small fire in the Anfield Road stand. The joke was that Hopkin was to blame as people were so shocked he had actually scored in what was his 78th appearance for the club. Smoke clouded the field of play, but the fire brigade extinguished the blaze and the game was played to a finish.

In 1926, Hopkin was described thus in the *Derby Daily Telegraph*: "Hopkin has turned out to be one of the best investments Liverpool have ever made. His head is now losing its hair, and he may not be as fast as he was, but he can still pull out a rare turn of speed, while as a dribbler he can be elusive. Clings to the touch-line, drops perfect centres, and rarely scores a goal."

The chant 'he's one of our own' often echoes around football grounds in salute to a local hero these days. Seventies star Joey Jones was certainly an adopted Scouser. He may have been born in Bangor but his mother was from Dingle and he grew up a staunch Red, to the extent that he had the letters 'LFC' tattooed on his arm when he was a teenager in the days before 'getting inked' was a common occurrence.

And his exploits on the road to Liverpool's first European Cup triumph in 1977 were of course immortalised in the famous 'Joey ate the frogs legs' banner.

"I always felt like I was representing the supporters," he told *LFC Weekly* magazine in 2010. "It was the absolute dream for me to play for Liverpool because that's what I dreamt of as a kid. I never ever thought that I would get that opportunity, but I did. Most of the players that I played with had come off the terraces themselves so they knew what it meant to those people. It used to be an honour to go and sign autographs for people after games. It was an honour to be asked."

In the summer of 1983, Brighton forward Michael Robinson was in dreamland when his boyhood favourites came calling. Reds manager Joe Fagan remained patient when his new signing didn't score in his first nine games. Robinson eventually found the net twice in a 5-0 victory over Odense Boldklub in the first round of the European Cup before going on to score a hat-trick in a league fixture against West Ham at Upton Park two weeks later.

He would spend just over a year at Anfield, returning a goalscoring ratio of one in four (13 in 52 games) and was admired by supporters for his whole-hearted displays. He left with a hat-trick of trophies from his full season too: league, League Cup and European Cup.

"Ian Rush made me look brilliant in the air," he admitted. "When I jumped up and headed, the ball would always go to Rushie. He could read my body – the way I jumped. He worked it out before I had. Rush never knew which knife or fork to use, but on the pitch he was a genius."

Israeli striker Ronny Rosenthal became an instant cult hero after joining the Reds on loan from Standard Liege in March 1990. Signed to add to the Reds' attacking options as they pushed for an 18th league title, Rosenthal made an explosive start to his Liverpool career. He had been on trial at Luton Town where he had scored two goals in three games, but the Hatters couldn't broker a deal with Liege. Liverpool stepped in to take a closer look and after one reserve appearance, he was handed a debut at Charlton

Athletic. He later recalled: "Kenny [Dalglish] was disappointed with Peter Beardsley and told me an hour before the game I'd be playing. After 10 minutes I scored with my right foot, then again immediately after half-time with my left and finally with my head after combining with John Barnes. The perfect hat-trick, I believe they call it."

After adding another four goals in the last six games of the season, Rosenthal's late contribution was vital to Liverpool's league triumph and the Reds didn't hesitate to pay £1 million to secure his services on a permanent basis the following summer.

Dutch forward Erik Meijer was a popular figure on and off the field during his spell of just over a year at Anfield in 1999 and 2000. Despite only scoring twice in 27 appearances, 'Mad Erik' endeared himself further to fans in 2001 when, as a Hamburg player, he travelled to Dortmund for Liverpool's UEFA Cup final against Alaves and was seen partying with many Reds before the match as he sang songs in the Alter Markt town square!

Just before Meijer moved on, Liverpool manager Gerard Houllier made an unexpected move into the transfer market. In July 2000, he signed Coventry City midfielder Gary McAllister on a 'Bosman'. The Scot was a seasoned campaigner at top-flight level but a few eyebrows were raised at the Reds' decision to sign a 35-year-old.

On signing, he told the *Liverpool Echo*: "The average age of the Liverpool side last season was under 25, and that's very young indeed for a top-flight club. The manager explained that there was a need for some experience around the squad, an old head in the side."

He didn't disappoint. Although not a regular starter until the second part of the season, he led by example as Liverpool marched through all three cup competitions. He ensured his name would live long in Liverpool folklore when Everton and Liverpool were heading for a 2-2 draw in a league derby at Goodison Park on

16 April 2001. McAllister prepared to take a free-kick 44-yards out in stoppage-time. Paul Gerrard in the Everton goal expected a cross, but McAllister had other ideas and hit a dipping shot into the bottom right-hand corner to seal a 3-2 victory and send the travelling Kop into raptures.

In the following game at Anfield McAllister's confident penalty, placed past Barcelona's Pepe Reina, guaranteed the Reds a place in the UEFA Cup final. McAllister would be voted man of the match in Dortmund, where he was involved in four of Liverpool's five goals.

The Kop took Gary Mac to their hearts and it was a sign of their affection for him that when he made his Anfield farewell the following season, he was serenaded by tongue-in-cheek chants of: 'Go back to Cov-en-try!' and 'What a waste of money!'

'Igor, Igor, Igor!' A familiar chant that echoed around Anfield – and still occasionally does in pubs around the ground on matchdays. It was sung in tribute to utility man Igor Biscan, signed from Dinamo Zagreb in December 2000. Often used in defence by Gerard Houllier, he was utilised as a central midfielder by Rafael Benitez in his final season at the club which saw him named on the bench for the epic Champions League triumph against AC Milan. His long, galloping runs became a feature of his play as Kopites took the big Croatian to their hearts and nobody at Craven Cottage in 2004 will forget the shocked look on his face when Biscan scored from outside the penalty area in a 4-2 comeback win.

Peter Crouch, standing at 6ft 7in tall, became a cult figure between 2005 and 2008 after arriving from Southampton with Kopites singing 'he's big, he's red, his feet stick out the bed, Peter Crouch, Peter Crouch' in his honour.

Famous for his robotic goal celebrations, striker Crouch netted 42 goals for the Reds including an FA Cup fifth round winner versus Manchester United, a hat-trick against Arsenal and two spectacular scissor-kick goals at the Kop end against Galatasaray and Bolton Wanderers to cement his cult hero status.

Liverpool's most recent cult-hero is none other than Divock Origi. He spent much of the Jürgen Klopp era down the pecking order behind the likes of Mo Salah, Sadio Mane, Roberto Firmino and Diogo Jota, yet his propensity to appear from nowhere and produce big goals on big occasions is uncanny.

His injury time winner against Everton at Anfield in December 2019 - when Blues goalkeeper Jordan Pickford misjudged Virgil van Dijk's miscued volley and the ball came back off the crossbar - was so wildly celebrated that Klopp ran onto the pitch and jumped into the arms of goalkeeper Alisson!

Origi followed it up with a late winner at Newcastle, two in the remarkable Champions League semi-final comeback against Barcelona at Anfield and then came on to seal Liverpool's sixth European Cup triumph with a strike against Tottenham Hotspur in Madrid.

He has since scored two more in a 5-2 win against Everton, a remarkable scorpion-kick goal in the League Cup at Preston North End, a 94th minute winner against Wolves at Molineux, Liverpool FC's winning goal against AC Milan in the San Siro in the first match ever played between the two European giants in Italy and yet another Merseyside derby goal to seal a 2-0 win at Anfield in April 2022.

No wonder James Milner pondered the following question in his book *Ask A Footballer*: "What would anyone's life be like without Divock Origi? Would we have won the Champions League without him? Possibly not…"

38/130

Yerba mate

WHENEVER a journalist from the official club magazine had the privilege of interviewing Luis Suarez at Melwood, the Uruguayan always arrived carrying a flask of herbal tea.

Indeed, so seldom was he seen without it at the club's former West Derby training base that it could be said that yerba mate, derived from the holly family, truly fuelled his phenomenal goalscoring exploits.

The infusion, known simply as mate in Spanish-speaking countries, is prepared by filling a container up to three-quarters full with dry leaves (and twigs) of the mate plant, and filling it up with water at a temperature of 70–80°, hot but not boiling.

Suarez would typically carry his in a stainless steel Thermos flask and imbibe the liquid via a steel straw as he listened to questions.

If the man from Salto enjoyed his hot beverages, the Kop just couldn't get enough of Suarez's displays in a red shirt.

Handed the famous no7 shirt, he announced himself with a goal in front of the Kop just 16 minutes after his introduction as a substitute against Stoke City in January 2011.

However with three more goals in a dozen starts during the remainder of the 2010/11 season, doubts were actually raised about whether the recruit from Ajax was able to prove himself as a prolific goalscorer.

The following campaign saw him net 17 in 39 appearances as he helped the Reds lift some silverware in the shape of the Carling Cup. Along the way, he produced moments of brilliance, such as his brace in the fourth round win at Stoke and a brilliant hat-trick in a 3-0 defeat of Norwich City in a Premier League clash at Carrow Road.

When Suarez returned to Melwood following Uruguay's elimination from the 2012 Olympic Games, he delighted Kopites by signing a new long-term contract. Manager Brendan Rodgers declared: "I'm delighted that he has signed. I think he's one of the top strikers in world football."

The following season would be his best yet in LFC colours as he produced a stunning return of 30 goals from 44 appearances in all competitions. His tally may have been higher but for missing the final four matches as part of a 10-game ban. Even so, he became the first Liverpool player to score 30 goals in a season since Fernando Torres in 2007/08.

He repeated the feat in 2013/14 as the Reds made a concerted charge for the title, no mean feat considering he was unavailable until late September.

Overtures from Arsenal were rebuffed and by the end of the season, Suarez had scored 31 goals in 33 matches, a total that included hat-tricks against West Bromwich Albion and Cardiff City plus four more against Norwich City at Anfield. The Canaries could be forgiven for wanting to see the back of the striker – his final record against the East Anglians stood at an incredible 12 goals in six outings.

Suarez was named as the Football Writers' Footballer of the Year shortly after receiving a similar award from the Professional Footballers' Association, reward for his all-action endeavours which ensured opposing defenders never had a moment's rest when they lined up against him.

Sadly for Liverpool fans his appearance against Newcastle United at Anfield in May 2014 would prove to be his last for the club while another high-profile disciplinary incident at the 2014 World Cup left him with a four-month ban.

The Reds agreed a club record fee of £65 million with Barcelona and Suarez ended a memorable first season at Camp Nou by scoring in the 3-1 win over Juventus in the Champions League final. He went on to score 198 goals in 283 games for Barca, winning 13 pieces of silverware with the Catalans, and followed it up by helping Atletico Madrid to win La Liga in season 2020/21, his first at the Wanda Metropolitano.

After joining the Catalans, the striker penned an open letter to Liverpool supporters in which he said: "In good times and bad, I always felt supported by wonderful fans at a wonderful club. We will always feel close to the city: we feel proud of the fact that our daughter was raised in Liverpool and that our son was born there.

"To have had the opportunity to play, enjoy, smile and score goals at a stadium as unique and special as Anfield is an honour. We depart as Liverpool fans. You'll Never Walk Alone."

The relationship between Suarez and Liverpudlians was tested when the Reds played Barcelona and Atletico Madrid in the Champions League in 2019 and 2021 respectively - the Uruguyan's willingness to defend the badge he wears is always his priority - but deep down there will always be a mutual love, respect and admiration between the player and Kopites.

Suarez left Liverpool with a record of 82 goals in 133 matches and, no doubt, an endless supply of yerba mate – a drink that has more recently been seen at the AXA Training Centre following the arrival of Uruguay's Darwin Nunez.

"Always Uruguayan," wrote Nunez on Instagram under an image of him holding a yerba mate on the day he signed for LFC. "I was the first one!" replied Suarez. "But I hope you come first in goals."

39/130

The Liverpool Way

HAS football really changed that much over the last few decades? Way back in season 1978/79 the Liverpool FC matchday programme ran a series by the club's youth development officer Tom Saunders, explaining the rudimentaries of the game – the way it should be played at Anfield – for the next generation of stars.

Tom, a former schoolteacher and member of the fabled Boot Room brigade, played a key role in Liverpool's success in the 1970s and 80s – although he's perhaps more renowned as the club's European 'spy'. In 1993 he was elected to the board of directors and made vice-president of the club. He died aged 80 in July 2001, but his words of wisdom live on...

On goalkeepers: "It is important for the keeper to make the greatest use of his area, so that as he despatches the ball he has gained space which enables him to get it to a team-mate... The keeper also has to be decisive about when to stay on his line and when to come out. A general rule is that when you're not directly involved with play you stand on the six-yard line, ready to move in relation to the ball, while if the action is coming close you should try to ensure that you have covered as much of the goal as possible, by judging the angle.

"Goalkeeping is far from being a matter of just standing around – playing in goal demands sound judgement as well as agility, safe handling and concentration... The keeper is the one real specialist in the team."

On winning the ball: "You don't have to be a giant or a heavyweight to win the ball in a tackle. If a player is determined enough and knows just when as well as how to tackle, he can come out with the ball even though he is smaller than his opponent.

"When making a tackle, play a game of patience and weigh up the best moment to go in for the ball. When the moment comes, make your move decisively and swiftly. Two good tackles from a defender early in the game, and the man who has lost the ball spends as much time afterwards worrying about the next tackle as he does in thinking what he's going to do with the ball."

On running off the ball: "You can run without the ball...and simply make a sprint down the field which doesn't mean a thing, because it isn't going to support the team-mate who has the ball and is looking for someone anticipating a pass. Running off the ball requires intelligence.

"When a team-mate is in possession of the ball his attention may be concentrated on an opponent barring his way – so that's the time to use your voice, as well as your brain, by letting your team-mate know you're in a position to make a pass."

On pass and move: "Good players in good teams are prepared to move around as the flow of the game dictates – they don't just operate in straight lines like characters on a drawing board.

"If you're not much good at dribbling but can pass a ball extremely well, don't try to be clever and beat man after man – make the pass do the work to your side's best advantage."

On clever play: "If you are the man in possession of the ball, use your brains and ensure that you play it simply and safely but don't be afraid to bypass a team-mate who is too close, if you spot another in a better position a bit further away...

"Quickness of thought should be matched by speed of action

– meaning that a quick throw can reach a team-mate before the other side has a chance to mark him."

On controlling the ball: "The opposition doesn't stand around while you take your time to bring a bouncing ball under control – the secret is to make sure you move as quickly as possible towards it, and get as close to it as you can... The overall aim of every footballer should be to master the ball so he can control it in virtually any situation."

On playing for the team: "You can beat one man or even two men – but don't be greedy, or you'll find you've taken on one man too many. Keep your eye on defenders as well as the ball.

"What you've got to be careful of, even though you are confident in your ability to master the ball, is that you don't baffle yourself – or your team-mates."

On beating your man: "If you're sideways-on to your opponent, you may get the chance to back-heel the ball away from him and turn to get clear... And if it's a face-to-face situation, always keep your eye open as to the chances of 'nutmegging' him...

"If the defender is jockeying you face to face, he may well be standing with legs apart, body swaying, trying to kid you and find an opening for making the tackle. The 'nutmeg' comes in if he's got his legs apart, because that gives you the chance to slip the ball between his legs and nip round him while he's caught relatively flat-footed."

On scoring: "If you rely on your 'good' foot it takes time to get the ball to that foot when you receive it on your 'wrong' side. In that time you could have lost a chance to shoot at goal.

"If you receive a cross near the goal, head quickly and downwards into the goalmouth when you've got a chance of catching the keeper on the wrong side of goal... When attempting to head a ball, you should keep your eye on it until just before you make contact with your forehead. Remember that the idea is not to wait for the ball to come to you, but for you to go and meet it."

And, finally, on respect: "The referee's decision is always final, and if he doesn't give a penalty when you think you should have had one it's no use arguing the toss."

Football has changed in lots of ways now we're in 2022, but much of what Tom wrote in 1979 remains true although quite what he would have made of VAR would be interesting to know!

40/130

Crazy Horse

INSPIRATIONAL. Infectious. Enthusiastic. That was Emlyn Hughes in a nutshell. If the Kop of the 1960s and 1970s had actually been a footballer, it would have been Hughes.

On the pitch he encapsulated everything the Kop was off it – passionate, exuberant and desperate to see Liverpool win.

His natural enthusiasm rubbed off not only on those he played with but also those he played for. He was an infectious character.

When he was Liverpool captain Emlyn would lead the lads out of the Anfield tunnel and sprint towards the Kop as if he was trying to get there to find his spec before it was full. You couldn't help but get behind a player like that.

Bill Shankly saw the passion and enthusiasm in him as a 19-year-old playing for Blackpool. He didn't just sign the man nicknamed 'Crazy Horse' for his fantastic ability as a footballer. He signed him for his drive, determination and future leadership qualities.

When Shanks paid the Tangerines £65,000 for Hughes in February 1967 he claimed that he was afraid to go back to the seaside town in case they ran him in for theft. Instead, the Police almost ran Shankly in for a driving offence on the very day he signed Hughes.

Speaking in an interview with *shankly.com* in November 1999, Emlyn recalled the incident.

"We had to get to Lytham St Annes to complete the signing so I could play straight away in Liverpool's next match and Shanks drove us both down there. It's only about 10 minutes from Bloomfield Road, but he was the worst driver in the world. He had this old brown Corsair and just as we left the ground he half went through a set of lights and a woman shunted into the back of us and smashed all the lights in.

"They got out of their cars and exchanged numbers and so on, then we carried on. Next thing, a police car flags us down and the young officer comes up to the car and Shanks winds down the window. 'What is it, officer?' he asked. 'I'm sorry sir you can't continue the journey in that car as you've got no lights', said the policeman.

"Shanks explained what had happened but the cop was having none of it. 'Do you know who's in this car?' said Shanks, and I thought he was doing the old do you know who I am routine. 'No,' said the officer, 'I don't recognise you.'

"'No, not me you fool', he said, 'I've got the future captain of England alongside me!'"

The boy from Barrow joined Blackpool as an apprentice – rather than follow his father Fred into Rugby League – but it was at Anfield where he established himself as one of the greatest names in football. Put the *Official Liverpool FC History* DVD on and you'll hear Shankly saying "it's debatable if there's a better player in the game" because, to him, Hughes had everything.

His ability to play equally as well at left-back, centre-half or in the centre of midfield made him as complete a footballer as there could be. Elegant on the ball, solid in the tackle and able to make those barn-storming runs through the middle and finish them off with a ferocious shot, Hughes was a driving force in the Liverpool team.

Many Reds remember his contribution in a game against Everton in March 1973 as one that shaped Liverpool's second era of success under Shankly and then Bob Paisley.

Liverpool hadn't won the league since 1966 and travelled to Goodison Park on the back of one win in five games. With 10 minutes left the scores were level at 0-0 but Hughes popped up with a couple of crucial goals to give Liverpool the points and the momentum from that win carried them to the title. Success after success followed.

Emlyn's stamina levels were renowned with his natural energy coming from his determination to be a winner. In part it earned him the nickname 'Crazy Horse' – first given to him after he rugby-tackled Newcastle's Albert Bennett in one of his first games at Anfield – but Shankly had to drum into him that he needed to channel his energy and not chase every ball as he'd risk burning himself out.

With Emlyn in the team and a vast array of quality around him, Liverpool embarked on a fantastic era of success. Hughes won four championships, two European Cups, two FA Cups and a UEFA Cup with Liverpool and bridged the gap between the Shankly and Paisley eras at Anfield, enjoying success both at home and on the continent under both men and scoring 48 goals in 665 appearances.

He rated picking up the FA Cup as Liverpool captain in 1974 – in what turned out to be Shankly's final competitive game in charge of the club – as his proudest moment as skipper, but the sight of him lifting the European Cup in Rome in 1977 with a smile that lit up the Stadio Olimpico is the defining memory of Emlyn Hughes for Kopites.

Hughes was the first ever Liverpool player to get his hands on the European Cup on an eternally remembered night in the Eternal City. He was the man who raised the giant silver trophy high into the air in a moment that symbolised one of the greatest nights in the club's history.

A year later he lifted the trophy again, this time at Wembley, and although he passed away in 2004 at the age of 57 after being diagnosed with a brain tumour, Emlyn Hughes was the first Englishman to captain a side to two European Cup wins.

He'll never be forgotten.

41/130

Men in white coats

THERE'S a photograph from season 1985/86 belonging to former Reds striker Paul Walsh which shows him on a treatment table at Melwood being 'seen to' by Roy Evans, then on the LFC coaching staff.

"It was the double-winning season," recalled Walsh a few years after it was taken, "and I'd been going along nicely until I ruptured my ankle ligaments against Manchester United [in February 1986]. In the picture on my wall at home I'm in the dressing room with Roy dabbing my ankle with a cold sponge and wiggling it about and saying, 'It'll be alright.' I was hobbling around for months.

"The funny thing is, eventually this fella comes around [at Melwood] to test the ultrasound machine and it turns out it's not working. I'd been having the ultrasound on my ankle three times a day for three months and it wasn't even working! At the time, that's just how things were…"

Three decades later the contrast could not be more striking. Today the club's backroom staff runs into double figures, with specialists in strength and conditioning, fitness and rehabilitation, massage and physiotherapy, nutrition and sports science, and pitchside assistance (and that's just the medical department) working with the most cutting-edge technology available.

As Walsh's story shows, 'twas not always thus, even as late as that trophy-laden era of the 1980s. If football's fabled 'magic sponge' had at least been consigned to history by then, clearly the very latest gadgets and jargon still took some getting used to.

Bill Shankly, famously, could hardly bear to even acknowledge players sidelined with injury, such was his obsession with the task at hand – winning. Previously the only nod to physiotherapy had come in the white-coated form of Albert Shelley, who'd arrived at Anfield just before the Second World War with new boss George Kay, and whose cure-all method of treatment was to cover any injured area with scalding-hot then freezing-cold towels!

Shelley was eventually replaced by Bob Paisley who had retired from playing in the 1950s to reinvent himself at first as an odd-job man, of all things, then physio and reserve-team trainer. Bob learned his trade alright, spending time in hospital A&E departments to watch basic injuries like sprains and muscle tears being treated, and for a while even wearing the same white coat as his predecessor.

Modern equipment, though, was another matter. In an echo of the Walsh episode, the story goes that one fine day in the early sixties, Bob was treating the left leg of Jimmy Melia with a set of electrodes and, unable to read the German instructions, asked the midfielder to say if he felt anything when the dial was turned. Nothing, replied Melia, again and again, even with the dial at its highest.

The tale is taken up in the 2017 Paisley biography *Quiet Genius*, by writer Ian Herbert: "'Bob, the plug – it's not on at the wall', said Chris Lawler, the full-back who was one of the quieter ones but often compensated for lack of noise with quality of observation. A look of anxiety began to spread across Melia's face. Paisley reached down to introduce electricity into the equation and Melia's leg shot up in the air. 'Turn the bloody thing off!' shouted Shankly. The players who were not doubled-up by now joined in his plea."

What the Boot Room boys, as they became known, may have lacked in technical knowledge they more than made up for with intuitive genius. Paisley, Evans, Joe Fagan, Ronnie Moran and Reuben Bennett, in their various functions over the years, were a tight-knit group working towards a common goal codified by the manager: get players fit and keep them that way.

It worked best with minimum fuss and minimum changes to personnel, and the consistency it encouraged is breathtaking: Liverpool were never out of the top five for 26 consecutive seasons from 1965/66 to 1990/91, finishing first 12 times, ultrasound or no ultrasound.

There was even, at one stage, a self-appointed physician among the players. "My nickname was 'Doc'," reveals 1970s forward David Johnson. "In those days there weren't all the mod-cons there are now, so you took your own bag in the dressing room with all your own shaving gear, shampoo, hairbrush and stuff like that.

"I always used to suffer from a sore throat, so there were usually some cough sweets in my bag and everyone used to help themselves. Terry McDermott went in my bag one time and took out all these pills and stuff and said, 'It's like a flippin' doctor's bag' – or words to that effect – and after that it just stuck.

"Even Joe Fagan and Ronnie Moran took the mickey, and if we were travelling away they'd always give me all the headache tablets and things. If anyone had anything wrong with them, they'd always come to me."

42/130

Blown away

SATURDAY 2 September 1978. *You're The One That I Want* was top of the charts, Liverpool were top of the table, and Anfield was bathed in late-summer sunshine.

Along came Tottenham Hotspur, glammed-up with new signings Osvaldo Ardiles and Ricardo Villa – fresh from winning the World Cup with Argentina – and fancied to win the title that season themselves. They ran straight into a steamroller called Pass And Move.

Seven-nil. The goals came from Kenny Dalglish (eighth and then 20th minutes), Ray Kennedy (28), David Johnson (48 and 58), Phil Neal (64 from the penalty-spot) and Terry McDermott (76) – the latter labelled by Bob Paisley as one of the best he'd ever seen.

"This was the greatest moment even in Liverpool's long history of greatest moments," wrote the still-breathless *Daily Post* correspondent. "The locked-out thousands will never believe their bad luck. Only the lucky 50,705 can listen to the stories and know that there is no exaggeration…

"There is one nagging problem: after this, what can be left to inspire and stir the emotions? It could just never be equalled. All that is to follow could appear inferior. How can any team equal the majesty of the six-man move which brought the final goal from McDermott? That was a moment of soaring elation; perfection, the like of which we may never see again."

Fast-forward a decade, give or take six months, to Wednesday 13 April 1988. This time Brian Clough's Nottingham Forest were in town – another top, top side only narrowly defeated by the Reds in the FA Cup semi-final four days earlier.

Five-nil. Ray Houghton (18th minute), John Aldridge (37), Gary Gillespie (58), Peter Beardsley (79) and Aldridge again (88).

The *Liverpool Echo* felt that Liverpool's performance on the night was "so devastating that at times it seemed the two teams were playing different games... The results throughout 1987/88 speak for themselves but it has been the positive quality of Liverpool's play rather than the mere accumulation of points that has been so impressive. This latest exhibition, though possibly the most spectacular of the season, was only one of many that have delighted crowds everywhere."

If the 78/79 team blended craft with supreme efficiency, the all-conquering class of 87/88 was outrageously gifted, too. Built by player-boss Kenny Dalglish in the wake of striker Ian Rush's departure to Juventus in July 87, it had a new attacking dimension – between them Beardsley, Aldridge and John Barnes scored 64 times in all competitions as Liverpool went unbeaten in the league until late March.

The evening after the Forest match, the BBC hastily scheduled a highlights show with Preston North End legend Tom Finney, an old pal of Bill Shankly and a guest at Anfield, telling commentator John Motson that it was "one of the finest exhibitions of football I've ever seen. It was absolutely tremendous and I came away thinking I've been really entertained. I'm sure the spectators saw an exhibition that will never be equalled."

Motson then asked Tom: "Are Liverpool the best of all time?" To which he replied: "I think they are, yes. You couldn't see it bettered anywhere – and I've seen the Brazilians play."

Tom passed away aged 91 on 14 February 2014, four days after league leaders Arsenal arrived at Anfield for a 12.45pm kick-off live on Sky Sports. It was a match which may have made the great man revise his opinion.

Five-one. Martin Skrtel (first and then 10th minute), Raheem Sterling (16), Daniel Sturridge (20), Sterling again (52).

With proceedings barely past 1pm the Reds raced into a four-goal lead. After Skrtel's brace, Luis Suarez smashed an astonishing half-volley against the woodwork before Sterling and Sturridge scored through sublime passing, movement and finishing. Anfield positively pulsated, as TV millions around the world looked on with mouths agape.

In the second half Sterling added a fifth at the second attempt in front of the Kop before the shell-shocked visitors pulled one back from the spot.

Reds skipper Steven Gerrard later described it as "definitely in the top three performances that I've been involved in – we absolutely demolished a top team there from start to finish." *The Echo* declared: "The benchmark has now been set. And how. Liverpool were superb. From the first minute to last, they outmuscled, outfought, outthought and outplayed a shell shocked Arsenal who were left hurt, humbled and humiliated."

September 1978, April 1988, February 2014…and now so many incredible displays in the Jürgen Klopp era, including 5-0 and 4-0 wins over Manchester United in 2021/22, that will perhaps one day have a chapter or book all of their own.

43/130

'They shot the wrong Kennedy'

HE is best remembered for scoring the goals which won Liverpool the European Cup on two separate occasions. Alan Kennedy's effort against Real Madrid in Paris in 1981 won the club Ol' Big Ears number three and in 1984 he was at it again, sealing success number four with the winning penalty in a shoot-out against AS Roma in their own backyard.

The defender admits moving to the Reds from Newcastle United in the late summer of 1978 was the very definition of the term 'no-brainer'.

"It was Liverpool! They were the European champions of 1977 and 1978 so there wasn't really much of a decision to make," he explained. "It was more a case of: 'I have to go.' Once they agreed a fee with Newcastle [£330,000] then I was very, very happy. I knew a number of players at the club already. I'd played in the England Under-23s with David Fairclough, Phil Thompson, Terry McDermott and David Johnson, so it was just a question of getting myself into the team. I remember talking to those players and they all said it's difficult to get into the team but once you get in and become established, you should be okay. It was a tough start. Replacing Emlyn Hughes and Joey Jones wasn't easy. These were seasoned international players and I had to step into their boots."

And while we all know about 'AK' and his European Cup-winning exploits, it was definitely a case of going from zero to hero as he found the initial transition from St James' Park to Anfield a difficult one.

Just six days after putting pen to paper on his Liverpool deal, he was thrown straight into the action, being selected for the Reds' opening league game of the 1978/79 season against Queens Park Rangers in front of an expectant Anfield crowd of 50,793.

But an inauspicious start would lead to a memorable line from Liverpool FC manager Bob Paisley as part of that afternoon's half-time team-talk. The Reds returned to the dressing room locked at 1-1 after Hoops forward Paul McGee had cancelled out Kenny Dalglish's opener.

"My first game was against QPR at Anfield early on and I mis-kicked with my right foot – the one I use for standing on – and knocked a policeman's helmet off!" he recalled. "I also conceded a couple of corners and made a few errors. I just wanted half-time to come so that I could get some reassurance from the manager. But when I got back to the dressing room, Bob Paisley looked at me and said: 'I think that they shot the wrong Kennedy!'"

Thankfully, Steve Heighway grabbed a second-half winner and things steadily improved for the left-back, who also won five league titles, four League Cups and a couple of European Super Cups alongside those precious European Cups.

"I think the first league title is always the best one," he says. "When you look back at the team I played in [1978/79] and who I played with, it was fantastic. Bob Paisley only used around 15 or 16 players that season which was a bonus. It was a strong team.

"Everybody thought that scoring 85 league goals in that season was the highlight but when you look back at the games themselves there were plenty of good moments. There was the famous Tottenham game that we won 7-0 and other matches where we went to other clubs and absolutely pulverised them. It was a pretty decent season for us. We didn't lose at home and it was just special.

"Bob Paisley knew what sort of team he was assembling. It had mainly been put together the year previously when Kenny Dalglish and Graeme Souness joined the club and I was just lucky enough to be part of it. I think I completed 37 league games so 79 was very special.

"Of course, the 83/84 season was also very special with it being Joe Fagan's first year in charge and the fact that he won a treble. That was a pretty decent campaign as well."

Strong seasons were becoming The Liverpool Way.

"At the start of each season our chairman John Smith used to come into the dressing-room and say to the lads: 'This is the start of another season, this is where it begins now.' Bob Paisley used to reiterate what the chairman had said, explaining: 'We're starting again now. We don't think about what happened in the past or last season.' So we always had that hunger to try and emulate what had gone before."

That hunger would see Kennedy enjoy a starring role in two of the Reds' greatest eighties nights – not a bad way for things to pan out after that false start of sending a Bobby's headgear flying on his debut!

44/130

Glove story

THERE are visiting goalkeepers who get it – in the majority, still to this day – and a few unfortunates who don't or won't, earning them a short burst of pantomime boos.

We're talking genuine appreciation and applause from the Kop when the goalie for the other side trots towards that end of the pitch at Anfield, before kick-off or at the switch-around depending on which captain won the toss. It's all about respect, and it's a matchday ritual going back years.

Long before social media one of the quickest ways of transmitting information was the electrical telegraph. Every big organisation had its own particular telegraphic address and Liverpool FC's was 'Goalkeeper – Anfield'. Former chairman John Smith once revealed that the choice of address symbolised the tradition of respect for great keepers, be they Liverpool's own or in nets for the opposition.

The rapport between crowd and keeper – or at least the man between the posts for the home side – can be traced way back to the first half of the last century.

In 1934, after the final appearance of an illustrious 22-year career with Liverpool FC, goalie Elisha Scott addressed the crowd thus: "Last, but not least, my friends of the Kop. I cannot thank them sufficiently – they have inspired me. God bless you all."

Subsequent goalkeepers with LFC longevity included Tommy

Lawrence, Ray Clemence and Bruce Grobbelaar. More recently Pepe Reina developed a bond with the fans because he'd celebrate goals just like a Kopite – and because previously with Barcelona he'd been applauded as he ran towards his goal in front of the Kop for the second half of a UEFA Cup semi-final second leg in April 2001. And now Alisson Becker is regarded by many Reds as not only the best goalkeeper in the world, but second only to Clemence in the pantheon of LFC goalkeeping greats.

One of high points of this tradition, according to football historian and Norwegian Reds fan Kjell Hanssen, was the 1964/65 season and specifically an FA Cup six-round replay for Liverpool against Leicester City.

"Gordon Banks was in goal for them and whenever Leicester had visited Anfield he was unbeatable," he explained. "He produced another brilliant performance in the cup tie, saving almost everything except for a Roger Hunt goal 18 minutes from time. When the final whistle blew Banks turned to the Kop and applauded them for their loud support. He instantly became a hero.

"Rumours then started that Bill Shankly wanted to sign him, and every time Banks appeared at Anfield either as goalkeeper or coach he got a tremendous ovation."

There was also plenty of mickey-taking between player and Kop, with Banks once sticking his tongue out at fans when they chanted "Clemence for England!" When he announced his retirement before season 1973/74 following a car accident, Banks was invited to Anfield as a VIP guest for the opening home match with Stoke City, his final club, and presented with a silver salver on the pitch. "It was a tremendous moment for me when I walked out and saw that crowd again," he told the LFC matchday programme a few weeks later. "I felt honoured and touched that Liverpool should think sufficient of me to make me a presentation."

Ex-Arsenal and Wolves goalkeeper Bob Wilson was a contemporary of Banks. A regular visitor to Anfield in the 1960s and early 70s, he recalls being fondly received: "Back then there were no warm-ups before kick-off, so your first sight of that stand [the Kop] was when you ran to the goal to start the game. It's a long run and when I reached the edge of the area the applause would be loud. By the time I got to the net it reached a crescendo.

"I could only imagine what it was like for the guys who played for the home side and were loved by the crowd. I found it simply inspirational. I used to say to myself: 'They've just given you a great ovation and you haven't done anything – you better play well now'. The Kop didn't care where you came from – once they saw you cared for your team as much as they did for theirs they gave you respect."

Joe Corrigan, latterly a goalkeeping coach at Anfield but in the 70s a fixture between the posts for Manchester City, was another acclaimed and teased by the Kop in equal measure. An item in an LFC matchday programme from 1980 reads: "Stoke City had Gordon Banks, Nottingham Forest have Peter Shilton, Arsenal have Pat Jennings...and all, in their time as top-level players, have commanded the unstinted respect of Liverpool supporters for their goalkeeping feats at Anfield. Recently the Kop, generous as ever, gave Shilton ungrudging applause when, in the League Cup semi-final tie, it was his turn to take over directly in front of our most vociferous supporters, who are renowned for their humour and knowledge of the game.

"Even more recently it was the turn of Joe Corrigan to face the Liverpool 'firing squad' – meaning our attack, as well as the Kop. Joe, the genial giant of Manchester City, came through the 90 minutes as a hero who prevented a massacre. Indeed Corrigan's display earned him an ovation which he described as 'fantastic, I've never had a reception like that before in my life'. And the man who has had to wait in the England queue behind our own Ray Clemence and Peter Shilton heard the fans chanting in fun: 'We all agree, Corrigan's better than Shilton!'"

Of course the most famous ovation of all for a visiting keeper was reserved for Clemence, the man who'd clocked up 665 appearances as Liverpool's no1 before returning as a Tottenham Hotspur player in May 1982. "Running down to the Kop always gave me a special feeling but I wasn't sure what reaction I'd get when I went back," he remembered.

"At the start of the second half when I came out and ran towards the Kop, a sea of hands went up and all sides of the ground rose to give me an ovation. I'll never forget them for that."

More recently, when Alisson suffered an injury against Norwich City on the opening night of the 2019/20 season, new signing Adrian had to come one and ran down towards a sea of arms on the Kop, an incredible welcome for a player making his debut.

Welsh international goalkeeper Paul Jones even turned down a two-year contract with Portsmouth in 2004 to join Liverpool for a month on loan from Southampton so he could experience a Kop ovation on his debut against Aston Villa.

"The fans in the Kop when I came out...I will never, ever forget that. The applause I got was incredible. It was very special and that summed the Kop up for me.

"I could have gone down the road for two years but that's why I'll never regret coming to Liverpool for a month. Just to get that feeling."

45/130

Kev and Berti

IF they had a common denominator it was absolute dedication to their sport, otherwise they were polar opposites on the pitch: Kevin Keegan, aka Mighty Mouse the bubble-permed striker, and Berti Vogts, blond-cropped stopper dubbed Der Terrier. Three times the former played a telling role in European triumphs for Liverpool, and on two of those occasions the Borussia Moenchengladbach man was the fall guy.

They first faced each other in a two-legged UEFA Cup final in May 1973, Keegan scoring twice for Liverpool's first European honour. It took Vogts another two years to win the same trophy, skippering BMG to victory over FC Twente in the 1975 final, by which time he'd also received a World Cup winner's medal with West Germany.

Season 1975/76 brought the fifth of six Bundesliga titles he'd win in seven years, while Keegan savoured a special double with Liverpool: having won the league for a second time in four years he then played a blinder in another UEFA Cup final, this time against Bruges – converting from the spot to make it 3-2 at Anfield in the first leg, then drilling home a free-kick to level in the return.

So to 1976/77 and a European Cup final in Rome which brought the two adversaries together again, Keegan aged 26 and Vogts 30. *Liverpool Echo* reporter Charles Lambert was in no doubt where the match was won and lost, and told the tale thus...

"The duel between Keegan and Vogts has already gone down in the football folklore of Merseyside. In due course it will also find a place in the history of the European Cup, alongside the scoring feats of Puskas and Di Stefano, the majesty of Beckenbauer and exhilarating skills of Cruyff.

"Keegan had a lot to prove in Rome. His stature on the domestic front had taken a series of knocks after a league season in which he seldom appeared at his best; abroad, the initial hubbub of excitement that had arisen when he announced his intention to quit Anfield had died almost to nothing...

"Thus Keegan's success was all the sweeter, and the fact that it was achieved against Berti Vogts made it the more dramatic. Vogts, the captain of Borussia and of West Germany, the man whose studs had pockmarked the shins of Europe, the man reckoned to be in a class of his own when it came to man-to-man marking, was made to look like a blundering novice by the skills of the Liverpool striker.

"Keegan was, simply, irresistible. Whether he received the ball on his head, on his chest or at his feet, he was in instant control, using his pace and his balance to perfection to keep Vogts out of tackling range or off balance. Keegan's use of the ball matched his control, his passes and centres being struck with absolute confidence and consistent accuracy.

"Keegan's contribution extended further. By giving Vogts such a hectic time in defence, he nullified the Borussia captain's counterattacking opportunities, and that in itself was a key factor in Liverpool's success. Further, Keegan's running to wide positions on either flank opened the way for the midfield men to move into the gaps left in the centre. Where Keegan went, Vogts followed; so too did the uneasy sweeper Wittkamp. With [full-back] Klinkhammer attempting to mark Heighway, the heart of the citadel was seriously undermanned, to the profit of Case, Kennedy, and especially McDermott, scorer of the first goal.

"The first 20 minutes were decisive, for it was in that time that Keegan established his mastery of Vogts that was to be maintained to the end. By the 20th minute he had run through an impressive repertoire, first nudging the ball past Vogts with a flick of the head; then, two minutes later, chesting down a pass from Emlyn Hughes, beating Vogts on the outside, and being felled from behind; then using his acceleration to beat Vogts to a Kennedy pass and enable McDermott to produce a shot.

"So it went on, with Keegan playing a leading part in almost all Liverpool's noteworthy attacks. He was involved in the move that ended with Kennedy forcing Kneib to tip his shot over the bar. Keegan it was who set up the chance for Heighway to fire his spectacular second-half drive. And finally it was Keegan who made the determined, balanced run that ended with the clumsy challenge of Vogts and the award of the penalty.

"When the French referee Robert Wurtz signalled the end of a marvellous match, the Liverpool followers united in the acclaim of one man. 'Kevin Keegan!' they chanted over and over again. It was a deserved tribute."

But not quite the end of the story. Keegan joined SV Hamburg that summer and would line up against Vogts three more times, losing on each occasion: in a 2-0 defeat for his new club at BMG's Bokelbergstadion in November 1977; then a 2-1 reverse for England against West Germany in a Munich friendly in February 1978; and finally a 6-2 home thumping by Berti's Borussia in April that year.

And Vogts would've swapped each and every one of them for another shot at that 1977 final.

46/130

This is Anfield

WHILE stood in the Anfield tunnel legendary Newcastle striker Malcolm Macdonald was once said to have looked at the sign above his head shortly after it was installed and mockingly remarked to his team-mates: "Oh we've got the right ground, lads. This is Anfield."

Bill Shankly, the man who had put up the now famous sign – which was first painted by maintenance foreman Bert Johnson – heard the comments and responded after the final whistle when his team had secured a 5-0 victory.

"After the game the boss goes and knocks on their door," Ian St John recalled. "He asks for Malcolm and when he has his attention tells him: 'You'll know where Anfield is the next time.'"

The Scottish manager's logic behind those three words hung above the players' tunnel was simple: "It's there to remind our lads who they're playing for and to remind the opposition who they're playing against."

The original sign, or plaque if you prefer, was said to have been put in place in March 1972 and remained there until 1998 when it was replaced with an updated version.

In the summer of 2012, just after succeeding Kenny Dalglish as manager, Brendan Rodgers reinstalled the initial sign. "The nostalgia around this football club is immense. I just felt that this was a sign and a symbol of what Liverpool was for many years," was the Ulsterman's logic.

LFC museum curator Stephen Done was also in attendance for the moment of reinstallation. "This sign has seen the greatest glory years of our club," he rightly pointed out. "It has been the talisman for some of our greatest players. It is arguably the single most important thing at Anfield. It still resonates, it still makes us emotional and means so much to so many."

Of course, since then the Main Stand has been comprehensively transformed into a stunning state of the art new facility which opened in September 2016. While that rebuilding work was going on the 'This Is Anfield' sign was put in storage for four months before once again taking pride of place above the tunnel in time for the visit of Leicester City, the maiden home fixture of the 2016/17 campaign. Later, Shankly's 'remind' quote was added to the wall next to the sign.

Current boss Jürgen Klopp had followed the long-held tradition of touching the sign when he brought his Borussia Dortmund side to Anfield for a pre-season friendly in the summer of 2014. He believes the history around the storied plaque is unique and that touching it can help to make LFC players "feel better, stronger and use the emotion of it" to achieve success, but also that they have to earn the right to touch it.

"Before the game when we went down the stairs, my Dortmund friends asked me 'do they all touch the This Is Anfield sign?', I said no," Klopp explained after Liverpool's 4-3 Europa League win against Borussia Dortmund in 2016.

"I don't really know exactly how it works but I think you need to win something before, I'm not sure. I didn't ask until now, but it's a sign of respect that we don't do it. Maybe these players one day will be allowed to do it."

The day came in August 2019 after Liverpool won the Champions League at the end of the previous season. "Boss wouldn't let us touch the sign until we won a trophy," wrote Gini Wijnaldum in a social media post before the first home game of the new season against Norwich. "Now is the time."

Rather than providing such inspiration though, the sign initially frightened Kenny Dalglish when he first arrived at the club from Celtic in the summer of 1977.

On his home debut against Newcastle that August he paused at the top of the stairs in the players' tunnel to see the sign lit up by a single strip of light. Beside him at that very moment stood opponent and fellow Glaswegian Tommy Craig. "The sign is supposed to frighten you," Dalglish said before admitting "but it terrifies me!"

Eventually, that feeling of dread went away. And Dalglish began touching the sign with two hands because he believed it would give him more luck than those who just used one hand. He said doing so lifted him and "made me feel six feet tall." And that, after all, was exactly what Shankly had hoped for.

47/130

Morecambe and Wise

"WOA-OH-WOA-OH-WOA-OH, we've got the best midfield in the world, we've got Xabi Alonso, Momo Sissoko, Gerrard and Mascherano-o-oh…"

The song dates from the noughties, of course, but three decades earlier the sentiment on the Kop was the same – it's just that in the late seventies there wasn't such a catchy song to praise the collective brilliance of Souness, McDermott, Kennedy and Case.

When the Reds swaggered through the record-breaking season of 1978/79 – going top in mid-August, staying there right through to the end of the season and accumulating a then-two-points-for-a-win-record points-haul of 68 – the quartet in midfield was the envy of the land.

Orchestrating from the middle with indomitable self-assurance, Graeme Souness, aged 25 at the start of the season. Charged with a roving role, 26-year-old Terry McDermott, Scouse joker par excellence and goalscorer extraordinaire. And out wide on either side, elder statesman Ray Kennedy (27), the big Geordie with the sweet left foot, and the baby of the group Jimmy Case (24), local lad with the cannonball shot.

Kennedy was an ever-present in the all-conquering league campaign, alongside Kenny Dalglish and Phil Neal with 42 appearances. Souness played 41 times, McDermott and Case both 37. Between them, the four midfielders scored 33 goals.

For Ray and Jimmy, the teamwork extended beyond the pitch. For the best part of seven years at Anfield – during which time they picked up three European Cup winner's medals each, among others – they were the closest of pals, rooming together on away trips and commandeering the back-seats on coaches and planes.

In his 2014 autobiography *Hard Case*, Jimmy revealed that they "were kind of thrown together in the first place, not long after I got into the first team [in 1975]." Left-back Joey Jones had been Jimmy's first room-mate, but when the Welshman was missing from one particular away trip, Kennedy took his place.

Case continued: "I realised I could learn a lot from a professional point-of-view from a player like Ray. He had won the double at Arsenal [in 1970/71] and I thought his experience could help me in my career.

"That's how it started, but it soon went much deeper than that. We just fitted together so well; we're both easy-going, plus we were both very tidy. Our room was always immaculate and anyone who travelled with footballers will know that is not always the case, usually they leave their rooms looking like a rat's nest. You know, we even polished each other's shoes. If Ray was watching TV, I would pick up his shoes and give them a shine, and vice versa."

In turn Kennedy would later reflect: "I have always picked my friends very carefully, and Jimmy Case and I built our lives around one another at Liverpool. The way we worked it out was that if the two of us stuck together we would be a stronger force than if isolated."

Case would always remember the class and distinct lack of ceremony with which Kennedy scored one particular goal for Liverpool at Bolton: controlling Jimmy's cross-field pass with his chest and calmly stroking home before acknowledging the assist with a little wave and trotting back to the halfway line.

The duo shared the same unassuming temperament and had similar interests: a love for Muhammad Ali and a taste for good food and wine on European trips. After a drink or two, though, they could be mischievous.

The night before one away game at Ipswich, recalled Kennedy: "We climbed through an open hotel window and turned Ray Clemence and Phil Neal's beds upside-down. Because they had their room keys with them they couldn't work out how it had happened. On another occasion we crawled along the verandah and set up a lamp stand so that we could switch it on and off from outside their room. When the two of them got into bed and the light started flashing on and off, they couldn't believe it and kept blaming one another…

"We were an explosive mix and when we went out together something always seemed to get out of control… [But] each of us would be there to help the other out in difficulties and Jimmy was able to calm me down in difficult situations."

That wasn't quite the case one weekend in March 1980 after Liverpool had beaten Everton 2-1 in the Goodison derby. On a team break in Llangollen in North Wales, the pair shared some late-night drinks, got embroiled in an altercation with hotel staff and ended up in the local police cells.

Even though it was an extreme incident, a one-off, Case felt Kennedy could be "a bit grumpy at times and overreact to situations. "There would be times when I couldn't understand why he was getting so worked up. I used to say to him, 'What's wrong, mate? Calm down, it's not worth it'.

"What no one knew at the time was it had nothing to do with Ray's personality: it was the first sign that physically, something wasn't right."

Kennedy was diagnosed with Parkinson's Disease in November 1984, three years after he had left Liverpool for Swansea City and Case had joined Brighton & Hove Albion. The latter also played for Southampton and settled down on the South Coast, while Ray returned to his native North East and became friends with Andrew Lees, the doctor who wrote his biography. Ray passed away at the age of 70 in November 2021 and Jimmy had always kept in touch.

As he wrote in his autobiography: "Me and Ray were inseparable, like Morecambe & Wise. If I came through a door he would be one step behind me. We were there for each other and everyone knew it."

48/130

Shooting stars

CAN you name the former Liverpool FC striker who scored an international hat-trick and also scored three goals in an Australian Cup final?

The Reds were blessed with fantastic strikers throughout the 1960s and 70s with Roger Hunt, Ian St John, John Toshack and Kevin Keegan all writing their names into Anfield folklore.

Their successes meant it was almost impossible for the men aiming to force their way into the first-team. Ted McDougall and Tommy Tynan were two examples of players who had to move elsewhere to prove their credentials in league football due to the excellence of the regulars in the Reds' senior side.

Injuries also play their part in the narrative of football. But had things played out slightly differently in that regard, Bill Shankly may not have needed to persuade the Anfield board to splash the cash on the Saint back in 1961.

Welsh international centre-forward Des Palmer was one of Phil Taylor's last major signings as Liverpool manager, moving to Anfield in March 1959. Sadly things did not turn out the way he had hoped and Palmer never played a first team game for the Reds.

Speaking to the club's matchday programme back in 2013, he explained: "Phil Taylor came in for me and took me to Liverpool from Swansea Town. I was 20 years of age at the time and the deal worked out at around £15,000 with wing-half Roy Saunders (father

175

of future Liverpool forward Dean) joining Swansea. I thought it was a great move for me, joining a bigger club like Liverpool and the chance to further my career as a centre-forward."

Des had been a prolific young striker for Swansea and also marked his home debut in international football by scoring a hat-trick in Wales' 1957 World Cup qualifier against East Germany at Ninian Park. However, his Liverpool career stalled from the start.

He explained: "In my first game at Anfield, a reserve match against Leeds United, I suffered a serious knee injury which required a double cartilage operation. In those days that was very serious. It took me months upon months of blood, sweat and tears to get back playing again, but eventually I was able to do so.

"Bill Shankly arrived as manager later that year and he quickly realised the situation with me. He arranged for me to go out to South Africa to play in a much warmer climate to help get me fit again. Shankly agreed to give me a free transfer. He knew that the former Liverpool goalkeeper Doug Rudham was managing a team out there in Johannesburg and it was arranged for me to sign for them."

Upon returning to the UK, Des had a brief spell at Derby County, where he was converted to a left winger by Rams' boss Harry Storer junior, the son of another ex-Reds goalkeeper.

However, the notoriously heavy pitches at the Baseball Ground did little to help Des' knee problems and he made the decision to emigrate to Australia in a bid to prolong his career. He did just that and enjoyed his time Down Under, playing in Melbourne and Sydney before eventually returning to Wales where he had a stint as player-manager of Llanelli.

"When I went to Australia, I signed for Slavia Melbourne," he recalled. "We had a mix of English, Scots, Welsh and Yugoslav players at the club! We blended together well and that season we won the Australian Cup final versus Palonia. We won 3-2 at the

Olympic Stadium in front of 55,000 and I scored a hat-trick. The winner came in extra-time and it was a great occasion."

Despite his career-threatening injury, Des looks back on his brief time at Liverpool with affection.

"The injury changed my direction from what I was anticipating, but the opportunity at Liverpool was brilliant. I lived in Old Swan – which was quite appropriate! – and a lot of the players were based around that area at the time. I enjoyed it but then had to re-adjust. I just wanted to keep playing. I had nothing else. That was my life. I felt I had to keep playing and I did until I was roughly 36 so I was pleased with that.

"Of course you think about the success Liverpool had under Bill Shankly and wonder what might have been. That was a great disappointment but injuries are part of the game."

49/130

You've been Tangoed

TIME to debunk a myth about footballs.

Think back to the early 1980s and matches at Anfield. Or try and find highlights of a few such games on YouTube. As you enjoy re-living the moments that Ian Rush, Kenny Dalglish and company put the ball into the opposition net, you will notice a familiar pattern to, or should we say, on, the goals.

That was the 'interlocking triads' on the adidas Tango matchballs favoured by LFC at the time.

During the 1984/85 season, Everton secured a famous victory at

Anfield with a long-range strike from Graeme Sharp flying beyond Bruce Grobbelaar and into the net at the Anfield Road end.

Several Everton players of that era have since revealed how the Blues received a delivery of Tango balls to their Bellefield training ground in the week leading up to that game and that the practice sessions helped them get to grips with it before that derby victory.

However, it was not as if they had not used Tango balls before. Watch the Goodison Park derby from November 1982 and you will find footage of Rush slotting one, two, three, four goals past his Wales international team-mate Neville Southall...all with a Tango.

In the early eighties there was no official matchball sponsorship deal in place with the Football League and so clubs were free to use whichever model took their particular preference.

A lot of clubs opted for Mitre matchballs, whereas Liverpool always felt that the Tango was better suited to their successful pass and move style.

In his book *Ian Rush: My Scrapbook*, the Reds' record goalscorer explained: "When I was at Liverpool, the adidas Tango was the ball that sticks out in my mind. We used to play with the Tango balls every week at Anfield and we loved them. We trained with them and we found that we could ping them far more easily than the Mitre balls of the time, which helped our passing game.

"Other clubs got on to this and it was amazing how often that, when we went away from home, we'd be up against sides who would use Mitre balls instead to try and stop us from playing. The Tango balls moved a lot quicker and they really suited the players we had at Liverpool. Opponents wanted to slow us down and the Mitre ball was a lot heavier, so they'd use them."

Considering all that the Reds achieved in the 1980s it's not a tactic that particularly worked! Nowadays all Premier League clubs use the same matchball with Nike having supplied them since the start of the 2000/01 season.

The ball Liverpool began their Premier League-winning season with in 2019/20 was called the Nike Merlin. This was subsequently replaced by the yellow winter ball in late October and the Nike Tunnel Vision ball in February, which was used right up until late July when the elongated-season finally concluded with the Reds as Champions, just like they were more often than not in the 1980s.

50/130

The write stuff

CHARLES Buchan, a former footballer of some repute with Sunderland and Arsenal, became a renowned sports journalist after hanging up his boots. Soon after the Second World War, he suggested a new award for the footballer of the year to be decided by members of the recently-established Football Writers' Association.

First awarded to Blackpool winger Stanley Matthews in 1947/48, it is now a feature of the end-of-season awards.

LFC have dominated the roll of honour with players from Anfield winning it more than any other club – the Reds ended the 2021/22 season with 14 wins compared to next-best Manchester United and Tottenham's nine apiece.

Ian Callaghan, the club's record appearance holder with an incredible 857 games to his name between 1960 and 1978, became the first Red to win the coveted honour in 1973/74, Bill Shankly's last season in charge at Anfield.

Cally recalled: "I had always played as a winger until I had a cartilage taken out in 1970 and in those days there was no microsurgery. I was in hospital for two weeks and then off for two months.

"Brian Hall was playing outside-right when I recovered and it was a struggle for me to get back into the team. As it happened John McLaughlin, a Liverpool kid, was playing in central midfield but then he got injured. I was moved into the central midfield and had a new career in that role.

"I'd had a fantastic season in 1973/74. It was probably my best season and winning the Football Writers' award was one of the highlights of my career.

"I remember the ceremony was held in London just before we played Newcastle in the FA Cup final. We were already down there preparing for the final and the dinner was on the Thursday evening.

"I always remember that night because we came in late, Mr Shankly and myself, just in time for the presentation as we'd been busy preparing for the final.

"When you looked around the top table and saw all the names who'd won the Footballer of the Year, it was nerve-racking, it really was. I'll always remember what Shanks said before we went in and they announced me as winner. He turned to me and said: 'You get out of life what you deserve.' And that was it!

"We both went in and it was unbelievable. I had to make a speech and it was one of the best moments of my life…the Football Writers' award is a big thing to win."

The Reds dominated the award throughout the seventies and eighties. Kevin Keegan (1975/76), Emlyn Hughes (1976/77) and Kenny Dalglish (1978/79) followed in Callaghan's footsteps before Terry McDermott began the 1980s with another LFC triumph as he became the first man to win both PFA Player of the Year and FWA Footballer of the Year in the same season.

However, Terry caused a stir when he didn't turn up to the awards ceremony in London – preferring a day at the races instead.

Speaking to the Reds' official matchday programme in 2017, he explained: "I didn't go to the Football Writers' do at the Cafe Royal. I got a call on the payphone in the players' lounge at Anfield telling me I'd won. The reporter calling asked if I had anything to say, so I said: 'How has a ragbag like me won both of these awards? I'm astounded'.

"I was elated, but they're still waiting for me to turn up to that do now! They got me rail tickets to go from Lime Street to London, but it was Chester Races that day and I was supposed to be going. I got to the station in my suit and I was moping about when I saw on the departures board that the train was delayed for over half-an-hour. 'I'm not waiting for that', I said to my brother Robert who was with me, so I went to Chester Races instead.

"What I didn't know was that Bob Paisley, of all people, had gone all the way down there to present it to me. Not turning up didn't go down well. Bob told the audience, 'He's gone on one of his famous blindside runs!'"

Dalglish won the award for a second time in 1982/83, while Ian Rush (1983/84) and Steve Nicol (1988/89) also carried it off in recognition of their efforts in those campaigns. A mark of the impact John Barnes made at Anfield saw him win the award twice in three seasons (1987/88 and 1989/90).

There followed a gap of 19 years before captain Steven Gerrard received the award in 2008/09, an achievement hailed by Callaghan in an era of the worldwide cast of the Premier League. The Liverpool skipper finished 2008/09 as the Reds' top scorer with his best-ever haul of 24 after playing in a slightly different position just off the main striker.

"It makes you particularly proud when you look around the Premier League today with so many foreign players," said

Callaghan. "The amount of games he changes on his own has been phenomenal over the years. He's grabbed games by the throat when they have looked as though Liverpool weren't going to do anything in them. He's like Roy of the Rovers…he changes games. I think he would have been selected in any team that Liverpool have had since I started playing in the 1960s. You can't really pay him a higher compliment."

Luis Suarez won FWA Footballer of the Year in 2013/14, polling 52% of the vote, and in season 2017/18 Mohamed Salah broke new ground. After scoring 44 goals in a truly incredible debut season with Liverpool, the Egyptian King became the first player to win a clean sweep of FWA Footballer of the Year, PFA Player of the Year, Premier League Player of the Season, Fans Player of the Year, Football Supporters Association Player of the Year and Football Supporters Federation Player of the Year.

"Mo Salah is the worthiest of winners," said FWA Chairman Patrick Barclay. "He is also the first African to receive the award and we congratulate him on a magnificent season."

Two years later, Liverpool's no14 Jordan Henderson became Liverpool's 14th recipient of the prize after leading the Reds to their first league title in 30 years and also lifting the UEFA Super Cup and FIFA Club World Cup during a magnificent 2019/20 campaign when Jürgen Klopp's men won 26 and drew one of their opening 27 league games.

"It is absolutely deserved," said Klopp. "He is one of the best players in the league and this year everybody acknowledged that. I am really happy for him and really proud of him."

Only Dalglish and Barnes had claimed the FWA Footballer of the Year award twice while at Liverpool, but in 2022 Salah added his name to that list after being voted the winner ahead of Manchester City's Kevin De Bruyne. Mo also added the 2022 PFA Player of the Year award to his list of individual honours.

51/130

Anfield Blues

UP to and including season 2021/22 there had been 30 Merseyside derbies at Anfield in the Premier League, and in them Liverpool had scored 47 goals against Everton: from a stoppage-time rocket by substitute Ronny Rosenthal that won the match in March 1993 to Andy Robertson's first Kop-end goal and a Divock Origi header in a 2-0 win in April 2022.

For the record, Steven Gerrard has the most goals in Premier League derbies at Anfield, with seven; then it's Origi with six, Robbie Fowler with five, Daniel Sturridge with three and Sadio Mane on two along with Patrik Berger, Luis Garcia, Dirk Kuyt and Philippe Coutinho.

But everyone knows that Merseyside derbies – home or away – didn't start in the 1992/93 season, just as everyone knows (or at least should do) about Liverpool's legendary FA Cup victories over their neighbours at Wembley and other neutral venues down the years: four in semi-finals (1950, 1971, 1977 and 2012) and two in the final (1986 and 1989).

For the very first encounter, you've got to go right back to April 1893 and another neutral setting: a Liverpool Senior Cup tie at Bootle's Hawthorne Road which the Reds (then-Blues!) won 1-0. Eighteen months later the teams drew 2-2 in the inaugural Anfield derby, Everton's first game on their old ground since 'the split'.

One of the earliest Anfield humdingers came in September 1925 when, a week after thrashing Manchester United 5-0 at home, Liverpool beat Everton 5-1. The city's *Evening Express* reported: "In the long series of games between Everton and Liverpool the Goodison club hold a great advantage in the number of victories on their opponents' ground, but Liverpool since the war have made desperate attempts to reduce the margin. The latest victory is their fourth out of seven matches at Anfield since the resumption of league warfare in 1919.

"For the second time, too, the Reds enjoyed a 5-1 win. Who would say [skipper Donald] MacKinlay and his men did not deserve their latest success? Under the present rules it is goals all the time, and it was because Liverpool adopted those methods and shot with accuracy that they triumphed.

"Everton made the mistake of keeping the ball too close. It was all pretty to watch, and most skilfully executed, but having reached the goal area the Everton forwards lost their shooting boots and their power to direct the ball at the target."

Two-and-a-half years later the teams drew 3-3 at Anfield in front of almost 60,000. Toffees legend Dixie Dean scored a hat-trick, but Liverpool recovered to draw level having been 3-1 down. This time the *Evening Express* wrote: "The atmosphere in which the issue was fought out was almost as wonderful as the game, for cheering ran round the ground in thrilling, swelling waves. It was as electrical as a cup-tie, and the good feeling which exists between the players was exemplified when both sides stepped onto the field together, skippers MacKinlay and [Warney] Cresswell trotting side by side. This was an innovation in the history of First Division football."

Then, on Saturday 11 February 1933, came the highest score ever in a Merseyside derby: Liverpool 7 Everton 4. For the hosts it was a first league victory over their rivals for six years; for the Blues, who were reigning top-flight champions, a heaviest defeat of the season.

The *Daily Post* called it "one of the best derbies, if not the best, of a long series. I have never seen a more thrilling game. When Liverpool announced their team one immediately thought that Everton's experience and the big occasion would master the youthful Liverpool side, but the Anfielders are noted for their contrariness... These young men demonstrated that the big occasion was not upsetting to them. They most likely forgot the nature of the match and had one thought in their minds – and that was to beat Everton."

The margin was much narrower in September that same year when the Reds beat the Blues 3-2 at Anfield in what was the second Liverpool appearance for their new South African winger Berry Nieuwenhuys, who scored on 32 minutes.

'Nivvy' later told the *Evening Express*: "Never before had I seen such a vast crowd, such brilliant football, or such clean football, and it was the thrill of my life when I managed to score the first goal...

"I confess I was rather staggered by the size of the crowd [53,698] at the start but I did my best to forget they were there. That was hard in view of the continuous roar of voices. Still you could play in front of a crowd like that for years. They are such sportsmen. I thank them for the encouragement they gave me and also for the wonderful reception I was accorded when I left the field. I don't mind confessing it touched me."

With the occasional exception, derbies tended to be more cagey and less goal-laden in the sixties and seventies. A 0-0 draw in April 1963 was notable for attracting the highest attendance for a league derby at Anfield – 56,060 on a Monday night. Indeed, of LFC's top 40 home league attendances thirteen have been for a derby with three in the top ten: this one, 55,994 in February 1939, and 55,975 in October 1972.

In March 1967 there was a 40,000-plus crowd at Anfield for a derby that wasn't even played there: an FA Cup fifth-round tie staged at Goodison Park (attendance 64,851) and also watched on the other side of Stanley Park on big screens.

On a surviving *Pathe News* reel, a reporter reveals: "TV engineers and technicians fought against gales to make possible an experiment which resulted in the biggest crowd for a cup tie in history. Eight huge screens, 30 feet by 40, were put up on the pitch at Anfield. Projectors would relay live from the Everton arena the entire game.

"As last-minute technical adjustments were made, crowds flocked to the Liverpool ground [and] the enthusiasm at Anfield was as electric as at Goodison Park where 22 men were battling for a place in the sixth round.

"There was a moment of drama as one of the screens, anchored by eight tons of steel, was slightly lifted for a second by a gust of wind. But for the 105,000 people watching the match live at Everton and over the direct TV link, the drama was being played out before their eyes. At last [Alan] Ball had it in the net for Everton [the only goal of the game]. The moment was shared as it happened by two massive crowds linked by modern science."

While the Reds subsequently proceeded to hoover up trophies at home and abroad, the Blues sought to blunt their domestic superiority – at least on Merseyside – and there was a particularly feisty derby in October 1979 when two players were sent off during a 2-2 Anfield draw.

Reds midfielder Terry McDermott takes up the story: "As a player I was always more desperate to win when Liverpool played Everton. I wanted it more. You live with Evertonians in this city, you go for a pint with them, you're friends with them and they like to gloat when they win!

"[Everton's] Garry Stanley made a tackle on David Johnson and everyone flew in with all kinds of punches thrown. I've still got a mark on my knuckle from Garry's tooth! There were all kinds of bruisers on the pitch – Graeme Souness, Jimmy Case, Mick Lyons – but the two biggest softies, myself and Garry, got sent off.

"They were the first red cards in the Merseyside derby that century, but as we were walking down the tunnel we were arranging where to go for a drink that night!"

52/130

Above us only sky

LIVERPOOL'S forays into European competition needed meticulous planning off the pitch as much as on it.

Before attention could switch to plotting how to conquer the continent with fine football, there was the fundamental requirement of actually getting from A to B.

For many years, the wind beneath the Reds' wing(er)s was guided by Irish airline carrier Aer Lingus.

Peter Robinson, former club secretary and later LFC chief executive who sadly passed away in January 2022, admitted the link had been established with the help of a little Irish blarney.

"The club had entered European competition in August 1964 and during my first season at Anfield, 1965/66, they were using scheduled flights including those operated by BEA which later became British Airways. The problem with being tied to scheduled flight times was that you could end up being away for two, three or, in the case of Iron Curtain trips, four days. So I suggested to the board that we charter our own flights so that we could travel at times to suit us and drastically reduce time spent away.

"Memories of Manchester United's Munich disaster on a charter in 1958 were still fresh in people's minds so quite understandably there was some resistance from some, including Bill Shankly. Eventually though the board agreed to my suggestion to charter and I asked several carriers to quote me prices. In the 1966/67 season we had a KLM charter to Romania to play Petrolul Ploesti and a BEA charter to Amsterdam to play Ajax.

"The reason we switched to Aer Lingus was down to Jim Kennefick, who was in charge of their new office in Liverpool. Jim's a charming man who became a friend and later joined the club as supporter liaison officer. He used to come to Anfield, usually after my secretary had gone home – ensuring that he'd get in to see me! He told me what Aer Lingus could offer and we decided to go with them not just through friendship, but also because they quoted the best price."

Liverpool's first charter trip into Europe with Aer Lingus was on a propellered Vickers Viscount airliner for a Fairs Cup game in Malmo in September 1967, the launch of a long and successful link with the Irish carrier. "It proved to be the start of a very enjoyable and efficient relationship, with the on-board food and standard of service top-class," added Robinson. "And Bill Shankly and the training staff were very pleased that by using charters we could drastically reduce our time abroad to just one night.

"Although the opposing club in Europe had to allow you to train at their stadium the night before the game, some could be awkward and make things difficult. So we decided on a pattern of the players training at Melwood in the morning before flying out early afternoon so that they didn't need a session at the stadium on the eve of the game. We honed our European travel to a fine art."

Captain Barney Croghan was the chief pilot for the majority of Liverpool FC's continental adventures with Aer Lingus.

"The players were supposed to sit up near the front, but Jimmy

Case and Ray Kennedy claimed to be nervous flyers and asked if they could be seated near the back because they'd read it was the safest place to be. Coincidentally, it meant Bob Paisley, Joe Fagan and Ronnie Moran couldn't see what they were doing.

"Over the years I got to know a lot of the players very well. Graeme Souness even bought me a bottle of champagne for my 40th birthday.

"It was a very warm relationship between the airline and LFC. I'm not 100 percent sure but I think the team never lost a two-legged tie when they flew with us.

"Naturally other airlines wanted the business – transporting the champions of Europe was very prestigious. I think some of them complained about the set-up because they felt an English club should go with an English airline.

"Technically I think they were correct – we didn't have permission to fly into Liverpool from Dublin and pick up passengers. However the arrangement continued for a long time.

"It was so good that when Liverpool came to Dublin to play in friendlies, which they did quite regularly, a lot of the airline staff would go along. After one of those, Kenny Dalglish got separated from the rest of the squad so I drove him to the hotel where the players were having a night out. On the way we found ourselves going in the wrong direction on a one-way street. A policeman stopped us and he didn't look too impressed until he spotted my passenger. Immediately he halted the traffic and waved us through.

"LFC became a big part of my life. I went to the European Cup finals and watched them play all over the continent. It was a wonderful time for the club and for me."

Barry Crowley was part of the ground operations staff for Aer Lingus which involved travelling as a loadmaster to various unusual locations, from carrying lamb carcasses to Libya, to UN troops to Cyprus to ships crews to Malta.

He recalled: "One journey was a Liverpool FC flight to Turkey for a game with Trabzonspor in 1976. The airport nearest the stadium was too small to handle a Boeing 737 – I think the runway there might have been just a grass strip. So the decision was made to fly with Aer Lingus as far as Ankara and then to transfer to a smaller local carrier for the final leg of the journey.

"It meant that the airline staff didn't go to the game. We stayed with the plane and during routine checks on the day of the match we noticed one of the wheels needed changing. The principle is the same as changing a tyre on a car but obviously on a much bigger scale. I ended up splitting my trousers while helping to lift the main wheel back into the cargo hold.

"Stocking the plane with drink for the flight back to England was also a challenge. The local catering services were unable to supply what we'd asked for, so it meant a trip to the duty-free shop. A member of the LFC party did comment on the price of the alcohol. However I recall looking out of the galley to see how the champagne had been received and getting the thumbs-up from the same person!"

"That was the only LFC flight that I did, so when I got back to Ireland and people asked me how the game went I couldn't tell them anything about it."

Bowled over

YOU may recall the footage on LFCTV of Jürgen Klopp trying his hand at crown green bowls when he first took charge of Liverpool. But did you know that a former LFC winger became one of the country's leading exponents of that sport after calling time on his Anfield career?

John Cox, popularly known as Jack, starred for Liverpool on the wing during the early years of the 20th century, blazing a trail for future Anfield favourites such as Billy Liddell, Ian Callaghan, Steve Heighway, John Barnes and Mo Salah.

Born on 21 December 1877 at 266 Vauxhall Road in Everton, he was the son of Irish parents and had two sisters, Ellen and Catherine, and a brother, William. At the age of nine, his family moved away from Merseyside to start a new life by the seaside in Blackpool.

A keen footballer, Jack had played for local non-league clubs South Shore Standard and Blackpool South Shore before agreeing professional terms with Blackpool in May 1897. He made an early impact on the right flank, prompting Liverpool to make an offer of £150 to bring him back to Merseyside just nine months later.

On 12 March 1898 he was handed his Liverpool debut – scoring in a 2-0 win against Notts County. It would prove to be the first of 361 matches for the club during which time he would contribute 81 goals to the cause.

During his spell at Anfield, Cox – who stood around five feet six inches tall and sported the handlebar moustache popular at the time – was most often deployed on the left wing and, after establishing himself in the first team, saw his displays draw regular comparisons to the England star of the day Billy Meredith.

Cox's performances eventually led to a national call-up of his own and he made his England debut in 1901 against Northern Ireland. He would win a further two caps for his country, both coming against Scotland in 1902 and 1903.

The wing wizard was the inspiration as Liverpool secured their first top-tier title win in 1901. He was a near ever-present in the all-conquering side, missing only two games and contributing 10 goals.

His prime role was skipping down the flanks and sending in crosses for men like Sam Raybould and Joe Hewitt to convert.

He repeated that tally in the promotion-winning season of 1904/05 to ensure that the Reds bounced straight back to the top-flight following their shock relegation. Cox had been one of the few to acquit himself during that disappointing drop year, playing in 33 of the 34 games and finishing as top scorer. He plundered another nine goals in 28 matches from his wide berth as Liverpool stormed to another championship success in 1905/06.

That was a fine Liverpool side with England international Sam Hardy coming in to replace veteran Ned Doig in goal. The previous year Doig had become the club's oldest debutant aged 38 and was a key player in the club's promotion campaign.

Loyal servant Bill Dunlop played behind Cox at left-back while Arthur Goddard complemented Cox on the opposite flank. Centre-forward Hewitt thrived on the service he enjoyed from the two wingers with 24 goals.

After a decade of service with the Reds, Cox played his final game for the club on 30 April 1909 in a 1-0 win over Newcastle

United at St James' Park after which he took a free transfer back to Blackpool, taking over as player-manager at Bloomfield Road.

He married Elizabeth Ann Barrett in Blackpool in April 1910 and the couple had one daughter, Mollie. He retired from playing in 1912.

An accomplished sprinter during his youth, Cox had always retained his keen interest in other sporting pursuits and turned his hand to crown green bowling where he quickly earned a reputation as a fine player. Indeed in 1925, he became the first man to win two of the sport's big prizes – the Waterloo Cup and the Talbot Cup – in the same year.

A report of his triumph in the *Blackpool Gazette and Herald, Fylde News and Advertiser* stated: "By winning the Talbot bowling championship yesterday, Jack Cox, the popular Blackpool sportsman, accomplished the fine feat of bringing off the double vent having won the Waterloo final last week. He has thus made bowling history. Cox's record may probably never be equalled.

"Cox thoroughly deserved his triumph for he bowled in championship style throughout the day and has maintained the form he showed in the Waterloo final last week."

Cox died of a heart attack on 11 November 1955. He made a significant contribution to Liverpool Football Club and was elected to join the club's Hall of Fame for the decade 1900 to 1910 alongside the legendary Alex Raisbeck. The pair had been awarded a joint benefit match in April 1909 when a crowd of 15,000 saw the Reds held to a 2-2 draw in their league game with Bury.

Record appearance holder Ian Callaghan was on the judging panel and said of his selection. "Nothing is more exciting for a supporter than seeing a winger surge past a full-back. From the team perspective, it puts that person in the most dangerous place on the pitch from which to cross the ball. Strikers love it when the ball is pulled back to them from the by-line, but you don't see too much of that in the modern game.

"The most exciting time for me as a player was when I was on the wing. Playing wide was special because of the reaction of the fans. They lift you and you lift them.

"Wing play was a vital part of football then. Jack Cox scored a goal every four games. That's a heck of a record for a winger and it makes him stand out from his rivals. It indicates he was in a different class."

54/130

Kenny's dink

IT wasn't the best European Cup final there'd ever been, not even the best one involving Liverpool.

After the previous season's glory that was Rome, the 1978 final between the Reds and Bruges of Belgium was more of a war of attrition played out at the old Wembley Stadium – but what a goal to win it, what a moment of sheer class from Kenny Dalglish. It just felt destined to be.

It was his 31st goal in his first season with the club, having played in all 61 of Liverpool's games, and it marked the tournament as LFC territory not for a solitary season but for the foreseeable future. Kenny described the 65th-minute winner like this in his 1996 autobiography: "It was such a tight game, one goal always looked likely to settle it. Fortunately one chance fell to me, just as I had dreamed it would. I was determined to take it.

"I noticed a habit of the Bruges goalkeeper Jensen that proved to be his undoing. Each of the two times Terry Mac [McDermott] ran through and shot low, Jensen dropped down to block the ball. So when Graeme Souness played me in, Jensen came out as he had for Terry and I knew he was going to go down early. I dummied to play it, Jensen fell for it, allowing me to lift the ball over the top of him.

"After the goal I wanted to run to our fans and celebrate. I don't even remember jumping over the advertising boards, but I do know that I was too tired to jump back."

Dalglish and Souness were two of Liverpool's exciting new trio of Scots, and all of them were involved in the match's key moments. Midfielder Souness, who'd celebrated his 25th birthday four days earlier, was appearing in only his second full European game for Bob Paisley's Reds, having joined from Middlesbrough that January.

With his natural swagger and wide range of passing, he looked born to play in big cup finals. At the end of the semi-final against old foes Borussia Moenchengladbach he'd refused to swap his shirt because he "felt so proud to be a Liverpool player." At Wembley he initiated the move that would lead to the goal, and in a frenzied penalty area had the presence of mind to find Dalglish for the finish that at last breached the Bruges rearguard.

Downfield there was Alan Hansen. The Reds had been leading for 15 minutes when one hair-raising moment of non-alignment with his goalkeeper and fellow defenders threatened to ruin the 22-year-old's evening. Hansen's hesitation allowed Bruges attacker Jan Simoen the chance to shoot, but Ray Clemence came to the rescue with Phil Thompson completing the clearance. It would have been cruel on the young Scot whose accomplished performance on the night belied his inexperience.

Hansen had signed for Liverpool from Partick Thistle in May

1977, moving into digs as young players did in those days. Four months later, upon his own arrival, fellow countryman Dalglish checked into the city's St George's Hotel (now the Holiday Inn) with his family and stayed there for the best part of the 1977/78 season. "It was brilliant," recalled Kenny. "We never got bored. The chambermaid used to baby-sit and the innkeeper was a Scot, Jack Ferguson, who really looked after us."

It was the summer of *Star Wars* and *Saturday Night Fever, Citizen Smith* and skateboards. Liverpool, ignoring the gossip linking them with Trevor Francis as a replacement for Kevin Keegan, had prised Dalglish from Celtic, and British football's new record signing made his debut in the Charity Shield against Manchester United and never looked back.

"An awful lot happened very quickly. I'd played for Celtic on the Tuesday, spoke to Liverpool after the game at midnight, then up early in the morning to pick up my boots. Jock Stein took us down to a hotel in Moffat [in Dumfries & Galloway] and John Smith and Bob Paisley drove us down to Anfield. Had a medical. Signed. Came in for training Thursday morning. Travelled Friday. Played Saturday.

"But I felt comfortable the very first time I walked into the place. That was the thing that struck me in training. They'd just come straight off two trophies the year before – European Cup, the League – and got to the FA Cup final. And they just said, 'You get nothing for last year'. The attitude was magnificent."

Kenny scored six minutes into his league debut at Middlesbrough. He was on target in his first game at Anfield, a 2-0 win over Newcastle United on 23 August 1977.

His 1978 Wembley winning goal meant that Liverpool became the first British team to retain the European Cup. "The year before I'd watched Liverpool win in Rome, so it was wonderful to help the lads win the trophy again in my first season here," said Dalglish when the dust had settled. "The thrill of scoring will stay with me forever because to win a European Cup medal had been my ambition since 1967 when Celtic lifted the trophy."

Ultimately he'd win three European Cups and eight league titles with Liverpool, scoring 172 goals in 515 games. He made his last appearance, as player-manager, on 1 May 1990 aged 39 years and 58 days old. But it was that deft dink over Jensen, when Kenny was 27 and at the height of his powers, that announced a very special talent to the wider football world.

55/130

Playing for Bill and Bob!

HAD things had worked out slightly differently, Peter Cormack would have been a Liverpool player long before he eventually put pen to paper at Anfield in the summer of 1972.

During his time at Hibernian, the attacking midfielder had played under two men who had Bill Shankly's ear and both had mentioned Cormack's progress to the legendary Liverpool boss.

Jock Stein, himself one of the game's greatest managers, had been impressed by the youngster he managed at Easter Road. And when Stein moved on to Celtic, his successor in charge of the green-and-white half of Edinburgh was Shankly's brother, Bob.

"Both Bob and Bill were magic and they knew the game inside out," Cormack explained. "As a player, it was just about the respect you had for them. People talk about a fear factor and I think that with all good managers there is a bit of that with the players, but you wanted to win things for them because of the respect you had for them.

"Of course, there was nobody like Bill Shankly! His brother was a quieter man more in the Bob Paisley mould. But they were similar in the sense that they knew the game tactically and also in terms of how they were when they were speaking to you. Sometimes you talk to people in football and wonder how they can be at that level as it's like talking to somebody in a pub. But with the Shanklys and Bob Paisley, you knew what they wanted from you, certainly in the big games."

The first interest in Cormack from an English club had come from Tottenham, but just when he was set to move to White Hart Lane, he was sent off while playing for Hibernian and handed a four-game suspension. When he eventually moved south of the border it was to wear the red-and white of Nottingham Forest.

"When I had just returned to the team after the ban, Forest came in and said to Hibs: 'There you go – there's £100,000.'"

The Scot had not been at Forest long when he heard that Liverpool were on the look-out for a new attacker.

"I think they were looking to play me off John Toshack but then Bob Shankly said: 'No, Peter's a midfield player, you play him in the middle of the field.' I think it was just with me scoring a lot of goals in the air that Liverpool thought I could play in attack."

They say all good things come to those who wait and in the summer of 1972, Cormack agreed a £110,000 switch to Anfield.

"When I first went to the club I think they were still going to play me up front with Toshack but then they had this wee guy Kevin Keegan too. People said: 'No, put Peter in the middle of the park and he'll just come from there and get the same amount of goals as he would up front.'"

He made the perfect start when he scored on his home debut

against Wolves. "Soon after that I scored the winner in the derby at Anfield and, after that, I think I had real acceptance."

Moving to Liverpool was a transfer Cormack would not regret as he collected two league championships, an FA Cup, a UEFA Cup and two Charity Shields during his spell of around four-and-a-half years on Merseyside, winning as much favour with Bill Shankly as he had done with his brother Bob!

56/130

Children of the Rafalution

OUTSIDE of England, Scotland and Wales, no other country has produced more first-team Liverpool FC players than Spain. A total of 22 different Spanish-born players have worn the Liver Bird upon their chest, yet that tally stood at zero for the first 112 years of LFC's existence until everything changed on 16 June 2004 with the appointment of Rafael Benitez as manager.

Madrid-born Benitez had been appointed as Valencia boss in 2001 at the age of 41. Although he'd guided Tenerife to promotion the previous season he wasn't the big name manager the Mestalla faithful were demanding, but he sent shockwaves through Spanish football by guiding Los Che to their first La Liga title in 31 years during his first season in charge.

In 2003/04 another La Liga crown and the UEFA Cup were landed, but after falling out with Valencia's Director of Football over transfers he resigned on 1 June, a week after Liverpool had parted company with manager Gerard Houllier. A fortnight later,

Benitez was in charge at Anfield and he immediately set about making wholesale changes. It became known as the Rafalution.

Fellow Spaniards Pako Ayestaran (assistant manager/fitness coach), Jose Ochotorena (goalkeeping coach) and Paco Herrera (chief scout) joined Benitez's backroom staff and in July tough-tackling Malaga right-back Jose Miguel Gonzalez Rey – better known by the first six letters of his name, Josemi – became the first ever Spanish player to sign, and make his debut for, Liverpool Football Club. Rafa was only just getting started.

Next in was right-winger Antonio Nunez as part of the deal that took Michael Owen to Real Madrid. Nicknamed 'Tony' by the Kop, injuries restricted Nunez's Anfield career to just 27 games but he does hold the unusual distinction of being the sole player to score his only Liverpool goal in a major cup final after netting against Chelsea in the 2005 League Cup final in Cardiff.

Benitez reinvested the transfer fee received for Owen towards two players, Real Sociedad's central midfielder Xabi Alonso and Barcelona's attacking-midfielder Luis Garcia. One newspaper back in Spain nicknamed Anfield's four amigos as 'El Benitels' after photographing them at The Cavern on Mathew Street while Kopites creatively reworked pop song La Bamba to 'Rafa Rafa Benitez, Rafa Rafa Benitez, Xabi Alonso, Garcia and Nunez (and Josemi!). Ra-fa Benitez, Ra-fa Benitez...'

"Alonso and Garcia will lift the team," said Benitez. "They will provide the team with more possibilities and in training they will improve the team.

"Xabi is important for us because he is strong and has experience and he wants to improve. With Gerrard, we have long passes and movement, with Hamann we have good positioning and short passes. With Xabi we have two possibilities; short passes, long passes, a lot of things.

"Luis is a very skilful player, a player with talent, clever in midfield.

He can play in a lot of positions, always with an attacking mentality. For us it is important to have this type of player. Normally he scores about 10 goals a season as a midfielder and if I was a supporter now I would want to see Luis Garcia. For sure."

It quickly became clear that Alonso's range of passing was the best Anfield had witnessed since great Dane Jan Molby had patrolled the centre-circle while Garcia earned himself a reputation as the little man for the big occasion, netting decisive Champions League goals in the knockout stages of the 2004/05 competition against Bayer Leverkusen, Juventus and, famously, in the semi-final victory against Chelsea.

On 25 May 2005 Xabi Alonso became the first Spaniard to score for Liverpool in a Champions League final when he netted the Reds' equaliser against AC Milan in Istanbul while Luis Garcia – who also played the full 120 minutes – plus Josemi and Nunez, who were both unused substitutes, ended an epic evening with winners' medals around their necks.

By then a fifth Spaniard, striker Fernando Morientes, had arrived from Real Madrid with a reputation for scoring goals, but he was cup-tied in Europe and struggled to adapt to the Premier League with his tally of 12 goals in 63 games not matching expectations of the Spanish international.

The same can't be said about Alonso who struck 19 goals – two from inside his own half against Luton Town and Newcastle United – in 210 appearances and Garcia, whose 30 goals in 121 games included another semi-final winner against Chelsea, this time in the 2006 FA Cup, and a couple of Merseyside derby efforts.

Two young Spanish defenders, Antonio Barragan and Miki Roque, arrived from Sevilla and Lleida in the summer of 2005. Both only made one first-team substitute appearance in Champions League games, Barragan against CSKA Sofia in 2005 and Roque against Galatasaray in 2006, but whereas Barragan went on to enjoy a career with clubs such as Valencia and Middlesbrough, Roque tragically died at the age of 23 after being diagnosed with pelvic cancer. Fans of his club at the time, Real Betis, raised funds to pay for his treatment and following the Euro 2012 final won by Spain against Italy in Kiev, goalkeeper Pepe Reina wore a t-shirt bearing Roque's name on the lap of honour.

Reina himself had arrived at Anfield in the summer of 2005 from Villarreal and was immediately installed as Liverpool's number one goalkeeper. He proved to be an inspired signing as during his first season Reina set new club records for keeping the most consecutive clean sheets in all competitions (11), the most consecutive clean sheets in the Premier League (six), the longest run without conceding (1,016 minutes) and saved three penalties in the FA Cup final as the Reds beat West Ham in a shoot-out following a 3-3 draw.

He also won the Premier League Golden Glove for the most shut-outs – an accolade Reina would claim again in 2007 and 2008 – and went on to keep 177 clean sheets in 394 games, putting the Madrid-born keeper third on Liverpool's all-time list behind Ray Clemence and Bruce Grobbelaar.

Full-back Alvaro Arbeloa, a £2.6m arrival from Deportivo La Coruna, was another shrewd Spanish acquisition in 2007 and proved his worth on his full debut when he marked Lionel Messi out of the game as Liverpool recorded a famous 2-1 Champions League victory against Barcelona in Camp Nou en-route to the final against AC Milan in Athens. Then, in the summer of 2007, came a new LFC golden boy.

Brought in from Atletico Madrid, Fernando Torres was a genuine world class signing. Pace, movement, goals – 'El Nino' had the lot and when he'd captained Atleti his armband had 'We'll Never Walk Alone' (adapted from You'll Never Walk Alone) written on the underside, something that made Liverpool supporters believe all the more that he was a perfect fit for LFC with a tribute song referencing his armband eclipsing 'Luis Garcia, he drinks Sangria...' for popularity on the Kop and eventually being turned into a Nike TV commercial.

Torres netted 33 goals in his debut campaign, scoring in eight consecutive Anfield games – a run which hadn't been seen since the days of Roger Hunt. He also fired home Liverpool's first ever winning goal in the San Siro as Inter Milan were beaten 1-0 in the Champions League.

A controversial transfer to Chelsea in 2011 took the shine off some of his goalscoring exploits, but Torres' tally of 81 goals in 142 games made him Liverpool's second all-time leading non-British goalscorer after Gordon Hodgson until his replacement, Luis Suarez, went on to surpass him with 82. Mo Salah, Sadio Mane and Roberto Firmino have since eclipsed them all bar Hodgson.

Albert Riera, Dani Pacheco and Daniel Ayala were other Spaniards to play for the Reds during Benitez's time in charge with one of Riera's five LFC goals being the first scored against Preston North End at Deepdale since the Bill Shankly Kop was built there in 1998.

Since then Suso, Jose Enrique, Luis Alberto, Iago Aspas, Pedro Chirivella, Sergi Canos, Javi Manquillo (loan), Alberto Moreno and Adrian have added to the Spanish contingent to play for the Redmen with various degrees of success.

Enrique was part of Kenny Dalglish's League Cup winning side in 2012 while in 2016 fellow left-back Moreno became the fifth Spaniard to have made a century of appearances for Liverpool FC. Adrian made himself a Reds' penalty shoot-out hero when he saved a spot-kick from Chelsea's Tammy Abraham in Istanbul, winning the 2019/20 UEFA Super Cup for the European champions.

A Italian-born Spanish international by the name of Thiago

Alcantara, the son of Brazilian World Cup winner Mazinho, has also captured the hearts of Kopites with his midfield artistry, class on the ball and no-look passes making him a key member of Jürgen Klopp's Liverpool team.

They all followed in the bootprints of Xabi Alonso, Luis Garcia, Pepe Reina and Fernando Torres – children of the Rafalution.

57/130

Time to fez up

WHO was the last man to score a goal in front of the standing Kop? Julian Dicks? Good try. Ashley Neal? Getting closer. Jeremy Goss? Warm, really warm. The answer? John Garner. That's right. John Garner.

But first things first.

Dicks was the last LFC player to score for the first-team in front of the standing Kop. The Reds failed to find the net in their final two home matches of the 1993/94 campaign, drawing blanks against Newcastle United (0-2) and Norwich City (0-1). And so it fell to Dicks to claim the honour of the last Red to net in a senior fixture in front of standing supporters on the Kop when he converted a late penalty to give Roy Evans' team a 1-0 win over Ipswich Town on Saturday 9 April 1994.

"It was a privilege to play for Liverpool," the full-back told the official matchday programme in 2014. "You look at people like Rushie who scored 300-odd goals, but I scored the last one for Liverpool in front of the standing Kop. For me that is a massive honour and whether people want me to be in there or not, I will always be in the Liverpool record books!"

However, the last Liverpool player to find the net in front of the old Spion Kop was actually Ashley Neal, who scored in a reserve game just days before that season finale against Norwich in which the Reds failed to find a way past Canaries keeper Bryan Gunn.

Neal, son of Reds legend Phil, recalled: "We played Nottingham Forest at Anfield shortly before the Kop's last stand and drew the game 2-2. I scored Liverpool's second goal at the Kop end and it came from a penalty. Of course, my Dad used to take them for Liverpool so there was a little bit of pressure on me. I stepped up and stuck it into the right corner of the net. I didn't know it at the time but luckily enough that was the last goal scored in front of the Kop by a Liverpool player.

"What does it mean to me? I look at it in relation to my Dad's career. He can turn round and say he's got these medals and those medals and that he's Liverpool's most successful footballer ever, but I wouldn't swap that for the little piece of history I've got. That's how much it means to me."

And so to Goss, the Norwich midfielder who spoiled Liverpool's party on the afternoon of 30 April 1994 as a colourful Kop bade farewell to the most famous terrace in the game.

His 35th minute strike decided the outcome and he admits that even as an opposing player, the fact that he can lay claim to having scored the final goal in front of the standing Kop fills him with pride.

Recalling the moment almost 20 years later in the matchday programme, the former Welsh international explained: "It was a special moment for me. I remember we were pleased to be a part of such a memorable day. Playing in front of world-renowned fans and in such an atmosphere was incredible but we were a decent team and were determined not to just make up the numbers.

"From what I remember, it was an entertaining, open game with plenty of chances for both teams. I hit the shot sweetly and to see it fly past David James and into the corner was fantastic. It is one of those things you look back on and think: 'Wow. I achieved that.'

"I knew Ian Rush from the Wales international team and we all felt that it would be fitting for him to have scored the last goal. He was the best of his time and a smashing guy as well. But I was fortunate that the honour of scoring that goal fell to me."

So where does John Garner come into it? The die-hard Red from Halewood takes up the story.

"The last day of the Kop was probably the most enjoyable day that any Kopite has ever had, but also the saddest," he recalled to the club's website a decade later. "I've never seen the Kop so colourful and fanatical as on that day. I knew when I got up that morning there was something special in the air. Even driving down Queens Drive, coming up towards the ground there was an atmosphere that only comes around once every three of four years at Anfield.

"What I did wasn't planned, but I was dressed for the occasion. I went as a Spion Kop war veteran, complete with fez, big colonel moustache, khaki kecks down to my knees, working boots and a nice army shirt with the Liver Bird on it. I thought I well looked the part!

"It was never my intention to get on the pitch because obviously it's wrong to encroach onto the playing surface. But at the end of the game everyone refused to leave the ground. We wanted to spend as much time there as we could."

Soon, a spark of an idea entered John's head: "When the players left the pitch, they'd left a ball in the Kop net. One of the stewards threw it into the crowd and some kids caught it near where I was standing. I asked for the ball and they told me where to go in no uncertain manner, claiming it was theirs. But I told them I was going to get on the pitch with it so they gladly handed it over.

"I got right behind the goal, waited until the copper turned his back and then I was away. I headed towards the centre circle as fast as I could. I was thinking: 'Am I going to get rugby tackled here?' but I could hear the roar of the Kop behind me and carried on.

"I just thought 'this is heaven', then had a bit of a juggle with the ball. The crowd were loving it, the flags came back out and it gave everyone a lift as it had been a bit of a flat ending to the match.

"My problem now was 'what do I do next?' I looked up and saw the wide-open goal before me and my eyes lit up. I'd always wanted to hit the back of that net. I made a charge towards the goal. The crowd were up for it. I was up for it. But just as I approached the 18-yard box, two coppers broke rank and one of the stewards, so I had to be careful.

"With them about to steal my moment of glory, I curled the ball into the top right-hand corner. Bang. In the onion bag and I'm on cloud nine. My first thought then was 'right lad, get off the pitch now' but just as I was about to dive back into the Kop, I was rugby tackled by two of our finest officers.

"Thankfully they saw the funny side of it and I was just given a slap on the wrists, told not to be silly again and to have a good night.

"So off I went to meet the rest of the lads in the Kop. When I got there someone pointed out to me that I'd just scored the last ever goal in front of the standing Kop. I must say we made the most of it that night.

"Was it the best moment of my life? Well put it this way, having kids doesn't even beat hitting the back of the net at Anfield!"

We've won this cup all over the place

THE Champions League final is played at a different venue every season. The League Cup final is played at the same stadium every season. So, when you add up Liverpool FC's overall trophy count – which takes longer to do so than at most other clubs – it's perhaps somewhat surprising to note that the Reds have won almost as many League Cups at different venues as they have European Cups.

Every Kopite knows their European geography. Rome. London. Paris. Rome. Istanbul. Madrid. But perhaps LFC's League Cup trail of glory – Birmingham. London. London. Manchester. London. Cardiff. Cardiff. London. London – isn't quite as well considered.

As of 2022, no club has won more League Cups than Liverpool's nine. No other club has won the League Cup at four different stadiums. And, had the Reds' first League Cup final appearance in 1978 ended with a victory, Liverpool would be the only club to have won domestic cup competitions at Manchester's Old Trafford and Maine Road.

Founded by Football League secretary Alan Hardaker in 1960, the League Cup wasn't compulsory to enter at first and although LFC did take part in the inaugural 1960/61 tournament, poor attendances persuaded the club's board – and manager Bill Shankly – not to bother for the following six seasons. LFC weren't the only club to opt out, but the introduction of an income-generating TV contract, replacing the two-legged final with a one-off Wembley showdown in 1967 and allocating the winners with a UEFA Cup place (from 1972) changed perceptions so from 1967/68 onwards the Reds have been involved.

Indeed, Liverpool were so successful in the competition during Bob Paisley's spell in charge that the League Cup spent more time at Anfield than the groundsman, despite defeat to Nottingham Forest in the 1978 final.

The Reds hadn't even made the semi-final before that campaign, but went all the way to Wembley only to be repeatedly denied by 18-year-old goalkeeper Chris Woods, a stand-in for the cup-tied Peter Shilton. The replay, held at Old Trafford, was settled by a controversial John Robertson penalty and Ian Callaghan was booked for the only time in his entire LFC career in what was the 856th of his 857 appearances!

By 1981 Bob Paisley's boys were back at Wembley again to face FA Cup holders West Ham and when Alan Kennedy netted an 118th minute extra-time opener it looked like the League Cup was finally heading to Anfield only for Terry McDermott to tip Alvin Martin's 120th minute goalbound header onto the crossbar. Unfortunately for the Reds Terry Mac was wearing number 10, not number one, so after Ray Stewart converted the penalty it was all back to Villa Park for a replay where Paul Goddard opened the scoring for the Hammers.

Kenny Dalglish's sliding volley levelled matters before the winner came from the unlikely source of Alan Hansen's head – via Billy Bonds' knee – to break LFC's League Cup duck in what remains the only domestic cup final Liverpool have won wearing a white away strip.

After that came complete and utter League Cup domination. Between August 1980 and October 1984 the Reds lost just once in the competition, a semi-final second leg at Burnley. Paisley brought the trophy home so often that wife Jessie must've thought it was part of the family silver.

In 1981/82 the competition had its first sponsor – the Milk Marketing Board – and that ended up earning Ronnie Whelan the nickname of the 'Milk Cup Kid'.

A Tottenham Hotspur side featuring Ray Clemence, Glenn Hoddle, Osvaldo Ardiles and Ricky Villa were the Reds' Wembley opponents and it took an 87th minute equaliser from 21-year-old Irishman Whelan, who'd only broken into the side that season as Ray Kennedy's long-term replacement, to send the game to extra-time. This time, however, no replay was needed.

Whelan scored again and Ian Rush netted a third to ensure Phil Thompson became the first Liverpool skipper to lead his men up the Wembley steps to lift the League Cup in London.

Paisley had told his players "you're turning the milk sour," at half-time and a year later it was the Reds boss himself who lifted the trophy at Wembley.

Again Liverpool went behind, this time to Manchester United in the first major cup final contested between the two giants, once again it took a late goal to send it to extra-time, this time from Alan Kennedy, and once again it was Whelan who scored in the additional 30 minutes, this time with a memorable right-footed curler.

By this point Paisley had announced it would be his ninth and final season as LFC boss before retiring so new club captain Graeme Souness gave up the opportunity to lift his first trophy with the armband on so that Anfield's quiet genius could enjoy the limelight. "It was purely spontaneous," revealed Souness. "We wanted him to go up because it was his last year and he deserved the credit as much as any of the players."

How could three-in-a-row possibly be topped in 1984? By beating Everton in the first all-Merseyside major cup final.

Joe Fagan was now in charge and the Milk Cup final represented the first leg of a potential treble of trophies that Liverpool could win with the championship and European Cup also in their sights. A crowd of 100,000 Reds and Blues filled Wembley Stadium with chants of 'Merseyside, Merseyside, Merseyside' ringing out but the match itself was a huge anti-climax, finishing 0-0 with Hansen lucky to get away with a handball on the goalline. A post-match photo of the teams posing together – without the trophy – after doing a joint lap of honour summed up the great camaraderie between the two sets of players and supporters.

The replay was held at Manchester City's Maine Road in front of just over 52,000 and was settled by a cracking first-half strike from Souness who turned his man after receiving a Phil Neal pass before lashing home a bouncing left-footed strike from 25-yards that zipped past Neville Southall. This time Souness himself lifted the trophy although it was a pint of beer rather than a pint of milk that was thrust into his hand as he gave a post-match TV interview!

Liverpool's run of success ended against Tottenham at White Hart Lane the following October and it was another 11 years – and three changes of sponsor from Littlewoods to Rumbelows to Coca Cola – before a Reds side managed by Roy Evans captured the trophy again, although there was a Wembley final defeat to Arsenal in 1987 during Kenny Dalglish's time in charge.

Steve McManaman played the starring role against Bolton Wanderers, netting two dazzling individual goals and walking away with the Alan Hardaker man-of-the-match trophy as the Reds ran out 2-1 winners. It was the third time Liverpool had won the League Cup in London and the last match LFC won beneath the Twin Towers at the old Wembley Stadium before it was demolished in 2000.

Cardiff's Millennium Stadium hosted domestic cup finals before the new Wembley opened in 2007 and Liverpool visited so often that it became known as Anfield South Wales. The travelling Kop's first trip there came in 2001 under the management of Gerard Houllier for the rebranded Worthington Cup final against Birmingham City with the Reds chasing a treble of League Cup, FA Cup and UEFA Cup.

Robbie Fowler's looping volley appeared to have the cup won but the Brummies equalised with a late penalty and, with replays having now been scrapped, it became both the first League Cup final to be settled by penalties and the first shoot-out the Reds had faced in a domestic cup final.

Goalkeeper Sander Westerveld emerged as the hero, saving from Andy Johnson after Jamie Carragher had put the Reds 5-4 ahead. "It was sudden death," recalled Carragher, "but I didn't have any nerves. I knew where I wanted to put it and thankfully it went in."

That sixth League Cup, won at a fourth different venue, was Liverpool's first trophy for six years – but the first of three in 2000/01 – and two years later Houllier's Reds were back in Cardiff to take on Manchester United in the Worthington Cup final.

For the first time in a major cup final, Liverpool played under a closed roof – the Welsh weather persuading stadium officials to shut it – and that made the atmosphere all the more feverish as songs echoed around the stadium, not least after Steven Gerrard opened the scoring. A late second from Michael Owen saw United off, but it took a string of saves from man-of-the-match Jerzy Dudek to keep Alex Ferguson's side at bay.

"It was my first cup final for Liverpool and as the team coach approached the stadium I could not believe the number of our supporters on the streets," recalled Dudek. "The Liverpool people were living for that game and it felt like the whole city had turned out in Cardiff."

Liverpool's 100% League Cup final record in Cardiff was ended by Chelsea in 2005 and when the Redmen next reached the final, during Kenny Dalglish's second stint as manager in 2012, it meant a first trip to the new Wembley where, ironically, Cardiff City were the Reds' opponents.

Martin Skrtel and Dirk Kuyt, in extra time, turned around a one-goal deficit but Ben Turner took the game to penalties and when Gerrard and Charlie Adam missed LFC's first two it looked like the Bluebirds were about to cause a cup shock. However, Cardiff missed three penalties themselves and when Anthony Gerrard – cousin of Steven – hit the post a record eighth League Cup, now sponsored by Carling, was on the way back to Anfield.

A first ever cup final defeat on penalties prevented Jürgen Klopp from winning his first trophy as Liverpool boss against Manchester City in 2016, but he took his men back to Wembley to face Chelsea in 2022 where the rebranded Carabao Cup was lifted.

In a pulsating 120 minutes Joel Matip had a goal disallowed by VAR for a foul by Virgil van Dijk, while Chelsea had three chalked off for offside by the assistant referee's flag and the video referee. So it went to penalties where the most incredible cup final shoot-out in Liverpool's history followed.

Held at the Liverpool end, after vice-captain James Milner won the toss, all 20 outfield players converted their spot-kicks, leaving goalkeepers Caoimhin Kelleher and Kepa Arrizabalaga – brought on by Chelsea boss Thomas Tuchel for the shoot-out – to step up.

Kelleher sent Arrizabalaga the wrong way to make it 11-10 and when the Chelsea keeper then blasted his penalty high over the crossbar a record ninth League Cup, won in four different cities, belonged to Liverpool FC.

59/130

Total football

JOHAN Cruyff in a Liverpool shirt, wouldn't that have been something? Had circumstances permitted in the 1960s it might just have happened – as the late, great Dutch genius revealed in his posthumously-published autobiography *My Turn*.

In the course of his career Cruyff played four times against Liverpool: twice in a European Cup second-round tie with Ajax in December 1966 and twice with Barcelona in a UEFA Cup semi-final almost a decade later. But it was his first visit to L4 with Ajax, when he was aged just 19, that left a lasting impression.

"At the time Liverpool were not just the best team in England but one of the strongest teams in the world," he wrote. "I can still recall pretty much everything about the legendary mistwedstrijd ('fog game') in the Olympic Stadium in Amsterdam and the return match at Anfield. In Amsterdam the final score was 5-1 and we had blown the English champions away in a technical sense, although I still remember their manager Bill Shankly saying after the end of the game that it was a freak result and it would be 7-0 in Liverpool."

Cruyff had scored twice in that chastening first leg for Liverpool, and he'd get two more – as would Reds striker Roger Hunt – in the return match at Anfield.

"A week later...I stood on the pitch at Anfield with goosebumps," he continued. "Not because I was scared of our opponents, but because of the atmosphere. The huge Kop stand where the most fanatical supporters were, and all their singing: Anfield was incredibly impressive. I really enjoyed it for ninety minutes, and we played a magnificent game. Even though it was a 2-2 draw, we were in complete control.

"My happiness at our progress and at getting into the next round was matched only by the impression Anfield left on me; from that evening English football had captured my heart. I had only played football at the highest level for a few seasons and I had never seen anything like this – the passion for the game, and how much the fans wanted their team to win, and it made me think that one day I would like to play in England. Unfortunately, that dream didn't come to pass, because in those days borders were still closed to foreign players. Even today I still think that was a terrible shame."

The tables were turned at Anfield in April 1976 when a 1-1 draw was enough to take Liverpool through 2-1 on aggregate to the UEFA Cup final, at the expense of Cruyff (then aged 28) and Barcelona. The game drew a crowd of 55,104 – Anfield's highest-ever European attendance.

Twenty-five years later Johan's son Jordi played for Alaves against Liverpool in 2001's UEFA Cup final, and a Cruyff quote adorned a wall at the Reds' old Melwood training ground: "There's not one club in Europe with an anthem like *You'll Never Walk Alone*. There's not one club in the world so united with the fans."

Cruyff isn't the only budding megastar to have appeared at Anfield for a non-British team. Future World Cup-winner Franz Beckenbauer was 25 when his Bayern Munich side – also featuring goalie Sepp Maier and ace striker Gerd Muller – lost 3-0 in a European Fairs Cup fourth-round first leg in March 1971. All three were back for a goalless draw in a Cup Winners' Cup second-round first leg six months later.

The 1996 European Championships brought Paolo Maldini

and Alessandro Del Piero to Anfield for Italy's group games, with Zinedine Zidane playing for France v the Netherlands in a subsequent quarter-final. More recently Lionel Messi played alongside Ronaldinho in the Barcelona team that won 1-0 in a Champions League first knockout round second leg in March 2007. He was 19, just as Cruyff had been back in 1966, but didn't enjoy his Anfield return as a 31-year-old in 2019 when an early Andy Robertson challenge left him sat on the turf and the Reds went on to win 4-0 to reach the Champions League final.

Real Madrid's Cristiano Ronaldo was applauded off by a sporting Anfield crowd after a sublime display and goal in a 3-0 Champions League victory for the Spaniards in 2014 with the three-goal deficit Liverpool's record home defeat in Europe. In 2022, following the tragic death of his twin son, Anfield held a minute of applause and sung *You'll Never Walk Alone* in a show of support during a game against Manchester United. "Thanks, Anfield. Me and my family will never forget this moment of compassion," he tweeted.

Appearing at Anfield in 1988 in a different capacity was Michel Platini, three-time Ballon d'Or winner and future French national-team coach and UEFA president. The former midfielder, just retired from playing for Juventus, was a French co-commentator in the press box, watching Liverpool beat Arsenal 2-0 along with 44,294 inside Anfield and a further 250 million on TV in 55 countries – a landmark figure in what was still the pre-Sky era. Of the Barnes-Beardsley-Aldridge era Reds he said: "They have some superb individuals, and I enjoy the way they play to feet."

Diego Maradona also visited Anfield, when coach of Argentina in 2010, to watch Javier Mascherano and Emiliano Insua play in a 3-0 Europa League win against Lille, while in March 2015 Pele visited Anfield to take in a Liverpool versus Manchester United game and was presented with a plaque by the club in honour of his contribution to the game.

60/130

Places I remember

THERE are places I remember. All my life, but some have changed. Some forever, not for better. Some have gone and some remain.

When you hear those lyrics, penned by Lennon and McCartney in 1965, you probably think of Istanbul. Of the video montage, partly narrated by Sean Connery, played on Sky Sports on the night of 25 May 2005 after Liverpool had stunned AC Milan to come back from 3-0 down to win the Champions League final on penalties. Hairs on the back of your neck standing up yet?

Istanbul is a city that no Kopite will ever forget, yet there are villages and towns that most Liverpool supporters have never been to – and probably never will – that also have a place in our club's illustrious history because of the sons they spawned.

Places like Glenbuck, an Ayrshire mining outpost on the A70 in Scotland that still exists in name, but not as a community. Formerly a thriving mining village with a population of 1,200, it was depopulated after the last mine closed in 1931, but not before it had – quite astonishingly – produced over 50 professional footballers, the most famous being Bill Shankly.

Many of them, including Shankly and his four brothers, played for the Glenbuck Cherrypickers on Burnside Park before going on to have careers in the game, but when the jobs went the people went too and by 1997 virtually every home had been demolished due to open-cast mining with only seven now remaining.

However, because it was the place where Shankly was born (in 1913) and raised, the name Glenbuck has remained in the psyche of Liverpool fans and on 27 April 1997 a memorial stone, featuring a plaque that includes the words 'The Legend, The Genius, The Man' plus his career achievements, was laid in the village in his honour.

On what would have been Shankly's 106th birthday in September 2019, and as part of work done by the Scottish Mines Restoration Trust, Glenbuck Heritage Village was opened. Landmarks such as the footprint of Shankly's childhood home have been marked out to guide visitors around the village.

Many Reds have since been to visit it, placing scarves and flowers on the site, and the same can be said of a memorial for Bob Paisley that was unveiled on 16 August 2008 in England's North-East village of Hetton-le-Hole following a fundraising campaign by Liverpool supporters.

Situated close to Sunderland and with a history that can be traced back to the 14th century, Hetton-le-Hole was, like Glenbuck, a mining community and home to Paisley, who was born there in 1919.

Travelling Kopites have made annual pilgrimages to the memorial, situated in Hetton-le-Hole town centre and featuring the words 'Proud son of Hetton-le-Hole and loyal servant of Liverpool FC for 52 years', en-route to away games at Sunderland, although the Black Cats' relegation from the Premier League in 2017 meant that routine has changed.

Would Glenbuck and Hetton-le-Hole be places you'd ever heard of if it wasn't for the Shankly and Paisley connections? Quite probably not, and that's almost certainly also the case with the Scottish mining village of Townhill in Fife, birthplace of Billy Liddell.

A memorial plaque honouring the Anfield great was unveiled on

22 May 2010 just 50 yards away from the home he grew up in, a reminder of the high esteem he was held in and his achievements in the game.

There are also plenty of places outside of the British Isles that have worked their way into the consciousness of Kopites thanks to LFC's overseas arrivals.

Gerard Houllier, Liverpool manager from 1998 to 2004, isn't from Paris or Marseille or Lyon. He was born in Thérouanne, a northern French commune that had a population of less than 1,000 when he arrived into the world in 1947.

Few Liverpudlians had heard of Porvoo before Sami Hyypia moved to Merseyside in 1999. The towering defender grew up in the Finnish coastal town 30 miles south of Helsinki – not a place that was commonly discussed on Merseyside, but clearly they make good centre-halves there!

Another little-known coastal town came under the spotlight in 2006 when Rafa Benitez signed Dutch international striker Dirk Kuyt. He arrived from Feyenoord in Rotterdam, but was born and raised in Katwijk aan Zee, a quiet North Sea fishing village that is now a popular seaside resort.

A year later Liverpool signed a lad from sunny Spain who gets the ball and scores again. Fernando Torres, Liverpool's number nine, as the song went, hails from Fuenlabrada, a municipality of Madrid situated 13 miles outside of the Spanish capital. Probably derived from the words Fuente Labrada (curved fountain), it has a population of almost 200,000 yet wasn't a place many had heard of before Torres signed for the Reds.

It's a similar story with Salto. Latin for 'to leap', Salto was founded in 1756 and lies in northwestern Uruguay. It is the South American country's second largest city with a population of over 100,000 but also the hometown of Luis Suarez, suggesting that whatever they put in the water over there leads to goals.

More recently the remote Senegalese village of Bambali, located in the Casamance region nearly 500 miles south of the capital Dakar, has become famous as the birthplace of Sadio Mane. The village now has a new school and hospital, officially opened by Sadio in June 2021, thanks to generous donations from the Liverpool striker.

Mo Salah also comes from a small African village – Nagrig in Egypt's Gharbia Province. Nagrig has become known by Liverpool supporters thanks to Mo and his Salah Charity Foundation has helped to fund projects in the local area from an ambulance station and sewage farm to sports facilities and oxygen tanks for COVID-19 patients in Basyoun Central Hospital.

If you don't know where the Black Forest village of Glatten is then it's time to check the map. Situated near Freudenstadt in South-West Germany, and home to less than 2,500 citizens, it was in that village that Stuttgart-born Jürgen Klopp was brought up.

Nestled between meadows and rows of trees, it may not have the mining background that the villages where Shankly and Paisley were furnaced do, but it has produced another fine Liverpool manager.

Glenbuck. Hetton-le-Hole. Thérouanne. Glatten. All have played a part in the history of Liverpool FC.

All are places to remember.

61/130

Shields of Anfield Road

WAS there ever a time in the eighties when Liverpool FC didn't contest the FA Charity Shield? Yes, amazingly: in 1981, 1985 and 1987.

In the decade's other seven years Wembley was 'Anfield South' for the traditional season curtain-raiser. Liverpool won it four times (1980, 82, 88 and 89 and always, it felt, in glorious sunshine), lost twice (83 and 84) and drew – hence shared the trophy – once (86).

For the record the Reds have won the Shield on ten occasions overall and shared it five times, and no one has appeared more times for the club than goalkeeper Bruce Grobbelaar, with eight games from 1982 to 1992 (Phil Thompson, Phil Neal, Alan Hansen, Kenny Dalglish, Ian Rush and Ronnie Whelan all have seven).

Back then the showpiece (now known as the FA Community Shield) also allowed Liverpool to blood new signings, many of whom would never quite become first-team superstars but still played their part in the side's virtual domination of the decade.

The 1-0 victory over FA Cup winners Tottenham Hotspur in August 1982 featured the debut of David Hodgson, signed from Middlesbrough and at the time an England Under-21 international striker.

He made a good start to the season with four goals in his first six games, but when fellow forward Michael Robinson joined Liverpool the following year – and made his own debut in the

Charity Shield – Hodgson felt his first-team chances were too limited and went back to the North East and Sunderland. A pity, because manager Joe Fagan had earmarked him as a right-midfield successor to Sammy Lee, a Scouser who won 10 major honours in his 295 games for LFC between 1978 and 1986 before working for the club in various coaching roles from 1992 to 2004 and again from 2008 to 2011.

Robinson was a summer of 1983 signing from Brighton & Hove Albion, who'd just lost to Manchester United in the FA Cup final. He'd lose to the same opposition with Liverpool in the subsequent Charity Shield, but he became a favourite with the Kop who affectionately dubbed him 'Fatty Robbo'.

Like Hodgson he remained a back-up for the dynamic duo of Rush and Dalglish, but he did come on as a substitute in the 1984 European Cup final against AS Roma before moving to QPR then carving out a new career in Spain.

The Liverpool side that finished the Charity Shield match of August 1984, against Everton, had Paul Walsh – another England Under-21 regular – making his debut upfront having moved from Luton Town. "I came on as a substitute after 53 minutes, replacing David Hodgson," he remembered. "We ended up losing 1-0 after Alan Hansen cleared a ball off the line, straight into Bruce Grobbelaar's shins and back into the net just five minutes after I'd come on!"

Starting for Liverpool that day was John Wark, who'd joined the club five months earlier from Ipswich Town and was staying in the same hotel as Walsh. The Scotsman with the Ming-the-Merciless moustache had been prolific in front of goal for the Tractor Boys and he continued his form for Liverpool, even outscoring Rush in 1984/85 with 27 goals including three hat-tricks.

An Achilles problem then a broken ankle curtailed Wark's Anfield career, and Walsh too was bedevilled by injuries including a torn cartilage and damaged hernia. He'd been bought, it was believed, as Dalglish's long-term replacement, and he did score 18 goals when Liverpool won an historic league and FA Cup double in 1986. But his contribution feels largely forgotten.

"Only a few games were televised in that era whereas now every minute of every match is recorded," he said. "If you look back at the double-winning team, people only remember Kenny chesting the ball down and volleying the winner at Stamford Bridge to win the league and Rushie scoring twice at Wembley against Everton. They were the iconic moments.

"The contribution of Kevin MacDonald gets overlooked, too, so if you asked most people to name that double-winning team I probably wouldn't get a mention. I missed the FA Cup final but I made the PFA Team of the Year which showed my peers thought I was one of the best players that season."

Dalglish did single out Scottish midfielder MacDonald, a November 1984 signing from Leicester City, for praise following the Wembley win over Everton that clinched the double.

He later wrote in his autobiography: "Headlines were being prepared in salute of Rushie and Jan Molby [but] in the dressing room we all rushed to congratulate Kevin MacDonald. He got in among Everton's midfield, taking the fight to Reidy [Peter Reid], reclaiming the ball time after time. Never one of the most celebrated footballers, Kevin Mac will always be remembered fondly for turning the 'blue tide' back at Wembley in May 1986."

MacDonald would also play in the August 1986 Charity Shield draw with the Toffees – the game in which full-back Barry Venison made his Liverpool debut. This particular England Under-21 international thought the original call from Anfield, to sign from Sunderland, had been a wind-up.

"It was ten o'clock at night and I'd been asleep. The phone rang: 'Hi Barry, this is Kenny – Kenny Dalglish'. And I said: 'Yeah, sure it is!' He insisted it was, and I'm thinking, well it sounds like him…

"Kenny didn't have to do anything. I was honoured to join a legendary club and an absolute winning machine. You knew you were a part of a winning establishment, but there was a quiet dignity about the players. That was one of the things I learned at Liverpool: you win with grace."

LFC's next Charity Shield match, against shock FA Cup-winners Wimbledon in 1988, saw two local lads in central defence: Gary Ablett and Alex Watson. The Reds had romped to the previous season's league title – with Ablett and Nigel Spackman among the unsung heroes as Barnes, Beardsley, Aldridge and Houghton grabbed the headlines. Watson, the younger brother of former Everton captain Dave, made just six more appearances before moving to AFC Bournemouth while Ablett, who tragically passed away in 2012, went on to play for Everton (he's the only man to win the FA Cup with both Merseyside clubs) and coach Liverpool Under-21s to a Premier Reserve League North title in 2008.

The last Charity Shield of the eighties was Glenn Hysen's first game for Liverpool. A 1-0 victory over Arsenal at Wembley in August 1989 provided a modicum of revenge for the previous season's title finale, and *The Times* reported: "The arrival of Hysen from Sweden promises to tighten the already solid security of Liverpool. On his debut, he was immaculate.

"Hansen, restored as captain, and the equally elegant Hysen give the impression that if a hand grenade were lobbed in their vicinity, they would casually await the explosion and check in which direction the shrapnel was flying before taking evasive action. They epitomise composure, almost nonchalance, under stress."

It was a central-defensive pairing, aided and abetted by the equally classy Ablett and Gary Gillespie, that would anchor Liverpool's 18th league title win.

Others to have made their Liverpool debuts in the showpiece

occasion since the 1980s include Paul Stewart (v Leeds United in 1992), John Arne Riise (v Manchester United in 2001), El-Hadji Diouf and Bruno Cheyrou (v Arsenal in 2002) and Fabio Aurelio (v Chelsea in 2006), while Takumi Minamino scored his first goal for the Reds against Arsenal in the FA Community Shield in 2020.

62/130

Plenty at steak

SINCE the turn of the 21st century, conventional thinking on how to fuel and refuel the body has seen leading football clubs employ large staffs of sports science experts.

In the summer of 2016 the club appointed Mona Nemmer as the Premier League's first full-time head of nutrition. Mona, who'd previously worked for the German national team and Bayern Munich, was soon hailed by Jürgen Klopp as "one of the most valuable team members at LFC."

Her job, she explained in her subsequent hit book *A Taste of the Liverpool Way*, was "to make sure the players eat the right food at the right times." Her dream, she added, was "to help the next generation of fans and footballers learn more about where good food comes from, why a healthy, well-balanced diet improves our wellbeing and sporting performance, and how it can be simple, easy and affordable to grow our own produce and even cook our own meals."

She continued: "At Liverpool FC there is so much history and tradition but also a modern, open-minded perspective among the players, management and staff which has helped to give nutrition a great profile and lots of respect and makes my job so fulfilling.

"Jürgen Klopp is the reason for this because he gives us a real family vibe at LFC, along with the opportunity and freedom to work hard and responsibly and achieve the highest standards we possibly can. He's a very smart leader who empowers, supports and pushes you in equal measure. None of it is possible without him. It's incredible to work with him and for him."

In the post-war period of rationing however, Liverpool FC chairman Bill McConnell had a brainwave ahead of the resumption of league football.

With malnourished players reporting back for training in the summer of 1946, he decided to arrange a pre-season tour of the United States and Canada. McConnell had visited America on official catering business 12 months earlier and was convinced of the nutritional benefits to be gained by undertaking such a trip.

He explained to manager George Kay that he believed it would give Liverpool an edge and the trip saw the squad tucking into plenty of foods such as steaks and eggs. By the time the team returned to England after eight weeks away, it was reported in the *New York Times* that they had averaged "a gain in weight of seven pounds a man."

How much of a factor that was in what was to follow is hard to gauge, but it can certainly have done no harm to the Reds. More than 12 months after leaving Anfield to set sail from Southampton to the States on the Queen Mary, they had won the 1946/47 championship in incredible fashion.

Years later, Bill Shankly and his staff had their eye on a young player who they felt had the potential to one day replace Ian Callaghan in the Liverpool line-up.

The only problem was that the young talent was a little bit on the thin side and Shanks, Bob Paisley and Joe Fagan all felt that he needed beefing up. A high-protein diet was called for with plenty of steak on the menu.

Paisley was given the task of ensuring the steak was delivered to the player's family every day. The diet was prescribed until the end of the season and through the summer.

When the squad returned for pre-season training, the lad concerned asked to go and see Shankly.

"You look like physical poetry, son," Shankly declared. "You're muscular. Those steaks have worked a treat!"

However, the youngster then explained to Shanks that the reason he had come to see him was that he had a bit of a problem and wanted a week off to sort things out – he had got a girl pregnant.

Shankly is said to have responded by darting to the door of his office and shouting down the corridor: "Joe, Bob, come here quickly. We've created a bleeding monster!"

63/130

Sweeper-keepers

THE popular computer game *Football Manager* has made 21st century fans familiar with the term 'sweeper-keeper'.

In a nutshell, it describes a goalkeeper who plays on the edge of his penalty area, constantly on alert to sweep up opposing breaks and advanced enough in their starting position to cut out threatening through balls before launching their own team's attacks.

Yet while the phrase has become part of the modern footballing lexicon, it was pioneered in the 1960s by legendary Liverpool manager Bill Shankly who saw an opportunity to pilot the approach using his number one Tommy Lawrence, aka 'The Flying Pig'.

Lawrence, who passed away in 2018, believes the seeds of the idea were sown during Shankly's beloved five-a-sides at Melwood.

"Back in those days the 10 outfield players would play five-a-side," he recalled. "That meant my team was myself, Bill Shankly, Joe Fagan, Bob Paisley and Reuben Bennett. We played against the apprentice professionals and we would take them on almost every day.

"I must have been playing in this team for well over a year. At the start of one season, I think it was 65/66, I was getting changed to go out training with the other lads when Cally came over to me and told me the boss wanted me."

It was in this meeting that Lawrence believed another example of Shankly's powers of perception came to the fore.

He explained: "I went into the room and Bill, Reuben, Bob and Joe were all sat behind a desk and there was a chair placed on the other side for me. At first I thought our five-a-side team must have been off to play in a big competition or something!

"Shanks said: 'We've got you here today son because we're trying to work something out. You know the way you play with us where it's as if you've got to cover for the whole back four? Well we're going to start trying that. We'll try it in training and then, if it works, we'll take it into the games. We want to you to play further up and the back four to play further up and to play square.'"

Shankly went on to reveal that in order to play a square back four, Liverpool ideally needed quick defenders. However, given that they had nobody renowned for their pace, Lawrence's job was to cover them.

"He'd worked out that if I was on my 18-yard line and the defenders were all on halfway that I could probably get there before an attacker if a ball was played through.

"Shankly said: 'You only have to run 15 or 20 yards and they'll be looking at you thinking: 'I'm not going near this fella,' because you'll be coming full pelt at them and you're not going to stop are you?' I just said: 'No boss, I'm not going to stop!'

"In those days, if anyone did get through you could just hit them because referees didn't take any action. I remember hitting Colin Bell on one occasion when we were playing Manchester City. I nudged him over and I never even got my name taken because the referee only saw it as a foul. And if you knocked them over that high up the pitch it was only a free-kick, so you wouldn't be giving away penalties!

"I hit Alun Evans one day before we signed him and I genuinely felt sorry because I really did clatter him. Then Jimmy Greaves always tells a story when he does his sportsman's dinners about a time he played against us. He says: 'The ball was shoved through and I just got there before Smithy, I went round Smithy [Tommy Smith] and then I woke up in the morning. I'd forgotten all about Tommy Lawrence!'"

The former Reds custodian, who went viral on the internet in 2015 when he was randomly stopped in the street by BBC reporter Stuart Flinders for a vox pop and asked if he remembered a Merseyside derby in 1967 only to reply, "I do, I played in it!" believed the reasoning behind Shankly's ground-breaking tactical approach was a desire to see the Reds improve on their goals against column. The team were regularly shipping 40 goals a season. In the championship-winning campaign of 1963/64, 45 were put past them. The following season, that figure was 73.

"When we tried this new system in 1965/66, that number came down to 34 as we won the league again," he said. "Three years later, we broke the record by getting it down to 24 goals for a 42-game season.

"Of course, Ray Clemence hammered that record later on with

229

16. Nobody gets near that now, even with 38 games rather than 42. To think we cut that figure down to almost half was absolutely amazing. And it was only because we started playing like this from an idea born from the five-a-sides.

"Shankly then started playing the Reserve team in exactly the same way so that when Ray came in, he had played that way in the Central League."

Lawrence admitted the new system also encouraged him to improve his skills with the ball at his feet.

"I wasn't a bad outfield player because I played rugby league at school and was a full-back so I was used to catching the ball, picking it up and kicking it. Playing as we did also got the goalkeeper in the game, whereas beforehand you could be kicking your heels against the post while the ball was at the other end."

Using the high line took a bit of getting used to however, not least for the fans on the Kop.

He recalled: "The first time I played that way at Anfield, it took a couple of months for the fans to accept it. The Kop weren't half giving me stick, shouting: 'Get back on your line!' But the system worked and continued with Ray and then Bruce Grobbelaar. Really, Liverpool had three goalkeepers in 30 years which was remarkable."

In the 2000s Pepe Reina was another fine exponent of the sweeper-keeper concept, though he preferred to think of himself as a 'goal player'.

The Spanish ace explained: "I've always tried to be ready to make a save at any time. Playing for a club like Liverpool means you are not going to be busy too many times, so it is really important to keep your concentration levels high at every moment.

"Maybe I was more involved in terms of building our game up from the back [under Brendan Rodgers]. But from time to time, sometimes for periods of up to 15 minutes, as a goalkeeper you might not even use your hands. So you have to be focused because when you need to be called upon to make a save or a catch, you have to be ready for it. It's not always easy but you have to keep that level of focus very high.

"Of course in the last 20 years or so since the backpass rule, the keeper's role has changed. I grew up in the Barca academy with that rule, and it helped me a lot because I practised building from the back with my feet. But today you have to be more involved in the game and we are not goalkeepers any longer – we are 'goal players'.

"Brendan liked to say that when we had the ball we are eleven vs ten, and that meant I counted as an outfield player sometimes. We had to create that superiority, use the ball well and look for the spaces that were always there."

More recently, Alisson Becker has become a fine sweeper-keeper playing behind Liverpool's high defensive line and has taken Reina's concept of being a 'goal player' to a new level with two assists for Mo Salah and scoring an unforgettable late header winner against West Bromwich Albion at The Hawthorns in 2021.

If Shankly was still here now picking five-a-side teams you suspect he might have Alisson upfront!

64/130

Eighteen carat goals

WE all know the line 'Rush scored one, Rush scored two, Rush scored three and Rush scored four' from *Poor Scouser Tommy*, but can you name the man who holds the Liverpool FC record for netting the most goals in a game?

First things first. Can you hazard a guess at the number of goals that record is made up of? Five? Perhaps six? How about 18 or, in other words, six hat-tricks in one fixture?

Picture the scene. A cold January day at Melwood and a young striker is lining up for the Reds youth team trying to impress. He scores goal after goal, ruthlessly taking every chance that comes his way. By the end of the game Liverpool have won 19-0 and the centre-forward has helped himself to a haul of 18 goals – one every five minutes!

It sounds like something taken from a script of *Scully*, the 1980s TV series created by Liverpool playwright Alan Bleasdale which centered around Francis Scully, a teenage boy with his heart set on playing in a trial match for the Reds.

Well, they say the truth is sometimes stranger than fiction and that 19-0 win did happen – on 31 January 1959 – as Liverpool's youth team hammered Pilkington Amateurs and the 18 goals were scored by Alan Bleasdale's older brother, Terry.

Speaking to *Liverpool FC* magazine at his Huyton home in 2014, Terry recalled: "I'm flabbergasted this story has come out but yes

– it's true. The thing is, the club only credited me with eight of the goals as they didn't want me to get big-headed!"

Brother Alan was among the spectators in West Derby that day but aside from a handful of others watching and the players involved, only one other person knew what really happened.

"I told my wife Joyce but never thought anyone else would know," adds Terry. "Eighteen goals in one game? You're joking aren't you!"

When statistician Jonny Stokkeland discovered Terry's 'eight' goal haul, LFC museum curator Stephen Done contacted Terry, a personal friend.

"I told Stephen that it wasn't eight but eighteen," he recalled. "The youth team was coached by the former great Liverpool centre-forward Jackie Balmer but the coaches told him they would give me eight goals to prevent me getting carried away, and they'd divvy out the rest between the other players."

Also in the LFC line-up that day was a certain Ian Callaghan, but although he supplied crosses for some of Terry's goals he wasn't one of the players 'awarded' a goal by the Reds' coaches!

The official records credited Terry with eight, Laurie Madgin with six, Tony Almond and William Hubbert with two apiece and Peter Price with the other: "I remember that the opposition were a very poor team and that I didn't miss a chance," said Terry. "I was banging them in – I remember a few were headers – and started keeping count. When I got to 10 I was thinking: I wonder how many I could end up with here… It's funny looking at the names in the team that day because I could have sworn Johnny Morrissey and Len Ashurst played in that game.

"In the end it never worked out for me and it is a regret of mine that I didn't make the grade. I think I've been a frustrated footballer all my life!"

Terry came from good footballing stock. Grandfather George,

a First World War POW, played for Blackburn Rovers. Two of Terry's sons also played professionally – Steven for Sheffield Wednesday (he later managed Peterborough and Chester) and David (an ex-LFC apprentice who cleaned the boots of Kenny Dalglish and Graeme Souness) for Preston North End.

Terry's father had taken him to Anfield during the Second World War and, more than 60 years on, he could easily reel off the names of the Reds starting XI for the 1950 FA Cup final. "People talk about Louis Bimpson, Jackie Balmer, Albert Stubbins and Billy Liddell and I used to love them," he said. "You'd come out of the ground when you were eight or nine and you'd feel as though you were a player yourself. You'd skip along and kick an imaginary ball because you'd been watching Liverpool."

Little wonder then that becoming a regular at Anfield himself was Terry's dream. "A hell of a lot of lads went through the Liverpool youth teams at the time. I played at Anfield in the Catholic Cup for St Aidan's in Huyton. I also played for Huyton & District Boys and started training with Liverpool on Tuesdays and Thursdays soon after that.

"I initially played for the C team, the 'colts' and the youth team, but in 1956 Wolves manager Stan Cullis came to see me and I went on their groundstaff for 12 months. But I couldn't settle in Wolverhampton and, being a Liverpool lad, wanted to get home.

"I played a couple of games on trial for Bolton's reserves. They wanted to sign me but Liverpool asked me to go back into their youth set-up. I was 17 then. I was an apprentice bricklayer at McAlpine's and played for 12 months but it didn't work out. Liverpool released me and after that I joined Prescot Cables."

Terry's displays for Prescot took the eye of Tranmere and he joined the Prenton Park club for a while before deciding to cut his ties with the professional game. "The ex-Everton captain Peter Farrell was manager. I stayed at Tranmere part-time for 18 months.

The money was £8 a week and they asked me to sign a contract, but the money wouldn't have been any more. I had two sons by then and with a family to support I needed a 'proper' job so took one on the buses. I played part-time for various non-league teams but got a knee injury at about 22 and had to pack it in.

"That's life, but it's nice to look back and know I hold a small piece of Liverpool Football Club history."

65/130

Is that all you take away?

THE UEFA Cup first round draw of 1995/96 presented plenty of challenges for club staff and supporters.

First of all there was confusion about Liverpool's opponents.

Initial reports suggested that the Reds had been paired with Spartak Vladivostok, a team based in a city on Russia's Pacific coastline 12,000 miles and nine timezones away – further east than any part of China.

Instead it was Russia's Spartak Vladikavkaz – a mere 5,000-mile round-trip in total – that the Reds had drawn. Either way, Liverpool manager Roy Evans remembers thinking: 'It could be a tricky one, this,' as he watched the draw on Teletext at his Aughton home.

The Home Office advised Liverpool supporters not to travel due to security concerns in the region. In the end, an intrepid 38 made the journey, which at 2,260 miles from Anfield was the second-furthest LFC had ever travelled in Europe (behind Dinamo Tbilisi at 2,320 miles).

Among the 38 travelling Kopites were Dave Murphy and John Pearman: "We flew with the team," Murphy told *Liverpool FC* magazine. "And the plane had to be Russian because it was entering their airspace. I think it was an old Aeroflot model. The players sat at the front with the fans at the back.

"When we landed I was first down the steps and as I got to the bottom an important-looking man from the British Embassy asked if I was [LFC chairman] David Moores!"

After swiftly passing through customs and negotiating a 20km bus-ride across barren terrain, the 120-strong convoy of players, officials and supporters sped to a hotel where authorities placed armed guards at its entrance and on all floors.

Yet Pearman recalled: "We'd been advised not to travel, but outside the hotel there were a large crowd of locals holding up placards saying 'Welcome', 'Hello' and 'YNWA,' which was also chalked on the pavements. And when we arrived for the game the coach was surrounded by hundreds of home supporters who started applauding."

Inside the unimaginatively named Spartak Stadium the following evening, 1,000 police surrounded the pitch.

The Reds' record against Russian (or former Soviet) clubs was poor. Knocked out of Europe by Dinamo Tbilisi in 1979 following a 3-0 reverse in Georgia, they suffered defeats both home and away to Spartak Moscow in 1992. Form ahead of the tie had also been erratic with Liverpool losing two of their opening five Premier League games against Leeds United and Wimbledon.

Liverpool, who wore 1-11 in the UEFA Cup as squad numbers had only been introduced for Premier League games at that stage, struggled to settle initially and when the hosts, backed by a capacity attendance of 33,500, took the lead after 20 minutes through Mirjalol Qosimov, the travelling support feared the worst.

However, Liverpool recovered with Steve McManaman

equalising after rounding the goalkeeper to convert from an acute angle. Then in the second-half a 30-yard thunderbolt from Jamie Redknapp secured what had seemed an unlikely victory.

Despite having their plane impounded upon arrival at Speke Airport for licensing reasons, Vladikavkaz were in confident mood for the second leg after moving towards the Russian title, seven points ahead of second place.

The day before the match in Vladikavkaz, a crowd of just 21,000 had been at Ewood Park to watch Blackburn Rovers lose to Spartak Moscow in the Champions League. As a result, Liverpool chief executive Peter Robinson decided to slash prices for the Anfield return: "Ewood was half-empty and the lack of atmosphere didn't help Blackburn," Robinson reasoned. "We need to make sure the same thing doesn't happen to us."

Liverpool struggled to a goalless draw at home, but the result was enough to come through one of their most tricky European engagements that 38 intrepid Reds will never forget.

66/130

Joy and despair

TEENAGE goalkeeper Chris Pile thought that something was afoot as he reported for training at Melwood one morning in May 1985.

The 18-year-old had been at Liverpool Football Club since joining as a schoolboy three years earlier.

As part of his Youth Training Scheme schedule, the Huyton lad would carry out various jobs such as painting, learning how to grow grass properly and laying out kits for the senior players.

Yet on this particular occasion, sideways glances in his direction meant that Pile couldn't help but detect it was he, rather than stars such as Kenny Dalglish, Phil Neal, Alan Hansen and Ian Rush, that was the centre of attention.

"A few apprentices were whispering. I didn't know what they were talking about so I asked them," he explained.

He discovered the cause of the chat was an injury which Bob Bolder, Bruce Grobbelaar's back-up, had suffered in a reserve game the previous evening. It meant Pile would now be on the bench for the upcoming European Cup final against Juventus.

"There was no coverage of the ressies on TV then, no internet or mobile phones, so I didn't have a clue about any of it."

In what was the typically understated LFC style of the time, none of the coaching staff made a big deal of it. It wasn't even mentioned until after training when Pile was putting some gloves away and Ronnie Moran told him he should keep himself fit and not to speak to anyone he shouldn't.

So unexpected was the youngster's inclusion for the match that he didn't even own a club suit and had to wear one of his own.

Sadly, what could have been a cherished occasion at the Heysel Stadium proved to be exactly the opposite as 39 Juventus fans died. The suddenly meaningless game still took place, the Italian side winning 1-0.

It took Pile a long time to speak about what happened on that evening in Belgium. "Clearly, it must have been very difficult for the lads who played. I remember doing a warm-up during half-time and there were imprints of horse hooves on the turf.

"The medals – which obviously nobody really wanted – were handed out in the dressing room. Craig Johnston and I were walking out of the stadium afterwards and took a wrong turn; we ended up in a gym where some of the bodies were being laid out.

"People sometimes criticise the fact that the game went ahead. But I think the authorities were worried that if it didn't there would have been more trouble."

When Pile returned for pre-season a new manager was at the helm with Kenny Dalglish succeeding Joe Fagan.

Nobody spoke of Heysel. Instead the chat centred on what to call the new gaffer. "Kenny told us to call him Kenny," Pile explains. "But Roy Evans said we should address him as boss. The biggest problem was in training when you'd be asking him for a pass. We all hesitated because we weren't sure which title to use."

Bob Bolder's decision to leave in search of first-team football meant Pile was set to be the regular number two goalkeeper. Then a slipped disc ruled him out. During his absence, the Reds bought Mike Hooper from Wrexham.

"That's life," Pile reflects. "I had to get on with it and when I recovered I played a few games for the reserves."

However, a first team appearance would elude him and he departed in 1987.

"Obviously it was disappointing and, for about 30 seconds, I had a little bit of resentment. Then I moved on. But I wouldn't swap those five minutes of fame for anything as I got to work with some of the best players in LFC's history."

67/130

The unlikely lad

MATCH-WINNING goals can come from the most unlikely of sources, especially when Liverpool FC are involved in a European final.

It all started in the 1973 UEFA Cup final when centre-half Larry Lloyd headed home what proved to be the decisive goal in the first leg of a 3-2 aggregate victory against Borussia Moenchengladbach.

Three years later it was 22-year-old substitute Jimmy Case who made the difference in the first leg of a 4-3 aggregate UEFA Cup final success against FC Bruges when he netted one of three goals the Bob Paisley boys struck in six minutes to turn a 0-2 deficit into a 3-2 victory in front of a bubbling Anfield cauldron.

Tommy Smith hadn't scored since 1974 when Liverpool travelled to Rome for the 1977 European Cup final so when he headed the Reds 2-1 up from Stevie Heighway's corner it was perhaps no wonder BBC commentator Barry Davies was so surprised: "Case and Keegan in the box. Kennedy, Smith and Joey Jones outside. Oh yes! And what a delighted scorer. It's Tommy Smith!"

Kenny Dalglish's dinked Wembley winner against Bruges in the 1978 European Cup final breaks the unlikely heroes rule, but left-back Alan Kennedy's shock winner against Real Madrid in Paris 81 continued the theme before fellow full-back Phil Neal got the Reds' goal against AS Roma in Rome 84 with Kennedy converting the European Cup clinching penalty after the match went to a shoot-out.

As for 2005 in Istanbul then goalscoring substitute Vladimir Smicer and penalty shoot-out hero Jerzy Dudek weren't the players that most Kopites travelling to Turkey expected to emerge as heroes (Smicer also scored what proved to be the winning penalty), although it was hardly a surprise that Mo Salah scored Liverpool's opening goal from the spot against Spurs in the 2019 Champions League final in Madrid.

Perhaps Divock Origi's match-clincher was an eyebrow raiser to some, but none of the aforementioned players were as unlikely match-winners as the man who settled the 2001 UEFA Cup final between Liverpool and Deportivo Alaves in Dortmund.

His name? Delfi Geli.

In what would still be regarded as the craziest European final Liverpool had been involved in if Istanbul had never happened, it was another unlikely goalscorer who put Gerard Houllier's side – semi-final winners against Barcelona – ahead in the fourth minute.

Markus Babbel was up from the back to head in a Gary McAllister free-kick and when a shaven-headed Steven Gerrard rifled home a second echoes of 'We shall not, we shall not be moved' boomed around Borussia Dortmund's Westfalenstadion.

Spanish minnows Alaves, playing in their first ever major final, looked shell shocked, but the arrival of 22nd minute substitute Ivan Alonso and a change of formation had the 'Potato Aphids' feeling chipper as Alonso pulled one back.

Suddenly Michael Owen was clean through only for Alaves keeper Martin Herrera to haul him down. Herrera somehow avoided a red card, but couldn't stop Gary Mac from making it 3-1 from the penalty spot. Alaves were far from beaten, though, and two goals in six second half minutes from Javi Moreno pegged the scoreline back to 3-3.

What next? A tactical change from Houllier. Stephane Henchoz was replaced by Smicer with Gerrard switched to right-back – something similar would end up happening four years later in Istanbul – before Robbie Fowler was introduced for Emile Heskey.

With 72 minutes on the clock Fowler latched on to a McAllister pass, cut inside from the left, shimmied past a defender and coolly slotted the ball into the net with his right foot. 4-3. However, God's divine intervention didn't see the plucky Basques off with Jordi Cruyff – son of the late Johan who was due to present the UEFA Cup to the winning captain that night – rising highest from an 88th minute corner to head the ball past Sander Westerveld. 4-4.

Could this game get any more ridiculous? Absolutely.

UEFA had introduced an extra-time 'golden goal' ruling meaning that, for the first time, Liverpool were playing 'next goal wins' football. Which made it quite a relief when a linesman's flag went up for offside after Ivan Alonso put the ball into Westerveld's net in the 94th minute.

Alaves, though, were beginning to tire. Brazilian substitute Magno was dismissed in the 98th minute for a second bookable offence. Fowler had a 104th minute goal chalked off for offside. And then, with five minutes to play, the Spaniards were down to nine men with skipper Antonio Karmona sent for a (not so) early bath for a cynical foul on Smicer. McAllister stepped up to curl in the resultant free-kick from a wide position on the left. Herrera came to punch it clear, but before he could full-back Delfi Geli, a 1996 double-winner with Atletico Madrid, rose in front of him and glanced the ball into the top corner to score a golden own goal.

5-4. Game Over. 30,000 travelling Kopites went wild. McAllister was mobbed by his team-mates. And Geli, who is now the president of Spanish second division club Girona, had inadvertently written his name into the history of Liverpool Football Club as the most unlikely match-winner of them all.

'That's the new boss, Bill Shankly'

VICTOR Gill's first meeting with Bill Shankly came in the unlikeliest of places: the gents' lavatories at Melwood.

A few years later his stomach was dancing with nerves as he sat in Shankly's living room awaiting his reaction to some life-changing news.

After scoring numerous goals for the Boys' Brigade as a teenager, a dream came true for Gill when he was signed by Liverpool FC in 1957.

He recalled: "Phil Taylor left in 1959 and one evening I was in the toilets at Melwood when this guy with training kit on stood at the urinal next to me. I thought: 'Blimey, they're signing some old players.' In a broad Scottish accent he asked how old I was. We went out onto the pitch together and ran a few laps of the pitch chatting away and he seemed like quite a nice bloke. Eli Wass, the groundsman, then told me: 'That's the new boss, Bill Shankly.' The following week we were playing a midweek match at Blackpool. In the team that night were Tommy Lawrence, Tommy Smith, Ian Callaghan, Willie Carlin and Frank Twist. While we were changing, Tom Bush, who ran the junior team, said: 'The new boss is coming to watch and he's going to say a few words before you go out.'

"This was quite a surprise because in the previous two years we had rarely seen Phil Taylor let alone spoken to him. Bill Shankly entered the dressing room and said: 'Ok lads, keep it simple and pass to a red shirt.' We did and won the game 3-2."

Much to his disappointment however, Gill was released by LFC in the summer of 1962 but his path would cross with the legendary Liverpool manager once again – as his son-in-law!

He explains: "I had a particular mate during my time at Liverpool called Bobby Oldham who lived next door to Everton's training ground in Bellefield Avenue, where the Shankly family also lived. Bobby and I would occasionally play head tennis in the entrance to Bellefield and sometimes this young girl would come and watch. We chatted and she told us her name was Barbara Shankly.

"I met her again at The Lowlands club in West Derby Village and we would have a dance and a coffee and sometimes I would walk her home. By the time I was 21 and Barbara was 18 our relationship was very serious. I asked her to marry me, Mr and Mrs Shankly gave their approval and a date was set for summer 1965."

Before the wedding however, Vic feared the full force of Shanks' ire.

"In December 1964 I went to the house and Mrs Shankly told me Barbara was pregnant. Liverpool had a game at Stoke the following day so Mr Shankly wasn't there. I turned up at the Shankly home the next evening not knowing what to expect.

"After the meal, Mrs Shankly broke the news and there was an ominous silence. He paced up and down and I was waiting for a punch in the back of my head. Then he said: 'Well, it happens in the best of families.' I was shocked but relieved.

"Later he told me Mrs Shankly was having great difficulty living with the fact that we were having a church wedding and that Barbara would walk down the aisle in a white dress. He said that if we cancelled the church wedding and had a register office ceremony instead, he would give us the deposit on any house of our choosing. Eventually Barbara agreed. We found a lovely three bedroomed terrace in Inigo Road off Queens Drive. It was £2,200 and a 10-minute walk from the Shankly home. Mr Shankly paid the deposit (£450) and I got a mortgage for the rest at £14 per month over 25 years."

Which wasn't where Victor Gill imagined his life would lead to when he bumped into Bill Shankly in the Melwood toilets!

69/130

Strings to their bows

BILL Shankly may have found it hard to agree, but several men who have pulled on the Red shirt throughout LFC's proud history also showed that there was more to life than football...

Jim Harley: The Reds have employed some fairly pacy players over the years but few were as quick as Jim Harley. One of many players to have had their careers cut short by the Second World War, Harley was a member of the 1946/47 squad that claimed Liverpool's fifth league championship. His sprinting skills paid off elsewhere too. The Fife-born full-back once won the Powderhall Handicap, a well-known sprint in Scotland which had been contested since 1870.

Gordon Hodgson: The Johannesburg-born forward first came

to Liverpool's attention when he was part of a team of touring South Africans that played a game at Anfield in October 1924. He caught the eye and Liverpool later agreed a deal to sign him. It was a shrewd move as he went on to score 241 goals in 377 games, putting him third in the list of the club's all-time record goalscorers. While his football abilities were never in doubt, Hodgson also excelled in another sport: cricket. He played first-class cricket for Lancashire between 1928 and 1933, taking 148 wickets for the Red Rose county.

John Hughes: The Welshman was a regular in the Reds' defence during the 1903/04 season and he quickly earned a reputation for his hard-work and courage. His bravery also helped him win accolades off the field. Hughes was awarded a certificate from the Royal Humane Society for life-saving after he saved four people from drowning, including two from the River Mersey and a child that had fallen into a clay pit.

James Jackson: An all-action defender, Jackson was also a man of the cloth. He established himself in the Liverpool team towards the end of the 1920s and missed only two out of 126 First Division games from August 1928 until May 1930 while captaining the side. He had three further seasons at Anfield before leaving to be ordained as a minister in the Presbyterian church in 1933. Jackson had started his divinity studies at Aberdeen University and continued them in Liverpool. Because of his church connections, he was nicknamed 'The Parson' around the club.

Craig Johnston: A part of the 1986 double-winning team, the colourful character's creativity stretched beyond the football field. The South African-born Aussie's entrepreneurial skills took root after he took the decision to retire from football aged just 27 in order to care for his sick sister. Co-writer of the 1988 hit record *The Anfield Rap*, he has also invented a football boot, created software for hotel businesses to monitor minibar thefts and established himself as an award-winning photographic artist.

Tommy Younger: Goalkeeper Younger was much-loved by Liverpool supporters during his four-year spell with the club and had the honour of captaining Scotland during the 1958 World Cup finals. In April 1959, the same month that he made the last of his 127 appearances for the Reds, he dabbled in politics and was adopted as the prospective Conservative candidate for Picton Ward (now Liverpool Wavertree). Younger was also a successful businessman after his football career ended and served the Scottish Football Association in various capacities, eventually becoming president.

70/130

Liverpool's fallen

EVERY November, Anfield falls silent to remember those who gave their lives for their country.

Records show that 13 men registered with Liverpool Football Club were killed during World War One. It was supposed to be the war to end all wars. And yet barely two decades later, hostilities resumed. Once again it took years rather than months and came at a cost of 73 million lives, including 11 more of those on the books of LFC.

Having been through the experience of 1914 to 1918, Liverpool

Football Club were well prepared by the time war was declared.

A number of players had signed up for the Territorial Army throughout the 1938/39 season but Liverpool were the first to join up as a club. Their 20-player entry into the 9th King's Regiment Liverpool was also supplemented by manager George Kay and assistant secretary Jack Rouse.

Germany invaded Poland on Friday 1 September 1939 but a Home Office bulletin stated that the situation did not warrant the cancellation of sporting fixtures.

Liverpool were due to play Chelsea the following day: it turned out to be the Reds' last league game until 1946. The club had a number of players due for sentry duty at the time the game was set to kick-off but thanks to the generosity of some Territorial friends who volunteered to take their places, Dirk Kemp, Bernard Ramsden, Matt Busby, Tom Bush, Jimmy McInnes, Willie Fagan, Jackie Balmer and Cyril Done were able to start the match.

Done marked his debut by scoring the only goal of the game and would have a prolific spell in front of goal during the war years.

Stationed somewhere 'in the north' the players had slept on a railway station floor before starting four hours' sentry duty at 5am. It didn't seem to have any adverse effect and the Reds held on to their 1-0 lead despite having defender Jim Harley sent off. Perhaps surprisingly, manager Kay made no mention of anything besides football in his programme notes.

However, the political landscape was changing on a daily basis as the impact of the war effort was constantly re-examined. Later that week, a ban on the assembly of crowds was enforced after a Government order to close places of entertainment.

The footballing authorities were keen to change that situation and on 14 September permission was granted to stage friendlies so long as there was police approval. A couple of days later, Liverpool won 5-0 at Chester.

Employees of Liverpool FC were keen to play their part in active service and several players were promoted within days of the war effort taking shape.

Of those who volunteered for the 9th King's Liverpool Battalion of Territorials, Riley and Kemp were made sergeants, while Tom Cooper, Fagan, Ramsden and Bush were promoted to lance corporals.

Several players developed key skills. Fagan became a trench mortar expert, while Balmer and (future manager) Phil Taylor learned to drive tanks. Berry Nieuwenhuys worked as a driller on Merseyside, drawing on the trade he developed during his days in South Africa.

There were incredible acts of courage.

Utility player Bill Jones was honoured with a military medal for rescuing wounded comrades under fire.

Full-back Ted Spicer, a lieutenant in the Marines, captured a German non-commissioned officer, who turned out to be a football international. A Commando, Spicer had been commissioned in May 1942 and was later promoted to the rank of captain.

Yet the grim realities of the conflict became all too real. Cooper had been England captain when Liverpool signed him from Derby County in 1934. He lost his life in a motorcycle accident near Aldeburgh, Suffolk. Serving as a sergeant in the military police, the full-back's vehicle was involved in a head-on crash with a lorry. A subsequent enquiry led to an order that despatch drivers were not allowed to ride motorcycles without wearing crash helmets.

While Anfield came through the war relatively unscathed, the proximity of L4 to the docks saw some damage at Goodison Park.

Football's popularity continued to see large numbers pour through the turnstiles and derby matches were a major draw. In January 1944, 45,820 witnessed Liverpool's win at Goodison while in 1945/46, a crowd of 60,926 saw a 2-2 draw at the same ground.

By the 1940/41 season, regional league football had been established in the north of the country – occasionally landing LFC in hot water.

When Northern Ireland star Peter Doherty went to watch a Liverpool match at Blackpool, the inside forward was asked to play for the Reds. He did so, but the club were later censured when it came to light that George Ainsley had been due to play before Doherty's surprise appearance. The RAF had granted Ainsley special leave and were furious, threatening never to grant leave to any of their footballers again. The club apologised to the RAF and the League.

Another episode saw Reds winger Nieuwenhuys banned for life. The South African's crime was to ask for more than the regulation fee of £2 per game. He was, however, soon reinstated.

Some notable matches were held during this period. The legendary Tom Finney made his Preston debut at Anfield against a Reds team that included future boss Don Welsh, then of Charlton Athletic, and Wolves' Stan Cullis.

There were successes too. Inside-forward Willie Fagan was a regular guest in the Northampton Town team that won the 1941/42 Cup qualifying competition.

As for themselves, Liverpool enjoyed a strong 1942/43 season. After finishing second to Blackpool by four points in the 18-game North One League which ran until Christmas Day 1942, the Reds topped the North Two League, played over 20 matches, between Boxing Day and May.

Two key men of the future also made an early impression. Bob Paisley had impressed during 1939/40 trial matches, but spent most of the war overseas in the Army. He served in North Africa and Italy as a gunner in the 73rd Medium Regiment of the Royal Artillery.

Meanwhile, a teenage winger by the name of Billy Liddell was described by manager Kay as 'the best thing that has come out of Scotland in the past 10 years.'

The terrible conflict eventually ended on 2 September 1945. League football was reintroduced in August 1946 with Liverpool embarking on an extraordinary season which would see them crowned as champions.

But the effect of the hostilities had left a lasting impression. The Kop paid its own tribute to those who lost their lives in the shape of the popular terrace anthem *Poor Scouser Tommy*.

Originally penned in the 1960s, the first verse goes: "Let me tell you the story of a poor boy, Who was sent far away from his home, To fight for his king and his country, And also the old folks back home..."

LFC'S FALLEN

Players killed in World War One

George Bradley (Aged 23)
Born: 1892, Aughton, Ormskirk.
Died: 25/9/1915, France.

James Francis Brennan (32)
Born: 10/9/1884, Templemore, North Tipperary.
Died: 6/9/1917, France.

Jack Tosswill (24)
Born: 6/10/1890, Eastbourne, Sussex.
Died: 28/9/1915, Brighton.

Tommy Gracie (26)
Born: 12/6/1889, Glasgow.
Died: 23/10/1915, Glasgow.

David Murray (33)
Born: 4/12/1882, Busby, Lanarkshire.
Died: 10/12/1915, Flanders, Belgium.

Joseph Barker (age not known)
Born: Liverpool.
Died: 13/1/1916, France.

Don Sloan (33)
Born: 31/7/1883, Ayr.
Died: 1/1/1917, Arras, France.

Wilfred Watson (24)
Born: 15/8/1892, Wigan.
Died: 24/7/1917, Belgium.

Arnold Dargie (26)
Born: 1891, Bangor.
Died: 18/9/1917, France.

Alfred Honess (31)
Born: 1886, West Derby.
Died: 22/10/1917, France.

William Morris (28)
Born: 13/2/1890, Arnold, Nottingham.
Died: 21/9/1918.

Joe Dines (32)
Born: 12/4/1886, King's Lynn, Norfolk.
Died: 27/9/1918, France.

Wilf Bartrop (30)
Born: 22/11/1887, Worksop.
Died: 7/11/1918, Warcoing, Belgium.

Players killed in World War Two

Tom Cooper (35 years)
Born: 9/4/1905, Fenton, Staffordshire.
Died: 25/6/1940, near Aldeburgh, Suffolk.

Richard Siddall (30)
Born: 1911, Warrington.
Died: 3/1941.

Harry Race (36)
Born: 7/1/1906, Evenwood, Durham.
Died: 24/10/1942, El Alamein, Egypt.

Ronald Soo (23)
Born: 22/10/1920, Liverpool.
Died: 14/1/1944, Germany.

Cecil McCaughey (34)
Born: 18/11/1909, Bootle.
Died: 8/2/1944, Christchurch, Hampshire.

David Murphy (27)
Born: 19/7/1917, South Bank.
Died: 19/9/1944, Italy.

Joe Donnachie (31)
Born: 1913, Liverpool.
Died: 12/10/1944, Chedborough, Suffolk.

Albert Yoxon (22)
Born: 10/4/1922, Liverpool.
Died: 7/12/1944, Bourne, Lincolnshire.

Ronald Dandy (22)
Born: 1923, Ormskirk.
Died: 5/4/1945, India.

Stanley Sheldrake (19)
Born: 1926, Liverpool.
Died: 5/1945, Germany.

George Collister (23)
Born: 21/3/1922, Liverpool.
Died: 13/5/1945, Holland.

71/130

All change

WHILE Liverpool began life in a blue and white home shirt before switching to red in 1896, the traditional change colour of white jerseys has been in place since LFC was founded in 1892.

That tradition has changed over the years with a variety of colours and designs introduced by different kit manufacturers, but in the 1890s it was always a white-buttoned shirt that Liverpool changed into although initially the players still had to wear the same shorts – or knickers as they were called at the time – and socks that belonged to the home strip.

At various stages those shorts and socks varied between dark blue, black and white with the first significant shirt change occurring in the early 1900s when a white jersey with a red yoke (the collar and shoulder area) was introduced along with white shorts and red socks.

Newspaper reports and cartoons also suggest that Liverpool wore red-and-white and black-and-white striped away shirts in one-off games at Arsenal, Middlesbrough, Burnley and Aston Villa between 1911 and 1920, although a lack of pictorial evidence makes those claims hard to confirm.

It was the 1931/32 season when black shorts and red socks were introduced to accompany red-collared white shirts and, but for design changes and sock colours varying from red to red-and-white and plain white, that fundamentally became Liverpool's change strip until 1982, with a few notable exceptions.

In 1966, having been paired against Dutch champions Ajax in the European Cup second round, Liverpool wore yellow shirts, black shorts and yellow socks during the second leg at Anfield.

"Liverpool tonight are playing in yellow shirts, an unusual colour for them," said the television commentator. "They've had to change because there is some red in the Ajax strip."

UEFA rules stated at the time that home teams should wear their change strip in event of a kit-clash and with Johan Cruyff and co turning up in their famous white and red strip the Bill Shankly boys took to the pitch in yellow, more commonly associated with submarines on Merseyside in the 1960s, drawing the game 2-2.

Perhaps yellow stuck in the mind of someone as when Liverpool drew Manchester United in the 1979 FA Cup semi-final they ran out onto the Maine Road pitch wearing a new all-yellow third strip despite United donning their white and black change kit. The match also finished 2-2 and both sides wore the same colours again during the replay at Goodison Park. Bob Paisley's men got a bit of extra use out of it away to Southampton later that month.

Yellow remained the club's third choice colour until 1981/82 when all-yellow with red pinstripes became the official away strip before a change of kit manufacturer in 1985 prompted the return of white shirts with white shorts (in 1985/86) and black shorts (in 1986/87). Then it was time for something completely different.

The introduction of a stylish silver-grey strip in 1987 coincided with a Kenny Dalglish team inspired by John Barnes, Peter Beardsley and John Aldridge winning trophies of the same colour while playing perhaps the finest football of any Liverpool side.

In 1991/92 the surprise introduction of green shirts, white shorts and green socks divided opinion on the Kop – Liverpool failing to win a single away league match wearing it that season didn't help – while a gold and black third strip debuted at Sheffield United's Bramall Lane on Boxing Day 1993 at time when the away strip was a unique combination of white and green with six black diagonal stripes.

A green and white number was produced as a part-throwback to Liverpool's first ever strip in 1995/96 before another change of kit manufacturer that summer saw the previously unheard of colour of ecru – a fancy word for cream – becoming part of Kopites' vocabulary.

By now, a new away strip was being released every season and that meant a variety of colours including all-yellow (1997/98), white, red and black (1998/99), green and navy (1999/2000), yellow and navy (2000/01) and white and navy (2001/02). Liverpool beat Arsenal in the 2001 FA Cup final in Cardiff wearing yellow and navy, making it only the second away kit the club has ever won a cup final in, the first being the traditional white-black-red ensemble at Villa Park in the 1981 League Cup final replay against West Ham United.

The summer of 2002 saw the unveiling of Liverpool's first ever black away strip – worn with grey shorts and black socks – before four seasons of rotating between white and yellow kits. Then, in the summer of 2006, came the annual introduction of official third strips, branded as European away kits, with Rafa Benitez's side switching between all-yellow and white and green on their travels that year.

All-black with a red trim was a new development in 2007/08 while the retro silver-grey kit that returned in 2008/09 instantly evokes memories of a famous 4-1 Liverpool win away to Manchester United in the same week that Real Madrid were beaten 4-0 in the Champions League at Anfield.

There was controversy in 2011/12 when a white and blue third kit was revealed, although the manufacturer at the time insisted the colour was 'cyan' and it became a best-seller, before a radical design of nightshade, orange and white was conjured up in 2012/13. For those of you reading in black and white, nightshade is another word for purple.

A deeper shade of purple appeared on the 2013/14 third kit alongside white and black harlequin panelling while a white, black and red away kit featured a rather unusual diamond print before only the third all-yellow strip of the Premier League era was reintroduced for the 2014/15 campaign.

In 2015/16 a new kit manufacturer made their mark by launching an all-white away strip with a red trim before going back to black in 2016/17 while also unveiling an eye-catching luminous green third kit.

Orange was the new black for 2017/18 – Liverpool's first ever all-orange third strip marking the arrival of a colour previously only used for goalkeeper kits – and provided contrast to an away strip designed to mark Liverpool Football Club's 125th anniversary with a green and white quartered shirt, inspired by the class of 1892, complemented by black shorts and white socks.

Perhaps it was somewhat appropriate, then, that the first player to score while wearing it, at Hoffenheim in a Champions League qualifier, was a Scouser, 18-year-old Trent Alexander-Arnold providing a neat link between the past, present and future of LFC.

A deep-violet away kit with orange panelling followed in 2018/19 with a grey third kit, featuring a steel gradient print, worn for European away matches, notably Liverpool's 3-1 victory against Bayern Munich in the Allianz Arena with Sadio Mane and Virgil van Dijk on the scoresheet.

The traditional white shirts, this time with navy shorts and white socks, returned for Liverpool's 2019/20 Premier League title winning season while the third kit was phantom black with another new colour introduced for the trim – vibrant tidepool.

Nike took over kit manufacturing duties in 2020/21 and their first offering was a teal and black away strip with a swirling pattern on the front inspired by the Shankly Gates. The third kit, featuring black and anthracite checks with crimson side panelling, was influenced by the chequered flags Kopites have waved on many European occasions.

The checks were retained for the 2021/22 third kit, but this time in red and yellow on the collar and sleeve cuffs of a striking all-yellow strip. Liverpool's away kit also proved to be hugely popular.

Inspired by the ecru kit of 1996/97, but officially 'stone' coloured as a nod towards the Three Graces on Liverpool's waterfront, it also features a teal and crimson collar and will forever be recalled as the strip that Mo Salah scored a hat-trick in when the Redmen beat Manchester United 5-0 at Old Trafford - a scoreline Liverpool had never previously achieved in that fixture no matter what colour kit they were wearing.

72/130

Young Bob Paisley

EIGHTY years ago probably the last thing on Bob Paisley's mind was football. Dug into a trench at El Alamein in North Africa during the Western Desert Campaign of 1942, he ducked when an enemy plane strafed his regiment's position and thought for one terrifying moment that he'd been blinded. Thankfully it was only sand in his eyes.

The second-oldest of four brothers, Bob was in his early 20s and serving with Field Marshall Montgomery's Desert Rats. After El Alamein, while stationed in Naples he watched Mount Vesuvius erupt. Later he rode aboard an Allied tank when Rome was liberated in June 1944 – an occasion he famously recalled in 1977 when he returned to the Italian capital for the first time for a European Cup final contested by the team he managed.

World War II marked a rite of passage for Bob from his formative years as an amateur footballer in the North East of England to his subsequent calling on the other side of the country with Liverpool FC.

Born in Hetton-le-Hole and commemorated both there and by Anfield's eponymously-named gates and a statue of himself carrying Emlyn Hughes on his back, Paisley remains the most successful English football manager of all-time and was the first man to guide one team to three European Cups. Before he reluctantly inherited the top job from Shanks in the summer of

259

1974, and prior to a two-decade spell in LFC's legendary Boot Room as first the reserve-team trainer then a first-team coach, he was an esteemed post-war player with the Reds. His position was half-back, usually the left side of a defensive-midfield pairing in a 3-2-2-3 or so-called 'W-M' formation because of its shape, and he was noted for his toughness and formidable long-throw.

Having signed for Liverpool as a 20-year-old in 1939, he had to wait seven years for his 'real' debut for the Reds, a few days before his 27th birthday in January 1946 when league football resumed at the end of the war. Liverpool immediately won the top-flight title with Bob shining in the side alongside the likes of Billy Liddell, Jackie Balmer, Albert Stubbins and Laurie Hughes.

Ultimately he made over 250 appearances in all competitions, scoring 12 goals…and might easily have played all those games for Sunderland had things transpired a little differently.

In 1933, upon leaving school as a 14-year-old, Bob played regularly with Durham County Schoolboys and worked briefly with his father Samuel at the local pit. When Paisley senior was badly injured in a mining accident he urged his son to seek his fortune in football. Bob took a job in bricklaying and joined Hetton Juniors.

Later in life he revealed: "Where I come from in the North East we were all brought up with the need to better yourself. That, and the belief in football as a religion, produces a kind of driving force for this job. It gives you that little spark of ruthlessness – a need to win." Bob could reflect on his childhood and admitted: "Although we never went short of life's essentials there was never much money left over by the end of the week."

This understates the difficulties the family faced, with his parents having to scrimp and save to buy kit. Paying for a proper football was also a problem, forcing young Paisley and his pals to improvise for kickabouts with an inflated pig's bladder from his uncle's butcher's shop. When that was worn-out, the resourceful lads would play with rolled-up newspapers or just old rags.

Younger brother Hughie would later remember: "Bob was always kicking a ball about. That's all his mind was set on: football football football. Nothing else mattered." He wasn't alone. "They used to say at one time you just had to shout down the pit shaft and you'd get half-a-dozen footballers," added Hughie. "There was rarely anything else for them to do."

The only football club that mattered, for Bob and most others, was Sunderland, six-times champions of the Football League and on the brink of winning their first-ever FA Cup in 1937. The story goes that Bob had a trial at Roker Park but was deemed too small in stature. There'd been interest too from Tottenham Hotspur and Wolverhampton Wanderers, but the same verdict. Bishop Auckland FC, based further upstream on the River Wear, and for whom Hetton were a nursery side, felt differently. They signed him for the start of 1937/38 and Bob would stay behind after training to work on his leap and improve his performance in the air.

When he duly helped 'the Bishops' to win a record 10th amateur championship plus two cups the following season, Sunderland's flame was rekindled. By then, though, Paisley had promised Liverpool manager George Kay that his future lay on Merseyside.

On Monday 8 May 1939 he boarded a train bound for the North West to begin a half-century association that would go down in footballing history. The signing-on fee was £25, with wages of £8 per week during the season and £6 in the summer.

Two reserve games into his LFC career, war broke out. It would become a grave recess lasting over half-a-dozen years, but for Paisley a glorious destiny awaited.

For all that, he never forgot his roots. Hanging on the wall by the bar of The Twelfth Man pub near Anfield on Walton Breck Road is a photograph of Bob in his late 50s, back in the North East and posing with flat-capped pals and some very familiar silverware.

"He was very good when he brought the cups here in 1977," recollected one old Hetton neighbour, Joe Lormore. "He went round and showed everyone, took his time and shook hands. He said: 'I wish my father had been here to see this'.

"My best memory is Bob coming into one of the working men's clubs with the European Cup and his brother Hughie. It was choc-a-bloc. 'You don't forget where you came from', he said. Then they had a party in the council chambers. It was a proud week."

73/130

Hat-trick heroes

THE last player to open his goalscoring account for Liverpool FC with a hat-trick? It was Divock Origi with three in a 6-1 League Cup win at Southampton in December 2015. Twenty-five years earlier, incidentally, Ronny Rosenthal did the same thing for the Reds against Charlton Athletic.

Now hands up who remembers Tony Rowley and his LFC claim-to-fame? He was the Welsh-Italian striker (full name Antonio Camilio Rowley) who scored all three goals in a 3-2 win over Doncaster Rovers at Anfield in August 1954 – Liverpool's opening game in the old Second Division following their relegation from the top flight the previous season. It was only his third appearance for the club.

In total Rowley would score eight goals in six appearances that season. But the standout scorer in 1954/55 was John Evans with 33 in all competitions, including five at home to Bristol Rovers in September 1954 – a feat only two other post-war Liverpool players have managed. Their names? Ian Rush and Robbie Fowler.

Rushie scored his five against Luton Town in October 1983, a week after his 22nd birthday, in a season which would see him net 47 goals in total. His overall stats are phenomenal: most goals for Liverpool FC with 346; most goals in a Merseyside derby with 25, famously including four at Goodison Park in 1982; most FA Cup final goals with five (1986, 1989 and 1992); most League Cup goals with 49 (shared with Geoff Hurst). Goal. Machine.

A decade to the month after the Welshman's five-in-one-game, Fowler repeated the feat against Fulham in the second leg of a League Cup second-round tie in October 1993. He was just 18. Less than ten months later he scored a hat-trick against Arsenal at Anfield in four minutes and 33 seconds – a record that stood until May 2015 when Sadio Mane, then with Southampton, bettered it with three goals in two minutes and 56 seconds versus Aston Villa. No one has scored more goals for Liverpool FC in the Premier League than Robbie: he has 128, although Mo Salah is fast catching him.

Rush got 16 hat-tricks for the Reds, Fowler ten – the same as Michael Owen. The daddy of them all was Gordon Hodgson with 17. Still third in the all-time LFC goals table – he was top scorer in seven out of the nine whole seasons he played at Liverpool – the South African registered his first hat-trick at home to Sheffield United in September 1926.

"He looks years older than he is [22]," mused the *Football Echo* at the time, "and he will do the club much good... Liverpool have found him a cute, strong, combining forward who can give and take a bump with impunity." His 17th and final hat-trick came in a 4-2 Anfield win over Leeds United in February 1935.

Third behind Hodgson and Rush in the hat-tricks table is 'Sir' Roger Hunt with 12, five of which came in the promotion-winning 1961/62 season under Bill Shankly. He was LFC's top scorer for an incredible eight consecutive seasons, 1961/62 through to 1968/69, and while Rush eventually overtook him for goals scored in all competitions, Hunt's total of 245 in the league is unlikely ever to be beaten.

Back in the first half of the 20th century there were four who loved to score. Sam Raybould was the first Liverpool player to get 30 goals in one season, 1902/03, and subsequently the first to score 100 league goals for the club. He hit six hat-tricks, including four goals in a 9-2 win over Grimsby Town at Anfield in December 1902.

Jack Parkinson, who was prolific in front of goal just before the First World War, claimed seven hat-tricks. So too Dick Forshaw, one of the stars of LFC's back-to-back title-winning team of 1921-23 along with Harry 'Smiler' Chambers, who got five.

The fifties belonged to Billy Liddell, invariably the club's talismanic top scorer in that decade. After one hat-trick – he got five all told – in a 5-2 win over Nottingham Forest at Anfield in December 1955 the *Echo* commented on the fading daylight during the second half then added: "None of us needed to strain our eyes to see that Billy Liddell had again donned his old mantle of match-winner. It was Liddell who helped to make victory certain for his side when it seemed not beyond probability that Forest might salvage a point."

Billy turned provider for one of Anfield's most famous goals – the second of a hat-trick by Albert Stubbins in an FA Cup win over Birmingham City in March 1947. "We won 4-1 and all who saw that match will never forget an amazing goal by Albert," recalled Liddell.

"I put the ball over and it was going a bit off course, but he literally threw himself through the air to meet it with his head when parallel with the ground, about two feet above the turf. It went in like a rocket and Albert slid on his stomach for several yards on the frozen pitch before coming to a stop."

In the modern LFC era the most hat-tricks belong to Fernando Torres, Luis Suarez and Steven Gerrard. The Spanish striker notched three in 2007/08 (and four in total) while three of the six LFC hat-tricks scored by Suarez were against the same opposition, Norwich City, in the space of 20 months – including four goals in the last of those matches in December 2013.

As for the five trebles by Gerrard, the most memorable has to be against Everton in the Anfield derby of March 2012, closely followed by his Europa League hat-trick as a second-half substitute against Napoli in November 2010, making him only the second LFC sub to notch a treble.

Of the current team Mo Salah (3), Roberto Firmino (2), Sadio Mane (1) and Diogo Jota (1) have all hit trebles, but only one forward opened his goalscoring account for Liverpool with a hat-trick – that man Origi.

74/130

Oggy, oggy, oggy

ON the opening day of the 1959/60 season, Liverpool started their Second Division schedule in Wales, taking on Cardiff City, and a new LFC record was established. The Reds lost 3-2 at Ninian Park that afternoon despite the best efforts of Bluebirds defender Danny Malloy.

The Scottish centre-back scored two own goals in the space of four minutes to give Phil Taylor's side a 2-1 half-time lead to the bemusement of Cardiff keeper Graham Vearncombe.

Malloy gained an unfortunate reputation for putting through his own goal, doing so an incredible 14 times in six seasons with Cardiff. He had also scored for Liverpool when the teams had met at Anfield in August 1957 in a game the Reds won 3-0!

There have been plenty of other well known own goals in the club's history, not least Delfi Geli's 'golden goal' winner in the 2001 UEFA Cup final.

The Merseyside derby has produced a few memorable 'oggys' down the years. The Reds took control of the December 1969 clash at Goodison Park when Blues defender Sandy Brown spectacularly headed a Peter Thompson cross from the left beyond goalkeeper Gordon West just seven minutes after Emlyn Hughes had put Liverpool ahead early in the second-half.

In March 1981 John Bailey put through his own net with 13 minutes of the game at Anfield remaining to give the Reds a 1-0 victory. Then, in March 2006, Phil Neville was another Blue to head past his own keeper when he diverted Xabi Alonso's corner past Richard Wright at the Anfield Road end in a game Liverpool went on to win 3-1 despite playing most of the match with 10 men.

However, the most famous of all Anfield own goals came in December 1967 when Liverpool defeated rivals Leeds United 2-0.

Roger Hunt had opened the scoring before the Reds' position was strengthened in a moment that took place one minute before half-time as goalkeeper Gary Sprake somehow contrived to throw the ball into his own net.

Sprake advanced to the edge of his area to collect a back-pass and shaped to throw the ball out quickly to left-back Terry Cooper. But instead the ball slipped out of his control and flew into the far corner of the net.

Recalling the incident in 2011, *The Guardian* reported: "Whether he changed his mind mid-throw – Cooper was being pressurised by Ian Callaghan, while Roger Hunt was sniffing around the area – or simply lost his grip has never been fully explained."

With the incident happening so close to the interval, and following prompting by the Reds' PA announcer during the break, The Kop proceeded to serenade Sprake with a rendition of *Careless Hands*, Des O'Connor's hit single of the time, and local band The Scaffold's *Thank U Very Much*, when the teams returned to the field.

Own goals can also be crucial in title races and two of them were important for Bill Shankly's champions of 1973. West Ham's Bobby Ferguson and Stoke's John Mahoney both scored own goals in games that Liverpool won 3-2 and 1-0 respectively that season.

Shanks' side went on to win the title by three points but without those two victories (it was two points for a win) they'd have gone into the last game of the season (which LFC drew 0-0 with Leicester) level on points with Arsenal.

An 89th minute own goal by Manchester City's Dave Watson also had an impact on Liverpool's 1977 title success. The City defender's error gave Bob Paisley's side a 1-1 draw at Maine Road in December and the final table shows that it was City who finished as runners-up that year, just one point behind the Reds.

Liverpool had won the league with a game to spare so fielded a slightly weakened side in the final game of the season at Bristol City (who won 2-1 to avoid relegation) before the FA and European Cup finals, but who's to know how things would have panned out if Watson hadn't handed Paisley's men that point and they'd needed to win at Ashton Gate?

Other opponents also hold rare, if unlikely, distinctions in Liverpool's history. For instance, when Leeds United's Gordon Strachan back-heeled the ball over his own goal-line in the 1992 FA Charity Shield, he became the only man to have scored an own goal for Liverpool at Wembley. Then in 2020, Liverpool's first ever victory away to Ajax in Amsterdam came courtesy of an own goal by Argentina left-back Nicolas Tagliafico

Of course, it hasn't all been one-way. Talking of Wembley, Liverpool keeper Bruce Grobbelaar put through his own net in spectacular style to win the 1984 FA Charity Shield for Everton when Graeme Sharp's shot cannoned off Alan Hansen and in via his leg.

More recently, not helped by the modern day Dubious Goals Panel, Jamie Carragher ended his fine career second on the Premier League list of own goal scorers, while Martin Skrtel holds the dubious record for most own goals in a single season, firing four past Simon Mignolet throughout the 2013/14 campaign.

However, as far as records show, Liverpool FC has benefitted from 205 own goals during the first 130 years of the club's existence.

Indeed, to put that into context, own goals is now fifth on the Reds' all-time list of goalscorers after overtaking Steven Gerrard when Burton Albion's Tom Naylor put through his own net during a League Cup tie at the Pirelli Stadium in August 2016.

Maybe Ian Rush's club record of 346 goals will be under threat during the next 130 years after all...

75/130

Our bread and butter

IN the early seventies, in a TV interview at Anfield, Reds boss Bill Shankly said: "I would like to win the European Cup, naturally, because that's the ultimate in Europe. But the main thing, and our bread and butter, is this…"

He pointed to his left and the old league championship trophy, the camera panning up from its base, past red ribbons to the gleaming silver figure at the top.

"And that's what we want to win all the time. Never mind Europe. I'm glad we're in Europe. It's been a great thing for Liverpool, great thing for the country. But this is our bread and butter, and this is the one that we want…"

Winning leagues: a Liverpool thing. It began in 1901, less than ten years after the club's foundation, with Sunderland pipped by two points after a 12-match unbeaten run under manager Tom Watson as forward Sam Raybould top-scored with 17 league goals.

Five years later, in their first season back in the big time, the Reds claimed the First Division crown again, finishing four points clear of runners-up Preston North End following a final-day 3-1 win over Sheffield United at Anfield.

The early twenties brought back-to-back titles. The team went top on Saturday 17 December 1921 with a home win over Manchester United and stayed there until the end of the season, with the *Liverpool Courier* newspaper of 18 April 1922 noting: "All honour then to the wearers of the Red shirt. It has been a long and strenuous struggle and the side has not been free from injuries. Yet all have given of their best, with the result that the championship returns to Merseyside after an absence of many years."

The following season, 1922/23, the Reds went top in mid-September and stayed there under Matt McQueen, who'd replaced David Ashworth as boss halfway through the campaign. The *Liverpool Evening Express* reported: "Consistency is the watchword of the side. They have always finished in the first four for seven consecutive seasons, and after coming out on top in 1921/22 have led the field a merry dance."

Success eluded LFC for the following two decades. But in 1946/47, the first 'proper' season since the war, the Reds under George Kay claimed their fifth title as the average Anfield gate topped 40,000 for the first time.

They had to wait, mind: after a 2-1 win at fellow title-chasers Wolves in their last fixture of the season on Saturday 31 May 1947, it was a further two weeks (in mid-June!) before it was confirmed by fourth-placed Stoke City's failure to win at Sheffield United.

The *Liverpool Evening Express* hailed "a triumph of teamwork, consistency and individual ability...it was a storming finish with eleven out of the last 12 points won despite the fact that the last four matches were away from home."

The fifties were spent mostly in the old Second Division. Then along came Bill Shankly. Having guided the club back into the big time in 1962, the charismatic Scot secured top-flight title number six in 1963/64. This time the Reds moved into first place on 30 March 1964 and ultimately finished four points ahead of runners-up Manchester United.

They were crowned champions on Saturday 18 April 1964 with a 5-0 win over Arsenal in front of almost 50,000 at Anfield; all the goals were scored before the hour-mark. On the day of the game the *Echo* described the scenes before kick-off: "Thousands were locked out when the gates were closed at 1.45pm with a capacity crowd inside. Scenes outside had been bordering on chaos with mounted police busy controlling the crowds, reinforced by special constabulary. From 1.45pm onwards the ground was tightly packed with an exultant crowd waiting for the kick-off. 'They are just singing their heads off – they love it', said an official."

Two seasons later, following an historic first FA Cup win, Liverpool were champions again, finishing six points clear of Leeds United, their erstwhile foes at Wembley. They clinched the title with a 2-1 win over Chelsea at Anfield on 30 April 1966. Roger Hunt got the goals, bringing his total to 32 – the sixth of nine seasons in which he'd be top scorer.

The fans, though, were the stars for the *Daily Post*: "Bill Shankly is right. There's no football crowd anywhere to compare with the Anfield throng for their fervour and spontaneous wit. Entirely original, they are not so much part of a scene as scene-stealers." Naturally Bill felt the best team lost in the following Thursday's Cup Winners' Cup final against Borussia Dortmund.

That was the final flourish of Shankly's first great team. It took seven years, but he duly built another one which would win the league. On Saturday 28 April 1973 a goalless draw at home to Leicester City clinched an eighth title, the Reds ultimately three points clear of second-placed Arsenal.

The *Daily Post*: "For colour – Liverpool's vivid red of course – fervour, song and sound, this was the day of days… The league trophy was not unveiled to public view until the final triumphant blast of the referee's whistle. Then out it came to the players in the centre-circle, closely followed by Mr Shankly, whose appearance increased the bedlam to deafening volume. As the swaying Kop stretched their scarves end to end, off came the manager's coat to reveal a striking red shirt." Three weeks later Liverpool lifted the UEFA Cup, beating Borussia Moenchengladbach 3-2 on aggregate.

So to the most sustained period of Liverpool FC's domestic dominance. Shankly had built the foundations, and successor Bob Paisley continued the all-conquering work. Season 1975/76 saw another league and UEFA Cup double: a ninth top-flight title with Keegan and Toshack once again the dynamic duo upfront and Bruges beaten over two legs.

After the dramatic title-clinching win at Wolves the *Echo* reported: "On a night of a thousand memories one outstanding fact emerged. This was the night when the Liverpool fans, particularly the Kopites, finally took Paisley to their hearts, recognising him as the great manager he is. They will always have a special affection for Bill Shankly but now they have their own regard for Bob as well. Perhaps it will never be as flamboyant as the Shankly links with the Kop, but it is deep, sincere, and based on a recognition of this man's special qualities."

It just kept getting better. In 1976/77 the Reds paired title number 10 with a first European Cup success. In 1978/79 they accumulated a record 68 points under the old two-points-for-a-win format and established a record for conceding the fewest goals, 16, by a top-flight side. And in 1979/80 a twelfth title was clinched with victory over Aston Villa, just like the previous season.

Villa took the crown themselves in 1980/81, after which Liverpool won three titles on the run for the first time in their history – indeed they became the only club to achieve this feat since the war. Number 13 was won on Saturday 15 May 1982 with victory over a Spurs side featuring Liverpool old boy Ray Clemence in goal, a rapturous Kop saluting goals by Mark Lawrenson, Kenny Dalglish and Ronnie Whelan.

Manager Bob Paisley called it "the hardest of them all to win. This season we have changed the team about and brought in new players. The toughest part of this job is producing new players at the right time. In this job you've always got people telling you what you should do. They tell you to bring in new players, but it isn't as easy as that. There comes a point when you have to say to the youngsters: 'You've had your education – now go through with it'."

In 1982/83 the Reds finished eleven points clear of Graham Taylor's Watford, having stayed top since the end of October. In 1983/84 the title formed part of a treble with the European Cup and League Cup. This time fans on the Kop stayed behind for 40 minutes after the final home game against Norwich City to hail their heroes – one of whom, Ian Rush, had scored 47 goals in all competitions.

While banned from European competition after the Heysel disaster, Liverpool pipped neighbours Everton to the league and FA Cup double in 1985/86 under player-manager Dalglish. The title was won at Chelsea on Saturday 3 May 1986, the *Daily Post* describing the celebrations as "so familiar that anyone who had been isolated from the English game for the past year or so could have found no reason to believe Liverpool Football Club had suffered a catastrophe last May. No club in the country was better equipped to take such a blow and recover so quickly."

Two years later, having finished runners-up to the Toffees the previous season, a scintillating new side assembled by Kenny finished nine points clear of Manchester United, although another double was thwarted by Wimbledon in the FA Cup final.

The 18th title triumph was confirmed with a 2-1 win against QPR before, on Tuesday 1 May 1990, a 1-0 victory over Derby

County at Anfield featured an 19-minute cameo by 39-year-old player-manager Dalglish as a substitute in what proved to be his last game for LFC. This, remember, was just 12 months after Hillsborough and the last-gasp title-costing defeat by Arsenal at Anfield that, somehow, hadn't seemed to matter so much.

When the Reds were next crowned champions – after a 30-year wait in 2019/20 – we had also been reminded by the COVID-19 pandemic that sometimes football isn't the be all and end all.

Lockdowns and the temporary suspension of normal life as we knew it meant the Premier League trophy wasn't eventually picked up by Jordan Henderson until a Wednesday night in July after a 5-3 home win over Chelsea. It wasn't the title-winning party we had all hoped for with the season ending behind closed doors, but finally the Premier League trophy was being lifted at Anfield by a Liverpool skipper.

In truth, that moment becoming a reality had looked likely months earlier as Jürgen Klopp's men – reigning European champions after winning the European Cup for the sixth time in 2019 – started the season with eight consecutive league victories.

None of their rivals could live with such a pace, a fact demonstrated perfectly in a 3-1 demolition of Manchester City that November which began with Fabinho's thumping drive.

Mo Salah headed in to round off a magnificent length of the pitch move and Sadio Mane nodded in at the back post completed the emphatic win.

A 2-1 victory at Aston Villa the previous weekend – with late headed goals from Andy Robertson and Mane turning defeat into victory – had already demonstrated exactly what the manager was referencing whenever he described his squad as 'mentality monsters'.

During a campaign littered with highlights another standout was a 5-2 December Merseyside derby win that saw the Reds put four first half goals past our neighbours, Divock Origi scoring twice.

The same month saw a quick trip to Qatar for the World Club Cup where the Reds were crowned the planet's best team. If their domestic rivals hoped that might prove a distraction they were sorely mistaken as the return to league action saw Klopp's men inflict an emphatic 4-0 Boxing Day win over second placed Leicester City.

There was simply no stopping this team and wins over Spurs, Man United and Wolves in January cemented their position at the summit. The second of those victories featured a thumping header from Virgil Van Dijk and a clinical Salah finish. Even more tellingly, the Anfield crowd saluted the win by bellowing out: 'we're gonna win the league'.

Impressively, a league reversal would not materialise until the end of February away at Watford. In truth, it was only delaying the inevitable title triumph as the Reds were still 22 points clear, having won 26 of their opening 28 fixtures and set all kinds of records along the way, taking 79 points from the first 81 available.

A few weeks later the season was paused due to the pandemic. When it eventually resumed in June, with empty stadiums, a 4-0 home win over Crystal Palace - lit up by a free-kick from Trent Alexander-Arnold - edged that title success even closer.

Just 24 hours later Man City's failure to defeat Chelsea meant the job was done; Liverpool were champions of England for an incredible 19th time!

The players rightly enjoyed the moment with a big party at a Formby hotel as Kopites all over the world celebrated the achievements of their heroes and Klopp reflected on the long-awaited triumph.

"I thought a lot about what we did in the last few years and I think one of the most important things I said – I had no idea how important this was when I said it – was we have to write our own story and create our own history. Because that's what was necessary and that's what these boys have done now."

99 points was a staggering tally to finish with and the Reds won the title with a top-flight record seven games to spare: a real indication of their dominance from start to finish in a season that ran from early August to late July and concluded with us once more enjoying our 'bread and butter'.

76/130

Something fishy

LIVERPOOL'S biggest league win over Stoke City came back in January 1902 when they ran out 7-0 victors in a Division One fixture at Anfield.

On the face of it, the result reflects a dominant display from the home side. However, that doesn't begin to tell the whole story as the scoreline was just one aspect of a day that the Potters found hard to stomach in just about every way.

The match also saw Scottish striker Andy McGuigan break new ground for Liverpool Football Club when he became the first Reds player to score five Football League goals in one game. McGuigan only played 37 times for LFC, netting 14 goals, and later returned to serve the club as a director.

However, his goalscoring feat was perhaps not as impressive as it sounds. A number of Stoke's players were apparently suffering from food poisoning having eaten bad fish prior to the match. During the game a number of Liverpool's opponents had to leave the field through illness and at one point there were only seven Stoke players left!

The *Liverpool Echo's* match report stated: "There were no less than six alterations to the Stoke team from that which was advertised. It transpired that just before the teams were due on the field, two or three Stoke players were seriously indisposed but they pluckily turned out with their comrades." The headlines at the top of the article told the tale, proclaiming: "Extraordinary attacks of sickness," "The Stoke Team Depleted," "Goalkeeper and several others retire" and "Liverpool forwards have an afternoon out." A sub-header in the analysis of the game also screamed: 'Evidently Ill."

A cartoon in the newspaper portrayed a Stoke player drawn as a clay pot after the club's nickname, taunted by a fish saying: "Have another before you go!" whilst a Liverpool player in the background was shouting: "Thanks aw'fly for the goals." The caption underneath read: "Liverpool and Fish! Ugh!! What with the two of 'em – it's poisonous!"

In a *Liverpool Echo* article previewing a game between the Reds and the Potters in December 1915, the fishy business was recalled.

"Next Saturday's game at Anfield brings to our memory a fishy smell," it explained. "Stoke and Liverpool will ever be associated with one of the few fiascos ever played. Considering the number of games played, the number of fiascos is small and this fact is due to the admireable *(sic)* control of the League by the businesslike Management Committee and its head, our own Mr John McKenna. The twenty-year-old Liverpool youth does not know why Stoke and Liverpool are connected with a fishy match. Therefore, I will put them 'wise'. The teams met on 4 January 1902, at Anfield, and Stoke were beaten by seven goals to nil, four being scored in the first half. Stoke were not well. They were ill before the game, during the game, and afterwards. They had had fish.

"Fin did not agree with them, and a semblance of poisoning troubled them in the Narrows. The weather in the Dardanelles that day was terribly rough, and player after player had to leave the field and 'heave to'.

"At one time Stoke had but seven men on the field. No wonder Liverpool won by a clear margin and by seven goals!"

77/130

Missed matches

THERE are some Liverpool fans who haven't missed a match for years, clocking up the miles to follow their beloved Reds home and away. Such commitment is hugely impressive as even team managers from Bill Shankly to Jürgen Klopp haven't seen every 90 minutes the team has played under their charge.

There have been various reasons for their one-off absences while Graeme Souness and Gerard Houllier were also absent for longer spells after undergoing heart surgery.

Shankly was left in a rage after his time away in 1965 as an FA Cup run which ended in glory was almost derailed in its early stages.

Liverpool's reward for a drama-filled victory over West Brom at The Hawthorns in round three was a home draw against Stockport County.

The Hatters were propping up the Football League, five points adrift of Bradford City and had won only four of their 28 Division Four fixtures to that point of the season. Therefore their third round win over Bristol Rovers had been something of a surprise.

For their part, the Reds had made a stuttering start to their own league campaign and were ninth in the First Division table. However, they also had the demands of European football to contend with for the first time and had progressed to the quarter-finals of the European Cup where they were set to face Cologne.

Of course, half-a-century ago Shankly was unable to call upon the kind of scouting network all Premier League clubs enjoy today.

Therefore, given that 83 places separated Liverpool and Stockport in the Football League standings, the Scot decided to make a trip to Germany to run the rule over the Reds' next Euro opponents – leaving Bob Paisley and Reuben Bennett in charge of events at Anfield.

But as things transpired, Liverpool's passage to round five was anything but smooth. Stockport player-manager Trevor Porteous had brought in veteran ex-Newcastle and Huddersfield striker Len White to add know-how to his side's attack. After 18 minutes, White fired County ahead after goalkeeper Tommy Lawrence had parried a cross-shot from Johnny Watt.

Following several good saves from County keeper Ken Mulhearn, Liverpool eventually levelled six minutes into the second-half thanks to a fine piece of opportunism from Gordon Milne, who swivelled to hit a low shot through a ruck of players and just inside the post.

However, the Reds' efforts to find a winner proved to be in vain and Liverpool even needed a last-ditch clearance from Gerry Byrne to protect the 1-1 scoreline and earn a replay. Mobile phone technology was still decades away and the first Shankly had heard of the result was on his return from the Cologne spying mission.

In his autobiography, *The Saint*, Ian St John recalled: "As he was coming through the airport in Manchester some of the workers greeted him.

'Hello, boys,' he said, before asking if there had been any cup surprises while he was away.

'Only your draw with Stockport, Bill,' he was told.

'Aye, you have a nice sense of humour today, boys,' he replied as he collected his bag and strode off in his best Jimmy Cagney style. Then he turned on the car radio and realised the baggage handlers hadn't been joking. He came rushing back to Anfield for a crisis meeting. There, Bob Paisley and Reuben Bennett took quite a bit of time assuring him that in his brief absence the world he had been building with such force had not fallen off its axis completely.

"Naturally Bob and Reuben didn't dwell too long on how near we had been to catastrophe while he was away – or how Gerry Byrne kept us alive by kicking the ball off the line in the last minutes."

With Shanks back in the dugout, Liverpool won the replay at Edgeley Park 2-0 with goals from Roger Hunt towards the end of each half. The team would go on to lift the FA Cup for the first time in the club's history.

The next Reds boss to miss a first-team fixture was Graeme Souness in 1993. Once again the reason for the absence was scouting-related, but this time the Liverpool manager was literally sent to Coventry.

The Scot missed the Anfield curtain call on the club's debut Premier League season of 1992/93 against Tottenham Hotspur in order to run the rule over Coventry City's game against Leeds United at Highfield Road, leaving Ronnie Moran in charge.

More than 43,000 were at Anfield and they witnessed a 6-2 Liverpool victory, the team's highest-scoring league win of that season, which included Ian Rush's 300th league goal for the club.

Fast forward more than 15 years and Rafael Benitez was forced to miss the pre-Christmas Premier League game at Arsenal due to surgery to remove kidney stones. Despite being more than 200 miles from the Emirates Stadium, it later transpired that Rafa had been making substitutions and tactical adjustments via regular calls to goalkeeping coach Xavi Valero!

Despite falling behind to a goal from Robin van Persie, Liverpool responded with an equaliser from Robbie Keane as they picked up a solid away point with a 1-1 draw against one of their title rivals.

When Liverpool travelled to Queens Park Rangers for their final game of 2012, assistant manager Colin Pascoe took charge with boss Brendan Rodgers absent with a stomach virus.

Two goals from Luis Suarez and one from Daniel Agger inside the first half-hour will have helped Rodgers feel better but Pascoe was unable to congratulate the team at half-time. The virus had also affected him and so he was unable to enter the dressing room during the interval for fear of infecting the players.

There was no further scoring in the second-half and the Reds returned to Merseyside with a good three points added to their tally.

A more recent occasion when Liverpool were without their leader in the technical area came in February 2016 when the Reds hosted Sunderland in a Premier League fixture.

Jürgen Klopp had only been at the helm for four months but was unable to make it to Anfield after entering hospital to have his appendix removed.

In his absence, coaching staff including Zeljko Buvac, Peter Krawietz, Pepijn Lijnders and John Achterberg took over with Roberto Firmino and Adam Lallana netting in a 2-2 draw.

Klopp was back in charge for the Reds' next fixture, their final ever game at West Ham's Upton Park, three days later.

The Liverpool boss has since missed a second game through illness when COVID-19 ruled him out of the Reds' trip to play Chelsea at Stamford Bridge in January 2022. Lijnders took charge and Liverpool drew 2-2 with Klopp returning for an FA Cup tie at home to Shrewsbury Town the following weekend.

78/130

The perfect storm

ELEVEN-NIL v Stromsgodset, European Cup Winners' Cup first round 1974... Ten-nil v Fulham, League Cup second-round first leg 1986... Nine-nil v Crystal Palace, First Division 1989... Eight-nil v Swansea City, League Cup 1990...

Every Reds fan knows about the big victories and probably the stories behind them. But next to these emphatic scorelines on lists of LFC records, there's usually this entry too: Record defeat: 1-9 v Birmingham City, Second Division 1954. It will never go away, so we may as well face up to what happened.

The fifties was not the best decade in LFC history, even though it was book-ended by an FA Cup final appearance and the arrival of Bill Shankly. By the end of season 1953/54 the club had been relegated, finishing rock-bottom with 28 points from 42 fixtures.

Defender Laurie Hughes, a title winner with Liverpool in 1946/47 and FA Cup finalist in 1950, later recalled: "We were in a poor way and had come close to [the drop] in previous seasons. Great players had left and weren't replaced. Simple as that."

In their first season in the second tier the Reds came a lacklustre eleventh. They did at least boast a standout goalscorer in John Evans, with 33 in all competitions that season, including five in one game against Bristol Rovers in September 1954. Three months later came another milestone moment, for all the wrong reasons.

The omens weren't good in the week beginning Monday 6

December 1954. By the Wednesday, the *Liverpool Echo* banner headline was 'Blizzard sweeps over Merseyside and North Wales' as high winds and the first snow of winter besieged the city and heavy seas pounded the coast.

A tram keeled over in Everton, the Cunard liner Franconia's voyage to New York was delayed, and 'over the water' in Wallasey the seawall was breached. By Friday the 'great tempest', as it had been dubbed, had suspended cross-Channel ferries amid fears of the Thames bursting its banks – long before London's flood barrier was built.

Could things get any worse? If you were a Liverpool supporter, unfortunately yes. To be fair, manager Don Welsh's team had made a steady start to the season and the *Echo* chief football writer, pen name 'Stork', was finding cause for optimism. In his midweek column he insisted: "With Everton getting the run of the ball at last and returning to winning ways [in the First Division] and Liverpool setting up a new 'record' for the season, the Goodison and Anfield horizon is brighter today.

"What is Liverpool's 'record' did I hear someone ask? A small one, but acceptable. By beating Middlesbrough [the previous week, 3-1] they took five points [from three games] for the first time… Let us hope this is a pointer to still better things in the second half of the season. The Reds are now only six points behind the Second Division leaders".

By Thursday that same week the paper was hailing the victory of middleweight boxer Pat McAteer, uncle of future Red Jason, over Les Allen at Liverpool Stadium, which gave him a shot at the British and Commonwealth title. And Liverpool, 12th in the Second Division table, were preparing to face 14th-placed Birmingham City at St Andrews on the Saturday, looking for a first away win of the campaign.

Which is where it all went horribly askew, as 'Stork' would relay in the following Monday's *Echo*: "It is easy to be wise after the event, but who was to know that the St Andrews ground would be frost-bound? There was no suggestion of frost when we left Liverpool, otherwise I am sure the rubber boots would have been packed.

"Would they have made all the difference? Would they have prevented this heaviest-ever defeat? It is true to say that Birmingham kept their feet much better than did Liverpool, but this is not the time for conjecture. It is bald facts we have to face up to in this slaughter.

"We cannot blame the bone-hard ground, for it was the same for both, but City were much more adaptable. They sped over the treacherous turf (well sanded) as though it was luscious grass. They tackled quickly and confidently; in fact their speed and enthusiasm soon had Liverpool three goals in arrears – two of which should never have been scored.

"I don't think I have ever seen so many goals scored so easily. There was no real approach work to any one of them and the last two were definitely suspect – the eighth undoubtedly offside, allowed after a consultation with the linesman.

"I am not making excuses for there are none to make. Birmingham were good winners over a Liverpool team which had the heart knocked out of them in the first fifteen minutes. They acknowledged the burden was too great and although they battled on gallantly until the interval, there they finished.

"It was not good football which beat them: just honest endeavour by a team which had set seal to victory by getting in their blow first – a deflected goal to which [goalkeeper Doug] Rudham never made a move. He was also at fault with the third for he pushed the ball up against his crossbar and [Blues striker Eddie] Brown met it as it came down and tapped it over the line.

"Every thread of confidence had been knocked out of the

Anfielders. Right from goal to outside-left there was ineptitude, [Billy] Liddell apart, for he strove like a hero without any assistance whatsoever.

"The defence could not build up any barrier to check the surging tide and goals came at regular intervals from the feet of those rampant City forwards. When I tell you that all were shot from inside the penalty area you will have some idea as to the sketchiness of the Liverpool defence. It just could not hold down the speedy City forward line, which in the end did almost as it liked. I think I am right in saying that Liddell's goal was the best of the bunch, for not even the England goalkeeper [Gil] Merrick could do anything to prevent it – such was its power.

"Brown, the Birmingham centre-forward, was like greased lightning off the mark: in fact the whole forward line was slick moving and they had only to see the white of the goalpost to let fly with everything they had, so their nine goals apart they hit the woodwork twice. Two weeks ago I gave high praise to the goalkeeping of Rudham. At St Andrews he was anything but impressive. He was not alone, however, for the team as a whole failed lamentably. But shall I say it was Birmingham's day, for it is only a truth to add that whatever they did came off, which was in direct opposite to Liverpool's efforts – not many I admit."

Years later, Reds winger Alan A'Court remembered "slipping and sliding all over the place. Billy Liddell pulled one back for us and I still say that was the best of the ten! He kept his balance beautifully on that surface, turned like an ice-skater and hit a screamer into the top corner. It was a one-off game. I cannot explain why it happened. It kept slipping away, literally."

Birmingham would go on to win the Second Division championship and promotion back to the top flight. For Liverpool, at the end of the storm there would be a golden sky. It would just take five more years to arrive.

79/130

Getting shirty!

OVER the years, Leicester City have proven something of a bogey side for Liverpool.

The Foxes became a regular thorn in Bill Shankly's side during the sixties and early seventies and also sparked a rare fit of pique from one of the Reds' greatest goalscorers.

Notwithstanding the East Midlands side's shock title success in 2015/16, Liverpool have found it hard to overcome Leicester over the years. Even during the Reds' dominance during the 1980s, Leicester registered two league wins at Anfield and during the 90s and noughties, they posed further problems as Martin O'Neill's sides enjoyed various successes at Liverpool's expense.

In just over a decade with the Reds Roger Hunt scored 285 goals in 492 games. Five of those goals came against Leicester, including the quarter-final replay winner that helped Liverpool take a huge step towards winning their first FA Cup in 1965.

In March 1969 however, the Foxes' Indian Sign over the Reds struck once again when the teams were paired together at Filbert Street in the FA Cup fifth round.

Remarkably, the inclement weather had led to an astonishing seven postponements before the tie was eventually played on 1 March, the date set for the quarter-finals. Indeed, when the semi-final draw was made, it read: Liverpool or Leicester City or Mansfield Town versus West Bromwich Albion!

A lively goalless draw was played out with teenage goalkeeper Peter Shilton carrying on the form of Foxes keepers against the Reds previously displayed by the likes of Walter Smith and Gordon Banks with a string of saves.

Even so, Liverpool were confident of victory in front of their own fans in the replay at Anfield the following Monday night. In the event, things didn't pan out as planned.

Forward Andy Lochhead put Leicester in front just after the half-hour mark but the Reds were afforded a quick opportunity to draw level when John Sjoberg handled in the penalty area and referee Jack Taylor pointed to the spot. However, Shilton saved Tommy Smith's effort and the Reds' cup run was in jeopardy.

Speaking to the LFC matchday programme, Shilton recalled: "It [the penalty] was in front of the Kop and I think I dived to my left. After that, it was the story of the Alamo again. We were defending for most of the time and I think I had a decent game.

"I can remember the noise. It was deafening for 90 minutes, I always like to shout and did so at Anfield, but our defenders couldn't hear a word from me.

"The Kop were terrific towards me that night. I was a 19-year-old keeper in an electric atmosphere and I'm sure they felt for me. Liverpool's attacks were rolling in like waves, one after another, but we got through. Anfield was a ground I always enjoyed. I was never nervous there and the fans were good to me."

To make matters worse for Kopites, the red mist came down from ace marksman Hunt who threw his shirt down in front of the dugout in disgust after being substituted for Bobby Graham in the 73rd minute.

Hunt felt humiliated as it was only the second time Shankly had made a change for tactical reasons since the introduction of substitutes two-and-a-half years earlier.

The boss refused to comment on the incident at the time with

Liverpool chairman Harold Cartwright saying: "We have every confidence in whatever action our manager may take which he thinks is in the best interest of the team at any particular time. There is no controversy as far as we are concerned."

Shankly addressed the brouhaha in his 1976 autobiography. He recalled: "We were fighting a battle for our lives. We were a goal down and Roger wasn't playing well. On the bench we had Bobby Graham, a quick-fire player who might have broken through. We needed a little pace.

"I could have picked any of the players to bring off, but I thought Roger was doing nothing by his standards. I sat for five or six minutes and thought: 'It's got to be Roger.' To take Roger off at Anfield was quite a difficult job but I did it, and of course he threw off his jersey, which didn't help any.

"Roger probably regretted that, because he did well for Liverpool and Liverpool did well for him. But I didn't say: 'He'll get fined' or 'He'll get this, or that, or the other.' I said: 'I took Roger Hunt off. Nobody else but me. I take the blame for him. I'm responsible for the whole thing'. What's more, if the same situation cropped up again and he was playing the same way as he was then, I'd do the same thing again.

"I caused a hullabaloo. If we had been winning the match, nothing would have been said about it. But we were losing and Roger knew he was having a lean time. He was one of the kingpins of Liverpool, make no mistake about that, but sometimes it is possible for a good player to play badly."

Hunt started the Reds' next game at Sunderland and the incident was quickly forgotten. He finished that 1968/69 campaign as the club's leading goalscorer for the ninth time in 10 seasons.

80/130

What should the captain of Liverpool do?

BY the start of May 1981, the European Cup had been to many destinations. Madrid. Milan. Lisbon. Amsterdam. Liverpool and Munich, to name just six. But by the end of May 1981 the most iconic trophy in European football had visited a couple of places where you'd never expect to see it – establishments UEFA president Artemio Franchi probably didn't envisage it ending up in after handing it over to LFC skipper Phil Thompson following Liverpool's 1-0 victory against Real Madrid in Parc des Princes, Paris. But then the Redmen have always done things differently.

It was the third time Bob Paisley's Reds had won the European Cup in five seasons and afterwards an official reception was held at the team hotel. But, after scores of joyous supporters invaded the party, the players made their excuses and decided to celebrate their success in different ways elsewhere.

"I went back to one of our hotel rooms with a few beers and had a bit of a sing-a-long with Alan Hansen and his family," recalled left-back Alan Kennedy, the scorer of Liverpool's winning goal. "My girlfriend at the time said we were not going out! Some of the other players went to the Lido club in town, a disgraceful place with six-foot dancing girls. They even took the cup with them! Thank goodness they brought it back."

'Le Lido' is a cabaret and burlesque show situated at 11 Avenue des Champs-Elysees. First opened in 1946, albeit a bit further down the most famous street in Paris, stars such as Eartha Kitt, Laurel and Hardy and Elton John have performed there down the years, but on the night of 27 May 1981 – well the early hours of 28 May 1981 anyway! – all eyes were on the three-time European Champions.

Graeme Souness and Phil Neal had remained at Parc de Princes when the team bus departed as both had been selected to take UEFA's random drug test but were unable to produce urine samples for quite some time due to dehydration. They ended up hitching a lift with some gendarmes to get back to the hotel but after discovering the invasion of Kopites, Souness – aka 'Champagne Charlie' – took a group of players to Le Lido where they found themselves confronted by some blues. And we don't mean Evertonians!

"When we walked in the Bluebells were performing, but the spotlight was switched onto us," recalled David Johnson in *Liverpool In Europe*. "We were given the best tables, close to the stage, and enjoyed a brilliant end to a perfect day."

Skipper Thompson chose to stay at the team hotel with his family, but when he returned to Merseyside he took 'old big ears' – as Kopites have lovingly christened the European Cup – back to his hometown.

Despite being captain of Liverpool Football Club, Thommo was still living in a modest semi-detached house in Kirkby with wife Marg and was managing his local pub team, Falcon, something he did for 12 seasons from the age of 21. He'd spend Sunday mornings, having played for the Reds the day before, on the touchline at Arbour Lane and would often bring the team kit and balls with him in the back of his Ford Capri. Indeed, such was his commitment that after being ruled out of the European Cup semi-final second leg against FC Zurich at Anfield through injury, Thompson went off to manage Falcon at Prescot Cables instead of attending the match!

So, after lifting the European Cup in Gay Paree – and spotting some of the lads from the pub waving a flag with 'Kirkby' on it from the front row of the Parc des Princes balcony opposite where the trophy was presented – he decided to take the celebrations to them.

"On the Thursday night I took the European Cup to The Falcon in Kirkby. We'd won the League Cup earlier that season against West Ham after a replay at Villa Park and the most important thing to us after the game when we got back to Liverpool was which nightclub we'd be going to for a drink! We got off the bus, rolled into the night and celebrated winning. The next morning I got a call from club secretary Peter Robinson: 'Phil, do you happen to know what happened to the League Cup last night?'

'I've not got a clue where it ended up Peter.'

'You're the captain, Phil, but I'll tell you what happened to it. When the bus driver was cleaning the bus back at the depot he found the League Cup on the back seat.'

'Well what did you want me to do with it?'

'Take it home if necessary Phil, you're the captain.'

"So when we won the European Cup in Paris I didn't need telling twice to look after it."

Liverpool's open-top bus parade took place on the Thursday and after it had finished there was only one place that Thompson was heading to next: Bewley Drive, Kirkby.

"I packed the cup into its red velvet bag, put it in the back of my Ford Capri and off to The Falcon I went. I walked in with the cup above my head and the whole place was bouncing. It was a wonderful night – I think we were in there until four or five in the morning – and I took the European Cup home with me."

It's unknown precisely how much beer was supped from the European Cup that night, but it ended up sat behind the bar, pride of place next to the vast number of trophies that Thompson's Falcon Sunday league side had won.

"At 9 o'clock the next morning I got another call from Peter Robinson: 'Phil, do you happen to know where the European Cup is?'

"I had a phone in the bedroom and I was still that drunk that when I peered towards the end of the bed I thought we had five of them! 'I've got it here Peter, I'll bring it down to Anfield later.'

'Phil, I've got the world's press coming to see it at 11 o'clock...'

"What he didn't know was that I'd promised to take it back to The Falcon at 11 so all the kids could have their photos taken with it as obviously they weren't in the pub the night before. I thought to myself 'what should the captain of Liverpool do?' So I took the European Cup back to The Falcon at 11 o'clock!

"I'm not sure the press lads were too happy, but that's what the passion and emotion does to you when you've gone from standing on the Kop as a fan to captaining Liverpool to winning the European Cup."

81/130

Raising the roof

NOTICED anything different about the roof of the Kop since 2016? Before the Main Stand expansion work was undertaken, the Kop roof was trimmed back. Football's most famous stand is still completely covered, but doesn't loom quite so far over the pitch's Kop-end touchline as it used to.

It's not the first time the roof has changed. In its current all-seater guise the Kop dates back to 1994, when the old standing structure was demolished following the last game of the 1993/94 season and replaced by what was the country's largest single-tiered stand.

And it wasn't always called the Kop, not at first. The original structure was a vast bank of cinder and brick created along Oakfield Road in 1906 following Liverpool FC's second title triumph.

On Thursday 30 August that year the *Liverpool Echo* reported: "People who have not been permitted to view the ground except from the top of passing tramcars have marvelled and expressed astonishment when seeing the rise of the Oakfield-road embankment. It is far from complete yet, and even now towers to the extent of forty rows. More than double this number remain to be fitted up… The club will have completed the large bank by Christmas."

Two days later, on the first weekend of the 1906/07 season, the *Liverpool Weekly Mercury* newspaper featured a bird's-eye illustration of Anfield and described how the ground "has been completely walled in with fancy brick setting, with large exit gates on the four sides, as well as numerous entrances. The playing pitch has been raised about five feet, with a paddock all round. Roofed-in stand accommodation will be plentiful, and at one end, as seen in the sketch, will be an elevated terrace consisting of 132 tiers of steps, which will afford space for something like 20,000 spectators."

The first match in front of the new, roofless embankment was a punishing one for the first-ever Kopites, who watched their team beat Stoke City 1-0 in sunstroke conditions. The *Football Echo* reported that "the phenomenal heat...was so intense that it was a question whether the referee would not deem it advisable to postpone the game."

In time the Oakfield Road embankment was re-christened by *Echo* reporter Ernest Edwards after the site of a notorious Boer War battle in 1900. He called it the Spion Kop. It came from the Dutch Spioenkop, meaning 'Lookout Hill', in Natal, South Africa, where the British had suffered a harrowing defeat.

It wasn't until 1928 when the first roof, an iron cantilever design by Crosby architect Joseph Watson-Cabre, was added. It would give the Kop its imposing aspect, and the terrace itself was enlarged to measure 425ft x 131ft and house up to 30,000 spectators.

The roofed Kop was officially opened by the club's former manager and chairman John McKenna, who congratulated the LFC board on providing more covered accommodation than any other club in the Football League. The *Echo* noted that the roof also featured glazing that was "wire-woven to protect the spectators from broken glass if someone raised the roof shouting 'Goal!'"

Fast-forward forty years to June 1968 when the roof was dismantled and a new one put in its place. "Spectators need not worry about its famous acoustics being altered," declared the *Echo*. "It will still act as a sounding board to maintain its reputation of being the most notable terracing in football... The Liverpool directors considered it was time for modernisation [and] a figure in the region of £30,000 is being spent."

The first fixture under this, the Kop's second roof, saw the Reds beat reigning champions Manchester City 2-1 on Saturday 10 August 1968. The first under the third roof as we know it now – with the Kop only partly open as it was still being constructed – was record-breaking. Robbie Fowler scored a four-minute hat-trick against Arsenal on Sunday 28 August 1994 with all of his goals scored at the Anfield Road end, meaning it was John Scales – in a League Cup game against Burnley – who netted the first goal in front of the new Kop.

82/130

"I wonder what all the rest of the world does"

BILL Shankly's famous line about football, life and death has been misquoted and misappropriated more times than the AXA Training Centre canteen staff have made hot dinners. Here's what he said to Granada TV presenter Shelley Rohde in 1981, when he was being interviewed along with former Prime Minister Harold Wilson...

ROHDE: "What have you got out of football all these years?"

SHANKLY: "Everything I've got I owe to football. You only get out of the game what you put into it, Shelley. So I put in all my heart and soul, to the extent that my family suffered."

ROHDE: "Do you regret that at all?"

SHANKLY: "I regret it very much. Somebody said, 'Football's a matter of life and death to you'. I said, 'Listen it's more important than that'. And my family's suffered. They've been neglected."

ROHDE: "How would you do it now, if you had your time again?"

SHANKLY: "I don't know really. If I had the same thoughts, I'd possibly do the same again…"

ROHDE: "So what are the qualities of a good footballer?"

SHANKLY: "Aw, ability. And dedication to the game. And giving people their money's worth. The players have got an obligation to the public to do that."

ROHDE: "You sound as if it's more of an entertainment?"

SHANKLY: "Well, entertainment comes second for me. Entertainment, you can laugh at. I don't laugh at football."

WILSON: "It's a religion too, isn't it?"

SHANKLY: "I think so, yes."

WILSON: "A way of life."

SHANKLY: "That's a good expression, Sir Harold. It is a way of life. And it's so serious that it's unbelievable. And I wonder what all the rest of the world does."

The discarded European medal

WHILE many players understandably don't care for a runners-up medal, the majority of them will keep hold of their consolation prize.

Scottish midfielder Willie Stevenson thought differently after Bill Shankly's side had suffered an agonising 2-1 extra time loss to Borussia Dortmund in the 1966 European Cup Winners' Cup final at Hampden Park in Glasgow.

"I chucked the medal out the dressing room window," the former midfielder, who helped the Reds to two league titles and an FA Cup between 1964 and 1966, readily admits. "I never wanted loser's medals in my collection anyway. Somebody must have found it on the street outside and good luck to them."

His disappointment stemmed from the fact that the defeat to the Germans came in front of those closest to him.

"Of all the games we had around that time, that was the most disappointing for me because we just didn't play well. With a lot of us coming from Scotland we had loads of family there and that made the result even harder to take."

Stevenson, although he hailed from Edinburgh, had actually begun his professional career with Glasgow Rangers before arriving at Liverpool in October 1962 via Australia and a spell with Apia Leichhardt. He is by far the most successful of the eleven individuals who have joined us from the Ibrox club over the years.

Strangely, despite the success of both sides, we are yet to meet in a competitive encounter, whereas we have faced the Gers' crosstown rivals Celtic on three different occasions in Europe.

The first of those came in the aforementioned run to the final of the 1966 Cup Winners' Cup, with the men in the green and white Hoops providing our semi-final opponents over two legs.

The opening encounter took place at Celtic Park. It resulted in a 1-0 loss for Bill Shankly's side, before they turned the tie around five days later with a two goal victory coming courtesy of Tommy Smith's aggregate equaliser and a clearly injured Geoff Strong heading in the decisive goal, much to the disappointment of the huge away support who littered the pitch with beer bottles in protest after a late Bobby Lennox goal was ruled out for an apparent offside.

More recently, it's been the UEFA Cup that has brought the sides together. In 1997 a brilliant late Steve McManaman leveller, after he ran half the length of the field and curled in a left-footed finish, earned the Reds a 2-2 draw in Scotland that sent Roy Evans' side through when the second leg finished scoreless.

And in 2003 another draw in Glasgow – this time one each – was followed by a 2-0 win at Anfield for the Scottish side.

Those games displayed the close bond that has developed between the clubs; a link that was strengthened in the aftermath of the 1989 Hillsborough disaster.

Just a fortnight after that horrific day in Sheffield, it was Celtic who provided the opposition on Liverpool's return to action when we travelled to Glasgow on the last day of the month for a fixture that saw all of the gate receipts go towards the Hillsborough Disaster Appeal.

Of course there was already a strong relationship in place by then as Bill Shankly had been great friends with his Celtic counterpart Jock Stein. There was also the Kenny Dalglish connection, too.

Although he would go on to prove an inspirational player and later manager at Anfield, his decision to move south of the border didn't go down well with all of his former fans as he found out on his first return to Parkhead for Stein's testimonial in August 1978.

"Bob [Paisley] had made me captain for the night, which was very nice of him," Sir Kenny explained.

"I knew the lads might try something, an old trick like stopping in the tunnel so I would run out alone. When we came down the tunnel, I kept looking back to check they were still right behind me. Feeling confident that we would run out together, I came charging out of the tunnel onto the pitch, towards a pipe band, and was immediately engulfed by this nightmare realisation that the boys were still standing back in the tunnel, laughing their heads off. 'Oh no,' I said to myself as the boos rang in my ears.

"Then Terry Mac and Thommo ran onto the pitch, chuckling away, and saying: 'Nice to be home, is it? You must have done this club a right turn. You must have been a right good player for this club.' I suppose it was a compliment in a way; they don't boo bad players."

Kenny, of course, would effortlessly move into a player-manager role at Anfield, sensationally leading the team to the league and cup double in 1986 and staying in charge until 1991. There was also a second stint as manager from January 2011 until May 2012. Over the course of his two reigns he claimed three league titles, two FA Cups and a League Cup.

In between those spells he would take charge of Blackburn Rovers and Newcastle United, and briefly managed Celtic after John Barnes had been sacked; Dalglish leaving the director of football role he had accepted in 1999 to stabilise the club.

Seeing a member of our all conquering side of the late 1970s and early 1980s at the helm of a Glasgow giant wasn't something new. Graeme Souness had become Rangers manager in April 1986 and went on to make them the dominant force in Scottish football before he departed to succeed Dalglish at Anfield.

More recently, another ex-Liverpool boss has taken the reins in Glasgow. Brendan Rodgers became Celtic boss in the summer of 2016, winning the Hoops' fourth league, Scottish Cup and League Cup treble after an unbeaten maiden domestic season and following it up with the same treble again in season 2017/18.

Another League Cup followed in 2018/19, but then Rodgers left for Leicester City and Celtic's aim of making it a 10th Scottish League title in a row was denied by another ex-Red.

Appointed manager of Rangers in 2018 after a period working at Liverpool's Academy, Steven Gerrard led the Ibrox club to the 2020/21 Scottish league title, their first for a decade. Gerrard's Gers went through the entire league season unbeaten and amassed 102 points to finish 25 points clear of their Glasgow rivals with the title wrapped up in March. He left for Aston Villa in November 2021.

84/130

Wing wizards

"HE could go round you, or past you, or even straight through you sometimes!" The astute words of Bob Paisley when asked to discuss the ability of Billy Liddell on the left flank.

The Scottish great was LFC's star man between 1946-60 and for a chunk of that time Paisley operated in a deeper position behind him so he had a close-up view of just how good Liddell was.

With Liddell being so effective it was rumoured that manager George Kay's pre-match instructions usually amounted to: "Give the ball to Billy whenever you can, and he'll win it for us."

The only sad note from Liddell's time at the club was that it coincided with a less successful period when his talent surely deserved much more silverware. By the time Liddell was leaving and supporters were wondering who could possibly replace him a youngster named Ian Callaghan had emerged.

Ironically, local lad 'Cally' had idolised Liddell from the terraces so knew just how difficult his task would be. It was a challenge he proved up to; going on to make a club record 857 appearances.

For a lot of those games he was providing excellent service to the strikers from the wing; most notably when he set up the winning goal for Ian St John during the 1965 FA Cup final.

On the other flank that day was Peter Thompson, another great winger who had impressed Bill Shankly so much during Preston's elimination of the Reds from the cup three years earlier that the manager signed him. A right-footer who played on the left, he had an ability to dance around defenders seemingly as often as he liked.

Callaghan on one side and Thompson on the other provided the perfect balance and a major factor in the success that mid-sixties team enjoyed. Such was their ability to create chances for the strikers that former Everton great Dixie Dean once remarked: "If I could play between Ian Callaghan and Peter Thompson I'd still get my 60 goals a season."

If those two had come into the side through recognisable routes, the man who would succeed them as the superstar on the wing arrived via a more scenic path. Steve Heighway was with non-league Skelmersdale United when he was spotted by Bob Paisley's sons.

"I told our coaches he was the best amateur footballer I'd ever seen," Paisley recalled of the man who debuted in 1970. Lightning quick with perfect balance and the ability to deliver exact crosses or beat his man and go for goal, Heighway was a sensation who would go on to win two European Cups, a quartet of league titles, the FA Cup and two UEFA Cups.

While others such as Craig Johnston enjoyed some moments of brilliance, it wasn't until 1987 and the signing of John Barnes that a true heir to Heighway arrived on the scene.

Again, there was that almost unstoppable combination of perfect balance and sensational speed. The Jamaican born England international also possessed sheer power that allowed him to shrug off opponents or drive forward at ease. A superb goalscorer too, he netted memorable efforts against QPR, Everton and Arsenal amongst others.

If Barnes looked the part physically, Steve McManaman seemed far too slight to deal with the physical force of first division full-backs who were more than content to kick any winger who dared to run at them.

That approach failed to stop the kid from Kirkdale who had grown up supporting Everton. Instead, his close control, dribbling ability and pace made him almost impossible to contain.

Manager Roy Evans would eventually employ a 3-5-2 formation that got the best from McManaman in a free role and he isn't the only winger to have seen his position change during his LFC career.

Liddell was sometimes used as a striker, as was Heighway. Others such as Callaghan and Barnes suffered injuries that meant they had to adapt their game and move into central midfield, but it's as dazzling wingers that Kopites will best remember them.

In a past era, Sadio Mane, Mo Salah and Luis Diaz would have been considered wingers, but in Jürgen Klopp's 4-3-3 system they play as wide forwards with the wingers essentially now full-backs Trent Alexander-Arnold and Andy Robertson.

The pair have now provided over 100 assists between them, highlighting that while the role of traditional wingers may have changed, the number of Liverpool goals created on the flanks remains crucial to the Reds' success.

85/130

Plenty in reserve

BOB Paisley's first title as a team-manager at Anfield? The Central League championship, season 1956/57, not long after he'd retired from playing.

Ditto Roy Evans, who unlike Bob might not have achieved the ultimate top-flight success as senior-side boss (despite his teams playing thrilling football in the mid-1990s) but won the first of seven Central League titles in 1974/75.

As Bill Shankly famously said: "We had the two best teams on Merseyside – Liverpool and Liverpool reserves."

Formed as far back as 1911, the Central League still exists today, albeit as a reserve league primarily for lower-division clubs with six teams contesting the division in season 2021/22 after the 2019/20 campaign was curtailed due to COVID-19 and season 2020/21 cancelled. In its seventies and eighties heyday, though, it was a breeding-ground for younger players looking to break into their respective first teams and learn from old pros into the bargain – and it was competitive.

For Liverpool Football Club, it was also the environment in which Boot Room coaches and potential first-team managers could earn their spurs, not least Evans.

A strong reserve team meant a strong Liverpool, and under Roy the 'second-string' was a mirror-image of the seniors, winning pretty much everything in sight. The results and fixtures pages at the back of the matchday programme would always carry the latest tables and it felt like the Reds reserves, like the Reds first-team, were always on top.

Towards the end of season 1978/79 an April issue of the matchday programme profiled the reserves in detail as they chased down a sixth Central League title success in seven seasons. "This season we have called on more than two dozen players," it revealed, "including established first-teamers at times, but a dozen players or so have been mainstays of the side.

"Goalkeeper Steve Ogrizovic and Brian Kettle have already been featured in the *Anfield Review*. Like Steve, Howard Gayle has been an ever-present and chipped in with eleven goals, while other leading marksmen have been Kevin Sheedy, David Fairclough and Sammy Lee. In fact almost every one of the players featured on these pages has contributed to Liverpool's total of close on 80 goals…and the team's defensive record of having conceded fewer than 30 goals speaks for itself as well."

"Sammy Lee, Alan Harper, Colin Irwin, Kevin Sheedy, Colin Russell, Jeff Ainsworth, Robbie Savage [not that Robbie Savage!], Alex Cribley…players such as these have played their part, with their appearances ranging from more than a dozen to the 30-mark. And in close on a score of games the reserves have kept a clean-sheet – in fact, when they have conceded anything it has usually been only the one goal.

"Trainer Roy Evans refuses to count any chickens before they're hatched, adopting the Liverpool motto of taking each game as it comes. But it is not too much to say that he and his players can be optimistic about bringing the Central League trophy back to Anfield again, for the ninth time in little more than a decade."

Less than three weeks later the matchday programme ran two photos: one of a smiling Roy Evans with a glittering Central League trophy, and another of the reserve team celebrating in the dressing room after beating Leeds United 3-0 to clinch the title.

Among them in the shot is local lad and winger Gayle, who years later told the matchday programme: "Roy helped me immensely through my early years at Liverpool. He was like a father figure to me and when my head dropped he'd always be there to explain things. It helped that he was much younger than the rest of the staff.

"There's always been a learning period for any players at Liverpool, whether big money had been paid for them or they'd come up through the ranks, and it was no different for me. Our reserve side then was full of internationals, all really good players. Stevie Heighway was coming towards the end of his Liverpool career, as was Emlyn Hughes, while Alan Hansen was just starting his.

"Then there were the up-and-coming youngsters like Sammy Lee, Kevin Sheedy, Ronnie Whelan and Ian Rush. This was the standard of players I had to compete with."

86/130

Goalscoring subs

WHEN Geoff Strong headed home an equaliser against West Ham on 15 September 1965, Kopites witnessed an Anfield first. The versatile Strong became the first ever goalscoring substitute for Liverpool Football Club...wearing the number two shirt!

Because subs were such a new development there wasn't a number twelve jersey for Strong to pull on so he had to wear the shirt belonging to the man he replaced – Chris Lawler – and was told to lead the line by Bill Shankly. He responded by netting the equaliser to secure an important point. Liverpool went on to win the First Division title.

Subs were only introduced at the start of that 1965/66 campaign (Shankly didn't even bother naming a sub for four of the opening seven league games) with one change permitted for an injury, although the Reds first ever sub had actually been made exactly 13 months to the day earlier when Phil Chisnall replaced Alf Arrowsmith in the Charity Shield – also against West Ham at Anfield.

It seems incredible now, but it was another two-and-a-half years after Strong's strike until another sub netted again, Bobby Graham nicking a late winner at Leeds, whereas of season 2021/22, with three substitutions from nine options permitted in the Premier League and five from as many as 12 in other competitions, goals from the bench are taken for granted.

Indeed, when Roberto Firmino came on to score in Liverpool's 2-0 win at Arsenal in March 2022 it was the 325th goal scored by a Reds' substitute and those goals have included some of the most crucial, memorable and defining strikes in the club's 130 year history.

David Fairclough was so prolific after coming on from the bench he earned the nickname 'super sub'. The Scouse striker netted a club record 18 goals as a substitute – including arguably the most famous goal ever scored in front of the Kop.

"And Fairclough is onside," cried commentator Gerald Sinstadt as the Reds' number twelve ran clean through in the 1977 European Cup quarter-final second leg against St Etienne with Liverpool needing another goal to progress. "This now could be interesting. Fairclough! Super sub strikes again!" All roads led to Rome – via Zurich – after that.

Goals from substitutes in cup finals have also been vital to Liverpool successes, particularly in six-minute European comebacks as Jimmy Case and Vladimir Smicer can testify.

The Reds were 2-0 down at Anfield to Bruges in the first leg of the 1976 UEFA Cup final only to turn the tie on its head with three goals in six minutes, the second coming from substitute Case. Twenty nine years later something similar happened in the Champions League final when three goals in six minutes wiped out AC Milan's 3-0 half-time lead with substitute Vladimir Smicer firing in the second goal.

It's also worth noting that Liverpool's three penalty shoot-out scorers in the Ataturk Stadium – Didi Hamann, Djibril Cisse and Smicer – were the three substitutes brought on by Rafa Benitez that night and when the Reds subsequently took on CSKA Moscow in the Super Cup final in Monaco three months later it was again Cisse who came from the bench to net twice, helping turn a 1-0 deficit into a 3-1 victory.

The goalscoring contributions made by subs Florent Sinama-Pongolle and Neil Mellor in Liverpool's famous Champions League comeback win against Olympiacos at Anfield in 2004 shouldn't be understated either as without their efforts, and Steven Gerrard's stunning game-clincher, there never would've been Istanbul or that Super Cup final.

Ian Rush proved to be a cup final winner having been brought on in the 1989 all-Merseyside FA Cup final at Wembley. Rushie put Kenny Dalglish's men 2-1 up in extra-time after John Aldridge and Stuart McCall had exchanged goals and although Everton's Scottish midfielder struck a second equaliser it was that man Rush again who produced a winner. It was the first time Rush has scored as a substitute since his first Liverpool goal against Oulu Palloseura in 1981, although that was largely due to the fact that he was usually in the starting XI.

Only two Liverpool subs have scored hat-tricks – Steve Staunton against Wigan Athletic in 1989 and Steven Gerrard against Napoli in 2010 – while only five first-half goals have ever been scored by Reds' substitutes with Jordon Ibe becoming the only man to come off the bench and net in the opening 45 minutes of an away match when he notched a League Cup semi-final first leg winner at Stoke in 2016.

Ryan Babel became the next substitute after Fairclough to score more than 10 Liverpool goals, his tally of 12 including a late one-on-one finish against Arsenal in the 2008 Champions League quarter-final at Anfield, while Daniel Sturridge's 13 goals from the bench include the only league goal by an LFC sub in a Merseyside derby at Goodison Park, an 89th minute equaliser in a 3-3 draw in 2013.

Divock Origi came on to score against Everton in a 3-1 Anfield victory in April 2017 and famously got the only goal against the Blues in the 96th minute at Anfield in December 2019. Origi netted 12 goals from the bench, including in the 2019 Champions League final against Spurs, while Gini Wijnaldum's double after coming off the bench against Barcelona in the semi-final was huge in Liverpool reaching Madrid.

As of May 2022, 82 goals have been scored by subs under Jürgen Klopp's management with Roberto Firmino notching 12 of them including late winners at home to Paris St Germain in the Champions League and in the FIFA Club World Cup semi-final in Qatar against CF Monterrey in 2019.

Xherdan Shaqiri's most memorable goalscoring contribution in a red shirt came in December 2018 when he came off the bench to net twice in a 3-1 Anfield success against Manchester United, while both Takumi Minamino (against Arsenal in the FA Community Shield) and Harvey Elliott (against Cardiff City in the FA Cup) got their first Liverpool goals as substitutes.

It just goes to show that just because a player begins a game on the bench doesn't mean he can't end it as the hero, while you might be surprised to learn that Liverpool have not lost a Premier League game at Anfield in which a Reds substitute has scored since December 2001. Long may it continue!

87/130

The famous Kopites

THERE was an extra-special Kopite in the crowd on the night Liverpool played Bournemouth at Anfield on Wednesday 5 April 2017: none other than Sir Kenny Dalglish.

The Reds legend watched the first half from behind the goal at the famous end, chatting with fans and observing a minute's applause in memory of Hillsborough (ahead of the 28th anniversary) before heading for the Main Stand directors' box after the break.

It was a long-held dream for Kenny, who revealed in his 2013 book *My Life*: "The thing about the Kop is that you wanted to be in there, but you couldn't because you were playing.

"I know Bill Shankly once stood on the Kop when he retired. Who knows? I'd like to do it anonymously. I wouldn't want to do it with a fanfare or for any PR or publicity. I would just love to be in there with the fans, who have always chanted my name."

Many a local-born player was also an erstwhile Kopite – not least Phil Thompson, skipper of the side from 1979 to 1981. When the centre-half ran out onto the pitch before each home game he'd always wave to his brother Owen, who would be standing on the

Kop in the same spot. And even Everton legend Peter Reid was brought up a staunch Red: "I used to take a little stool in the Kop and stand on that; the atmosphere would be white hot."

While LFC has plenty of celebrity fans – *James Bond* actor Daniel Craig, Hollywood star Samuel L Jackson, Danish tennis player Caroline Wozniacki, *Neighbours* star Alan Fletcher (aka Dr Karl Kennedy) and singer Lana Del Rey, to name but a few – it's another thing to have stood or sat on the Kop in person to watch the Reds play.

Comedian John Bishop did so – despite a momentary flirtation with Everton after "the Bluenoses of the family" attempted to brainwash him when he was six! "I don't think you just start supporting Liverpool, it's given to you," he revealed. "When you're born, your dad says: 'Right, that's it!'"

Bishop was born a few miles from Anfield in 1966, three months after England had won the World Cup. So it's no great shock that his first hero was one of the Liverpool FC players in Alf Ramsey's squad. "I liked Ian Callaghan. Most of the time I liked people I was told to like. But Callaghan transcended that period when my dad made me watch him to the point where I chose to watch him.

"Then like a lot of people of my generation I fell in love with Kevin Keegan. Then it was Kenny. In fact anyone beginning with a 'K'! Then at school I always wanted to be Graeme Souness. He always seemed to be the one who could grab hold of the game and lift the team before Kenny would work some magic."

Bishop, in turn, isn't the only Scouse funnyman who's been on the Kop. The terrace was captured in its mid-1960s heyday by TV cameras for the BBC current-affairs show *Panorama* – and in mid-shot as the fans sing along to a Cilla Black hit is a young, soon-to-be stand-up star Stan Boardman.

Around the same time, Ricky Tomlinson was another regular. The actor, who would become a household name for his role in

The Royle Family, said: "I graduated from the old Boys' Pen to the Kop in the early 1960s and I still remember Bill Shankly walking up to the Kop [after the Reds had just clinched another title] and picking up a fan's scarf."

From today's music world there's young singer-songwriter Louis Berry, who told the BBC2 programme *The Premier League Show*: "Most musicians dream of playing at Glastonbury, but there's only one better place if you're a football fan to hear your music – and that place for me is Anfield."

Rock royalty Elvis Costello had "my place on the Kop just behind the goal in the early 1970s, the atmosphere then was something else," and the late DJ John Peel caught the bug while stationed at Anglesey for his national service in the late 50s, riding to Anfield and the Kop on his motorbike.

Austin Powers star Mike Myers, meanwhile, finally made the pilgrimage in the early nineties just before the standing Kop was demolished (his parents were originally from the Liverpool suburb of Old Swan); while West Indian cricketing legend Viv Richards once stood there for a Liverpool-Manchester United game and revealed: "I was a fan on that day and I remain a devoted follower."

88/130

Summer of love

THE city of Liverpool is used to welcoming foreign football fans in their hundreds and often thousands. But it's only rarely that Anfield has played host to an entire stadium full of non-Reds fans. That's how it was, four times over, in the summer of 1996 when 'football came home'.

England's grey change-strip for Euro 96 feels most synonymous with Paul Gascoigne, Gareth Southgate and a semi-final defeat by Germany when Gazza was agonisingly close to diverting home a low cross during extra-time for what would've been a golden-goal winner for a side containing LFC's Steve McManaman, before Southgate missed the decisive spot-kick in the ensuing shoot-out.

Over those memorable few weeks Liverpool FC's home played its part. The only previous international tournament to take place in England had been the 1966 World Cup finals, with Goodison Park picked as a venue for games.

Three decades on, it was Anfield's turn to welcome a host of countries, having already staged a play-off between the Netherlands and the Republic of Ireland for the final place in the tournament. That December 1995 night, backed by huge travelling support, Jack Charlton's Eire team were undone by the Dutch, with Patrick Kluivert scoring in each half to seal a 2-0 victory.

Three Group C fixtures would take place in front of the Kop: Italy v Russia, Italy v Czech Republic and Czech Republic v Russia.

The action began on Tuesday 11 June with a 4.30pm kick-off for the Italians and Russians. The Azzurri, featuring a 27-year-old Paolo Maldini who would play against the Reds in two Champions League finals a decade later, edged the encounter thanks to a double from Pierluigi Casiraghi. Two years later a Casiraghi goal for Chelsea at the Anfield Road end would result in Phil Babb unforgettably – and painfully – colliding with a post.

Later that same week it was the Italians again on L4 soil, this time against Czech opponents who included Patrik Berger and Vladimir Smicer among their squad. Borussia Dortmund's Berger, who'd registered eight goals in a dozen internationals, was one to watch, with Ivo Viktor, the Czech assistant-manager, declaring: "I am sure he will be up to the task in England. He has a super temperament and an extraordinary range of skills. Patrik is the sort of richly talented player who comes along extremely rarely."

On this occasion, though, it was Pavel Nedved who caught the eye, opening the scoring after five minutes as his side went on to register a 2-1 triumph over an Italy side reduced to 10 men when defender Luigi Apolloni was red-carded.

There was more excitement to come in the last group fixture, Russia against the Czechs. Two goals to the good inside 19 minutes, Berger and co then found themselves trailing 3-2 and facing elimination with the final whistle in sight. That was until Smicer came off the bench to net a late equaliser, 3-3, which ensured progress (and ultimately a place in the final where they lost to Germany despite Berger opening the scoring). It was third-place Italy who went home early.

With the opening-round formalities completed, Anfield had one more fixture to fulfil, a quarter-final clash between the winners of Group B and runners up in Group A: France v Netherlands.

A subsequent 0-0 draw, on the same day that England overcame Spain on penalties at Wembley, may have lacked the previous levels of excitement at Anfield, yet there was the drama of a shoot-out to decide which team reached the last four. It would be the French who held their nerve best to emerge 5-4 victors, Dutch midfielder Clarence Seedorf the only player to miss.

That shoot-out victory for a team containing greats such as Marcel Desailly, Zinedine Zidane and Lilian Thuram extended their unbeaten run to an impressive 27 outings, a sequence that would only be halted by the Czechs in another penalty shoot-out in the semi-final. Even so, Les Bleus had shown enough to make their World Cup success on home soil two years later far from a surprise.

89/130

One direction

AHEAD of season 2020/21 there was a fond farewell in the Liverpool FC boardroom as Peter Moore stepped down from his role as chief-executive officer after a successful spell overseeing the club's off-pitch business operations. Succeeding him was Billy Hogan, previously LFC's managing director and chief commercial officer, supported by a strong, experienced leadership team.

Back in the summer of 2017, local-born Moore had joined principal owner John Henry, chairman Tom Werner plus fellow directors Michael Gordon, Mike Egan, Sir Kenny Dalglish MBE and Andy Hughes on the Reds board, and in a subsequent interview with the matchday programme his lifelong passion was abundantly clear – not least when it came to watching 12:30pm kick-offs live from his previous home on America's west coast!

"I had a great room that was a shrine to Liverpool," he revealed, "and my regimen would be: set my alarm for 3:45am; put my [Liverpool] shirt on; and I had to watch it on my own. Seriously. It's such an intense experience for me. And so I would make sure that I was there, watching Twitter in real-time so I was getting the feedback from the fans here.

"I soon realised that Twitter was 30 seconds ahead of the American broadcast – enough to see that somebody had just scored before it happened on the TV. That's the worst thing in the world! Great if we scored, but not so good when it was the opposition.

"So that was my ritual in San Francisco when I was a hardcore, five-and-a-half-thousand-miles-away Liverpool fan. People would ask why I didn't record the game if it was at 4am. I'd say: 'No – they need me'. I can't watch a recorded game because there's nothing I can do to change the outcome. It's this weird thing that a lot of football fans have. If I'm there and it's real-time when we're in trouble, I get closer to the television!"

Upon his decision to return to the US with wife Debbie, he paid tribute to his fellow directors and said: "I've loved every minute… To think we have won the UEFA Champions League, FIFA Club World Cup and now the Premier League title during my time here is way beyond my dreams. It's been a phenomenal achievement by the manager, players and staff. The team fully deserves the plaudits and recognition – and the memories I will cherish forever."

An abiding love for LFC tends to characterise those who have served the club in positions 'upstairs' over the years. Peter Beckett Robinson (known to his peers as 'PBR'), an Anfield administrative stalwart for over three decades as first club secretary then chief executive between 1965 and 2000, always ensured that Liverpool FC's activities ran as smoothly off the pitch as on it.

It was with a heavy heart that the club announced his passing in January 2022.

"Peter Robinson was the focal point in the development of Liverpool FC," tweeted Sir Kenny Dalglish on the day that one of Anfield's longest and finest servants passed away. "He made decisions that shaped the club and we simply wouldn't have enjoyed as many successes without his massive influence. PBR – thank you for everything you've done for me, you'll be sorely missed."

Robinson's successor in 1998 was Rick Parry, who'd played a major role in the formation of the Premier League and oversaw the accumulation of ten major trophies as well as the development of the Academy in Kirkby – a project first instigated by his predecessor.

The club's first post-war chairman, WH McConnell JP, was previously a caterer who ran a string of dockside cafes before joining the board in 1933. It was 'Billy Mac' who proposed that the team escape the austerity of food-rationed Britain for a tour of North America in the summer of 1946; by the end of the following season they'd won the title.

In the fifties and sixties, Thomas Valentine ('TV' for short) Williams was the chairman who put Liverpool FC on the road to the most dominant spell of success in its history. A city cotton-broker and proud Liverpudlian, he instigated the purchase of what became the Melwood training ground and appointed Bill Shankly as manager in 1959. 'TV' became the club's second President, between 1965-1975.

Sir John Smith CBE, JP assumed the chairman's role in 1973 and worked tirelessly to ensure the highest standards were maintained. He was a firm believer in the continuity of promoting from within, appointing first Bob Paisley then Joe Fagan and then Kenny Dalglish as manager. He also brokered a groundbreaking shirt sponsorship deal with Hitachi in 1979 and worked to safeguard the club's reputation after Heysel and Hillsborough.

The nineties saw Noel White succeeded as chairman by David

Moores, nephew of Sir John Moores, creator of the Littlewoods Organisation. Sir John, who had long maintained a keen interest in both of the city's football clubs, was chairman of Everton FC in the 1960s and early 70s and also a shareholder at Liverpool FC. It was he who recommended Eric Sawyer to the Anfield board in the early sixties, and it was Sawyer who persuaded LFC (and a hesitant TV Williams) to invest in Shankly's ambitious plans.

It was the destiny of David Moores to preside over a period of change and turbulence that resulted in the sale of the club to owner/investors that ultimately proved short-lived and unsatisfactory. However, regardless of the club's fortunes before it was acquired and stabilised by Fenway Sports Group, his love for the Reds was never in doubt.

Like Peter Moore he'd stood on the Kop as a kid, and in the matchday programme at the start of season 2001/02 – following the cup treble under manager Gerard Houllier – he paid his own tribute to the fans.

"Amid all the rightful and richly deserved praise for team, manager and backroom staff, I feel one vital ingredient in our success has been somewhat overlooked: our support has been absolutely tremendous.

"Commentators used to say the Liverpool support was worth a goal start. I certainly thought that was the case last year. There were so many great games and occasions it's difficult to single out individual favourites [but] I thought our supporters saved their best until the finals.

"That [FA Cup] final against Arsenal really should've been over and out of reach, but our fans – like the team they adore – would not give in. Wave after wave of sound roared the boys on and I do believe our support was worth at least a goal to us. And then that unforgettable evening in Dortmund.

"What I would like to say is thank you, sincerely. Your unstinting

Coming home

OF the many amazing photographs taken when the Reds returned with the UEFA Champions League trophy on Sunday 2 June 2019, one in particular stands out.

Taken from the top of one of the newer buildings in Liverpool ONE overlooking the Strand, it shows the sunshine glinting on the waters of Salthouse Dock, tall ships moored to the left, the Museum of Liverpool and the River Mersey in the background and a red sea of supporters all along the Dock Road (as it's still often known).

Through the drifting pales of rose-coloured smoke from countless flares you can just make out an open-top bus of players, coaches and officials from LFC who can hardly believe their eyes.

The night before, when crowds at home came out in force following the 2-0 win over Tottenham Hotspur in the final over in Madrid, one adopted Scouser tweeted: "I might not be a Liverpool FC fan, but the city's tendency to go completely mad is a big reason I've called it home for 23 years. Don't go changing..."

As if we would... Although actually, to be geographically pedantic, we did. Previously the focal point for Liverpool's victorious homecomings had been elsewhere in the city: St George's Hall when 'Ole Big Ears' had last been brought back in 2005, and the Town Hall when the Reds won the FA Cup for the very first time in 1965.

On that momentous day in May all those years ago, after Bill Shankly's boys had beaten Don Revie's Leeds United 2-1 after extra-time at Wembley, the scenes had to be seen to be believed. The *Echo* newspaper reported: "Skipper Ron Yeats and the team were greeted by roars of 'Liverpool! Liverpool! Liverpool!' from 50,000 throats in the vicinity of Lime Street station alone, and St George's Plateau was a solid mass of people. One senior police officer said: 'This makes The Beatles' reception look like a vicarage tea party!'"

Black-and-white footage showed fans on almost every rooftop as the open-top bus finally reached Castle Street before Yeats raised the famous old trophy aloft from the balcony of the Town Hall.

But it was FA Cup final heartache – and on both occasions following defeat to Arsenal – which best seemed to illustrate the love and unswerving loyalty of Kopites. After the 2-0 loss to the Gunners at Wembley in 1950, the *Echo* reported: "One hundred thousand people showed the team that, far from being forgotten, their effort was thought worthy of this reward… This will go down in Liverpool FC history because, despite all they say about the fickleness of the football public, 'they still cared'…"

In 1971 the score was 2-1 to Arsenal after extra-time, but when the Reds returned empty-handed the next day it was to a heroes' welcome once more. Photographers took messianic shots of Shankly on the steps of St George's Plateau as the Liverpool manager proclaimed: "Yesterday at Wembley we lost, but you the people have won everything."

Hushing the crowd to absolute silence, Shankly added: "Since I came here to Liverpool, and to Anfield, I have drummed it into our players time and again that they are privileged to play for you.

And if they didn't believe me, they believe me now." Spine-tingling stuff.

Two years later, as his team paraded the 1972/73 league and UEFA Cup trophies, Shanks told the massed ranks: "If there is any doubt you are the greatest fans in the world, this is the day to prove it. We have won something for you and that is all we are interested in – winning for you. The reason we have won is because you believe and we believe."

Only a European Cup triumph could top what had gone on before, and of course it happened for the first time in 1977. By then Bob Paisley was in charge and the players, coaching staff and civic figures celebrated from the balcony of Picton Library, adjacent to St George's Hall.

The *Daily Post* described it as such: "Emlyn Hughes still grinning, Terry McDermott clowning, Joey Jones singing and Tommy Smith compering, as each player was introduced to his own personal deafening roar. [Then] the cry 'Shankly! Shankly!' went up and there was the Grand Old Man himself, fist clenched, face proud but impassive, hailed witness to the culmination of his carried-on dreams."

The Eighties was the era of more elaborate open-top bus tours from the airport and Anfield then into the city centre. During the long parade following the 1981 European Cup win, captain Phil Thompson had to leave the bus with his wife to use the toilet of a random house en route. "When we came back out of the house the bus was miles away," he recalled. "So I stood in the road and flagged down an ice-cream van. The door was shut and we had to climb through the hatch!"

Season 1985/86 saw Liverpool pip Everton to the domestic double, with both teams embarking on a circular route around the city the day after the FA Cup final at Wembley. The *Daily Post* felt "the agreement to come home side-by-side was a gesture badly needed by a game and city bruised in the last year [by Heysel]."

The paper continued: "Touchdown in Liverpool was accompanied by the Royal Liverpool Philharmonic Orchestra, assembled inside a ring of red and blue streamers on the airport apron, and bursting into a medley of *Here We Go* and *You'll Never Walk Alone.*

"There was a quick civic reception in the airport's new terminal before each squad boarded its own bus ready for an 18-mile tour laughingly scheduled to take two hours. More than 20 police motorcyclists escorted the motorcade into Speke Hall Avenue. Bang on cue, the heavens opened, but heavy rain was not going to drive the teams off the top decks. Liverpool players began a chorus of *Singin' In The Rain.*

"An ecstatic crowd drummed up a deafening roar. There was no room left on the pavements. They climbed onto phone boxes and bus shelters. They stood on parked cars. They set off burglar alarms as they scrambled onto factory and house roofs. No traffic light, signpost or tree stood alone.

"Buses stopped so driver and passengers alike could yell out of the windows. The crowds at Scotland Road took action when they decided the motorcade was going too fast: they swarmed in front of the Liverpool bus and brought it to a halt. Reds manager Kenny Dalglish said: "It was unbelievable, the best homecoming I have ever seen. There were thousands of Evertonians around, too. It was nice."

The FA Cup was paraded again in 1992 and in 2001 there was the treble tour with tens of thousands lining the route to the Strand to see Sami Hyypia, Robbie Fowler, Danny Murphy, Sander Westerveld and co show off the UEFA Cup, FA Cup and League Cup. Then came 2005.

Around three-quarters-of-a-million people were thought to have welcomed the Reds back from Istanbul after the dramatic victory over AC Milan in the Champions League final, with 300,000 of them gathered around St George's Hall.

Earlier, the *Echo* was there when the LFC plane landed at John Lennon Airport: "Captain Steven Gerrard held aloft the trophy with manager Rafael Benitez. The pair were dressed in regulation tracksuit trousers and red fleeces, with Gerrard wearing a pair of flip-flops. Both wore broad grins as they descended the aircraft steps clutching the trophy between them. Staff climbed on fire engines and baggage trucks to get a better view of their heroes."

Following the scenes in the city centre, Gerrard echoed Dalglish's sentiments from two decades earlier, calling it "unbelievable. None of the players imagined there would be so many people there. I'd been sitting on the plane with my medal and thinking 'life can't get any better than this'. And then you saw those fans everywhere."

Many of those hailing their heroes along the Strand in 2019 hadn't been born back in 2005. Some had been here before – a few right back to the days of Shankly – but for thousands lining the route it was the first time they'd seen the trophy and perhaps even Jürgen Klopp and his players 'in the flesh'.

Goal hero Divock Origi told LFCTV: "Liverpool is celebrating today and we can feel it. It means a lot to the people – I can see it in their eyes and in their reaction."

Defender Virgil van Dijk declared it "unbelievable, already past my expectations. I'm very proud to be sitting on this coach and I'm just taking everything in and enjoying every bit of it with all of these fans."

The boss was in his element. Having fulfilled his promise in 2015 to bring a major trophy to Anfield within four years of his appointment, he sang along with the crowds and was filmed playfully counting to six on his fingers. What did he make of the day?

"I cannot really describe it because I cried a little bit as well because it's so overwhelming what the people are doing. When you have a direct-eye contact and you see how much it means to them, that's touching, so intense. Today – wow! It's crazy."

At a little past 7pm, and with the bus convoy's speaker-system playing *You'll Never Walk Alone*, fireworks were set off from one of the Royal Liver Building's towers as red confetti filled the air. Klopp duly made his way to the front of the bus and raised the cup aloft. A new generation of fans now had their own homecoming parade to cherish and in May 2022 those Kopites lined the streets again to celebrate Liverpool's Carabao Cup and FA Cup successes.

91/130

Bill's gates

IT was all-change at Anfield when the expanded Main Stand was completed in 2016. The areas around the stadium underwent major redevelopment with a couple of famous landmarks relocated in the process.

The Hillsborough Memorial is now on 97 Avenue, which links the Stanley Park end of the stadium to Paisley Square, a space named after the most successful English football manager in history. The three European Cups Bob Paisley won features in the decorative ironwork of the nearby Gateway named in his honour and that was unveiled in 1999 by his wife Jessie. You can read more about two new statues that have been installed elsewhere in this book.

At the corner of the Sir Kenny Dalglish and Anfield Road Stand, which is now also undergoing an expansion, stand the magnificent – and similarly repositioned – Shankly Gates. They were officially opened in August 1982 by Bill's widow Nessie accompanied by their grandchildren plus Liverpool FC chairman John Smith, manager Bob Paisley and skipper Graeme Souness.

"Mrs Shankly was keen for a memorial which showed Bill's affiliation with the supporters," club secretary Peter Robinson told a subsequent matchday programme. "It is not thought a similar honour exists in football. A comparison would be the Grace Gates at Lord's in honour of WG Grace."

There in spirit that day was Ken Hall, the man who'd designed and built the gates – which weigh more than three tons – from his foundry in Somerset.

Ken, a lifelong Liverpool fan, kept his original blueprint for the design as well as some old snaps of the gates being offloaded by crane from the lorry which had transported them 200 miles north to Anfield. From commission to completion, between the end of one football season and start of another, the job had taken ten hectic summer weeks.

"I was 25 at the time and I'd been a Liverpool fan for years, since the Keegan and Toshack era of the early 70s," he later recalled. "It was my father who originally saw the advert in the paper for a Shankly memorial. We rang up and eventually got through to Peter Robinson who gave us the number of the architects [Mather & Nutter].

"They gave us the brief and our design was one of ten which were submitted. The story goes that they were all laid out on a table in front of the selection committee which included Mrs Shankly, who chose ours. There was nothing to touch it, she said. I remember when we got the phone call my dad said I went as white as a sheet – we were in shock!"

On 13 August 1982 the *Somerset Standard* newspaper reported how County Forge had "gained the contract in the face of tough opposition from all over the country" and approached a master blacksmith, Chris Brooks from Melksham in neighbouring Wiltshire, to assist with the most technical and elaborate elements of the job.

The paper remarked upon the "astounding" detail of the ironwork with the most ornate part, the overthrow, sitting atop and apart from the 14ft x 16ft gates. It always gleams in the sunshine. Above the legend 'YOU'LL NEVER WALK ALONE' and embellished with swirling gold acanthus leaves is to all intents and purposes the Shankly heraldic device: the white cross of St Andrew and a green-stalked thistle with a bluish-purple flowerhead, together denoting Bill's Scottish roots, and a crest bearing a blood-red Liver Bird to symbolise his sustained passion.

"Originally the club were only thinking about a set of gates, but we came up with the idea of the overthrow and they liked it," said Ken. "We both had apprentices so there were four of us working on it in the end. Chris did the leafwork on the overthrow and I forged the gates, which we had to make one at a time, laid flat on top of each other like a big table because my workshop was quite small."

The overthrow was coated with primer but not painted until the entire structure was loaded by crane onto the lorry which took it to Anfield before the start of the 1982/83 season. Less than 12 months after Bill's death aged 67, Nessie unlocked the gates.

Today you can still make out, at waist-height next to the central deadlock, a small brass panel engraved with the words 'SHANKLY GATES DESIGNED & MANUFACTURED BY COUNTY FORGE 1982' and followed by an old telephone number with an obsolete area code.

"Enthusiasm got us through it," admitted Ken. "We were shattered at the end but always confident about completing the gates on time. The only worry was about getting them to fit. We were nervous but the installation was perfect – just 3mm out on one of the hinges.

"I've only been back to Anfield twice since. The last time, we were in a taxi heading for the ground and when we told the driver he wouldn't charge us for the fare. I've still got an enamel brooch of a Liver Bird that was given to me by another chap who came down [to the forge] when we were still making the gates, just to be photographed next to them. He told me his grandfather had given it to him. I'd love to return it to him some day."

The key to the Shankly Gates went on display in Liverpool city centre after being placed in a glass case and buried in the floor of the lobby of the Shankly Hotel. Opened in 2015, Bill's grandson Chris Carline is the hotel director.

92/130

The late late show

DURING the Premier League era, Kenny Dalglish, in his role of team manager, has had cause to celebrate two last-minute Liverpool FC winners in fixtures against Blackburn Rovers.

In 2011, Dalglish was grinning broadly after Andy Carroll popped up with a thumping header in the final throes of a game at Ewood Park to give his side a 3-2 win in an incident-packed encounter.

Back in May 1995, he was punching the air on the final day of the season when Jamie Redknapp slotted home a free-kick at

Anfield to give LFC a 2-1 win against title-chasing Blackburn. Only thing is, Kenny was in charge of Rovers at the time. Had he lost the plot? Did his Liverpool links run so deep that he couldn't bring himself not to celebrate a last-minute winner scored by the Reds? As it turned out, Manchester United's failure to win at West Ham United that afternoon meant Rovers' defeat was immaterial. Blackburn were champions and so, soon after the final whistle, Kenny was able to parade the Premier League trophy around the Anfield turf with Kopites lapping up his success.

There's simply nothing quite like the buzz of a last-minute winner. Think back to the week before Christmas 2016 and Sadio Mane pouncing to give the Reds a derby victory at Goodison Park with virtually the last kick of the match. What a moment!

Since the advent of the Premier League era in 1992, Liverpool have scored more last-minute winners than any other team (Divock Origi's winner at Wolves in December 2021 was the 39th such goal) and the very first of those came at the expense of the Blues too, in the first Anfield derby played under the Premier League banner.

Ronny Rosenthal was the man who broke Everton hearts that afternoon, 14 minutes after coming on as a substitute to replace boyhood Blue Steve McManaman. To the delight of the majority among a raucous crowd of 44,619, the Israeli forward found a way past goalkeeper Neville Southall with time almost up following good work from John Barnes and Ian Rush.

No Red will forget Gary McAllister's extraordinary free-kick that gave Gerard Houllier's Reds a 3-2 victory at Goodison Park on Easter Monday 2001, while the 2007/08 season also saw Liverpool claim local bragging rights in their neighbours' back yard. The pressure was piled on forward Dirk Kuyt, who was given the chance to win it from the penalty spot after Phil Neville had been sent-off for producing a spectacular save to tip away substitute Lucas' goalbound effort.

Kuyt, who had beaten Blues keeper Tim Howard from 12-yards earlier in the game, kept his nerve to secure a memorable 2-1 victory for Rafael Benitez's team.

Andy Barlow created an unwanted record when he became the first non-Liverpool player to settle a game in the final minute by putting through his own goal in the dying seconds of the Reds' league clash with Oldham Athletic in October 1993.

We say first and not only because future Red Steven Caulker, who had a brief loan spell in 2016, also matched Barlow's feat by scoring the winning goal in a crazy finish to Liverpool's 3-2 victory at QPR in October 2014 while in the Hoops. Three goals were scored in added time with two of them being 'oggys' as Reds' skipper Steven Gerrard also deflected an Eduardo Vargas effort beyond Simon Mignolet before Caulker's decisive intervention.

They say lightning doesn't strike twice. The statistics would beg to differ. Take Liverpool v Newcastle United games at Anfield in the mid-1990s for instance. The Kop was bouncing when Stan Collymore scored a dramatic last-minute winner in April 1996. When the teams met again the following March, a repeat didn't look on the cards as Roy Evans' Reds raced into a 3-0 half-time lead. By the 88th minute, however, Newcastle, now managed by Dalglish, had fought their way back to level the scores at 3-3. Cometh the hour-and-a-half, cometh Robbie Fowler. Cue scenes of mayhem inside Anfield.

Less feted but just as satisfying were home games against Chelsea in 2002 and 2003 which both resulted in 1-0 wins which saw the Reds claim the three points with the final kick. In March 2002, Vladimir Smicer smashed a spectacular volley past Carlo Cudicini to put Liverpool top of the table and fuel expectations among Reds supporters.

Just seven months later, Liverpool repeated the dose with Michael Owen's predatory instincts helping him to be first on the scene to tap home the rebound after Cudicini had pushed Emile Heskey's left-footed drive onto the post.

Chelsea's London rivals Arsenal have also been on the wrong end of some late Liverpool interventions during the past quarter-of-a-century.

Robbie Fowler was the man who had proved the Gunners' undoing at Anfield early in the 1994/95 campaign with a blink-and-you've-missed-it hat-trick. So the North Londoners could be forgiven for being sick of the sight of Fowler when he won the corresponding fixture at Highbury the following April – his last-gasp shot defeating keeper David Seaman.

In November 2004, Anfield was the venue for the Gunners' late woes. The game seemed to be heading for a draw after Patrick Vieira had cancelled out Xabi Alonso's opener, but then a young Liverpool striker made a name for himself. Neil Mellor, handed a start in attack, latched on to Harry Kewell's late flick-on before unleashing a venomous shot beyond the despairing dive of Jens Lehmann to secure a memorable 2-1 victory.

Legendary Liverpool captain Steven Gerrard was responsible for four 90th minute winners in the Premier League – more than any other Red.

The first gave his team a 2-1 victory over Charlton Athletic in April 2003, the Reds having trailed entering the final five minutes. In typically all-action style, he burst into the penalty area and skipped between two tackles before lashing a low drive past goalkeeper Dean Kiely.

His next late show came on Boxing Day 2007 and secured another 2-1 win, this time against Derby County at Pride Park.

In the first Anfield league game of the following season, he capped an all-Scouse fightback against Middlesbrough. Going into the final five minutes, the visitors led 1-0 through a Mido goal before Jamie Carragher produced an equaliser. Then, in the closing seconds, the ball dropped to Gerrard just outside the penalty area at the Kop end. You know the rest.

His final winning intervention came at Fulham in the 2013/14 campaign to keep the Reds on course for a tilt at the Premier League title.

The fixture at Craven Cottage was locked at 2-2 when home defender Sascha Riether brought down Daniel Sturridge in the area. Gerrard took responsibility from the penalty spot and slotted his effort past keeper David Stockdale to the delight of the away fans in the Putney End of the ground.

The 2008/09 season produced the Reds' biggest tally of late winning goals with four – meaning eight points were secured in those final seconds, testament to the way Rafael Benitez's side refused to give anything up.

That Gerrard winner against Middlesbrough preceded three away days the travelling Kop won't soon forget.

First up came a 3-2 success at Manchester City with Dirk Kuyt sweeping in the winner to complete a rousing second-half comeback after Liverpool had trailed 2-0 at the half-time interval.

In February 2009, Fernando Torres headed home in the dying embers of a game against Portsmouth at Fratton Park to give the Reds another 3-2 victory.

Then in early April, Yossi Benayoun took Benitez's team to the top of the table when he made the most of finding himself in space late on by turning and re-directing the ball past Fulham keeper Mark Schwarzer.

Other Reds to savour that feeling of coming up with the all-important moment in the 90th-minute of Premier League action include: Ian Rush v Man City (1993/94), Steve McManaman v Barnsley (97/98), Sami Hyypia v Wolves (2003/04), Milan Baros v Crystal Palace (2004/05), Fernando Torres v Aston Villa (2009/10), Joe Cole v Bolton Wanderers (2010/11), Adam Lallana v Norwich City (2015/16), Christian Benteke v Crystal Palace (2015/16), Ragnar Klavan v Burnley (2017/18), Origi v Everton (2018/19), James Milner v Leicester (2019/20), Mane v Aston Villa (2019/20), Roberto Firmino v Spurs (2020/21) and Trent Alexander-Arnold v Aston Villa (2020/21).

Then, in May 2021 at The Hawthorns, came Liverpool's most incredible, most ridiculous, most memorable last minute Premier League winner yet...

93/130

Klopp's game changers

"SOMETIMES there are things you can't explain," was how Alisson Becker attempted to sum up his stunning 95th minute winner away at West Brom in May 2021.

The goal was crucial in the Reds' attempts to secure a top-four place and Champions League qualification at the end of an injury-hit season played behind closed doors, but meant even more to the Brazilian goalkeeper after the tragic death of his father just a few months earlier.

Not only was the headed effort past Sam Johnstone important and the first occasion a 'keeper had ever scored for Liverpool FC, it was also of an extremely high quality.

"It was an unbelievable header, I've never seen anything like that, good technique!" said Jürgen Klopp.

Such a feat may have surprised some people. But perhaps it shouldn't have been a massive shock as 'Ali' – as his teammates refer to him – has been a crucial contributor ever since arriving at the club.

Time and time again he has produced vital match-winning moments like the one at The Hawthorns, albeit at the other end of the field.

Think of the closing seconds of the must-win game against Napoli in the 2018/19 Champions League group stages. When Arkadiusz Milik found the ball at his feet six yards from the net he must have been certain he would score. Instead, Alisson spread his limbs to block the effort, earning a 1-0 victory which was enough to progress. Liverpool eventually went on to lift the trophy. "I have no clue how he made that save," Klopp later remarked with admiration while at the end of the 2018/19 season Alisson ranked it as his favourite save of his career so far.

If such big stops aren't enough there are the one-on-ones where he dominates despite opponents seeming to have the advantage. And then there is his ability to cover the whole area behind the defence to allow them to regularly maintain a high line.

Going the other way, his ability to find a team-mate with a throw-out or pass is often pinpoint accurate; as assists for Mo Salah against Manchester United in 2019/20 and Norwich City in 2021/22 demonstrate perfectly.

Really, there isn't any aspect of the goalkeeping job he can't perform to perfection and that's why LFC were so keen to acquire his services from Roma in the summer of 2018.

One of the decisive factors in Alisson's decision to move to Merseyside must have been the knowledge that he'd be playing with Virgil van Dijk leading the defence in front of him.

At that stage the Dutch centre-back had only been a Red for six months after joining from Southampton in January 2018, but had slotted in so effectively that it felt like he'd been there much, much longer.

After netting a headed winner against Everton on his debut in an FA Cup victory he quickly became the leader of the back four; expertly marshalling those around him, snuffing out attacks before they had even begun and starting moves with unerringly accurate long raking passes.

Rarely does he ever look under pressure with opposition strikers often completely bamboozled by his combination of anticipation, pace, strength and ball control. Those who appear full of confidence as they face him often meet a dead end. "I like to look them in the eyes," says Virgil, and that's normally before he whisks the ball away.

Combative ex-Watford frontman Troy Deeney admitted that facing van Dijk was an impossible task. "Too big, too fast, loves a fight and smells nice," he declared.

If opponents worry about van Dijk then his approach is the complete opposite. "I'm never nervous any more," he explains. "With experience the nervousness is not there. If you're nervous you think: 'I don't want to make mistakes or give the ball away.' But you limit your own qualities then."

Similar to Alisson, he's not only effective in the defensive third. VVD also makes a huge contribution at the other end. During the title-winning season, when he didn't miss a minute of league action, the centre-back netted five goals including both in a vital 2-1 win over Brighton and an opener against Manchester United at the Annie Road End.

The last of those displayed his excellent timing and spring to outjump the visitors' defence before planting the header beyond a helpless David De Gea. "van Dijk steamed imperiously through United's defence like a majestic liner arriving up the Mersey, cheered by crowds of onlookers," wrote Henry Winter in *The Times*.

It was a brilliant goal although whether it was as good as our goalkeeper's effort at West Brom is open to debate.

What is beyond any doubt is that Virgil van Dijk and Alisson regularly deliver at the crucial moments in the biggest matches. They have been brilliant signings; turning a good team into a great one. They are Klopp's game changers.

94/130

The leaving of Liverpool

CHANCES are, if you're old enough, you can remember where you were and what you were doing on Friday 22 February 1991 when Kenny Dalglish shocked the football world with his resignation as manager, barely 48 hours after Liverpool's FA Cup fifth-round replay at Everton had finished 4-4. It was just ten days before his 40th birthday.

Ian Rush remembers it well. "We'd all come in for training and were told to meet in the dressing room," recalled the Welshman, who was 29 and at the peak of his playing career. "Kenny walked in and said he was leaving. It was complete shock and surprise in there. He couldn't say too much, but there were tears in his eyes as he spoke.

"As players you just get on with it – that's the nature of football. We were sat in the dressing room in silence and Ronnie Moran [soon-to-be caretaker boss] said, 'Okay, let's go training now', and we all got on the coach. No-one had a clue it was coming."

The Reds were reigning champions and top of the table by three points, and if Rushie was shocked, new boy Jamie Redknapp was downright devastated. The midfielder, then yet to turn 18, had been signed by Dalglish from Bournemouth the previous month and was heading back to his digs when he heard the news.

"I was in tears. I thought my Liverpool career would be over before it started. Not only had Kenny signed me, but he was like a father figure to me. We played golf together, his lovely wife Marina would cook food for me and he took an interest in me beyond the call-of-duty, because he knew my dad [Harry] and how close we were.

"I was 17, away from home and he took special care of me. Then he was gone. But that day – the day he resigned and his world was caving in – he found time to call me. In the days before mobile phones I was in my room at my digs and my landlady said: 'It's a call for you – it's Kenny'. I remember thinking: Kenny who? I was overwhelmed that he took time to call me. He said: 'You will be alright, I'll make sure of that'."

In the aftermath of the Dalglish bombshell, it's hard to imagine anyone at Anfield raising a smile. Alan Hansen did. He was, after all, a close pal of Kenny and a habitual practical-joker. He just couldn't help himself. "The bookies had made me 6/4 to be the next manager but I didn't want it, I wanted to retire," he recalled. "But before I retired, I wanted to leave a parting gift for the players.

"So I told them I was taking over and went round the room, saying: 'No more Kentucky Fried Chicken for you, no more going to The Crown for you, we'll be doing double training sessions in the afternoon, every Sunday we'll be watching a video of the match...'

"Their heads were going further and further down and I was laughing all the way to the lounge."

Was Kenny's resignation a bigger shock than the retirement of Bill Shankly, aged 60, in July 1974? It's so hard to call. But perhaps the latter was the more unexpected even though, it would later transpire, Shanks had threatened to walk away before. Sundry LFC grandees had filed away previous letters of resignation before, this time, they accepted his decision with what club chairman John Smith called "extreme reluctance."

Bill was about to make an addition to his first-team squad, not a young prospect like Redknapp but a relative veteran in the shape of Arsenal forward Ray Kennedy. It was the summer close-season and his Liverpool team were still basking in the glow of their victory over Newcastle United in a one-sided FA Cup final on Saturday 4 May 1974.

Two months later, at a midday press conference at Anfield on Friday 12 July 1974, he said, simply: "I feel it is time I had a rest from the game."

Earlier that day, in an uncanny prelude to Dalglish's decision seventeen years later, Shankly gathered the players in the dressing room to break the news. Tommy Smith, then 29 and a stalwart in the side, remembered thinking "he was about to give us a pep talk for the season ahead. He wasted no time in getting straight down to the point. 'Boys, I've got a big meeting at Anfield this afternoon', he informed us. 'I have decided to retire. My time here is done'.

"Like every player in the room, I sat there absolutely stunned. I felt my forehead prickle as adrenaline rushed to my head. No-one had expected this. Shanks didn't say much more. He simply told us that he'd wanted to tell us first before his decision was made public.

"One of the things I recall about that day was the evening news on TV. A crew had gone onto the streets to obtain reaction from Liverpool supporters to the news. One young fan was asked: 'What do you think about Bill Shankly retiring?' He had obviously not heard the news and looked straight into the camera with a shocked look on his face.

"'Shankly?' he said disbelievingly. 'Bill Shankly?' The camera stayed fixed on his face. The lad just shook his head. Tears welled, and he couldn't speak another word."

Gerry the Brave

THREE minutes into the 1965 FA Cup final between Liverpool FC and Leeds United at Wembley, Reds midfielder Willie Stevenson was dispossessed by Bobby Collins. Leeds' Scottish midfielder, who had been with Everton from 1958 to 1962, chased after the loose ball that was rolling in the direction of Liverpool left-back Gerry Byrne. What followed next was truly shocking.

Collins went in studs up, over the ball and clattered Byrne at knee height before following through with a body-check. If you've never seen that tackle look it up on YouTube – *British Pathe News* have uploaded colour footage on there – but be prepared to wince.

The force of the challenge left Scouse full-back Byrne with a broken collarbone. That he didn't end up with a broken leg too was quite remarkable, but with bone-shuddering tackles considered to be acceptable in the 1960s referee Bill Clements simply awarded a free-kick and gave Collins a bit of a talking to.

Bob Paisley, Liverpool's trainer at the time, rushed on and initially thought he was dealing with nothing more than a leg injury. "I went on and Gerry's shin was bruised and skinned," he was quoted as saying in the *Liverpool Echo*. "I bandaged it up and he carried on. But only a few minutes later I saw him take a throw-in and wince with pain.

"I took the first opportunity to get onto the field and when a Leeds player went down I dashed over to Gerry. As soon as I felt his shoulder I knew he had broken his collarbone. I told him of the injury and warned him that if it was hit the broken bone could puncture his lung.

"The anguish, not from the injury, but from the horrible decision that faced him was mirrored on Gerry's face. He turned to me and said 'what would you do, Bob?' Suddenly the memory of 1950 came flooding back and I remembered how I would have gone through anything to have been out there playing in the Cup Final. Quite solemnly and sincerely I replied 'Gerry, if it were me, I'd play even if I had a wooden leg'. That was the decision made so I put a figure eight bandage on his damaged shoulder and told left-half Willie Stevenson to cover for Gerry if necessary and not to let him take throw-ins. Gerry went on to play the game of his life."

Byrne played for one hundred and seventeen minutes of an FA Cup final with a broken collarbone knowing that one inadvertent collision could puncture his lung. What's more, he didn't let on to his opponents that he was injured.

"At half-time the doctor tried to freeze it but he couldn't," said manager Bill Shankly. "The bones were grinding together, but Leeds United didn't know he was injured."

There was a good reason for that. "It was a bad tackle and Bobby Collins was a dirty player," recalled Roger Hunt, the scorer of Liverpool's opening goal in a 2-1 victory after extra-time. "Gerry was a brave man but, Leeds being Leeds, they would have exploited it had they found out."

Incredibly it was Byrne who created Hunt's goal when he got to the byline and crossed for 'Sir Roger' to head in. That his assist came in the third minute of extra-time, having been injured in the third minute of normal time, was ironic and as Byrne ran towards his team-mates to celebrate he did so with his left arm in the air and his right arm by his side in the style of a Subbuteo figure.

Billy Bremner equalised, but a 111th minute header from Ian St John was enough to earn Liverpool a historic first FA Cup in a game that will forever be remembered for Byrne's bravery.

"I didn't really feel the pain until after," he revealed. "I couldn't lift up my hand, I was running with it across my chest. I made the mistake of trying to take a throw-in and it nearly killed me. At that point I knew something was broken. No-one tried to get me to come off – it was the last year before substitutes – and anyway, I didn't want to come off. They put a bit of padding on me. It didn't help much!"

Never mind a winner's medal, perhaps the Queen – who presented skipper Ron Yeats with the FA Cup – should've given him a George Cross, but joking aside it was another Anfield hardman in Tommy Smith – no stranger to playing through the pain barrier himself as you will read elsewhere in this book – who put Byrne's performance into true context.

"At half-time they had his arm in a sling but as we were going out Gerry said 'Boss, I'm alright to carry on'. Can you imagine that now? I mean, how the hell do you play with a broken collarbone? It was the bravest thing I ever saw."

It completed a remarkable FA Cup campaign for Byrne who had a rather unusual calf problem before the 1965 FA Cup semi-final against Chelsea at Villa Park. Strangely, it wasn't his calf that was the problem.

On the Wednesday night before the cup semi the Reds had played Cologne in a European Cup 2nd round replay, held in Rotterdam, after both legs had finished 0-0. The replay also finished level, 2-2 this time, before famously being settled on the toss of a disc.

Afterwards, Shankly decided to take his players away to a quiet hotel in the countryside to let them recharge their batteries before preparing to take on Tommy Docherty's much-vaunted young Chelsea side that were two points off the top of the table and had

Peter Bonetti, John Hollins, Ron Harris, George Graham, Terry Venables and Bobby Tambling in their ranks.

On the morning of the match, a traditional 3pm kick-off that attracted a sizeable 67,686-strong crowd to Villa Park, Byrne and Ian Callaghan decided to stretch their legs by going for a post-breakfast wander down a quiet country lane. What could possibly go wrong?

Moments later, the steely Reds' full-back was rugby tackling a cow before putting it in a headlock. As you do on the morning of Liverpool's biggest FA Cup game since the final in 1950.

Now why, you may ask, was Byrne doing a spot of cow wrestling? Shankly was a manager who liked his players to have a steak three hours before kick-off, but surely sending them out to catch their own lunch was taking things a bit far?

The *Liverpool Daily Post* revealed all...

"How easily the plans of a manager to take the team to a quiet hideout, free of distractions and disturbances, can be upset was shown on Saturday morning," they reported. "While Byrne and Callaghan took a leisurely morning stroll, along came a cattle truck. Down fell one of the doors and out jumped a calf into the road. Immediately Byrne was after it and with a rugby tackle around its head, held it until the driver could return to claim it. 'It was a perfectly fair tackle,' said the ice-cool full-back."

If Byrne suffered any ill-effects from his bovine encounter he didn't milk it while you could say that playing in an FA Cup final with a broken collarbone was previously un-herd of.

Moo-ving on (sorry!), there have been numerous other occasions when Liverpool players have defied the pain barrier to continue playing, many before substitutes were introduced in the 1960s, with another famous example coming from Geoff Strong in the 1966 European Cup Winners' Cup semi-final second leg against Celtic at Anfield.

Versatile midfielder Strong had damaged his knee in the first-half but, with UEFA not permitting substitutes, had stayed on and was hobbling around up front, essentially for nuisance value. With the tie locked at 1-1 and 23 minutes left to play, Callaghan crossed from the right and Strong sprung off his good leg to head the ball home and send Liverpool back up to Glasgow for the final.

If you think hard enough you can probably still picture centre-halves like Sami Hyypia and Martin Skrtel rising to head the ball clear with bandages wrapped around their foreheads to protect wounds – Skrtel had staples inserted into his head to be able to complete a 2-2 draw against Arsenal in 2014 (his bandage scoring a 97th minute equaliser!) – but Jamie Carragher had taken things to a new level in 2003 when he tried to run off a broken leg at Blackburn Rovers following a horror tackle by Lucas Neill. Only the realisation that it wasn't physically possible to run on a broken limb prevented Carra from continuing but he still refused to get on a stretcher, instead being helped off up the touchline by physio Dave Galley and first-team coach Sammy Lee.

A couple of more recent examples of courageous displays occurred in major cup finals.

Carragher was riddled with cramp in his groin during extra-time of the 2005 Champions League final in Istanbul, but still threw his body in front of goalbound AC Milan shots, and there was also a Liverpool player on the Ataturk Stadium pitch that night who continued to play on with a broken foot.

"I actually broke a metatarsal in my foot landing after a header about six minutes from time," revealed Didi Hamann. "But there was no question about going off – we just had to hang on in there and get to penalties."

Despite his injury, Hamann stepped up to take Liverpool's first penalty-kick in the shoot-out and calmly placed it past Dida. "I made up my mind I was going to my left because I thought it was easier to generate pace [with a broken foot] going across my body. Fortunately it worked out."

A year later, in the 2006 FA Cup final between Liverpool and West Ham in Cardiff, the Reds were trailing 3-2 as the clock ticked into stoppage time when a clearance bounced towards Steven Gerrard over 35 yards from goal.

"I was cramping up, had nothing left, but I had to be around for the scraps," he wrote in *Gerrard: My Autobiography*. "Morientes and Gabbidon fought for Riise's cross and the ball flew back out. Towards me. Oh God! I stood there, legs stiff as boards, tank empty, thirty-seven yards from goal with this ball coming my way. Everyone raves about what happened next, but they don't realise one crucial thing; if my legs hadn't been riddled with cramp I would have brought the ball down and tried to build an attack. I was a long way out, too far to shoot, but the cramp made up my mind."

His shot fizzed past Shaka Hislop to send the game into extra-time and Rafa Benitez's side emerged victorious on penalties with Gerrard having also stepped up to successfully convert a spot-kick.

Perhaps it wasn't quite on a par with what Gerry Byrne did 41 years earlier, but as acts of footballing bravery go little else ever could be.

96/130

South Liverpool

FROM Alisson in goal and Fabinho in midfield to Bobby Firmino and Luis Diaz in attack, South American aces have become staples of the successful Liverpool teams of the modern era.

But back in 1913 it was a Merseysider going the other way who made a name for himself. Wavertree-born Harry Welfare had made just four appearances for the LFC senior side before he decided to take a teaching post in Rio, Brazil. The PE teacher at the boarding school, J. A. Quincey-Taylor, was also the coach of Fluminense and quickly signed up Welfare who was particularly apt at the then legal practice of charging goalkeepers into the net to score.

Such was his impact in the still amateur league that Brazilian officials wrote to LFC to confirm that he hadn't been at the club on professional terms. In a decade at Fluminese he provided 163 goals in just 166 outings.

Post-playing, Welfare coached Vasco da Gama to success, played a major part in helping Brazilian football transform from amateur to professional status and worked behind the scenes on the hosting of the 1950 World Cup. Fluminense's website still features him now, a sign of the impact he had in a land over 5,000 miles away from his home.

Despite Welfare's success it wasn't until 2005 that a South American would represent LFC. Argentine centre-back Mauricio Pellegrino, appointed Southampton manager in 2017, arrived

344

from Valencia in January 2005. To date, four of his compatriots have followed in his footsteps: Sebastian Leto, Emiliano Insua, Javier Mascherano and Maxi Rodriguez.

That Argentine contingent has been outnumbered by Brazilians, with Fabio Aurelio leading the way for his countrymen in 2006. Lucas Leiva arrived the following year and since then Diego Cavalieri [2008], Doni [2011], Philippe Coutinho [2013], Roberto Firmino [2015], Fabinho and Alisson Becker [2018] have all become members of the Liverpool dressing room.

The latter trio are undoubtedly amongst the best South Americans to wear the Liver Bird upon their chests. The trio were integral parts of Jürgen Klopp's side that became European champions for the sixth time and UEFA Super Cup winners for a fourth occasion in 2019, FIFA Club World Cup champions for the first time in the Reds' history later that year and then Premier League winners at last in 2020, plus League Cup victors in 2022. Firmino has been an essential part of Klopp's style, leading the press and providing a link between midfield and attack.

He was crucial to Liverpool's inaugural FIFA Club World Cup success in Qatar, netting a late winner in the semi-final against CF Monterrey before popping up with the only goal of the final in extra-time against Flamengo. Si Senor!

Fabinho, meanwhile, quickly forged a reputation as one of the leading defensive midfielders in the game as he offered protection to the back four, breaking up opponents' attacks and launching Liverpool's own.

Alisson was briefly the most expensive goalkeeper in world football when the Reds brought him to Anfield from AS Roma for a reported £65 million in 2018. That fee has proven to be a bargain as he has established himself as one of the best in the business with his calming presence, command of his area and shot-stopping abilities. He won the Premier League Golden

Glove award in 2018/19, after keeping 21 clean sheets, and the 2019 Copa America Golden Glove. In 2019 he also became the inaugural winner of France Football's Yashin Trophy for the best goalkeeper, an award presented on the same night as the Ballon d'Or.

Another of Liverpool's South American greats is Uruguayan striker Luis Suarez who lit up Anfield on a regular basis and inspired the Reds' 2013/14 title challenge. Kopites just couldn't get enough of Suarez who scored 82 goals in 133 games for the Reds. He was later joined at the club by fellow Uruguayan Sebastian Coates.

In January 2022, Liverpool expanded their roll call of South Americans by bringing in the club's very first Colombian. Luis Diaz had impressed while playing against the Reds for FC Porto in the UEFA Champions League and he quickly made an impact.

After playing a big part in a goal for Takumi Minamino on his debut in an FA Cup fourth-round tie against Cardiff City, Diaz soon added his first Reds' goal in only his second Premier League start, clipping an assured finish beyond Norwich City goalkeeper Angus Gunn at the Kop end to complete a 3-1 Liverpool victory. He also scored in a 4-0 home win against Manchester United.

Uruguayan striker Darwin Nunez, signed from Benfica in the summer of 2022, is the latest South American star aiming to write his name into Liverpool history.

Moving away from Latin America, another area of the southern hemisphere that has produced LFC players is Australia. Harry Kewell was probably prevented from regularly displaying his true ability by injuries, but in 2005 became the first Australian-born Champions League winner. Brad Jones was an able back-up to Pepe Reina, most notably deputising in the 2012 FA Cup semi-final win over Everton. And left-back Brad Smith enjoyed an 11-game LFC career before moving on to Bournemouth in the summer of 2016 and has since been an MLS Cup winner with Seattle Sounders.

97/130

The Boys' Pen

AS a young Liverpool supporter, Phil Thompson would always arrive at Anfield two hours before a Saturday 3pm kick-off. He would immediately head to the area of the ground known as the Boys' Pen, a separate section for youths within the Kop.

It was here that the next generation of fans congregated to see their heroes perform, although they all had only one goal; to make their way into the actual Kop via whatever means necessary.

"My aim was to watch football regularly from the most famous terrace in world football," Thommo says. "To get there, a fan would have to progress through the Boys' Pen. I was desperate to stand on the Kop.

"I used to get to the ground really early and do a runner from the Boys' Pen. The earlier you got in, the easier it was because there were fewer stewards around. We used to call them guards. I frequently managed to get to the game for about 1pm so I could maximise my chance of escaping the Pen.

"I was a good climber and nifty on foot so I have to say, quite proudly, that I was a prolific escapee."

Thompson wasn't the only Scouser to go from a youth in the Pen to one day playing for the first XI. Roy Evans – who vividly recalls watching Ronnie Moran playing at left-back from there – Terry McDermott, Jimmy Case and John Aldridge were some of the others to do the same.

The man who wrote the screenplay for the 1996 *Hillsborough* docudrama, Jimmy McGovern, was another local to sample the unique setting. He has since recalled paying six pence for the pleasure of seeing his heroes up close, although he found himself being laughed at by the other members of the Pen because the school uniform scarf he was wearing was the same maroon and blue colours as that of the away side on the day, Burnley!

That was probably one of the tamer experiences in the kids-only section which had been in existence at the stadium since first being opened in the paddock area at the Anfield Road end of the old Kemlyn Road Stand in 1922. With a capacity of 4,000 it ran half the length of the pitch and was seen as a way of ensuring a new generation of fans were being nurtured.

Legend has it that an incident where the Pen inhabitants – who were often referred to as bearing a striking resemblance to the street kids in the *Oliver Twist* movie – threw fruit at Wolves players in the late 1930s eventually made LFC relocate the juvenile section to the top corner of the Kop in the post-War 1946/47 season, where it had a separate entrance from Lake Street on the Main Stand side of the ground.

An undoubtedly tough environment, it was where kids learned lessons about football and, to a further extent, life. Peter Hooton – avid LFC fan and lead singer in The Farm – described it as thus: "The Kop was an all-welcoming society, the Pen – a caged jungle – was a holding ground for frustrated juveniles and sometimes a lonely place for newcomers."

With safety at football grounds around the UK understandably becoming more of a concern, the Boys' Pen was shut down in 1978. By then it had more than served its purpose in providing affordable access to football for thousands of youngsters who would go on to support the Reds long after leaving their childhoods behind.

98/130

Heroes and villains

WRITHING around the turf near the Annie Road end goal, the image of Arsenal's Michael Thomas celebrating his last-second title-grabbing strike at Anfield in 1989 is one that, unfortunately, will never be forgotten by Liverpool supporters.

If, at that very moment, you had told those same fans he would one day become their hero by scoring in the 2-0 FA Cup final win against Sunderland just three years later, most of them would have found it hard to believe.

That, though, is the nature of football with its completely unpredictable transfer market; one week you despise a player as he strives to do his best for your rivals, a few days later you can be overjoyed by his actions for your own side.

If Thomas is perhaps the finest example of that scenario, there are plenty of others who have completed similar transformations.

Nicky Barmby had played for Everton against LFC on five different occasions before Gerard Houllier shocked everyone by signing him in July 2000. It didn't take the midfielder long to endear himself to Kopites, his first league goal for the club coming in the 3-1 Anfield derby win that October when he reacted superbly to head in a deflected Christian Ziege shot and enrage Evertonians even further.

If crossing the Merseyside divide always guarantees controversy, then daring to experience both sides of the LFC-Manchester

United rivalry is probably even more incendiary. Perhaps that's why it hasn't happened directly since Phil Chisnall did so in 1964, when he moved to Anfield.

Despite doing so via Inter Milan, Paul Ince was still seen as an ex-Red Devil before he won over Liverpool fans and went on to captain Roy Evans' side, even netting a late Kop end equaliser in a 2-2 draw against his former club in May 1999.

Across Manchester, Robbie Fowler and Steve McManaman both had spells with City after leaving Anfield and in 2003 it was Fowler who haunted Houllier – the man who had sold him – by netting a 90th minute equaliser in a 2-2 draw at the City of Manchester Stadium. He isn't the only ex-Red to have scored past Liverpool since departing.

Peter Beardsley was a brilliant player in red, scoring 59 goals in 175 games, but when Graeme Souness deemed him surplus to requirements he switched to Everton in 1991. December of the following year saw him make his former manager regret that decision when he provided the winner in the Goodison derby. Beardsley's replacement, Dean Saunders, was sold on to Aston Villa in 1992 only to net twice on his home debut against the Reds 10 days later and follow it up with an Anfield winner in the same season.

More recently – in 2017 – Christian Benteke, who had only enjoyed one season on Merseyside, scoring 10 goals, returned to do similar, scoring twice for Crystal Palace at Anfield in a 2-1 win. Raheem Sterling, who scored 23 goals in 129 games in Red, netted against Liverpool for Manchester City at Wembley in 2019, the Etihad in 2020 and Anfield in 2021.

But when it comes to the most painful of those types of transformations two names sit top of the list for LFC fans: Michael Owen and Fernando Torres. Owen had come through the academy ranks and been a phenomenal goalscorer for the club before going on to play for rivals Manchester United, while Torres' January 2011 switch to Chelsea left many Kopites feeling upset after they had taken him to their hearts.

However, in the 14 games the pair played between them against Liverpool since moving on, neither found the net, proving that some exes are more troublesome than others!

99/130

We won it in Qatar

UPON landing in Japan for the 2005 FIFA Club World Club Championship the LFC squad were handed a pair of sunglasses each. It wasn't a welcome present from the locals. Instead, Rafa Benitez was the man behind the 'gift', as Jerzy Dudek explained.

"The coach that was taking us from the airport to the hotel had its curtains closed too," the Pole recalled. "Apparently, the strength of the light at that time of day is far stronger in Japan than we were used to in Europe so we had to protect our eyes. This was the level of detail Rafa and his staff went into."

Anyone who dared risk exposing themselves to the light suffered the wrath of the manager.

"As the coach set off I pulled back the curtain," Dudek continued. "A couple of the other lads did the same. Rafa gave us a rollicking! 'We are not here to be tourists. We are here to do a job so do as you're told. You can come back another time', was his warning."

Unfortunately, not even such detailed preparation could help land a trophy that had previously eluded LFC. After a comfortable

3-0 win over Costa Rican outfit Deportivo Saprissa in the semi-final, Peter Crouch netting twice, the Reds lost 1-0 in the final to Brazilian side Sao Paulo despite dominating much of the encounter. Afterwards some of the players headed out to sample the local nightlife.

"Chelsea v Arsenal was on TV so we found a boozer and had a few shandies to drown our sorrows," Didi Hamman recalled. Later that night when the bar shut there was a bit of aggro.

"Within a minute there was police all over the place, so everyone ran away including some of Carra's mates. I was injured at the time so I couldn't run, even if I was fit, I still would have been caught because most others were probably quicker!

"Anyway I got caught by a copper. So there I was at 3am and the bus was leaving from the hotel about 8 o'clock so I was a bit nervous before I got back.

"Carra kept ringing the room [I was sharing with Sami Hyypia] every 15 minutes because he was worried he might be in trouble too.

"Sami wasn't too happy that he was getting called throughout the night because he loves his sleep. I made it back just in time."

No such escapades were reported from Liverpool's previous experiences of the competition in 1981 and 1984 when it was just a one-off game between the champions of Europe and South America rather than a tournament.

In 1981 Bob Paisley's team lost 3-0 vs Brazilian outfit Flamengo in Tokyo, with all the goals coming in the first half.

Joe Fagan was in charge when they next made the same journey east via an 18-hour flight from London. This time it was Argentine club Independiente who stood in the way. Another defeat – 1-0 – ensued and was swiftly followed by another 18-hour flight back to London which touched down at 5.15am before the players boarded a coach for a five-hour journey to Merseyside.

So when Jürgen Klopp's European Champions headed to Qatar in 2019 - leaving the U23s to play in a League Cup quarter-final at Aston Villa due to an unresolvable fixture clash - for a tournament rebranded as the FIFA Club World Cup they did so knowing history could be made. Insead of being handed sunglasses, this Liverpool side were intent on being handed medals.

Liverpool's semi-final, against Mexicans CF Monterrey, was played on National Qatar Day, an annual celebration of Qatar's unification in 1878. A huge parade on Doha's seven-mile corniche (waterfront) featured a military fly-by with hundreds of flag-waving Qataris leaning out of car windows as they drove by Souq Waqif, the city's traditional Middle East market squeezed into narrow alleyways and backstreets.

The Khalifa International Stadium, with its 300ft high Aspire Tower – also known as 'The Torch Doha' due to the way it is shaped like a flame at the top – hosted the semi and for surely the first time in Liverpool's history the match was played with giant air vents, built into the stands, pumping cool air onto the pitch.

A huge number of Egyptian fans in the stands made Mo Salah the star of the show although with Virgil van Dijk taken ill and Joe Gomez the only fit centre-half, skipper Jordan Henderson had to play at the back with James Milner at right-back.

Salah created Liverpool's opening goal for Naby Keita, but a Monterrey equaliser and a dull second half, featuring the Mexican fans starting a Mexican wave, seemed set to take things to extra-time until substitute Trent Alexander-Arnold clipped a sensational pass for fellow sub Roberto Firmino to convert at the near post.

"It was always going to be a tough game," said Adam Lallana, Liverpool's holding midfielder for the night with Fabinho injured. "They had won something to get to Qatar and teams from Central and South America play differently, but you've got to deal with different dynamics."

It was back to the Khalifa for the final where Brazil's Flamengo, the team that defeated the Reds in 1981, awaited. It was the biggest match in their history as with the Brazilian league title and Copa Libertadores already won a victory over the Reds would give them a first-ever treble and make it the most successful in their esteemed history.

As a result, Doha was full of Flamengo fans. With an estimated 40m followers in Brazil around 15,000 of them travelled to Qatar, many via 20-hour indirect flights, and for once Liverpool supporters were completely outnumbered at a major cup final.

The Reds, with van Dijk back in the side, should have won the game in normal time, but Firmino scooped an early chance over, hit the inside of the post in the second half and in the final minute Sadio Mane was awarded a penalty…only for the referee to go to the screen, review the footage and – after replays showed Mane was fouled just outside the box – bizarrely award an uncontested drop-ball instead.

Finally, in extra-time, came the historic moment. Henderson's 99th minute pass sent Mane through and he teed up Firmino to find the net and secure Liverpool's first FIFA Club World Cup. Never before had the line 'the best in the world is Bobby Firmino' sounded more apt when his song rang around the stadium.

It was Liverpool FC's 47th major trophy - a new English record - and the man who made it possible enjoyed the celebrations.

"We don't fly 3,000 miles not to show up," said Jürgen Klopp. "It's a wonderful night for us, the club, for everybody who is with us. I said before the game I don't know exactly how it would feel to win it. Now I can say it's outstanding, absolutely sensational."

100/130

Out of Africa

IN mid-February 2022, Liverpool trailed at home to Norwich City with more than an hour gone and an air of anxiety was just beginning to grip Anfield.

A couple of minutes later all was well again as Liverpool's two African striking sensations, Sadio Mane and Mohamed Salah, had scored in front of the Kop to put the Reds 2-1 up and pave the way for an eventual 3-1 Premier League win over the Canaries.

The duo went one better in the next Premier League game a few days later, each scoring twice in a 6-0 rout of Leeds United. Salah moved into ninth place in the Reds' all-time scoring chart in the process, while Mane became the only player to score 10 or more Premier League goals in each of the past eight seasons!

The duo were not long back from the Africa Cup of Nations tournament in Cameroon where Mane's Senegal had triumphed over Salah's Egypt with Liverpool's no10 scoring the decisive kick in the penalty shoot-out. It gave Senegal their first triumph in the competition and Mane was also named player of the tournament.

The pair had announced themselves as a dual threat in red shirts during the opening Premier League game of the 2017/18 season when both put their names on the scoresheet in their first competitive fixture together. They were on target in the 3-3 draw at Watford, giving Liverpudlians a taste of things to come as the speed merchants illuminated the team's display at Vicarage Road.

Both African aces were recruited for fees in excess of £30 million and each made an immediate impact at Anfield.

Mane's displays during his debut season of 2016/17 were such that he was a unanimous choice as the winner of LFC's Player of the Year award. Twelve months later, Salah claimed that honour himself after one of the most sensational debut seasons in the Reds' history. The no11 was a prolific goalscorer despite starting most games on the right wing. Salah scored 44 goals in all competitions, including 32 in the Premier League.

In the years since both men have passed 100 goals for the Reds and played starring roles as Liverpool won the UEFA Champions League, UEFA Super Cup, FIFA Club World Cup and the Premier League across 2018/19 and 2019/20.

Salah's goal against Norwich referred to above took his tally at Liverpool to 150 in only his 233rd game. Only 'Sir' Roger Hunt managed to achieve the milestone in a quicker time (226 games) and some of his early appearances took place in the second tier of English football.

The impact made by both Africans has seen both catapult themselves into any conversation about the Reds' all-time greats and you can pay them no greater compliment than that.

They are among the latest in a line of African players who have been part of the LFC story.

South Africans such as Gordon Hodgson, Berry Nieuwenhuys and Arthur Riley became crowd favourites, mainly between the two world wars.

Part of an amateur South African touring side that arrived in the UK in September 1924, Hodgson was only 19 at the time when he caught the eye of Anfield officials during a 5-2 victory over the Reds. The following December he became a Liverpool player and would go on to feature in 11 seasons, usually finishing as top scorer.

The prolific forward wasn't the only member of that South

African side to relocate to Merseyside. Goalkeeper Riley debuted in October 1924 after the *Liverpool Echo* newspaper had declared him "a tall, keen fellow who has reach, anticipation and a safe pair of hands." Initially understudy to the legendary Elisha Scott, he eventually dislodged him and went on to make 338 appearances.

The Riley influence didn't end there either. Arthur's English-born father lived in South Africa and spotted and recommended two more individuals who would sign for the club; wingers Nieuwenhuys and Lance Carr. The pair arrived on 11 September 1933.

The former was quickly nicknamed 'Nivvy' and created two goals on his debut away at Spurs. He made 257 appearances for the club, a tally that would have been much higher were it not for the outbreak of World War II. His sporting talent wasn't limited to the football field. A talented golfer, he participated in The Open in 1946.

Carr didn't enjoy as much success making just 33 appearances; the highlight of those undoubtedly being a 6-0 win over Everton in which he created two goals.

During a time when foreign players were far from the norm, the South African quartet paved the way for others to follow in their footsteps.

Two men from the same country were major contributors to our league and cup double in 1986; Bruce Grobbelaar and Craig Johnston. The former was born in Durban, but spent his childhood in Zimbabwe, while Johnston – who grew up in Australia – was born in Johannesburg. Another South African wide-man with impressive acceleration was Mark Gonzalez, who was born in Durban (but later played for Chile) and enjoyed one season at Anfield in 2006/07.

Of all the interesting backgrounds of Liverpool players, few can compare with that of Bruce Grobbelaar, who spent two years on active service in the Rhodesian National Guard during the

Rhodesian Bush War. His experiences of fighting in the African jungle shaped his perceptions of playing football. While always eager to win, he played the game with a smile on his face and was affectionately nicknamed the 'Clown Prince' in response to some of his on-field antics. During twelve-and-a-half years' service at the club, Grobbelaar became known as one of the Reds' all-time goalkeeping greats.

His 628 games puts him in the top 10 of the Reds' all-time appearances list and between August 1981 and August 1986, Brucie achieved the astonishing feat of playing 310 consecutive first-team games.

Johnston was another colourful character. A South African Aussie who won representative age group honours for England (yes, really!), 'Skippy' became the first 'Australian' to score in an FA Cup final in 1986 and won nine major honours as a Red, including the 1984 European Cup, and is LFC's most decorated African-born outfield player.

At the back end of the 1990s, Liverpool manager Gerard Houllier also looked to a couple of African players in a bid to bolster his squad.

Cameroon defender Rigobert Song made 38 appearances for the Reds between January 1999 and September 2000. An international regular for 17 years, he won an incredible 137 caps. He also appeared in a record eight Africa Cup of Nations tournaments, captaining Cameroon in five of them. He was on the winning team on two occasions – in Nigeria in 2000 and Mali in 2002.

Meanwhile, Guinea's Titi Camara became a firm favourite with fans admiring his repertoire of silky skills. He made a fine start, scoring on his debut against Sheffield Wednesday. His most memorable moment however came on an October night in 1999 when he slumped to his knees at the Anfield Road end after scoring what turned out to be the winning goal against West Ham. It later transpired that he had been told only hours earlier that his father had died. Houllier explained after the game: "Titi lost his dad during the day but he told me, 'I want to play for my father.' He was crying after he scored because it was such an emotional day."

The Guinea international made 37 appearances during the 1999/2000 campaign, including 13 as a substitute. He scored 10 times with other memorable strikes including a curling effort against Leeds United at Elland Road and a screamer against Coventry City at the Kop end on the day the club celebrated the fortieth anniversary of Bill Shankly's arrival at Anfield.

Senegal's shock performances at the 2002 World Cup caught the eye and Houllier swooped to sign two of their star turns in attacker El-Hadji Diouf and midfielder Salif Diao. Neither managed to live up to their billing with Diouf, twice African Footballer of the Year, scoring six times in 80 games in return for a £10 million outlay.

Far more successful was French-born Mali international defender Djimi Traore, who was another brought to the club by Houllier. Capable of playing at left-back or in the centre of defence, he went on to become a UEFA Champions League winner with the Reds under Rafael Benitez in 2005.

Another French-born Malian international who played his part in a run to a Champions League final was Momo Sissoko, a defensive midfielder brought to Liverpool by Benitez who had also worked with him at former club Valencia.

Momo played 87 times for the Reds between 2005 and 2007 and figured in eight Champions League games as the team reached their second final in three seasons. He was also a member of the 2006 FA Cup final winning team despite suffering a serious eye injury earlier that season which saw him wear special protective goggles during a 7-0 win at Birmingham City...only to have to take them off after they steamed up!

Brendan Rodgers' reign at Liverpool saw three more Africans brought in to varying degrees of success.

Moroccan winger Oussama Assaidi made little impact after becoming the Northern Irishman's third signing as LFC boss in August 2012. He was the second Moroccan to play for the Reds after Nabil El Zhar, who had scored once in 31 games between 2006 and 2010.

Twelve months later, fellow wide man Victor Moses arrived on a season-long loan from Chelsea. The Nigerian scored on his debut at Swansea City, but was predominantly a bit-part player during a season that saw Liverpool mount a strong challenge for the Premier League title.

Also arriving at Anfield that summer was central defender Kolo Toure. The Ivory Coast international joined on a free transfer from Manchester City and became a popular figure during the next three seasons, making 71 appearances under Rodgers and Jürgen Klopp. His one goal for the Reds – in a 6-0 rout of Aston Villa in February 2016 – was celebrated wildly!

Toure bowed out of international football in style by helping the Ivory Coast to victory in the 2015 Africa Cup of Nations in Equatorial Guinea. He had announced it would be his final assignment for the national team ahead of the competition. His last match, his 120th cap, saw the Ivory Coast defeat Ghana 9–8 on penalties in the final after the game had ended in a 0-0 draw. Kolo scored the Elephants' seventh penalty.

By the start of the 2017/18 season, Klopp had signed three players of African heritage who became linchpins of his side.

Mane's pace, goalscoring ability and work rate saw him become a key part of the team from 2016/17 and, as explained earlier in this chapter, he has gone on to become a Liverpool legend.

Meanwhile, Joel Matip had also become a regular in the heart of defence. The centre-back was called up by Cameroon for the 2010

Africa Cup of Nations in Angola but declined to take part. At the time, the German FA were hoping the Bochum-born stopper would play his international football for them, but in March 2010 Matip opted to represent Cameroon and made his debut in a friendly against Italy. He also played at the 2014 World Cup, scoring against hosts Brazil.

Matip has become a key member of Reds' squad and is surely one of the best free transfers in the club's history, arriving at Anfield following the expiry of his contract at Schalke 04. Although injury restricted his appearances in the Premier League title-winning team of 2019/20, he provided a goalscoring assist for Divock Origi to seal the Champions League triumph over Tottenham Hotspur in Madrid in June 2019.

Prior to his Anfield move, Salah had been part of the Egypt squad which reached the 2017 Africa Cup of Nations final, scoring twice and providing two assists as the Pharaohs reached the showpiece game in which they fell to a 2-1 defeat at the hands of Cameroon. He then helped his country reach the 2018 FIFA World Cup finals in Russia and also the final of the 2022 Africa Cup of Nations, where they fell just short in losing to Mane's Senegal in a penalty shoot-out. He has already broken numerous records in a red shirt and may well go on to set many more.

In the summer of 2018, Mane and Salah were joined at Anfield by Guinean midfielder Naby Keita. A versatile player, his club RB Leipzig were so reluctant to let him go that the Reds agreed a deal in excess of £50 million and also allowed the German side to keep the player for another 12 months. Injury prevented Keita from being a part of Liverpool's triumphant Champions League final-winning side in his debut campaign. However, the following season saw him help the Reds to become club world champions for the first time. He started both matches of the tournament in Qatar and scored in the semi-final victory against CF Monterrey.

Christened 'Naby Lad' by supporters, he also played 18 times as the Reds ended their long wait for a Premier League title in 2019/20 and in season 2021/22 opened the scoring in a record 5-0 win against Manchester United at Old Trafford.

Liverpool's Africans have made an incredible impact at Anfield, particularly in recent times, and Kopites will be hoping there is even more to come from them in the years ahead.

101/130

Spotified

ICE-COOL LFC penalty-takers. Think the Egyptian King – particularly in the 2019 Champions League final - 'Milly' and even more recently Fabinho during the Jürgen Klopp era. Think Big Jan and 'Zico' back in the day.

Those opposing supporters who took great delight in singing about Steven Gerrard's slip at the end of season 2013/14 conveniently forgot that it was his successful penalties in the second half of that campaign that helped put Liverpool within touching distance of the Premier League crown. He made eight conversions between 12 January and 6 April 2014.

Three in particular stood out. There was the 95th-minute winner in the howling wind at Fulham on Wednesday 12 February 2014 that sent the travelling Kop wild. Then the first of his two successful penalties in the 3-0 win at Manchester United on 16 March 2014 – his 12th consecutive conversion from the spot, although he did hit the post with a third. The second of his two pens at West Ham on 6 April 2014 also kept LFC's title-chasing momentum going.

Other sensational Stevie spot-kicks include the one swept past Manchester City's Joe Hart at the Etihad, after a bit of pre-kick banter with his England team-mate, in the Carling Cup semi-final first leg of 11 January 2012 (he also scored from the spot in the second leg at Anfield).

And could anyone ever forget his penalty in the 4-1 win at Old Trafford on 14 March 2009, celebrated with that camera-kiss?

No one has scored more penalties for Liverpool than Gerrard, his 47 successful conversions five more than previous record-holder Jan Molby. But if anyone could match him for composure under pressure, it was Dirk Kuyt. A 112th minute opportunity to put Liverpool level from the spot? No sweat.

In normal play Kuyt converted eight times for the Reds, including three against Mersey rivals Everton in two games either side of Stanley Park: two at Goodison Park in a 2-1 win in October 2007 and one at Anfield in a 2-2 draw in January 2011. He also missed one at Goodison in October 2011, but Liverpool won 2-0.

His finest moment from 12 yards – not counting shoot-outs against Chelsea in the 2007 Champions League semis and Cardiff City in the 2012 Carling Cup final – has to be that late, late equaliser against Arsenal at the Emirates on Sunday 17 April 2011.

With the game goalless going into the eighth minute of stoppage-time, Robin van Persie put the Gunners ahead with a penalty...only for his unflappable compatriot to do the same four minutes later up the other end! No wonder goalkeeper Pepe Reina sprinted 100 yards to celebrate with Kuyt, his team-mates and Liverpool's travelling fans.

With eight dispatched, Dirk is 18th in LFC's list of all-time successful penalty-takers. Third behind Gerrard (47) and Molby (42) at the top is former skipper Phil Neal, whose record of 38 conversions stood for eight years before the great Dane finally overtook him.

Ironically Molby's first-ever spot-kick for Liverpool, against Spurs on 28 September 1985, came just 21 days after Neal's last LFC penalty, against Watford on 7 September that same year. And, slightly spookily, in the same game that Neal scored his 35th penalty for Liverpool to surpass Billy Liddell's previous club record of 34 – against Norwich City on 25 August 1984 – Molby actually made his LFC debut.

Time and again in the 1970s and 80s full-back Phil – nicknamed 'Zico' by Kopites after the Brazilian legend – stepped up when it mattered, at Anfield or elsewhere, to coolly dispatch the ball past the keeper. His most important pen? There have been a few special ones by Liverpool players in Europe – Mo Salah v Tottenham Hotspur in 2019, Gary McAllister v Barcelona in 2001, Alan Kennedy v AS Roma in 1984 and Kevin Keegan v FC Bruges in 1976 – but arguably Neal's spot-kick v Borussia Moenchengladbach in 1977 to win that first European Cup is the greatest.

"As I ran up to the ball I then did something I never did and which you should never do – I changed my mind," he revealed. "Instead I hit it low to the other side of the keeper, but it went in and up came Ian Callaghan in delight. I still get a tingle when I see the videos of Bob Paisley and Ronnie Moran and the lads leaping up off the bench with joy."

"Know your keepers, stay cool, and enjoy it." That was the mantra of Molby, who with 42 conversions from 45 kicks had a success-rate of 93.33% from the spot - a ratio only bettered by Danny Murphy (100%, 8/8), Mark Walters (100%, 6/6) and John Aldridge (94.44%, 17/18).

"Over the years you'd gain a knowledge of goalies," recalled former midfielder Molby. "Peter Shilton, for example, would never move before you'd hit the ball – he wouldn't give you the pleasure of sending him the wrong way. But I always put it in the same place: it hit the back of the net, then Shilton dived, but never the wrong way.

"These days there's more video analysis but I'll guarantee that won't bother the really good penalty-takers. You could have all the information you wanted about me, but it's still about that moment and I'd always back myself.

"The biggest thing is whether you can handle the pressure. Screaming crowds and match situations can't be replicated. You can practice and make people more confident of being able to hit the target in a certain place, but the moment you walk up to take the kick, all that changes. I genuinely believe you're either born to take penalties or you're not. You must enjoy the responsibility and that game of cat-and-mouse with the keeper."

Dietmar Hamann, one of the heroes of Istanbul, always insisted it was about being focused and sticking to a plan. Three of the four penalties Didi took for Liverpool were in cup final shoot-outs: a miss v Birmingham City in the 2001 League Cup and conversions against AC Milan in the 2005 Champions League and West Ham United in the 2006 FA Cup.

"The fact that I'd missed in the League Cup final didn't enter my head four years later in Istanbul. Rafael Benitez asked if I wanted to take one and I nodded. From that moment on I wasn't aware of what was happening around me. I was, as they say, in the zone – completely focused on my job. Rafa came around again and told me I'd be going first. Because I was so focused I didn't know who was next. I was like a supporter looking to see who was stepping up each time.

"Regardless of which penalty you're taking, I always felt the most important thing was to commit. I never thought: I just need to hit the target. Instead I decided where I was going to hit the ball and went for it. If you do it properly there is every chance of scoring a goal that helps your club to victory."

Of course, every kick in a shootout isn't just about the taker. There is also a man on the line with their arms outstretched ready to be the hero. Such an opportunity unexpectedly came the way of Adrian in August 2019.

Just a few weeks after being without a club he had arrived at Anfield and found himself playing in the UEFA Super Cup final against Chelsea as Alisson was injured.

With the match finishing 2-2 and the Reds having converted their five penalties, Tammy Abraham needed to score to force sudden death. The goalkeeper thwarted those hopes and the silverware was ours, with the manager celebrating by shouting 'Adrian' in a way that suggested he could have been a much better Rocky than Sly Stallone.

Just 10 weeks later another shootout came around and this time it was Caoimhin Kelleher between the posts, saving decisively from Dani Ceballos to help the Redmen eliminate Arsenal from the League Cup after a 5-5 draw.

In 2021/22 the same competition witnessed the Irishman once again be the hero in shoot-out situations. Saves from Luke Thomas and Ryan Bertrand earned a quarter-final spot-kick victory over Leicester City at Anfield when the Reds had been 3-1 down at half-time. In the final against Chelsea he couldn't repeat those stops. Instead, Kelleher netted the final kick, before rival goalie Kepa Arrizabalaga missed, to provide an 11-10 victory after a goalless contest.

Remarkably, the 2022 FA Cup final between Liverpool and Chelsea was also settled on penalties after a 0-0 draw and this time it was Alisson, with a save from Mason Mount, and Kostas Tsimikas, with an ice-cool sudden death spot-kick, who added their names to LFC's ever-growing list of penalty shoot-out heroes.

102/130

Camp Nou conquerors

CAMP Nou. A true cathedral of football. One of the game's great arenas and a venue where the Reds went unbeaten in four visits, finally losing on their fifth trip to Barcelona.

The most famous – or should that be infamous – of those games occurred in February 2007. Barca, under Dutchman Frank Rijkaard, were reigning European Champions and had Ronaldinho, Samuel Eto'o, Xavi, Deco and Lionel Messi within their impressive ranks.

Yet, it would be a Welshman who ended up as the star of the evening. Liverpool's Craig Bellamy had been involved in a disagreement with team-mate John Arne Riise while at a training camp in preparation for the fixture, a difference of opinion that had reportedly led to a golf club being brandished.

So when Bellamy cancelled out Deco's opening goal with a close-range first half header he celebrated with a cheeky golf swing, much to the amusement of his team-mates. The drama didn't end there; Bellamy teeing up Riise for the decisive strike of the evening 16 minutes from time. LFC went on to reach the Champions League final.

The Reds' maiden trip to Camp Nou came in March 1976, for a UEFA Cup semi-final first leg. Again, Barca were supposed to possess the 'stars' in Dutch talents Johan Cruyff and Johan Neeskens. However, it was Bob Paisley's team, and another

Welshman in particular, who were celebrating at the end. 'Fans in fury as Liverpool stroll home' one newspaper report proclaimed after John Toshack's 13th minute goal had earned a 1-0 away victory. That fury of the Barca faithful was demonstrated by the sight of hundreds of cushions being hurled from the stands onto the pitch below.

An unused sub that night was Welsh left-back Joey Jones. "They started throwing objects because we were playing quite well," he explained. "I started getting nicked by objects, in the back of the head. They were gob-stoppers, hard-boiled sweets. [After full-time] they started to throw the cushions first and then parts of the seats. I'd had enough then. I was angry because I wasn't playing. I got these cushions and threw them back. Bob Paisley grabbed me by the collar and said 'get in that dressing room before you cause a riot'. I said: 'I'm not having them throw seats at us'. He said: 'They're throwing the seats at them because we beat them. Now get in the dressing room!'"

It would not be until 2001 that we once again found ourselves back in Catalonia, with Gerard Houllier's team – wearing an all-white kit – on their way to an unprecedented cup treble. Again, it was a UEFA Cup last four meeting. Once more Barca – spearheaded by Patrick Kluivert and Rivaldo – were favourites and incredibly the kick-off was moved to 9.15pm so the BBC, who had the TV rights, could show a 40-minute *Eastenders* special revealing who shot Phil Mitchell in the programme's normal 8.30pm time slot!

This time it was a much more disciplined Liverpool display that brought about a 0-0 draw – and loud boos of disapproval from the home fans at the final whistle – before the Reds finished the task thanks to a 1-0 victory back at Anfield in the return match.

The draw for the following season's Champions League second group stage handed Liverpool a swift return journey to Barca's home and another scoreless encounter materialised.

Liverpool's unbeaten record at Camp Nou ended in 2019 when Luis Suarez and Lionel Messi (2) gave the hosts a 3-0 Champions League semi-final first leg win...but it all worked out in the end after a sensational second leg at Anfield...and as of May 2022 the Reds remain the only English club to have beaten Barcelona on their home turf.

103/130

Hardmen

PORTUGUESE side Vitoria Setubal were the visitors to Anfield for a 1969 Fairs Cup second leg tie which Bill Shankly's side won 3-2, although the result saw them exit on away goals after a 1-0 reversal in the first meeting. But that European departure wasn't the biggest shock of the evening.

That came when news emerged that Tommy Smith, the team's teak-tough defender, was injured and wouldn't play again until January. The Scouser had picked up a fractured kneecap just 20 minutes in. Typically, he played on and even converted a penalty.

Such a feat was a sign of the durability and steel the boy from Scottie Road brought to Shankly's successful units. Others such as Peter Thompson, Ian Callaghan, Roger Hunt or Ian St John may have provided the magic moments, but they were only able to do so because of Smith's presence.

A gifted player in his own right, the ability to intimidate opponents seemed to come naturally to 'the Anfield Iron' and it was a useful weapon for the side to have. In fact, some of the best LFC teams over the ages have also possessed similar types of characters; guys who could play or battle equally well.

Jimmy Case was another local lad – he hailed from south Liverpool – who played in the first team between 1975-1981. Having learned the game with dockers' club team Blue Union, he relished the rough and tumble of a midfield battle as demonstrated by the fact he once punched team-mate Alec Lindsay in training!

Case's game was about far more than just putting his foot, or fist, in though. His standout quality was tremendous long-range shooting, as demonstrated by a stunning goal in the 1977 FA Cup final.

As if the side of the late 70s wasn't good enough or tough enough already, Scottish midfielder Graeme Souness was added to the ranks in the January of 1978. His compatriot and friend Alan Hansen once remarked of him: "Graeme had some battles in midfield with players and nobody got the better of Souness."

That tenacity, desire to win, ability to control games and produce both superb goals and assists meant he eventually became captain of the side. When asked about Souness's ability to inspire colleagues Steve Nicol summed it up by saying: "When you're walking behind Souness and he's walking towards the enemy, 30-40,000 of them, with a big smile on his face... he gave the impression he enjoyed walking into a stadium full of people that hated him. It seemed he got more pleasure turning over opponents that didn't like him.

"You can imagine what that did for someone like me. I'm looking at our captain and he's got that, 'I can't wait for this' look on his face. You know you're going to be okay.

"The thought of defeat never crosses your mind. Losing was not something we contemplated, even for a second."

Souness' departure for Sampdoria at the conclusion of the 1983/84 campaign meant a new presence was required in the centre of the park and the following year Kenny Dalglish signed Steve McMahon from Aston Villa. Following on in the mould of Smith, Case and Souness, the Scouser – who had previously appeared for Everton – was a mixture of grit and talent.

When required he could make a bone-crunching tackle. The next minute he would be providing an inch perfect pass or scoring a sensational goal such as his lob in the 9-0 win over Crystal Palace in 1989 or the cracking low drive in a derby victory at Goodison Park in 1985. They were just two of his 50 goals in a red shirt.

While McMahon was a key component of the LFC side under Dalglish, a local youngster looked on in admiration. Little did Steven Gerrard know then that he would one day become the man who set the tone in the centre of the park himself.

Initially, Gerrard was sometimes used as a right-back and made an early impression in the side with some fearsome tackles including one in a League Cup semi-final win over Crystal Palace that left a lasting impression on assistant manager at the time, Phil Thompson.

"Palace had a lively Latvian winger in Andrejs Rubins, who had caused us some trouble in the first leg," Thompson explained. "In the return we played Igor [Biscan] in centre-midfield and put Steven Gerrard at right-back to deal with the wide threat. I remember Stevie putting in this tackle early on that took me back to the old days of Tommy Smith when players could take the ball and the man and put them in the stands.

"Stevie's sliding tackle carried all of his bodyweight behind it and this boy ended up on the track. He wasn't much of a threat after that. We had shown our intent and won 5-0."

Of course Gerrard's game was about much more than tackling. The ability to do everything was what made him stand out and helped him become the ideal captain. Like Smith, Case, Souness or McMahon he could play whichever way the opposition preferred.

If they wanted a battle all those players were happy to go down that route and be enforcers. Or they could just as easily play football instead. That was what made them so difficult to get the better of.

104/130

The Rafatollah

RA Ra Ra Ra-fa Benitez...the *La Bamba* inspired tune effortlessly rolled off the tongue and between 2004 and 2010 it was belted out by Kopites as they journeyed across England and Europe in support of the Reds.

It was that involvement – and success – in continental competitions that will remain Benitez's legacy at Anfield. Most memorably, obviously, was Istanbul and the incredible scenes that led to Liverpool's fifth European Cup triumph thanks to a still hard to believe penalty shoot-out win over AC Milan.

Just what words did the coach produce during the interval to help transform a 3-0 deficit into an eventual victory? "I said to try to score a goal, because the game would be reopened and our fans would do the rest," is how he has modestly described his input on that famous evening.

Success in the 2005 UEFA Super Cup and another Champions League final appearance in 2007 also followed. But it wasn't just the results, it was the breathtaking nature of some of the European fixtures under the Spaniard that have stayed in Kopites' minds and hearts – even when he managed Chelsea and Everton!

Olympiacos, Juventus, Chelsea more than once, AC Milan,

Barcelona, both Inter Milan and Real Madrid home and away, Arsenal; so many great nights that helped make LFC a side to be feared whenever UEFA were hosting a draw for the next stage of club football's biggest competition.

Prior to one of those ties in 2007, Barcelona at Anfield in the second leg of the first knockout round, a group of supporters dressed as cardinals to canonise Benitez.

It was a humorous display of the esteem he was held in at the time and part of their ceremony involved carrying a large framed photo of the boss – nicknamed 'the Rafatollah' – around the city streets to visit famous venues such as The Cavern (after it had first been paraded around Cardiff before the 2005 League Cup final). In the process, they were met by both LFC and Barca fans who wanted to pose with 'the Rafatollah' for photos.

Martin Tsang was one of 'the cardinals' in question and he explained: "This was a silly idea, but it's now grown into something big that lots of supporters can associate with."

Despite the delays due to the crowds in town, the group eventually made it to the ground in time for kick-off where they did some laps of the stadium. Unfortunately, that was where 'the Rafatollah's' journey came to a halt as safety concerns meant it wasn't allowed past the turnstiles.

If supporters revelled in the cult of Rafa and the results he masterminded, his wife Montse was probably just as pleased to see silverware being collected because if it happened it meant she received a new watch.

"When I was at Valencia my wife said that we would win the league," Benitez explained in April 2005 ahead of the Champions League semi-final with Chelsea. "She was right and to mark the occasion she asked me for a new watch. I bought her the watch, but then she said that we would win the UEFA Cup [which they also did in 2004] and that when we did she wanted another watch.

"Now she says that we will win the Champions League and that she will want an even more expensive watch. My wife has a lot of confidence and a lot of watches!"

During Rafa's time at LFC Montse expanded her collection of timepieces, although she never received one to mark the occasion of a much longed for league title. The closest Benitez came was during 2008/09 when the Reds only lost two league games and accumulated an impressive 86 points. Eleven draws, though, ultimately cost them top spot.

Nonetheless, Benitez is still viewed affectionately by Kopites on Merseyside, where his family home remains, as he possesses a human side as witnessed when he visited a pub in Germany and had a beer with supporters the night before a Champions League last 16 tie with Bayern Leverkusen. Or there was his insistence on sitting down on the sideline during a penalty shoot-out with Chelsea in the 2007 semi-final so fans behind could see the Anfield Road end spot-kicks.

There is also the fact the he illustrates his passion for the club – at times when others in similar situations might have chosen the easier option of hiding their feelings – and his support of the Hillsborough Family Support Group is well-known with Benitez even inviting HFSG chair Margaret Aspinall to be his guest of honour when Newcastle United faced Liverpool at St James' Park in October 2017.

And during his short-spell as Everton manager in 2021/22 it was the travelling Kop who sang Rafa's name during the Merseyside derby at Goodison Park – although there was an element of mischief involved as Liverpool beat the Blues 4-1.

105/130

Euro Kop

"**I'VE** been saying it for years," stated Jamie Carragher. "Sami Hyypia will go down in history alongside the likes of Ron Yeats, Alan Hansen and Emlyn Hughes. In all the time he's been at Liverpool you could probably count his bad performances on one hand."

When Hyypia became the first man from Finland to sign for LFC in 1999 – after a TV cameraman filming his Dutch club Willem II tipped off chief executive Peter Robinson and chief scout Yeats was sent over to watch him – he was dubbed by some as Sami 'Whopia?' Little did the critics know that the giant Finn would become the defensive rock that both Gerard Houllier and Rafa Benitez built their trophy-winning eras upon at a bargain cost of just £2.5m.

Dominant in the air, comfortable on the ball and outstanding at reading the game, Hyypia formed superb central defensive partnerships with Stephane Henchoz and then Carragher as he clocked up 464 appearances for the Reds, the second highest total of any non-British or Irish born Liverpool player behind Bruce Grobbelaar.

He also weighed in with 35 goals in five different competitions, including three in Champions League quarter-finals against Bayer Leverkusen (2002), Juventus (2005) and Arsenal (2008), and captained Liverpool regularly between 2000 and 2003, lifting the 2001 UEFA Cup with Robbie Fowler plus the Charity Shield (2001) and League Cup (2003) before Steven Gerrard took over as skipper.

In the end it was another Nordic-born centre-half, Denmark's Daniel Agger, who edged Sami out of the team, but the ovation he received in May 2009 following his final LFC match against Spurs was one of Anfield's finest with the Kop's trademark 'Oh, Sami Sami' chant ringing out as loud as ever.

Agger was 22 when brought in from Brondby in 2006 and his composure and ability to run with the ball earned him early comparisons to Alan Hansen. He became a popular figure on the Kop, making 232 appearances in a red shirt, a tally that would've been far higher had persistent injuries not compromised the left-footed defender's game-time during an eight-and-a-half season stint in L4.

His most memorable moment came in 2007 when he netted a Champions League semi-final second leg winner against Chelsea at Anfield to take the tie to penalties, the Reds advancing to the final in Athens, and Agger proved how much playing for Liverpool meant to him when he had YNWA tattooed across the knuckles of his right hand.

Of course Kopites already knew a thing or two about great Danes thanks to Jan Molby, regarded by some observers as the most technically gifted midfielder ever seen in a Liverpool shirt.

Joe Fagan brought the Danish international to Anfield from Ajax in 1984 and although he battled with his weight, Molby's passing ability, technical skill and ferocious shooting were second to none with one of the two goals he scored in a 2-1 League Cup victory at home to Manchester United in 1985 regarded by many who witnessed it live as the best they had seen.

Molby pressed two United players, won the ball off Norman Whiteside in his own half and powered his way past Clayton

Blackmore before unleashing a rocket from the edge of the box into the roof of the Kop-end net. It was one of 21 goals 'Big Jan' scored from midfield during Liverpool's 1985/86 double-winning season.

Another technically-gifted Nordic-born player to grace the Anfield turf was Jari Litmanen, widely regarded as Finland's greatest ever footballer. Brought in from Barcelona in January 2001, having won the Champions League with Ajax in 1995, he was strangely underused by Houllier – and caretaker boss Phil Thompson when Houllier was recovering from heart surgery – and made just 43 appearances for the Reds, scoring nine times.

As spectacular goal collections go, few other Reds can match John Arne Riise. Of the six Norwegians to play for LFC – Stig Inge Bjornebye, Bjorn Tore Kvarme, Vegard Heggem, Oyvind Leonhardsen and Frode Kippe being the others – left-back Riise had by far the most successful Anfield career, winning two UEFA Super Cups (2001 and 2005), the League Cup (2003), Champions League (2005) and FA Cup (2006) during his 348 appearances.

Norway's most-capped player (110) will forever be remembered, however, for his venomous, thunderbolt strikes including a free-kick against Manchester United at Anfield in 2001 that almost took the crossbar off as it flew over Fabien Barthez. Signed from Monaco, Riise also netted League Cup final, FA Cup semi-final and Community Shield goals against Chelsea, a Super Cup goal against Bayern Munich, and the winner against Barcelona in Camp Nou in the 2007 Champions League with his weaker right peg.

Torben Piechnik (Denmark), Christian Poulsen (Denmark) and Lauri Dalla Valle (Finland) also had brief Liverpool FC careers, but the only Swedish footballer to have played first-team football for the Reds is centre-back Glenn Hysen, who arrived from Fiorentina in 1989 after Kenny Dalglish swooped to secure his signature ahead of Manchester United's Alex Ferguson.

Sweden's captain missed just three league games in 1989/90 as Dalglish's side landed an 18th league title and Hysen scored the first of his three Liverpool goals, in 93 games, against Crystal Palace in a 9-0 win at Anfield.

Other European countries to have had one player appear for Liverpool FC include Estonia (Ragnar Klavan), Poland (Jerzy Dudek), Slovakia (Martin Skrtel) and Ukraine (Andriy Voronin) while there have been a couple of players from Croatia (Igor Biscan, Dejan Lovren), Greece (Sotirios Kyrgiakos, Kostas Tsimikas), Hungary (Istvan Kozma, Adam Bogdan) and Turkey (Nuri Sahin, Ozan Kabak), plus three Serbians (Milan Jovanovic, Lazar Markovic, Marko Grujic), three Swiss (Stephane Henchoz, Philipp Degen, Xherdan Shaqiri), three Belgians (Simon Mignolet, Christian Benteke, Divock Origi) and three Czechs (Patrik Berger, Vladimir Smicer, Milan Baros). Some of these players, such as Bosnian-born Lovren, have represented countries other than the one they were born in.

The Netherlands has provided LFC with eight players including another whose name can be added to the Reds' family tree of great European centre-backs alongside Hyypia and Agger. When Virgil van Dijk signed for a club record fee of around £75 million in January 2018, his pedigree was already established following successful spells in the UK at Celtic and Southampton. However, few could have predicted the impact he would have as he quickly became a lynchpin in the backline and a key foundation on which the successes of the Jürgen Klopp era were built.

The Dutch captain's partnerships with Joel Matip and Joe Gomez proved vital as the Reds won the Champions League, UEFA Super Cup and FIFA Club World Cup in 2019, the Premier League in 2020 and the Carabao Cup and FA Cup in 2022. His performance in the Carabao Cup final, his first at Wembley, also saw him receive the Alan Hardaker Trophy as player of the match. That transfer fee now looks like an absolute steal for a player who was narrowly beaten to the Ballon d'Or by Lionel Messi in 2019.

The other seven men from the Netherlands to play for the Reds are Erik Meijer, Sander Westerveld, Dirk Kuyt, Jan Kromkamp, Bolo Zenden, Ryan Babel and Gini Wijnaldum.

Germany has provided LFC with seven players (Karl-Heinz Riedle, Markus Babbel, Dietmar Hamann, Christian Ziege, Samed Yesil, Emre Can, Loris Karius), while there have been five Italians (Daniele Padelli, Andrea Dossena, Alberto Aquilani, Fabio Borini, Mario Balotelli) and five Portuguese (Abel Xavier, Raul Meireles, Joao Carlos Teixeria, Tiago Ilori and Diogo Jota) to ply their trade at Anfield. Fabio Carvalho will make it six when making his Liverpool debut following his move from Fulham in July 2022.

With the exception of Spain, which has provided the most players of any European nation with 23 (as you'll have read in the Children of the Rafalution chapter), all those other countries also trail France, though, with 17 Frenchmen all crossing the Channel to play for Liverpool.

The list comprises Jean Michel Ferri, Djimi Traore, Bernard Diomede, Pegguy Arphexad, Nicolas Anelka, Gregory Vignal, Bruno Cheyrou, Patrice Luzi, Anthony Le Tallec, Florent Sinama-Pongolle, Djibril Cisse, Charles Itandje, Damien Plessis, David Ngog, Mamadou Sakho, Aly Cissokho and Ibrahima Konate with Traore being the only one to make over a century of appearances (141) and Cisse netting the most goals (24).

106/130

A spot of bother

DID you know that the Kop ruined Liverpool's chances of winning a first FA Cup? It may have been unwitting and unintentional but some people felt that's exactly what happened in February 1964 when the Reds crashed out at the quarter-final stage at home to Second Division Swansea Town.

First of all, some context. The 1963/64 season saw the Reds fighting hard for the league title although they were suddenly afflicted by a strange problem – an inability to convert penalties.

Ronnie Moran had been the semi-regular man with the duties from 12-yards since 1960 (Kevin Lewis took on the role during his time at Anfield) and had converted eight penalties during his LFC career up to the start of that 1963/64 campaign.

But in the opening month of that season, Ronnie had missed three times from the spot (against Blackburn Rovers, Blackpool and West Ham) and so when the Reds were awarded a late spot-kick in the home game against Burnley at the end of November, a change of taker was required. Bill Shankly had extended his famous mind games to his own players by telling them he would only reveal who was to be Moran's successor when the team were next awarded a penalty. Roger Hunt was the man who got the nod and duly scored to seal a 2-0 victory over the Clarets, but Liverpool's problems didn't end there.

Hunt missed his next spot-kick in an FA Cup fifth round tie at

Arsenal but it didn't prove costly with Liverpool leading 1-0 and the award coming in the dramatic final exchanges which had also seen Reds skipper Ron Yeats sent-off for the only time in his Liverpool career, along with the Gunners' Joe Baker.

The quarter-final draw handed the Reds a home tie against Swansea and the quest for a first FA Cup victory seemed to be on track. The Welshmen however, had other ideas and took a shock 2-0 lead into the interval after two goals in three minutes from Jimmy McLaughlin and Eddie Thomas.

However, Peter Thompson halved the deficit 18 minutes into the second half and the rescue mission appeared set to be completed 10 minutes from time when the Reds were awarded a penalty.

Amid the uncertainty of who should take it, a cry came from the Kop of 'Moran, Moran, Moran...'

Unfortunately, however, he struck his effort wide for his fourth consecutive miss from the spot. Afterwards one press report pondered whether the full-back had been reluctant to take the kick given his record that season.

"Why did Moran finally step up and blast Liverpool's Cup hopes for another season high and wide? I believe he was swayed in his decision by some of those who are Liverpool's greatest fans and who, at the finish, were near to tears at the explosion of another Wembley dream.

"The drama of that penalty kick will stay with us and while there is no guarantee that another player would have scored the fact remains that poor Moran was the most reluctant taker of a penalty I have seen for many seasons."

Shankly, however, later dismissed that theory, saying: "If we had a penalty Ronnie was to be given the chance of taking it. If he did not want to take it, another player would have been delegated. It's unbelievable. I have never seen my boys play better. We could have scored 14 goals and yet here we are out of the Cup."

Liverpool's astonishing penalty woes would go on for some time. Remarkably, Hunt's successful conversion against Burnley would be their only goal from the spot in 10 attempts between 24 August 1963 and 20 March 1965. After Moran's miss against the Swans, Ian Callaghan, Gordon Milne (twice) and Tommy Smith all failed to score with the following four penalties the Reds were awarded.

Ironically the next penalty to be given in our favour after that sequence came in the following season's FA Cup semi-final against Chelsea at Villa Park.

Liverpool were leading 1-0 against Tommy Docherty's much-fancied team and knew a successful spot-kick, coming with 11 minutes left, would all but seal a place in the Wembley final.

Milne was still on penalty duties at the time. Speaking to *LFCTV* in 2015, he admitted: "It was one of those days when the ball is like a balloon and the goal shrinks. It was one of those pictures I had in my mind. Willie [Stevenson] was next to me and I said: 'Willie, I don't fancy this.'"

Stevenson admitted he had never taken a penalty in a competitive game before but felt confident, especially having had little time to worry about it.

"I thought I was having quite a good game so I said: 'I'll take it,'" he recalled. "The best thing about that was I meant to put it in the bottom right-hand corner, my right facing it, but my foot just slipped as I came to the ball and instead of going on the ground it went about six feet up straight back into the net. They are all great goals!"

Midfielder Stevenson stayed on penalty duties and solved Liverpool's quandary, finding the net with six of his next seven attempts before Smith became the regular taker at the start of the 1967/68 season, converting 22 in total.

107/130

By the way, you're the champions!

HEARD the one about the Liverpool side who had to be informed by a team-mate that they had been crowned league champions? Well that's exactly what happened in 2014 when Liverpool Ladies – now Liverpool FC Women – retained their Women's Super League trophy on the final day of the season after an amazing afternoon of twists and turns.

The Reds' triumph also took league officials by surprise and the team had to wait on the pitch for the best part of an hour while the trophy was brought to Widnes by a dispatch rider as the team jigged around in celebration before Liverpool captain Gemma Bonner finally lifted the coveted piece of silverware aloft.

Having won the league title in 2013 for the first time, Liverpool had mounted a spirited defence of their crown though it seemed set to fall short having been beset by injury problems.

The Reds, managed by Matt Beard, started the final day in third position, three points behind leaders Chelsea and one behind Birmingham City. Few gave them any hope at all, but Beard kept his focus on making sure the Reds kept their part of the bargain by beating Bristol Academy at the Select Security Stadium.

Ironically, Bristol had been the team they had defeated at home on the final day of the previous season to clinch the title.

At half-time, Liverpool were goalless but they received a tonic after being told both their rivals were trailing at the interval in their respective fixtures.

Second-half goals from Natasha Dowie and Lucy Bronze followed by a Fara Williams penalty gave the Reds a 3-0 win over Bristol and then they had to wait and hear what had happened elsewhere.

The Liverpool game was the first to finish. Up in the corporate boxes, injured midfielder Lucy Staniforth was following the closing stages of the Manchester City v Chelsea game on television. Two-one down, Chelsea were piling on the pressure – against a City team who had been reduced to 10 players for the final 19 minutes – knowing an equaliser would win them the league.

There were some agonisingly close shaves but when the final whistle blew, City's 2-1 victory seemed to have confirmed an unlikely Liverpool success.

As Staniforth emerged onto the balcony facing the pitch, she was met by the sight of the Liverpool squad looking up at her for news.

She gave them the thumbs up and the celebrations began.

What the Liverpool ladies didn't realise at the time was that Birmingham and Notts County were still playing! The scoreline there was 2-2 and a Birmingham goal in the dying embers of that fixture would have seen them crowned champions and left Liverpool red-faced.

"That would have been a bit embarrassing to say the least!," Staniforth admitted on the BBC's *Women's Football Show* the following evening. "Fortunately that didn't happen and we were able to celebrate a fantastic achievement."

Such were the odds against the Reds, the trophy had been in Manchester in anticipation of a Chelsea title triumph, albeit with the proviso that a quick dash to Birmingham may be required.

In the event however, it was re-routed to Widnes as the Reds finished level on points with Chelsea but with a goal difference of plus nine compared to the Blues' plus seven.

The team's Louisville-born goalkeeper Libby Stout recalls: "We needed to win by two goals and then required other things to happen for us but we were pretty focused on doing what we needed to. Beardy (manager Beard) said: 'I don't want anyone to be talking about the other games'.

"At half-time, everyone seemed quite positive. I asked my goalkeeping coach Pottsy (Joe Potts) what was happening and he whispered the scores to me! They were in our favour and at that point it seemed so real that we began to think it could possibly happen. It was still 0-0 in our match, of course, but we had dominated the first half and knew that we just had to be patient.

"We scored in the first few minutes of the second half and the second goal came quickly too. The crowd had started chanting that we were top of the league but with about 20 minutes to go they stopped. After we had won our game, I ran into the circle of players and staff and was asking everyone: 'What's going on?' Pottsy told me things were still in our favour but the other games were still going on. Everyone was standing around next to each other in a huddle not sure what to do.

"The coaches told us to stay grounded and humble and wait until we knew exactly what had happened in the other matches. That was a really tough time to stand and wait. My parents were up in the stands and I was looking at them for some sort of clue! The first thing I saw was someone in the hospitality boxes coming out giving us the thumbs up. Then I was thinking: 'Is it real?'

"Beardy started celebrating and then we all went nuts! It was nice that everyone was in it with us. It wasn't just us out on that pitch, it was our fans, our parents, everybody who was there rooting for us. It was an amazing moment I will never forget and absolutely the best day of my football career.

"That final day is hard to describe to people. You see it on paper and think: 'Oh, they won the league.' But that doesn't begin to explain the story behind it. I guess the stars were aligned."

Stout, Beard, Bonner and company were left to toast a second successive top-flight title and with it qualification for the UEFA Women's Champions League as Liverpool's ladies in red began to make their own mark in bringing success to the club.

108/130

The phone call that led to a future LFC legend

"THERE'S this kid in our Under-9s and he's outstanding. You'll have to see him play." LFC academy coach Dave Shannon had been sitting at home when the phone rang one evening. On the other end of the line was a guy called Ben McIntyre, who was involved with a local club called Whiston Juniors.

Of course Shannon had heard similar recommendations on countless occasions before that had come to nothing. Nonetheless, he decided to follow it up: "[Fellow academy coaches] Hughie McAuley, Steve Heighway and I used to go to a lot of Sunday league games in an attempt to find talented youngsters. Of course we couldn't cover every fixture, so we'd always ask those working in under-age football on Merseyside to let us know if there was a player they really rated. Ben was one of those people."

The boy in question was invited to the Vernon Sangster Centre in Stanley Park, where LFC youngsters trained at the time.

"Simply phenomenal," is how Shannon sums up his first sighting of a young Steven Gerrard in action.

"Full of energy, he was getting stuck into the older players. Obviously we had a lot of talented boys at the club, but from the first minute Stevie was special. It was natural talent. All we had to do was ensure he kept working on his technique and continued improving. He did because he loved training, he never wanted to be anywhere else."

The aforementioned McAuley believes it wasn't just ability that made the Huyton youngster stand out when, at the age of eight, he first began what would be a long-lasting association with the Reds.

"People who play for Liverpool need a winner's attitude and he had that. Then there is desire and commitment to play and train. Again, he had plenty of those qualities too.

"It was up to us to put other good players and teams around him to make him even better. Hopefully we did that. In such an environment he was able to express himself, improve and develop. Talent-wise there wasn't anything that he couldn't do. And tactically, which isn't the case with every youngster, he knew the game inside out.

"The only area that he really needed to work on was his decision-making regarding when to challenge for the ball. A lot of that came from his natural enthusiasm. He wanted to win every 50/50, 70/30 or even 80/20 in the opposition's favour and felt he could. He didn't want to hurt other players – he just wanted to compete. Football is an aggressive sport, but at times he was overzealous and we thought if he didn't curb that instinct he would end up getting injured.

"When boys are still growing up it can sometimes be hard to speak to them about their own game. But Steven eventually took our message on board."

Steve Heighway, who had been a major part of first Bill Shankly and then Bob Paisley's all conquering sides of the 1970s, was head of the Academy at the time and immediately realised that Gerrard was a boy blessed with unique abilities.

"His talent was there right from the beginning," he recalls, "but I never like predicting players will make it until they are slightly older. By the time he reached 14 or 15 I was certain he would go on to be a Liverpool player. The only other individual I've ever said the same about at that stage was Michael Owen.

"Working with Steven was a real pleasure. We saw him develop from an enthusiastic boy into a world-class player."

Naturally, the three coaches all have their own favourite moments from the years they spent helping Gerrard hone his ability prior to the Scouser becoming a part of the first team set-up under Gerard Houllier in 1998.

Shannon picks out "a shot in to the top corner from 25 yards in a B-team game against Man Utd at Melwood," McAuley goes for "his goalscoring ability, there are too many to pick just one," while Heighway opts for seeing "a 14-year-old Gerrard entertaining fans with his skills while at an U-18 tournament in Spain."

It wasn't just the 2005 European Cup winning captain who Heighway, McAuley and Shannon helped to bring through the ranks either.

The trio also played a major part in nurturing, amongst others, Steve McManaman, Robbie Fowler, Dominic Matteo and FA Youth Cup winners Jamie Carragher, Michael Owen, David Thompson and Jay Spearing. Their contribution to him becoming one of the game's greats hasn't been forgotten by Gerrard, the player they first learned of via a late evening phone call.

Gerrard went on to work at the Academy himself, managing Liverpool Under-18s in 2017/18, and will perhaps one day be recalled as being highly influential in the development of a 16-year-old midfielder who played in his side – Curtis Jones.

109/130

Specs appeal

A quick quiz question: what do Nuri Sahin and Christian Benteke have in common?

Both players spent a single season at Anfield and neither the Turkey international midfielder nor the Belgian striker were able to establish themselves in the club's longer-term plans. But that isn't what we're getting at. The answer is that both players left a lasting impression on Jürgen Klopp's vision – by breaking his glasses!

In January 2016, Benteke left Klopp's trademark spectacles in pieces after joining in the exuberant celebrations that followed Adam Lallana's last-gasp winner at Norwich City as the Reds edged a crazy encounter by five goals to four.

But it was not the first time that the German had needed new eye-wear as his specs were also on the receiving end during his days at Borussia Dortmund.

After the Premier League game at Carrow Road – just three-and-a-half months into his spell as LFC boss – Klopp explained:

"[At Dortmund when] we won for the first time against Bayern Munich, Nuri Sahin broke my glasses. Today it was Christian.

"Usually I have a second pair, but I couldn't find them. It's really difficult looking for glasses without glasses!"

The pair damaged in Germany now reside in Borussia Dortmund's club museum but the Reds' manager admitted that the frames he donned in East Anglia had to be binned.

Recalling the incident a year later, he joked: "They were absolutely broken! It was Christian Benteke who did it. So don't kill my glasses, otherwise you will be sold!"

Before the 2021/22 campaign kick off the Liverpool manager surprised supporters by returning for pre-season training without his trademark glasses.

It's actually totally private, but I can explain it to you once, too," he told German newspaper *BILD*. "I've been wearing glasses since I was ten years old - that's 44 years. The problem in recent years was that the glasses could no longer correct my poor eyesight. The solution to this was a minor intervention. It wasn't lasering or anything, but it made me see very well without glasses at the moment.

"I think my face is weird without glasses, but I don't need them anymore. I may need one more [intervention]. When that happens, I'll wear glasses again."

Whether you wear glasses or not, everybody can see that Jürgen Klopp is overseeing one of the greatest eras in the history of Liverpool FC.

110/130

Love supreme

WEDNESDAY 12 October 1966. European Cup first round second leg. Petrolul Ploiesti 3 Liverpool 1.

The result, in LFC's second foray into Europe's grandest club competition, meant the Reds had drawn 3-3 on aggregate with the team from Romania and, in the days before the away-goals rule had been introduced in the European Cup, had to play them again in a replay a week later on neutral ground. Liverpool won 2-0 at the Heysel Stadium in Brussels.

That away leg in Ploiesti is of particular interest to a very focused group of Reds fans: those who take their interest to another level altogether, chronicling a history of LFC through stats, information and memorabilia ranging from programmes and tickets to autographs and match-worn shirts.

These are the Anfield eggheads – the world's leading experts on all things LFC.

For three decades two of them, Dave Ball and Ged Rea, have been the club's official statisticians. Like many enthusiasts, both kept football scrapbooks as youngsters. Eventually they began to work professionally in sports trivia and they've also been researchers on the BBC programme *A Question of Sport* for many years.

A fellow 'statto' with a very personal connection to the club is Eric Doig, who was born and brought up a stone's throw from the Spion Kop. "My grandfather 'Ned' Doig was a former Liverpool

FC goalkeeper," he explains. "I always had an interest in his career, and since making contact with fellow statistician Jonny Stokkeland over 20 years ago we have been working jointly on all aspects of LFC history."

In turn Stokkeland, a member of the Norwegian LFC supporters club since 1980, has worked with colleague Sveinung Egeland to compile a comprehensive database with "a who's who of more than 4,500 names. Together with Eric I have visited libraries and archives all over England, looking for new information on Liverpool FC and correcting old errors. We collect match facts for all first-team, reserve and junior games going back to 1892, and recently our collection has become LFC's official archive."

Among other specialist Nordic Reds are Icelandic duo Gudmundur Magnusson and Arnie Baldursson, who run the go-to website *lfchistory.net* and published the acclaimed book *The Liverpool Encyclopedia*. "We've never been fascinated with just stats alone but more by the stories that surround them," reveals Arnie. "For example, when writing the Encyclopedia we discovered that when LFC won the First Division for the first time in 1900/01 they were only top of the league on two occasions – the first day of the season and the last."

Kjell Hanssen, originally from Oslo, says his friendship with Doig and Stokkeland inspired him to write *Dicky Sams: Liverpool FC in Blue and White*, covering the period 1892-95. He's also uploaded 10,000 historic newspaper articles onto his database *playupliver-pool.com*, although has been unable to update it since 2019 after suffering a severe stroke.

"One of my last big discoveries was in connection with the building of the 'new Anfield' of 1906," he said. "Some wonderful articles appeared in different newspapers and I now have a much better picture of what Anfield looked like in, for example, 1890, 1895, 1900 and 1906. Regarding the pitch itself, since 1892 to today it has moved almost 20 yards away from the Sir Kenny Dalglish/Centenary/Kemlyn Road Stand."

Closer to home, Anfield season-ticket holder Adrian Killen had a dad who collected football cuttings from newspapers and a grandmother who kept matchday programmes and ticket stubs. "Every collector has a niche and mine is compiling match reports in semi-professional scrapbooks as well as collecting images and film of every game," he says.

"In the early 1960s my brother bought a cine camera and filmed a few games in colour, then in 1979 I bought a video recorder and camera and from then on I've kept a copy of every Liverpool FC game shown on TV, as well as filming numerous live games in the last three decades."

Adrian even landed a dream job at the club museum, working there for six years. "I was privileged to handle everything at close quarters, including a Kenny Dalglish bench coat as well as Bill Shankly's blazer. But as a lifetime collector of LFC memorabilia, if I had to pick anything I'd love to own it would be David Fairclough's St Etienne shirt from 1977 which is signed by all the team and on display in the museum."

Over in Ireland, collector Gerard Scully boasts Bill Shankly's tracksuit from the 1972/73 season, while fellow Irish fan Jim Donnelly owns the great man's desk – "purchased by the club before the Second World War and used at Anfield until 1970. Don Welsh, Phil Taylor and Shankly all used the desk."

For George Rowlands, it's all about cigarette cards. In the early 20th century these were the most enduring portrayals of football stars. They were collected, swapped and traded by young fans like George, who produced a richly illustrated book about this bygone era. He estimates that there are 331 cards depicting Liverpool FC players.

The abiding passion for Keith Stanton is programmes. He's been collecting them since the mid-1950s and is the proud owner of a copy of the 1965 FA Cup final programme – and match ticket – signed by the players. Along with Robin Gowers he also formed the Liverpool Programme Collectors Club which publishes a 28-page bulletin four times a season.

Which brings us back to Petrolul Ploiesti. "European away programmes are the most interesting and expensive, and this one is very rare," says Keith. "I've only seen it once and never owned it. The copy I saw was obtained via a butcher's shop in Liverpool where I believe one of the club directors used to shop and hand in programmes from his travels. It had a match ticket inserted, further enhancing this rarest of Liverpool FC items.

"Another very rare programme is from the 1976/77 European Cup match in Trabzonspor, Turkey. A handful of supporters made the journey and I'm led to believe only about 12 programmes were brought back."

Fellow collector Alan Parkinson is the owner of a match ticket for both Petrolul Ploiesti and Trabzonspor and counts them among his top three most treasured items. Number one for him, though, is the ticket from LFC's first European game, against KR Reykjavik in August 1964. "I went over to Iceland and visited the supporters club before a game and managed to pick up two. They are just so rare! But my 'holy grail' is undoubtedly the tickets from Liverpool's Inter-Cities Fairs Cup game at Malmo in 1967, and the 1969 Fairs Cup game v Dundalk, if indeed they even exist – no one has ever seen either of them."

Time to take a closer look in the attic and also at Andy Marsden's 2022 book *Liverpool Football Programmes - The Definitive Guide*. Described as "a colossal, metatarsal-crushing, limited-edition paean to Liverpool FC matchday programmes," it took Andy five years to produce, catalogues 75 years of Liverpool programme history and all profits go to the LFC Foundation. Epic!

111/130

Graeme's gamble

DURING his six-years with Liverpool from 1978 to 1984, Graeme Souness was arguably the most complete midfielder in the country, if not Europe. His Anfield playing career culminated in him lifting the European Cup in Rome while only once in six seasons did the Reds fail to win the league with Souness in their side.

His second spell with Liverpool, as manager from 1991 to 1994, was less successful, and by his own admission he struggled to apply his methods to a club in transition at a time of change in English football as he worked alongside former Anfield team-mates Phil Boersma and Sammy Lee.

Big money signings such as Paul Stewart, Dean Saunders, Mark Wright, Mark Walters, Nigel Clough and Neil Ruddock didn't quite work out as planned, but Souness did give opportunities to young players such as David James, Nick Tanner, Mike Marsh, Jamie Redknapp, Don Hutchison, Dominic Matteo, Steve McManaman and Robbie Fowler.

In 1992 his side won the FA Cup – the only major honour that had eluded him as a player – and four weeks after heart surgery he was at Wembley to watch his team beat second-tier Sunderland 2-0 with Michael Thomas, another Souness signing, and Ian Rush, with his fifth goal in three final appearances, both scoring.

Also in the triumphant Liverpool team that day was Rob Jones, whose grandfather Bill had played in both the title-winning side of 1946/47 and the team that had lost to Arsenal in the 1950 FA Cup final. Full-back Rob had been signed by Souness from Crewe Alexandra in February 1991 and, less than 48 hours after putting pen to paper, was playing against Manchester United.

"Souness just took a big risk," he recalled. "I know he came to watch me a couple of times at Crewe and there was a slight injury-crisis at the time. But still, for them to gamble on a Fourth Division, young 19-year-old – to buy me on the Friday and throw me straight in at Old Trafford in a televised game on the Sunday – it just doesn't happen any more."

The game finished goalless and Jones put in a man-of-the-match performance to neutralise the threat of Ryan Giggs. By the end of 1990/91 he'd been capped by England. But for an injury picked up after the 1992 FA Cup final, in a friendly against Brazil, he would have been England's first-choice right-back for Euro '92.

Indeed it was injury that curtailed his playing career after 243 appearances for Liverpool, but Rob – who famously never scored for the Reds and has since coached at the Liverpool Academy – will always be grateful to Souness for changing his life. "Graeme gambled on signing me, it paid off for him, it paid off for me – and I never looked back after that."

112/130

Room with a view

LIVERPOOL FC's world-famous home has arguably changed as much in the last few years than at any time in its history – and still it's evolving.

As the revised edition of this book was being readied for print in the summer of 2022, expansion work on the Anfield Road Stand to increase the ground's capacity to 61,000 had been going on for six months – ever since Jürgen Klopp ceremonially put the first spade into the ground in September 2021.

First came the foundations, then the concrete cores, then new steelwork to support the structure and create space underneath to allow the existing stand to be accessed on matchdays.

The hubbub reminded fans of the stadium's last major upgrade – could seven years really have passed already? On a day of calm, favourable weather conditions back in late July 2015, three weeks before the Reds' first home game of the season against AFC Bournemouth, the look of Anfield had changed forever.

Up into place went a massive, 650-tonne roof truss, raised by two huge cranes then lowered onto two towers to form the new 'exo-skeleton' of the expanded Main Stand. It had taken months of planning, with the 140-metre long truss arriving in sections at Anfield and being assembled on site. The cranes, known as AK680 and AK912, had previously been employed upon projects such as the London 2012 Olympic Park and Wembley Stadium.

The truss dominated the skyline throughout the first half of the 2015/16 season: looming above Anfield's warren of historic terraced streets, straddling the horizon across the Wirral Peninsula and River Mersey, and visible from Knowsley and the East Lancs Road. With it in place, and the original two-storey building at the back of the existing Main Stand already demolished, work could begin on constructing the new roof, with cranes lifting and securing steel rafters into place. Layers of concrete, brickwork, cladding and glazing followed, and with each passing fixture Anfield matchgoers could see the changes for themselves.

Much had changed at the football club, and indeed in the city, since the last time the Main Stand was significantly altered, in 1973. Back then it underwent a facelift to become the most modern of the stadium's four stands at the time. Its old dugout was even built by a certain 'bricklayer' who took on almost every other role going at the club in those days: none other than Bob Paisley.

The preceding structure dated from 1906 when it was named after nearby Lake Street, off Walton Breck Road, and featured a mock-Tudor 'eyebrow' gable on its roof – a design-feature characteristic of the famous football architect Archibald Leitch. It was from a balcony along this Main Stand that Bill Shankly and his first great team celebrated their league title win in April 1964 before an ecstatic crowd.

Almost 50 years later, at the start of 2016/17, the expanded Main Stand was officially opened. Today, as one of the largest all-seater single stands in Europe, it boasts three tiers and two concourses providing space for supporters to gather and enjoy its many facilities. There are modern new dressing-rooms, a widened players' tunnel, new dugouts, a media platform and more bays for disabled spectators – not just in the Main Stand, but on the other side of the pitch in what is now the Sir Kenny Dalglish Stand, too.

For many fans, a redeveloped Anfield Road Stand felt like the next natural progression. But these things, quite rightly, take time. In December 2019 the club began a first-stage public consultation to share early ideas and listen to views from the local community, businesses, supporters and stakeholders. A second phase followed in February 2020 with proposals reshaped to reflect initial feedback, and new visualisations unveiled. At the end of that year the club thanked everyone who'd contributed and submitted its planning application to the City Council after it'd been paused in the spring due to the uncertainty surrounding the pandemic.

The stand's capacity would increase by around 7,000 seats, with the lower tier retained and refurbished and a new upper tier built above it. Careful consideration would again be given to Anfield's atmosphere – the best in the business – through the development of an acoustic and lighting strategy to match that of the remodelled Main Stand.

When permission was granted in late spring 2021, thanks to COVID-19, it was tough to imagine Anfield with a full house again. So what a tonic it was to think that eventually, all being well, the ground would be not only packed to the rafters but bigger than ever before.

The redeveloped Anfield Road Stand is anticipated to be ready for the 2023/24 season and when completed LFC will be on course to set a new record – never before has Anfield held 60,000-plus for a league match.

None of this will compromise the stadium's traditional four-stand configuration, and all along the expansion has sat at the heart of a broader masterplan for the Anfield neighbourhood. The ground has been reconnected with historic Stanley Park, which celebrated its own 150th birthday in 2020, and a vibrant area has been created for football fans and the local community.

All along the club's owners Fenway Sports Group have stressed the need to "retain the heart and spirit of Anfield and the city of

Liverpool itself. We've learned that it's possible to take a hallowed sporting ground, upgrade it and end up with the best of all worlds: a stadium that retains the essence of what made it special while providing an improved experience for everyone."

In the club's 130th anniversary year Anfield reflects the origins of the sport itself, but is very much a 21st-century venue. If the Main Stand has been a striking addition to the skyline in its own right, from its upper reaches it also offers spectacular new views of the city it calls home, overlooking the sweep of Liverpool's northern suburbs down to the docks and River Mersey.

113/130

Poetry in motion

OVER the years there have probably been more books written about Liverpool Football Club than any other English side. The LFC library includes tomes on statistical records, photo books and a vast array of player autobiographies taking you inside Anfield and Melwood during different eras.

A departure from the norm came in December 1976 when striker John Toshack indulged his love of poetry by publishing a book of his best self-penned work entitled *Gosh, It's Tosh!*

A quick search online shows that a pristine copy of the 96-page book will now set you back over a grand although well-thumbed copies can be acquired for a lot less.

The poems mainly recalled Toshack's exploits in the red of Liverpool and Wales. Earlier in 1976, Toshack's goal had helped

Liverpool become the first English side to beat Barcelona in Camp Nou in the first leg of the UEFA Cup semi-final. The Cardiff-born striker captured the feeling of that victory which came four days before an Anfield clash with Everton.

We're coming in to land at Speke.
My legs are feeling very weak.
We've just returned from Barcelona,
And now I'm going for a sauna.
But the Pressmen's questions are all the same:
'Where's your poem for the Derby game?'
I tell them 'Poems don't grow on trees,
And you ain't forthcoming with any fees!
You'll have to give me one more day'
They laugh and talk, then walk away.

Toshack isn't the only Liverpool player to have turned to verse, however – goalkeeper Elisha Scott is also known to have been a man who would occasionally transfer his thoughts to paper.

A big character who was not known for curbing his tongue, his colourful language had apparently embarrassed Reds defender James Jackson, who was training for the ministry while on LFC's books.

When Liverpool made the trip to South Wales to take on Cardiff City in October 1922, an away win seemed a banker with David Ashworth's Reds top of the table and the Bluebirds rock bottom, but Liverpool produced an insipid display and slumped to a 0-3 defeat in the Welsh capital. A furious Scott is said to have penned the following ditty as he let off some steam afterwards.

Twinkle, twinkle little star
How I wonder what you are

Wheel 'em in and wheel 'em out
Cardiff three, Liverpool nowt.

Those first 30 years of the club's history also saw the local press moved to rhyme on various occasions as they followed the Reds' ups and downs.

After the death of founder John Houlding in 1902, the club faced an uncertain future. In the years that followed – and with the ownership issues still largely unresolved – rumours began to circulate surrounding Liverpool's future at Anfield. In May 1904, with the Reds recently relegated, the *Liverpool Review* somewhat mischievously produced an imaginary sporting operetta featuring a gloomy manager, Tom Watson, who sang about the club's predicament.

McKenna's not smiled for a week
He thinks we'll sail off in a sloop.
We're all without fable,
Dressed in crepe and sable.
In the Second they've placed us
They've gone and disgraced us.
Because – and I have it on the very best authority –
We have all been drowned 'in the soup'.

Within a decade the tone had turned from melancholy to satire. With the club back in the top-flight, there was excitement around the Reds' prospects in the FA Cup. Having beaten Barnsley and Gillingham, a 1-1 draw at West Ham meant a third round replay.

The problem was that there were no floodlights in those days and a 3pm kick-off on a Wednesday afternoon presented problems for the city's workforce and schoolchildren. The *Liverpool Echo* suggested some of the inventive reasons which would be conjured up to ensure attendance [in the event, 43,729 turned up!].

There'll be grandmothers to bury,
At the Anfield Cemetree
And lots of sudden illnesses,
Next Wednesday at three.
There'll be reams of lies on paper
Special Spion Copper Crammers
There'll be lots of French leave taken
For the fun'ral of the Hammers

Moving into the 21st century, it is no surprise that such a storied club as Liverpool has remained the subject matter of many a poem. Poignantly, respected playwright Dave Kirby – a proud Liverpool FC supporter – wrote about the Hillsborough disaster in a work titled *The Justice Bell* which was published to mark the 13th anniversary of the tragedy in 2002.

Ten years on, Dave also put pen to paper to celebrate the Reds' first visit to the rebuilt Wembley Stadium for the 2012 Carling Cup final. *Footsteps of our Fathers* celebrated Liverpool supporters' 'million special memories' of England's national stadium.

In 2006, thirty years after the collected works of John Toshack had hit the bookshops, Liverpool FC took the unusual step of appointing the club's first official poet.

Liverpool JMU student Cheyelle Omar, then an undergraduate in imaginative writing, was appointed to the role after impressing LFC chief executive Rick Parry with a boardroom presentation.

And poetry is, of course, still mentioned on matchdays today in the form of the popular fans' song *We Are Liverpool* which features the words 'poetry in motion'.

So there you have it. Chapter and verse.

114/130

Irish Reds

LIVERPOOL FC's links with Ireland go back to the very foundations of the club.

The team's first managers, John McKenna and William Barclay, both hailed from the island of Ireland. Since then, a host of Irishmen have helped Liverpool hit the heights.

Elisha Scott, the goalkeeping great from the North, secured automatic selection into the club's official Hall of Fame.

Considered by some to be the club's best ever keeper, his Anfield career spanned an incredible 21 years. His tally of 468 appearances would have been even higher but for World War One.

The backbone to LFC's championship-winning teams of 1921/22 and 1922/23, Scott forged a friendly rivalry with the great Everton centre-forward Dixie Dean.

"Elisha was the greatest I've ever seen," he said. "You can have Swift, Trautmann, Banks, Wilson. You can have them all. I'll take Elisha Scott."

Kopites of the time agreed. When a survey was conducted among Liverpool supporters in 1939 to name the club's greatest player, Scott topped the list.

Flying winger Steve Heighway starred for the Reds in their European Cup triumphs of 1977 and 1978 before returning to LFC to serve the club with distinction in his role as academy director.

His name still rings out around the ground on a regular basis as part of the song *The Fields of Anfield Road.*

In 2005, Limerick-born Steve Finnan played in the Champions League final as the Reds were crowned kings of Europe for the fifth time. Between those times, players such as Mark Lawrenson, Steve Staunton, Jim Beglin, Ray Houghton, Ronnie Whelan and John Aldridge all shone in the red shirt of Liverpool as well as the green jersey of Ireland – although not all of them were born in Eire!

The Republic of Ireland's most capped player of all-time, Robbie Keane, spent the first half of the 2008/09 season at Anfield. Four of his 146 international games came while he was a Liverpool player. He scored seven times in 28 appearances for the Reds before returning to former club Tottenham Hotspur.

Liverpool Football Club were managed by Northern Irishman Brendan Rodgers between June 2012 and October 2015 with the Carnlough-born boss taking the Reds to within a whisker of the Premier League title in 2013/14.

Irish wingers Mark Kennedy and Richie Partridge made a combined 24 appearances for LFC between 1995 and 2004 and Cork-born goalkeeper Caoimhin Kelleher has not only set a club record for the most penalty shoot-outs won by a Liverpool goalie, but also struck the winning penalty as the Reds beat Chelsea on spot-kicks in the 2022 Carabao Cup final at Wembley.

The club has a huge fan base across the Irish Sea. There are official club stores in Dublin and Belfast and legions of supporters think nothing of making regular pilgrimages via boat or plane to see their beloved Reds in action.

As LFC prepared to kick-off their 125th year celebrations in 2017/18, the team played a 'home' pre-season friendly against Athletic Bilbao at the Aviva Stadium in Dublin while a new pitch was being bedded in at Anfield.

It was the third time Liverpool had played at the stadium in four years and manager Klopp was delighted with the reception the team received with a crowd of 51,333 watching their 3-1 victory.

He said: "I am well aware of the number of Liverpool FC supporters who make the journey from Ireland to Anfield on a regular basis to support the team so it seems right that we made the trip to see them!

"I had been told that LFC played a couple of other friendly matches in Dublin during the past few years and that the welcome the team received had been first-class. I really enjoyed experiencing that for myself."

An even bigger crowd of 51,512 returned a year later to see Liverpool beat Napoli 5-0 at the Aviva with Kelleher an unused substitute at the stadium where he now plays international football for the Republic of Ireland.

115/130

Sound as a pound

FOOTBALLERS don't do singing as a rule, and the vast majority of those at Liverpool FC, past and present, are no exception.

Only John Barnes has ever given it a go and still looked cool, with his cult-status-earning rap in England's official Italia 90 song, *World in Motion*: "You've got to hold and give but do it at the right time, You can be slow or fast but you must get to the line, They'll always hit you and hurt you, Defend and attack, There's only one way to beat them – get round the back..."

Two years earlier the winger had dipped his toe into the waters of musical stardom, along with several team-mates, for LFC's 1988 FA Cup final song *The Anfield Rap (Red Machine In Full Effect)*.

It was co-written by Reds midfielder Craig Johnston, who'd also been the creative force behind the rousing *Pride Of Merseyside* featuring the vocals of Joe Fagin (a long-time singer and not the LFC manager). And it featured two of the team's local-born players, Steve McMahon and John Aldridge, encouraging the others to learn Scouse: "Alright Aldo, Sound as a pound, I'm cushty, la, but there's nothing down, The rest of the lads ain't got it sussed, We'll have to learn 'em to talk like us!'

To which Barnes replied: "You two Scousers are always yapping, I'm gonna show you some serious rapping!"

The video featured dodgy tracksuits and even dodgier headgear, gold chains and gaudy shades, and it still managed to reach number three in the UK charts – despite one BBC entertainment reporter calling it "an inexplicably awful track which rhymes 'hard as hell' with 'Ar-se-nell'."

Barnesie was back on top form for the 1996 FA Cup final offering, *Pass and Move (It's The Liverpool Groove)* by The Boot Room Boyz. The less said about the actual game the better, but here's how it went…

"Straight out the Boot Room, To Wembley our second home, We come to conquer – you know we never walk alone, We dominate – the cream of the crop, Drawing all our strength from the roar of the Kop…"

Back in the day, there was no rapping nor even a video for *We Are Liverpool*, a 7in single recorded by the players in 1978 and gloriously revived by Kopites in more recent years.

It was one side of a double-A single, the other track being *Hail To The Kop*, and it appeared on a label called Logo Records when the Reds were champions of Europe – the first-team squad is pictured on the cover with 'Old Big Ears' as well as the League championship trophy and Charity Shield. The original melody came from the hit pop song *Brown Girl In The Ring* by Boney M.

The reason behind the song's special place in the hearts of the supporters? Who knows, but maybe these words from Bill Shankly provide an explanation...

"Above all, I would like to be remembered as a man who was selfless, who strove and worried so that others could share the glory, and who built up a family of people who could hold their heads up high and say...We are Liverpool."

116/130

Istanbul

WE won it at Wembley. We won it in gay Paree. In 77 and 84 it was Rome. We won it five times. We won it five times. In Istanbul, we won it five times. Goosebumps gone down yet?

Istanbul 2005. The greatest night in the 130 year history of Liverpool Football Club? In the eyes of most, yes, although Kopites of a certain age might offer the Reds' first FA Cup win at Wembley in 1965 or Liverpool's maiden European Cup triumph in 1977 in Rome as alternatives, while for younger Reds perhaps Madrid 2019 is the greatest of all.

Yet for sheer drama and the polarised emotional extremes of desolation and despair turning into unexpected ecstasy and elation – or vice-versa for AC Milan supporters – there has simply never been another night like 25 May 2005.

Every Red who made the pilgrimage to Istanbul has their own story, memories that will last for a lifetime. Sabiha Gokcen Airport. Rafa is the Bosphorus. Taksim Square rocking. Them Scousers Again. Kebabs and Efes. Queues of yellow taxis snaking through the hills. The lunar landscape surrounding the Ataturk Stadium. Pure excitement that the Redmen were in the Champions League final. The incomparable adrenaline rush that surges through your veins in the moments before kick-off. And then it all went from anticipation to agony in the space of 45 gut-wrenching minutes.

Maldini. 1-0. Not even a minute on the clock. Harry Kewell. Injured. On comes Vladimir Smicer. Penalty! Referee! Nesta handballed it, it should be a pen...2-0. Crespo. They've scored on the counter. Now we're in trouble. We need to hold out until half...3-0. Crespo again. Game over. Milan are too good. This is embarrassing.

Never had there been such a feeling of acute deflation for Liverpool supporters at the half-time interval of a big match. Ever. There was a stunned silence at one end of the Ataturk while the Milanese were planning their post-match party at the other. On Merseyside, some Reds turned their TV sets over while it was Evertonians, not Liverpudlians, ordering champagne in the pubs.

Chaos and confusion reigned in the Liverpool dressing room. Heads had gone. Djimi Traore was told to get changed, he was being hooked, but then it emerged that Steve Finnan wasn't fit enough to continue and the Frenchman had to put his kit back on. At one point, Rafa Benitez even had a team of 12 names written down for the second half. It seemed inconceivable that anything other than a heavy defeat would follow.

Outside, shortly before the half-time interval ended, the silence had ended. "When you walk," came a murmur from a corner of the stadium, "through a storm, hold your head up high..." As storms go, this was a category five hurricane for Liverpool, but the Anfield anthem caught on, getting louder and louder with each line. By the time "with hope, in your heart" was reached you would've thought it was Liverpool winning 3-0. What's more, the players could hear it and it lifted them.

Truth be told, *You'll Never Walk Alone* was sung in hope rather than belief during that half-time interval. It was sung in defiance as a reminder to the watching world that We Are Liverpool. That we stand shoulder to shoulder, in sickness and in health, 'till death do us part, in support of our team.

Amazingly, against all the odds, that faith was repaid.

Benitez introduced Didi Hamann at half-time and switched to a 3-5-2 system with Traore lining up alongside Jamie Carragher and Sami Hyypia at the back, Smicer and John Arne Riise as wing-backs, Xabi Alonso and Steven Gerrard being joined in midfield by Hamann and Luis Garcia playing off Milan Baros. It changed the game.

Kaka, the Brazilian midfielder, had destroyed the Reds before the interval with his passing and movement, but Hamann now had him under wraps, although it took a fine Jerzy Dudek save from Andriy Shevchenko to prevent an early fourth goal. And then? And then came six crazy minutes.

Good cross. Gerrard! 3-1! Great header Stevie lad. He's gesturing at us to make some noise. Come on Reds! Let's have a go. Liverpool, Liverpool, Liverpool. Hang on, Vladi's having a crack...3-2!

Suddenly hope turned into belief. This was really happening. Vladimir Smicer, playing at right wing-back for the first time, who hadn't scored a single Liverpool goal since 2003, had smashed the ball into the AC Milan net from Hamann's pass two minutes after Gerrard had brilliantly headed Riise's cross past Dida. As surreal as it seemed the comeback was well and truly on and Liverpool had all the momentum.

Carra's going forward. Go 'ead Jamie. Baros to Stevie, chance...penalty! Gattuso fouled him. Referee! He's given it! Oh my God he's given it. Xabi's taking it. Come on Xabi. Saved. But he's got to the rebound first...

The noise that erupted around three-quarters of the Ataturk when Alonso's left-footed shot from the rebound hit the roof of the net was almost guttural. There were exhalations of relief mixed in with screams and shouts of joy, but mostly there was complete and utter disbelief at what had just unfolded in those six minutes. Liverpool 3 AC Milan 3. And nobody was pinching themselves, just in case.

Liverpool's players, however, had expended so much energy, both physically and emotionally, to pull those three goals back that they couldn't sustain their momentum. The game settled down again and, as the clock ticked on, AC Milan began to recover from the shock they had gone into and asserted some control with Traore clearing off the line from Shevchenko. Then came extra-time.

Benitez switched Gerrard to right-back, to cope with the attacking threat of substitute Serginho, and Carragher threw his cramp-riddled body in the way of two goalbound shots, but with just three minutes left came the most glorious of glorious chances for European Footballer of the Year Shevchenko when he met Serginho's cross with his head.

"He met it well," recalled Jerzy Dudek in *A Big Pole In Our Goal*. "His header was pretty powerful. He directed it downwards, slightly to my right. I dived to block it and the ball bounced off me, just two yards in front of goal.

"I was on my knees. I think one of my legs was even a little behind the line. The odds were stacked against me. In that second, with the AC Milan player almost on top of me, I instinctively raised my hands up. It was pure impulse.

"I saw that it was Shevchenko who was running for the ball. It landed perfectly for him. He hit it as hard as he could, like he was channelling all his anger. His shot struck my hand. The ball could easily have broken my fingers and flown into the net. But it didn't. It flew upwards instead and landed behind the net. John Arne Riise raised his hands in the air like I'd just scored a goal. It felt like I had."

Dudek's save became known as the 'miracle of Istanbul' and his hero-status would be confirmed during the penalty shoot-out, but only after Carragher had wildly gesticulated in the Pole's face before a spot-kick was taken, telling him to mimic Bruce Grobbelaar's 'spaghetti legs' routine from Liverpool's 1984 European Cup final win against AS Roma to put the Milan players off.

Dudek did exactly that, but he also had goalkeeping coach Jose Ochotorena on the sidelines telling him which way to dive, based on their research into Milan's players, by getting substitute goalkeeper Scott Carson to raise one hand to dive left, two hands to dive right. A combination of both tactics worked wonders.

Perhaps distracted by Dudek's antics, Serginho blasted over. Hamann then stepped forward to make it one-nil despite having fractured his foot. Andrea Pirlo was up next, Dudek dived right to save it. Substitute Djibril Cisse made it two-nil, but with Jon Dahl Tomasson and Kaka converting either side of Riise's effort being saved by Dida it left the score at 2-2 with Smicer up next. He netted, meaning Shevchenko had to score.

Dudek handed the Ukrainian the ball, saying "will you shoot the same way as usual?" to him. Perhaps that, and the sight of Dudek bouncing around on his goalline and wobbling his legs created doubt in Shevchenko's mind, as at the very last second, after planning to shoot to the right, he changed his mind and went down the middle. Dudek, diving to his right, stuck out his left glove.

Saved. Saved! The European Cup was won and, under the UEFA rules of the time, was Liverpool's to keep after winning it for a fifth time.

Cast your mind back to that very moment. Picture yourself, wherever you were and whoever you were with, as the realisation hit you that Liverpool Football Club were champions of Europe for a fifth time after looking doomed at half-time.

Moments like that make all the bad days worthwhile. Moments like that make following Liverpool, wherever you are in the world, a habit you can't kick. Moments like that, even if you were too young to experience it in 2005, are what we're all hoping for again, but while crazy comebacks like that have only come along once in 130 years, European Cup successes have been more often.

We won it six times. We won it six times. In Madrid, we won it six times...

117/130

Reds' rivals: Leeds and Nottingham Forest

DISCOUNTING derbies, both urban (Everton) and regional (Manchester United), rivalries have come and gone in Liverpool FC's history.

In the 1960s and early 70s it was all about the games against Leeds. Redmen v White Rose. Bill Shankly versus Don Revie.

Anfield and Elland Road. Kopites never walking alone. Leeds marching on together. The 'Canal derby'.

Between August 1964 and August 1974 the rivalry was simply huge – season-defining in many cases. Liverpool and Leeds met in title-deciding league games, the FA Cup final, a European semi-final, the League Cup and in the Charity Shield. As Shankly put it, when asked by the BBC's John Motson about the rivalry between the two clubs in 1973: "It's been a kind of monopoly, you know? Possibly we invented the word 'monopoly', Leeds and Liverpool."

It began when Leeds returned to the top flight in August 1964. Shankly's men arrived in West Yorkshire for their first away game as defending champions and lost 4-2 – only the second time they'd conceded four goals in a game since being promoted. The Reds won the return 2-1 – a scoreline that would go down in Scouse folklore when the sides next met, in May 1965, when Liverpool prevailed in the FA Cup final at Wembley.

Liverpool won the league for the second time in three years in 1965/66, with Leeds runners-up. Three years later the title was at stake when Leeds were in town on a Monday night in April 1969. With three games left to play, second-placed Liverpool trailed Revie's men by five points, with a game-in-hand. A win would keep the Reds in title contention; anything less and Leeds would clinch their first-ever First Division championship. It finished 0-0 with goalkeeper Sprake making a flying save from Ian Callaghan to earn Leeds the point they needed.

The sense of disappointment in the ground was palpable but what happened next was legendary. As the Leeds players walked towards the Kop, unsure of what reaction they would receive, a ripple of applause was followed by the chant of "Champions!" Revie called it "a great gesture." Shankly told the press that "the best team drew," but later went into the Leeds dressing room to pass on his congratulations.

1970/71 saw the rivalry move to a different playing field. Liverpool and Leeds met in the last four of the European Fairs Cup (rebranded the UEFA Cup the following year) and a Kop-end Bremner header gave the Yorkshiremen a 1-0 first-leg win. Shankly's side couldn't break down a white wall of defenders in the second leg, and Leeds went through to the final where they beat Juventus on away goals.

If those games had been tight it was nothing compared to the title-race in 1971/72 when four clubs – Liverpool, Leeds, Derby County and Manchester City – went into their final games of the season with a chance of being crowned champions.

City beat Brian Clough's Derby 2-0 in their final match, but the Rams won their game-in-hand at home to Liverpool to go top. Liverpool could still pull it off if they won at Arsenal, as could Leeds if they drew at Wolves, both games on the same Monday night. Incredibly both teams blew it, Leeds losing 2-1 at Molineux, Liverpool drawing at Arsenal. Derby were champions, with Clough only learning while on holiday in Sicily!

When the Reds and Whites met at Anfield in April 1973, a Liverpool win would all but mathematically secure the championship and end Leeds' own faint title hopes. They got the job done. Peter Cormack notched the first shortly after half-time before Kevin Keegan slotted home a second following a collision between Leeds keeper David Harvey and a defender.

Remembering the reception they had been afforded when winning the title at Anfield four years earlier, the Leeds players lined up by the tunnel at full-time to give Liverpool a guard of honour. It may have been English football's fiercest rivalry, but such respect spoke volumes for both clubs.

The next season it was Leeds who won the title with Liverpool finishing as runners-up, five points adrift. But the late seventies brought a new force in football in the shape of newly-promoted

Nottingham Forest – with a familiar face in manager Clough.

"At Anfield the Forest will fall," went the line from the raucous Kop chant of the time, but more often than not Cloughie's visitors stood firm against relentless Reds pressure in front of feverish 50,000-plus crowds – Bob Paisley's Liverpool recorded just two victories over the East Midlanders in six encounters on home soil between May 1978 and November 1980.

Every other photo seemed to show Forest keeper Peter Shilton smothering the ball after another attack was foiled, with defensive duo Kenny Burns and Larry Lloyd (once of Liverpool) lurking nearby to frustrate the likes of Terry McDermott or Kenny Dalglish in what were invariably niggly, ill-tempered clashes.

The jinx began in season 1977/78 when the Reds finally seemed to take the League Cup seriously, edging a titanic two-legged semi-final over Arsenal; the 2-1 win at Anfield was the start of an 85-match unbeaten home run in all competitions over three years.

But in the final lay Forest. Beforehand Clough had dabbled in some mind-games by stating: "You have to face the fact that Liverpool have the experience of Wembley and cup finals and we haven't. I didn't even think we were good enough to get this far."

Liverpool duly dominated the game, but McDermott had a goal disallowed and Forest's 18-year-old goalkeeper Chris Woods, playing instead of the cup-tied Shilton, had a blinder between the sticks. Nil-nil. In the Old Trafford replay four days later it was Forest who prevailed with a John Robertson penalty after Phil Thompson had committed a foul later shown to be outside the box.

Terry Mac also had an equaliser disallowed for a very dubious handball and Forest also went on to win the title, finishing seven points ahead of the second-placed Reds.

In the following season's European Cup, Forest eliminated holders Liverpool at the first hurdle, the goalless return leg at

Anfield infamous for Shilton's heroics and Thommo's tears at the end. Liverpool exacted some revenge with a 2-0 league victory in December 1978, McDermott scoring twice, as the Reds went on to regain the title.

1979/80 brought four meetings in less than a month. The first and third were the two legs of a League Cup semi-final, which Forest edged 2-1 on aggregate. At the City Ground a last-minute Robertson penalty separated the sides despite Liverpool again dominating proceedings. "Shilton saved them," said Ray Kennedy. "We would've won by three or four if he hadn't turned it on." Another Robertson spot-kick extended their advantage at Anfield and although super sub David Fairclough netted in the 89th minute it wasn't enough.

In-between those League Cup games, Liverpool won 2-0 at the City Ground in an FA Cup fourth-round tie with Dalglish scoring for the first time in ten tussles with the enemy. Arguably more satisfying was match number four – a midweek league fixture at Anfield that was heading for stalemate before late goals from McDermott and Kennedy sent the Kop into raptures.

"We didn't have much success against Forest," recalled midfielder Graeme Souness. "We could hold the ball against them, play in their half all the game and pepper their goal with shots. They didn't come after us, just played us on the break. That's how they played their football. Frustrating."

The rivalry lost some of its needle as the years progressed but there were still some big and memorable games. Dalglish's Liverpool beat Forest 2-1 in the 1988 FA Cup semi-final at Hillsborough before following it up with a famous 5-0 Anfield league victory in the same week having lost just their second Division One game of the season at the City Ground earlier that April.

Liverpool and Nottingham Forest will always be connected due to the 1989 Hillsborough disaster when 97 Reds were unlawfully killed before the FA Cup semi-final of that year. Liverpool won the rearranged match 3-1, John Aldridge scoring twice, but it was only in March 2022 when the two clubs met in the FA Cup again with Forest leaving 97 seats empty in memory of those we lost before a quarter-final tie at the City Ground was settled by a Diogo Jota goal.

It felt like the rivalry between the two clubs, who also met in their first ever Premier League outing at the City Ground in 1992, was revived that night and when you've won eight European Cups between you – including five in five years from 1977 to 1981 – there will always be a rivalry no matter how long it is between drinks.

118/130

Never forgotten

THE 1989 Hillsborough disaster resulted in 97 Liverpool supporters losing their lives on Sheffield Wednesday's Leppings Lane terrace before the FA Cup semi-final against Nottingham Forest. It brought the whole city of Liverpool together. Thousands of Reds and Blues queued up at Anfield to lay flowers and scarves on the pitch in memory of those who had perished, prompting supporters from all over the country and beyond to do the same.

Liverpool FC has placed on record its gratitude to Everton FC for its support, solidarity and compassion down the years. No Liverpool fan will forget the young mascots in the Goodison Park centre-circle wearing blue and red jerseys before an Everton match in September 2012 (following the findings of the Hillsborough Independent Panel) nor the reading by Bill Kenwright at the Memorial Service at Anfield on Monday 15 April 2013. Thank you EFC: we never walked alone.

Following the 2016 Main Stand expansion, Anfield's Hillsborough Memorial was relocated in a cloister on 97 Avenue, named in honour of those we lost in 1989 and linking the stadium and Paisley Square to Stanley Park. It's a place of pilgrimage for supporters of every football club, providing moments of poignancy and reflection.

On the opposite side of the stadium, outside the Sir Kenny Dalglish Stand, is the Heysel Memorial unveiled in 2006 as a permanent tribute to the 39 who died at the 1985 European Cup final. Underneath the club crests of Juventus FC and Liverpool FC it reads: In Memoria E Amicizia – In Memory And Friendship.

Football tragedies strengthen the bond between supporters of different clubs worldwide. In 2007, before the Champions League final in Athens, Liverpool supporters paid their respects to the 21 Olympiacos fans killed in the 1981 'Gate 7 Disaster' – following a crush on a stairway at the Karaiskakis Stadium – by placing scarves and banners in tribute at the memorial there.

In 2016, on the eve of the 27th anniversary of the Hillsborough disaster, Borussia Dortmund fans inside Anfield for a Europa League game paid their own tribute by raising a '96' mosaic [this was before Andrew Devine became the 97th victim in 2021] before the unified pre-match singing of You'll Never Walk Alone earned an award from FIFA.

"It honours both sets of supporters, and the respect shown by our friends from Dortmund was absolutely typical of the world-class values that club upholds," said Jürgen Klopp. "To honour the 96 victims, their families and the survivors of Hillsborough was very poignant.

"I know we won the match and the tie, but I think everyone inside Anfield that night and watching at home – whether they were wearing red or yellow and black – knows that football can be very proud of how they represented their club. I hope the special memories created that night can serve as a perfect example of the joy and happiness football can bring."

In November 2019 former South Yorkshire police chief superintendent David Duckenfield was found not guilty of gross negligence manslaughter more than 30 years after he commanded the police at the 1989 FA Cup semi-final at Hillsborough.

The verdict came after a retrial at Preston crown court. A first trial on the same charge, heard by the same judge Sir Peter Openshaw, ended in April 2019 with the jury unable to reach a verdict. Duckenfield had been charged in June 2017 after a new police investigation into the disaster, Operation Resolve, and verdicts of unlawful killing returned by the jury in an inquest in Warrington.

In 2021, the trial of two former South Yorkshire police officers and the force's former solicitor, who had been charged with perverting the course of justice for amending police statements after the Hillsborough disaster, was halted by Mr Justice William Davis.

"He ruled that the offence could not have been committed, because the amendments were to prepare police statements for the public inquiry, chaired by Lord Justice Taylor. That was a non-statutory inquiry, which Davis described to the jury as "an administrative exercise", not a "course of public justice," reported *The Guardian*. "So even if the amendments meant the South Yorkshire police withheld important evidence from the Taylor inquiry, that could not constitute perverting the course of justice."

The acquittal brought to an end a 32-year fight for justice without anybody being held accountable for the loss of 97 lives.

"It is with huge disappointment that Liverpool Football Club notes the latest developments in the judicial process relating to the Hillsborough disaster," read a Liverpool FC statement in May 2021.

"While it would not be our place, legally or otherwise, to comment on those proceedings as they pertain to individuals, it is incumbent on us to forcefully point out that the 96 victims, their families, survivors and all those who suffered as a result of the Hillsborough tragedy have continuously been failed in their pursuit for justice.

"We salute all those who have campaigned for justice. They have been let down yet again. We have a situation in which 96 people were unlawfully killed and yet no individual or group has been deemed legally culpable for their deaths.

"As ever, our thoughts are with the families, survivors and campaigners and we would reiterate that, as established by the 2016 inquests, the behaviour of our supporters was not a contributory factor in the disaster, a truth for which the bereaved families had to fight for over a quarter of a century."

Two months later, Andrew Devine became the 97th victim of the Hillsborough disaster and in January 2022 his name was etched onto the Hillsborough Memorial at Anfield.

They may never get the justice they and their families deserve, but the 97 will never be forgotten.

119/130

Other trophies

SIX European Cups. 19 league titles. Nine League Cups. Eight FA Cups. Three UEFA Cups. Four European Super Cups. One FIFA Club World Cup. 15 Charity/Community Shields.

As of June 2022, Liverpool Football Club has claimed a vast array of silverware during the first 130 years of existence, but they weren't the only trophies to have been put on display at Anfield. The Reds have won a number of other competitions, many of which have been forgotten or are considered as lesser achievements so are rarely mentioned.

Indeed, Liverpool's first ever trophy success came in the club's maiden campaign all the way back in 1892/93 when Blackpool were pipped to the Lancashire League title on goal average in what proved to be a crazy end to the season.

William Barclay's side drew their final game at Southport Central – which was refereed by a local man after the referee failed to turn up – 1-1 meaning Blackpool needed just a point from their final game to be champions, only to lose 1-0 to Southport Central.

It meant Liverpool had earned promotion to the Football League Second Division and then had the opportunity to clinch a double by beating First Division Everton in the Liverpool Senior Cup final.

The first Merseyside derby was played at Bootle in front of 10,000 people and it was Liverpool who emerged victorious, winning 1-0 with a goal from former Everton man Tom Wylie although the trophy itself was not presented at full-time due to protests from Evertonians that they should have been awarded a late penalty.

Their appeal was later dismissed and Liverpool were presented with the Senior Cup, but they didn't have both trophies for long. On 1 September 1893, the day before the club's first ever Second Division game, both pieces of silverware were stolen from a pawn shop belonging to Charles Gibson in Paddington, Liverpool, where they had been on display. It cost the club £130 (about £2,000 in today's money) to have both replaced.

The Reds have won the Liverpool Senior Cup 41 times in total, most recently in 2009/10 when a side featuring future first-team players Jon Flanagan, Andre Wisdom and Conor Coady beat Skelmersdale United 3-2, but haven't participated in the tournament since 2011 having struggled to fit it into the fixture schedule following various restructurings of youth leagues, age-groups and the introduction of the NextGen Series and then the UEFA Youth League.

Liverpool also beat Oldham Athletic 3-0 in the Lancashire Senior Cup final in 2009/10, winning it for the 11th time having first lifted the trophy in 1918/19. They won it again in 2016/17, following a penalty shoot-out win over Fleetwood Town, and in 2021/22 with a 1-0 win against Burnley, James Norris scoring.

Having won 19 top-flight titles it is perhaps not too surprising that Liverpool's four Second Division championship successes in 1893/94, 1895/96, 1905/05 and 1961/62 have been somewhat overshadowed while you may not be aware that the Reds claimed three titles during World War I.

They were Lancashire Section Principle Winners in 1916/17 and Lancashire Section Subsidiary Winners in 1917/18 and 1918/19. Local lad Tom Bennett scored 77 goals in 70 games during those three seasons but only made one official first-team appearance, against Chelsea in 1919/20, after it transpired he was suffering from tuberculosis. He never fully recovered and tragically died in 1923 at the age of 31.

Another wartime title, the League North Second Championship, followed during the Second World War in 1942/43, a year after Bill Shankly had played his only game for Liverpool, against Everton, as a wartime guest.

The Bass Charity Vase has been held since 1890 in Burton-on-Trent to raise money for local charities and in 1897 Liverpool took part, winning the considerably sized piece of silverware at Peel Croft by beating Burton Wanderers 1-0 in the final courtesy of a George Allan goal.

Arguably the most random competition that Liverpool ever won was the ScreenSport Super Cup, held in 1985/86 and contested between the sides that would have played in Europe if English clubs hadn't been banned following the Heysel disaster. Screened live on a satellite TV channel, the two-legged final between Liverpool and Everton was postponed until 1986/87 due to fixture congestion.

The crowds of 20,660 for the first leg at Anfield and 26,068 for the return fixture at Goodison Park reflected the disdain the one-off tournament was held in, but it was Kenny Dalglish's side that emerged victorious, winning at home 3-1 (Ian Rush 2 and Steve McMahon) and 4-1 (Ian Rush 3 and Steve Nicol) at Goodison Park. It's fair to say an open-top bus tour didn't follow!

Various pre-season trophies have been won during the last 130 years, including the Carlsberg Trophy in 1998, 1999 and 2000, and it is a piece of silverware earned ahead of a new season that became the first Liverpool had won after the club's 125th anniversary had passed in June 2017.

Jürgen Klopp's team travelled to Hong Kong to play in the Premier League Asia Trophy where they beat Leicester City 2-1 in the final with goals from Mohamed Salah and Philippe Coutinho.

120/130

Memorable mosaics

JUST before kick-off of Liverpool's Premier League game against Burnley in August 2021 – the first time Anfield had been full since the COVID-19 pandemic began almost 18 months earlier – fans on the Kop raised cards above their heads. Together they spelt out the number 97 with two eternal flames displayed either side.

It was a tribute to Andrew Devine, the 97th victim of the Hillsborough disaster who had died a month earlier at the age of 55. Andrew wasn't expected to survive through the night from the injuries he suffered at Hillsborough in 1989, but spent a further 32 years with his brave family before passing away. The Anfield mosaic was a show of support and remembrance from his fellow Reds.

Since the mid-1990s, mosaics have made for some of the most spectacular sights seen on the Kop. From a giant yellow LFC back in 1995 to a salute to the late Ray Kennedy in December 2021, they have marked various historic events, anniversaries and farewells.

Created by cards being held up by each fan, the carefully-planned mosaics, organised by Kopite Andy Knott, have provided spine-tingling and eye-catching visions.

The Bob Paisley flag night for the UEFA Cup game against AS Roma in 2001 saw various trophies won by the legendary Liverpool's most successful manager cover the Kop, lower Centenary Stand and Anfield Road end lower.

Later the same year, the Kop paraded the letters 'GH' for a game against Manchester United in solidarity with manager Gerard Houllier, who had recently undergone major heart surgery.

In 2002, AS Roma were again the opponents when a returning Houllier was greeted with the word 'Allez' ahead of a Champions League encounter.

Houllier's final game as LFC manager against Newcastle United in May 2004 saw a tribute with the words 'YNWA, The Kop' being held aloft.

When the Reds were drawn against Juventus in the quarter-final of the Champions League in April 2005, the Italian word 'Amicizia', meaning friendship, was displayed as the 20th anniversary of the Heysel Stadium tragedy approached.

Four years later, ahead of a Premier League game against Arsenal, both sets of supporters honoured Ray Kennedy, to raise awareness of Parkinson's Disease. Kopites raised cards which produced a large number five, Kennedy's LFC shirt number, while the travelling Gunners lifted a mosaic showing the number 10, that of his Arsenal jersey. Ray was guest of honour that night to see it and, after he passed away in 2021, another mosaic displaying his shirt number paid tribute to him before a Premier League game against Aston Villa.

Bill Shankly was remembered with a mosaic in December 2009 exclaiming 'Shanks Legend' to mark the 50th anniversary of his arrival at the club and another in 2013 to mark what would have been his 100th birthday.

Local lads Jamie Carragher and Steven Gerrard were hailed as they played their final home games for the Reds after long and illustrious Anfield careers: 'JC23' marked Carragher's last game for the club in April 2013 while 'S8G' and 'Captain' signposted Gerrard's finale a little over two years later. A 'Sami' mosaic had previously bid farewell to Sami Hyypia in 2009.

The passing of Ronnie Moran in 2017 was marked with a mosaic spelling out 'Bugsy', his nickname, and in August of the same year LFC's 125th anniversary was marked with mosaics reading 'LFC 125' and 'YNWA' in the Sir Kenny Dalglish Stand and the Kop. The following month the mosaics were out in force again before Liverpool played Manchester United to mark the official opening of the renamed Sir Kenny Dalglish Stand.

Two years later, in 2019, the 100th anniversary of LFC's most successful manager was marked with a 'Paisley 100' mosaic and later that year the 2019/20 season kicked off with a Kop mosaic featuring the European Cup and the number 6 following the Reds' triumph in Madrid a few months earlier.

Fittingly, the most regular subject of the mosaics has been those who lost their lives at Hillsborough.

Ahead of a home game against Norwich City in October 2011, the phrase 'JFT96' was displayed, while in September 2012, 'The Truth', 'Justice' and '96' filled parts of Anfield shortly after the findings of the Hillsborough Independent Panel report. In May 2013, the Reds publicly acknowledged the support given to them by Evertonians since the disaster with 'Thanks' being lifted up from the Kop ahead of a Merseyside derby.

In April 2014, prior to an epic encounter with Manchester City, '96 – 25 Years' was the message from supporters.

As previously mentioned, ahead of their 2016 Europa League quarter-final and to mark the 27th anniversary, fans of both Liverpool and Borussia Dortmund showed their support with the number '96', one in red-and-white and one in yellow-and-black.

The following month, further tributes were paid ahead of the semi-final against Villarreal, with a mosaic being formed across the Anfield Road, Centenary Stand and the Kop spelling out the number '96' and the phrase 'The Greatest Football Family'.

In December 2019, after David Duckenfield - the match

commander on the day of the Hillsborough disaster - was found not guilty of gross negligence manslaughter at a retrial at Preston Crown Court there was another show of support with the number 96 held aloft on the Kop, and both sets of supporters chanting 'Justice for the 96', before the Merseyside derby between Liverpool and Everton.

In July 2021, the 96 became 97 and that emotional tribute to Andrew Devine the following months was paid with one of the most poignant mosaics of all.

121/130

The fields of Melling Road

AND they're off...to play another game of football on Grand National Day.

When Jürgen Klopp's Reds hosted Aston Villa on 10 April 2021 it was the 43rd time that LFC had played on the same day as the city of Liverpool's biggest one-off sporting event: The Grand National.

For the first time ever, though, neither Anfield or Aintree had spectators with both events held behind closed doors due to the COVID-19 pandemic. On a weekend when Liverpool should have been bustling with Reds fans and racegoers it almost feels like neither sporting occasion happened, but for the record goals from Mo Salah and Trent Alexander-Arnold gave Liverpool a 2-1 win while Rachael Blackmore became the Grand National's first female winning jockey onboard Minella Times.

Held at Aintree Racecourse since 1839, over half a century before Liverpool Football Club was formed in 1892, the Grand National sees 40 horses compete over fences in a gruelling four mile and 514-yard race and is the showpiece event of a three-day festival that, in 2019, attracted an attendance of over 150,000.

Perhaps 43 fixture clashes between the world's most famous steeplechase and England's most famous football club in a century-and-a-quarter doesn't sound a lot, but there have been numerous reasons for that including the fact that the Grand National – bar a one-off in 1858 – was traditionally held on a Friday until being switched to Saturday in 1947 following the end of World War II.

And so, on 29 March 1947, Liverpool played for the first time on the same day the Grand National was being held and it just happened to be the small matter of an FA Cup semi-final against Burnley at Blackburn's Ewood Park which resulted in 5,000 Reds queueing up for 2,500 train tickets at Exchange Station in an attempt to get to deepest, darkest Lancashire.

The match ended 0-0 and punters at Aintree probably went home with nil either as 100/1 shot Caughoo, ridden by Eddie Dempsey, crossed the line first in a race that was only covered live on BBC Radio after the government agreed to relax a post-war electricity ban due to a national interest in hearing the commentary.

Indeed, such was the interest in the Grand National that Liverpool FC's board of directors were so concerned it would reduce the Anfield attendance for the Reds clash with Blackpool in 1948 that they switched the kick-off to 5.30pm. It was a shrewd move. 48,725 turned up to see Blackpool's Stanley Matthews have a mare – he missed a first minute penalty as Liverpool won 2-0 with Albert Stubbins netting twice – while at Aintree Sheila's Cottage became the first mare to win the race in 46 years.

Bob Paisley was well known for his love of horse racing when he was Liverpool manager and Grand National day seemed to inspire him during his playing days too. On 25 March 1950 a crowd of 72,000 Scousers packed into Maine Road to watch Liverpool and Everton contest an FA Cup semi-final and it was Paisley who opened the scoring before Billy Liddell clinched a 2-0 win while Freebooter won at Aintree.

Paisley was also on target on Grand National day in 1952 as Stoke were beaten 2-1 on Anfield Road while 100/7 shot Teal was leading the way across the Melling Road – a road that famously crosses the Aintree track where, between 1955 and 1962, the Formula One British Grand Prix was also held five times on a circuit within the racecourse.

A year later the Liverpool board took a punt themselves and didn't move the club's home fixture against Charlton Athletic from the scheduled 3pm kick-off slot. It backfired. A crowd of just 23,204 came through the Anfield turnstiles – a drop of over 17,000 from the previous home game against Sunderland – and saw the Reds lose 2-1 while famous trainer Vincent O'Brien was landing his first of three consecutive Grand National wins having saddled up 20/1 hope Early Mist.

Liverpool's 2-1 defeat at Notts County on 24 March 1956 is easily forgotten but the Grand National that afternoon never will be. The race was won by E.S.B after Devon Loch – owned by The Queen Mother and ridden by Dick Francis – inexplicably half-jumped and landed on its belly just 40 yards from the winning post. Unable to carry on when victory seemed certain, it was the equine equivalent of missing a sitter.

Another poor Anfield attendance for a 5.15pm kick-off against Alf Ramsey's Ipswich in 1958 (although being in Division Two didn't help either) saw the Liverpool board trial Friday night football on Grand National weekend in 1959 with a crowd of 35,507 being deemed a success, unlike the 4-3 defeat to Stoke that they witnessed.

They tried the same trick again in March 1964 – 38,583 turning out to see the Bill Shankly boys edge another game closer to winning the First Division by beating Bolton 2-0 – as the desire to avoid schedule clashes had become even greater from 1960 onwards when the Grand National was screened live on BBC TV for the first time.

A year earlier FA Cup fever got the better of Aintree excitement as almost 50,000 packed into Anfield to see a West Ham side featuring Bobby Moore and Martin Peters beaten 1-0 courtesy of a late Roger Hunt strike while over in Sefton the Grand National was won by a 66/1 shot that would share a name with a future Liverpool player – Ayala.

Speaking of names, did you know that Tommy Smith rode the winner of the 1965 Grand National? No, not THAT Tommy Smith. The 'Anfield Iron' was part of the Liverpool side that beat Chelsea 2-0 in the FA Cup semi-final at Villa Park on a Grand National day that ended with jockey Tommy Smith riding 100/6 shot Jay Trump to glory.

After Friday night Anfield encounters with Newcastle (1967, the year when 100/1 shot Foinavon won the following day after a huge pile-up at the fence that is now named after him) and West Brom (1971), the Liverpool board tried something different again for the visit of Coventry City on 8 April 1972.

The game kicked-off at 11.30am on the Saturday morning and over 50,000 – plus a live TV audience – saw a 3-1 win that put the Reds top of the table with both players and fans alike having time to get to Aintree that afternoon where Well To Do galloped past the winning post first.

Then came Grand National day 1973, a memorable one at both Anfield and Aintree. Shankly's title-chasers, in a two-horse race with Arsenal for top-spot, faced Tottenham at 11.30am but ran into the human fence that was Pat Jennings.

The legendary Northern Irish goalkeeper made himself look bigger than Aintree's famous Becher's Brook fence that morning and saved penalties from both Kevin Keegan and Smith to ensure Spurs snatched a 1-1 draw. Later that day, a horse by the name of Red Rum – trained by Southport's Ginger McCain and ridden by Brian Fletcher – somehow made up 30 lengths on long-time leader Crisp to win the Grand National in a then record-time of nine minutes and 1.9 seconds. Many punters still regard it as the greatest renewal of all to this day.

'Rummy' won again in 1974 before finishing second in both 1975 (to L'Escargot) and 1976 (to Rag Trade) on a day when red-headed super sub David Fairclough scored a stunning 88th minute solo goal following a mazy dribble to give Liverpool a 1-0 Merseyside derby victory over Everton.

2 April 1977 was even more special. In another 11.30am Anfield kick-off Leeds United were dispatched 3-1 as Paisley's men went top of the First Division only for Red Rum to steal the headlines by winning the Grand National again.

Red Rum – who was pictured with Bill Shankly afterwards and had Reds' skipper Emlyn Hughes sit on his back as part of a publicity stunt – remains the only horse to have won the Grand National three times and Liverpool won two league titles, one European Cup, one UEFA Cup and one FA Cup during the three years he was successful. Horses for courses and all that!

Liverpool and Manchester United met on Grand National day in 1979, the FA Cup semi-final at Maine Road finishing 2-2 with Kenny Dalglish and Alan Hansen on the scoresheet on an afternoon when Rubstic became the first Scottish trained winner of the big race, but with more and more games being moved for TV coverage fixture clashes gradually became less frequent.

1984 was a sell-out at Aintree – a crowd of 54,583 coming through the gates – to see the first race limited to a maximum of 40 runners for safety reasons won by Hallo Dandy at 13/1. Liverpool won at Watford that day, John Wark scoring on his debut in a 2-0 win, and the following year the Reds played on the Sunday after the Grand National for the first time with the home match against Manchester United moved for TV coverage.

FA Cup semi-final day clashed with the Grand National again in both 1986 (Liverpool beating Southampton 2-0 at White Hart Lane and West Tip winning at Aintree) and 1988 (the Reds beating Nottingham Forest 2-1 at Hillsborough and Rhyme 'n' Reason winning the National) while in 1989 a Sheffield Wednesday side wearing an unusual green and white strip were thrashed 5-1 at Anfield in another 11.30am kick-off with Peter Beardsley netting a double ahead of Little Polveir's 28/1 success.

1993 was memorable for the wrong reasons. Liverpool lost 4-1 at Kenny Dalglish's Blackburn Rovers while the Grand National was declared void for the only time in the race's history after 30 of the 39 runners continued following a false start, forcing bookies to refund an estimated £75m in bets.

A year later and Liverpool played at Anfield on Grand National Day for what, until 2018, was the final time. Ipswich were beaten 1-0, Julian Dicks carving his name into history as the last Reds player to score in front of the old standing Spion Kop and the Freddie Starr owned Minnehoma winning at Aintree.

For te next 25 years, partly due to police recommendations, any Liverpool or Everton home games on Grand National day were rescheduled for the Sunday and 1997 provided a good example as to why when an IRA bomb threat forced Aintree Racecourse to be evacuated and the race, eventually won by Lord Gyllene, to be postponed until the Monday.

The Reds played six Premier League away games on Grand National day in the years that followed – arguably the most memorable being at Fulham in 2009 when Yossi Benayoun struck

433

a 90th minute winner just hours after 100/1 shot Mon Mome had triumphed over the Aintree fences – and one FA Cup semi-final at Wembley.

Dalglish's Liverpool beat Everton 2-1 that afternoon, Luis Suarez and Andy Carroll sending travelling Kopites into raptures following Nikica Jelavic's opener, while at Aintree the Paul Nicholls trained Neptune Collonges became the first grey horse to win the Grand National since 1961 in a photo finish at odds of 33/1.

In 2017, One For Arthur triumphed at Aintree after substitutes Philippe Coutinho and Roberto Firmino had come off the bench at the Bet365 Stadium to turn a 1-0 deficit against Stoke City into a 2-1 victory, helping the Reds to clear another hurdle en-route to ensuring Champions League football would return to the Fields of Anfield Road in 2017/18, and then in April 2018 came the first Anfield/Aintree fixture clash for half-a-decade.

With the Grand National now moved to a 5.15pm start and Liverpool's home Premier League game against Bournemouth kicking off at 5.30pm it was impossible for those who follow both sports to attend both fixtures. Shortly after Tiger Roll won his first of two consecutive Grand Nationals at Aintree, Sadio Mane, Mo Salah and Firmino got the Reds past the winning post at Anfield.

Perhaps some of Jürgen Klopp's players will have been keen to hear the result as it was revealed in 2021 that Jordan Henderson, James Milner, Alex Oxlade-Chamberlain, Andy Robertson, Alexander-Arnold and ex-Red Adam Lallana had bought a two-year old colt and named it Mr McCann, after Liverpool FC's head of press Matt McCann.

While it may never run over the Aintree Grand National fences, Mr McCann won three of its first seven races on the flat and is sure to give his owners a lot of fun.

122/130

Said and done

THURSDAY 14 April 2016. Time was almost up in the Europa League quarter-final second leg at Anfield between Liverpool and Borussia Dortmund, and with the score 4-4 on aggregate the Reds were going out on away-goals. Here's how LFCTV commentator John Bradley described what happened next...

"The Dortmund players are sensing they are almost home. [Fourth official] Serkan Ok puts up the board and tells us there will be four minutes. [Milner takes a free-kick] Liverpool now want to rock Anfield even more. Daniel Sturridge... Liverpool need a moment of brilliance, a moment of inspiration... Milner, there's the cross – Lovrennnnn! The roof has come off Anfield! It's Dejan Lovren! It is perhaps the greatest comeback that Anfield has ever seen! Amazing celebrations! Amazing scenes! It's been an amazing night at Anfield!"

As classic Reds-related TV commentary goes it is one of many memorable contenders. Some of them are short-and-sweet, like ITV's Clive Tyldesley when Michael Owen scored his second goal against Arsenal at Cardiff's sweltering Millennium Stadium in May 2001: "He has won the Cup for Liverpool all by himself!"

Others are a little longer, maybe not quite as memorable but still stirring enough to raise the hairs on the back of your neck. Another FA Cup final, another hero, this time in 2006 and described by the BBC's John Motson: "The fourth official has got the board.

Riise's cross, oh it's fallen... Gerraaaarrddd! He's got it! Oh Steven Gerrard, just when he looked injured and out of it, has equalised for Liverpool with 90 minutes gone. It's 3-3 in surely the best cup final of modern times!"

But then, when it comes to Stevie, nothing beats co-commentator Andy Gray's reaction on Sky Sports when the skipper struck against Olympiacos in December 2004: "Oohhhhhh you beauty! What a hit, son! What a hit!"

Which brings us, via a few more rounds of that Champions League campaign, to Istanbul on the night of 25 May 2005, and the Radio City commentary team of Steve Hothersall and John Aldridge.

In the penalty shoot-out, former Reds striker Aldo – much-loved for his passionate and partisan match-analysis – had managed to hold things together before AC Milan's Andriy Shevchenko stepped up to take his spot-kick. Hothersall: "Shevchenko...scored the winner two years ago. He's up against Dudek. Will he hand Liverpool the European Cup?" Aldridge: "Yeeeesssssssssssss!!!"

Back in the Premier League, the winner in one of Anfield's greatest-ever games was immortalised by Martin Tyler on Sky Sports. Rewind back to the dying seconds between Liverpool and Newcastle United in April 1996 and the score at a breathless 3-3: "Barnes, Rush, Barnes, still John Barnes... Collymore closing innnnn! Liverpool lead in stoppage-time!"

Of course, the past is another country and they do things differently there. The legendary David Coleman, doyen of dozens of unforgettable commentary soundbites, didn't waste his words when it came to one of Liverpool FC's finest double-acts ever.

Twenty minutes into the first leg of the 1973 UEFA Cup final against Borussia Moenchengladbach, full-back Chris Lawler launches one into the box and Coleman keeps it exquisitely simple: "Peter Cormack. Lawler. Toshack. Keegan. One-nil."

Perhaps the most memorable LFC commentary of all, though,

came from Coleman at the 1974 FA Cup final between Liverpool and Newcastle: "And Shanks' army, this Liverpool side, swarming forward now. Hall. Keegan! Goals pay the rent and Keegan does his share."

If that description of LFC's opening goal in a 3-0 win stuck in the mind, his description of the Reds' third is arguably iconic.

"Callaghan's available behind Keegan. Beautiful ball to Smith, he didn't have to move to get it. Hall to Smith. Heighway... Liverpool showing their party pieces, he wasn't offside, Smith... YES! Keegan's second and Newcastle were undressed. They were absolutely stripped naked."

In 2019, Barcelona were undressed by a Trent Alexander-Arnold corner that led to a four-word piece of commentary from LFCTV's Steve Hunter that went viral: "Corner taken quickly ORIGI!"

Such can be the power of commentary that if you say those four words to any Red they'll know exactly which goal it describes, which is quite something given Liverpool have scored over 10,000 of them.

123/130

Returning Reds

THEY say you should never go back. That if you've earned legendary status somewhere you've nothing to gain by returning, only everything to lose. But, when you're Sir Kenny Dalglish – as iconic an Anfield legend as there is – and Liverpool Football Club comes calling, you simply cannot say no.

On 8 January 2011, with the Reds languishing in 12th place, four points above the relegation zone, after 20 games of the Premier League season, LFC owners Fenway Sports Group reappointed Dalglish as Liverpool manager following the sacking of Roy Hodgson. He returned to the job a little short of 20 years since quitting in February 1991 when the stress of guiding the club through the 1989 Hillsborough disaster finally caught up with Dalglish, leaving him emotionally drained.

His first spell in charge – 1985 to 1991 – was an exceptional period for LFC. Appointed as English football's first player-manager at the age of 34, Dalglish inherited a side that had won nothing in 1984/85, had been banned from Europe following the Heysel disaster and, after 11 games, trailed Manchester United by 10 points in second place after United won their opening 10 fixtures.

A 2-0 home defeat to Everton in February appeared to have finished the Reds' title hopes off, but after restoring himself to the side in place of Paul Walsh, Dalglish's Liverpool won 10 and drew one of their final 11 games to pip the Blues to first place with Kenny himself scoring the title-winning goal at Chelsea's Stamford Bridge on the final day of the season.

It remains the only time a manager has scored the goal that wins his side a championship. Could you imagine that happening now?

The Reds went on to clinch a first league and FA Cup double, beating Everton at Wembley, and further success followed in 1988 (league title), 1989 (FA Cup) and 1990 (league title) with Dalglish's Liverpool two games away from winning three league and cup doubles in four seasons having lost the 1988 FA Cup final to Wimbledon and seen Arsenal snatch the league title in the final minutes of the season at Anfield. They also played some of the finest football, particularly in 1987/88, ever seen by Liverpudlians.

Living up to that level of success was always going to be impossible for Dalglish when he returned to the job in 2011, but he was happy to put his reputation on the line. "I'd have thought it would have been put on the line if I hadn't taken it," he said at his press conference unveiling. "I think it would have been disrespectful of me. For me, there was never, ever, any way I was going to disrespect this football club."

Luis Suarez, Andy Carroll and Jordan Henderson were Dalglish's first three signings and in 2011/12 he took Liverpool back to Wembley three times. Cardiff City were beaten on penalties in the League Cup final to secure LFC's first piece of silverware since 2006 and Everton were defeated 2-1 in the FA Cup semi-final only for Chelsea to run out 2-1 winners in the final. However, in the space of 16 months he had steadied the ship and when the Liverpool board decided it was time to begin a new era with the appointment of Brendan Rodgers that summer, the King of the Kop took the decision gracefully like the man he is: "I am here to help the club and if being of help to the club means Kenny Dalglish isn't the manager, then not a problem."

Dalglish wasn't the first Liverpool manager to have a second spell in charge. Following the death of manager Tom Watson in 1915, club secretary George Patterson took charge of the team although his appointment was only made official in 1918 and he still had to run the administrative side of the club. He guided LFC through the First World War period, even placing an advert in the *Liverpool Echo* for players, before David Ashworth was brought in from Stockport County in 1919 to manage the team with Patterson reverting solely to his secretarial duties.

He was still at Anfield in 1928 when Ashworth's successor, Matt McQueen, retired and with the club operating an 'appoint from within' policy, Patterson was asked to assume control again – while also taking care of administrative duties to save money on wages! – but it proved to be an unsuccessful eight seasons for the

Reds. Liverpool never finished higher than fifth (1928/29) and after slumping to 19th in 1935/36 Patterson again returned to his original position of secretary when George Kay was tempted into leaving Southampton to take charge at Anfield.

A number of players have also had two spells at Liverpool, most famously Ian Rush who was with the Reds from 1980 to 1987, Juventus from 1987 to 1988, and then Liverpool again from 1988 to 1996. Rushie hit 207 goals during his first stint with the Redmen and 139 following his return, which would've put the Welshman in the top 10 list of Liverpool's all-time leading goalscorers twice if his tallies weren't added together until Mo Salah came along and netted 150-plus goals.

That he scored twice in two FA Cup final victories against Everton either side of his year in Italy is remarkable in itself, but Rush was a truly remarkable goalscorer and went on to captain the club under Roy Evans.

Another goalscoring genius to make a much-heralded Anfield return was Robbie Fowler, known as 'God' around the Fields of Anfield Road. Red-hot Robbie burst onto the scene as a teenager in 1993/94, scoring goal after goal and looking every inch a natural finisher. Before his departure to Leeds United in 2001 he netted 171 goals, scoring over 30 times in each of his first three full seasons as a Liverpool player between 1994 and 1997, a feat nobody else (including Salah!) has achieved.

Fowler travelled to the 2005 Champions League final as a Liverpool fan and in January 2006 he was back in a Liverpool shirt after completing a free transfer from Man City. He added another 12 goals in 18 months to his LFC tally with his first coming against Fulham, the side he had scored his first ever Liverpool goal against in the League Cup at Craven Cottage in 1993 – and all five in a 5-0 second leg win at Anfield.

Steve Staunton was another to leave Liverpool and return at a later date. The Republic of Ireland international left-back made 90 appearances between 1988 and 1991, incredibly becoming the first Liverpool substitute to net a hat-trick when forced to play as an emergency striker in a League Cup game against Wigan Athletic in 1989. He was sold to Aston Villa in 1991 with a UEFA rule limiting the number of non-English players eligible to play in Europe partly to blame for his departure, meaning David Burrows was preferred at left-back with Steve Harkness in reserve.

Staunton returned to Liverpool in July 1998 – 13 days before Gerard Houllier was appointed as joint-manager alongside Evans – and made another 58 appearances before history repeated itself again and he rejoined Aston Villa, presumably making him rather familiar with the M6!

Another left-back, Fabio Aurelio, technically had two different spells at Liverpool but without playing for another club in-between. After four seasons and 110 appearances the Brazilian left in the summer of 2010 when his contract expired only to return a couple of months later on a new two-year deal as new manager Roy Hodgson struggled to recruit players.

Striker Craig Bellamy had two different one-season stints as a Liverpool player. The fiery Welshman spent 2006/07 at Anfield under Rafa Benitez's management, scoring nine times, and returned under Dalglish in 2011/12, again hitting the target on nine occasions with a goal against former club Man City in the League Cup semi-final second leg at Anfield taking the Reds to Wembley for the first time since 1996. He also played in the FA Cup semi-final win against Everton there.

"The way I saw it, playing for Liverpool was my destiny," wrote Bellamy in *Goodfella*, his autobiography. "This is what I was here for. I was born to play this game and Liverpool was my team. The semi against Everton was worth more than the final to me. The first FA Cup final I remember watching was 1986 when I was six years old and Ian Rush scored two against Everton. So that semi let me relive a lot of my childhood memories."

Which is why when they say you should never go back, not everybody listens.

124/130

Record breakers

OVER the last 130 years there have been so many footballing and club records set by Liverpool FC and its players that an entire book could be devoted to them. They range from impressive and seemingly unbreakable to the quirky and little known.

For instance, you might be aware that Liverpool's record victory is 11-0 versus Stromsgodset (1974) in the European Cup Winners' Cup and that Ian Rush is LFC's all-time leading goalscorer with 346 goals in all competitions, but do you know what footballing record was extended when Mohamed Salah netted the Reds' fourth goal against Watford at Vicarage Road in October 2021?

Salah's stunning solo strike in Hertfordshire meant that Liverpool had scored at least four goals in one league game for a 96th consecutive season, dating back to 1919/20, a unique feat in English football.

Another team record was established by forward Daniel Sturridge in the 2016/17 season. When the England international scored the winner in a 2-1 victory at Bournemouth, he helped the Reds become the first team to have won away games at 50 different Premier League grounds since the division was founded in 1992.

Another team effort saw Liverpool become the first side in top-flight history to go six consecutive seasons without any opponents inflicting a league double over them. The record was set in March 2022 when they defeated a West Ham United side who had defeated them the previous November and who had the last chance of any team to complete a double over the Reds that season.

The run dated back to 2016/17, Jürgen Klopp's first full campaign as manager, and saw 19 teams in each of those six seasons try and fail to beat Liverpool twice in a league campaign, 114 attempts in total. The next longest such sequence was recorded by Liverpool themselves, who avoided being doubled in five successive seasons from 1975/76.

Those records may one day be beaten, but there are a number of club highs that look unlikely to ever be broken, not least Ian Callaghan's 857 appearances in a Liverpool shirt. Born and bred in Liverpool, Cally made his Reds debut against Bristol Rovers in 1960 six days after his 18th birthday and his final appearance in the 1978 European Cup semi-final first leg three weeks before his 36th birthday. To put Callaghan's 857 games into context, only two other players – Jamie Carragher (737) and Steven Gerrard (710) have ever broken through the 700-appearance mark for Liverpool while to smash Cally's club record of 640 league games a player would have to appear in every one of the Reds' Premier League fixtures for almost 17 full seasons!

Nobody has ever come close to doing that and it seems nigh-on impossible that anyone will ever break the record Phil Neal set for the most consecutive LFC games. Between 23 October 1976 and 24 September 1983, Neal appeared in 417 games in a row, in all competitions, until forced to miss three matches through injury. When the right-back returned he followed it up with another 127 consecutive games, so it's perhaps no surprise that Neal, bought by Bob Paisley from Northampton Town, is Liverpool's most decorated player and the only Englishman to have won four European Cups.

Liverpool's six European Cup triumphs is, of course, a British record while no English team has won more League Cups (nine) either, and on the subject of long-serving men then it is Tom Watson who has managed the Reds for longer than any other manager – he was in charge at Anfield for 18 years and 262 days between 17 August 1896 and 6 May 1915, which was the day he died of pneumonia. Bill Shankly, however, holds the record for the most games having taken charge for, with the Reds playing 783 matches (compared to 742 under Watson) during his 14 years and seven months as LFC boss.

At the other end of the scale then the shortest individual reign of any Liverpool manager – excluding the 10-game joint partnership between Roy Evans and Gerard Houllier in 1998 – belongs to Roy Hodgson who took charge of 31 games in 2010/11. Despite this, he holds the record of being the only individual LFC manager not to have lost a single game in European competition with the Reds winning six and drawing four of the 10 Europa League matches he oversaw, although the best win percentage belongs to Joe Fagan, whose side won 73.68% of their 19 European games.

At international level Laurie Hughes became the first Liverpool player to appear in a World Cup when he represented England in the 1950 tournament in Brazil, Ian Rush (Wales) and Michael Owen (England) jointly hold the record for the most international goals while at Liverpool with 26 apiece and Steven Gerrard's 114 England caps is also a club record.

Roger Hunt, for England in 1966, became the first Liverpool player to appear on the winning side in a World Cup final, a feat matched by Fernando Torres in 2010 and the Spanish striker also became the first Red to score in a European Championship final in 2008 when netting the winning goal against Germany with team-mates

Xabi Alonso, Pepe Reina and Alvaro Arbeloa also becoming the first Liverpool players to pick up winners' medals at the Euros.

Rigobert Song, for Cameroon in 2000, was the first Liverpool player to be an Africa Cup of Nations Winner after scoring the winning penalty-kick in a shoot-out success against Nigeria. Another defender, Kolo Toure, for Ivory Coast in 2015, also scored in a penalty shoot-out success against Ghana while in 2022 two Liverpool stars went head-to-head in the final in Cameroon. Sadio Mane's Senegal triumphed for the first time in the tournament with the Reds striker scoring the winning penalty in a shoot-out against Mohamed Salah's Egypt.

Liverpool have also had Copa America winners. The first was Luis Suarez, who opened the scoring in the 2011 final as Uruguay beat Paraguay 3-0 with Sebastian Coates also in the Uruguayan side a month before signing for the Reds. In 2019, Liverpool goalkeeper Alisson Becker and forward Roberto Firmino were in the Brazil squad that went on to lift the trophy on home soil, beating Peru 3-1 in the final in Rio.

One of the most unusual Liverpool records concerns French goalkeeper Pegguy Arphexad who made just six appearances for the Reds between 2000 and 2002. Gerard Houllier's side won those six games 27-3 on aggregate (2-1, 8-0, 5-0, 2-1, 4-1 and 6-0) and Arphexad finished his Anfield career with six winners' medals having been an unused substitute in the League Cup final, FA Cup final, UEFA Cup final, Charity Shield and Super Cup (all 2001) and the League Cup final in 2003.

Other quirky records include Phil Babb scoring his only Liverpool goal against Coventry City, having netted his only Coventry City goal against Liverpool, Brad Jones being the only Reds player to have been an unused substitute in over 100 league games (103), Roberto Firmino holding the surprising record of being the first Red substituted in over 100 Premier League matches, Steven

Gerrard being sent off (7) more times that any other man and Ephraim Longworth going a club record (for an outfield player) 370 matches without scoring between his debut on 19 September 1910 and his final appearance on 21 April 1928.

In the 2021/22 season, Japanese forward Takumi Minamino extended his club-record sequence of scoring only away from home to seven goals before then netting his next six on home soil at Anfield, while in March 2022, defender Virgil van Dijk established a new Premier League record of 60 home games for a single club without tasting defeat. Ray Houghton's record of going 23 games in all competitions from debut without suffering defeat in a Red shirt was also beaten by Ibrahima Konate during the 3-2 win against Villarreal in the Champions League semi-final second leg.

As statistical highs go, however, there are perhaps none greater than the all-time top-flight English league table which, as of the end of May 2022, had Liverpool FC perched on top. The Reds were the first team to register 2,000 top tier league wins and amass 7,000 points. They also sat almost 200 points clear of nearest challengers Arsenal after 4,248 games!

125/130

Boss That

IN 2007 a Kopite called Dan Nicholson and some mates started a Liverpool FC fanzine called BOSS Mag. It was a simple black-and-white photocopied fanzine that sold for £1 but, unlike most fanzines, largely focussed on what happened off the pitch; the stories around Liverpool FC games, away trips and the culture around it.

Music is a massive part of that culture and BOSS Mag attracted a particular following - Reds who would go to the match on a Saturday afternoon followed by a gig on a Saturday night.

Many of them were in bands themselves and so they decided to put a gig on themselves, the first BOSS event being a beginning-of-season party in August 2011 after the Sunderland game at Anfield.

The Tea Street Band were one of the first to play at the sell-out gig at the Static Gallery on Berry Street. Not a single Liverpool FC song was sung at that first session, despite it being a post-match LFC crowd.

Promoted in BOSS Mag and through word of mouth, more gigs were arranged and in season 2012/13 Nicholson and co hit upon the name A BOSS Night. With the Reds in the Europa League that season there were a lot of Sunday league matches so BOSS Sunday Sessions were born, the first being held in OSQA, a complex off Renshaw Street. Cast's John Power even played at one gig.

Interest grew as the season went on and at the start of May, after the Merseyside derby at Anfield, a teenager who travelled on the coaches to see Liverpool's away games played his first gig. His name? Jamie Webster.

A BOSS Night moved to Sound on Duke Street in season 2013/14 and it was then, with the Reds flying in the Premier League, that football songs became a natural part of the gig with musicians on stage reacting to supporters singing Liverpool chants in the crowd.

When Webster started to strum along to the crowd singing 'here's to you Jordan Henderson,' and video footage of it spread on social media, the culture of terrace chants being part of BOSS Nights organically began.

A BOSS Night moved to District in the Baltic Triangle the following season and since Webster has been headlining the nights the football side of things has not only come to the fore, but led to one of the Kop's most famous chants.

Jamie, and fellow musician Kieran Molyneux, continued to go to away games on the coaches and it was one of them where the Virgil van Dijk song was thought up after The Pogues' *Dirty Old Town* happened to come on the radio. Many Liverpool songs have started on away coaches, but the difference now is that social media allows them to spread more quickly. Within weeks it became a Kop anthem.

In 2017/18, BOSS Nights went on the road for the first time when Liverpool reached the Champions League final in Kiev.

"The pre-match event in Shevchenko Park was the catalyst," said Nicholson. "Shevchenko Park wasn't really about BOSS, I wanted it to be about Jamie because he summed up everything that was good about our support. After the Roma semi-final I texted Tony Barrett, Liverpool's Head of Supporter Liaison, to say 'whatever happens musically in Kiev then Jamie should be involved', especially with his recording of *Allez Allez Allez* being released on iTunes.

"Tony agreed, put me in touch with some people at the club and that's how Shevchenko Park got set up. It went really well and in the days afterwards the club got back in touch with me and invited myself and Jamie to go on the pre-season tour of North America with them."

A year later, the Redmen were heading to another Champions League final and en-route they visited Bayern Munich and Barcelona in the knockout stages. Pre-match BOSS Nights were held in Munich's Reitknechtstrasse and Razzmatazz, a nightclub in Barcelona's Poblenou neighbourhood.

While Webster and co were performing on the stage, Klopp's Liverpool were performing on the pitch and when the Reds were Madrid-bound the opportunity to put on another BOSS Session before a Champions League final wasn't to be missed. It was arranged in collaboration with Liverpool FC, led by Head of Tourism Tom Cassidy.

"It was like a festival," Cassidy told *liverpoolfc.com*. "Whereas Shevchenko Park just kind of happened and was a bit of a blur, this was different. The stage was a proper stage, not a bandstand like we had in Kiev. Everything had to go up a couple of levels and it did. Although we were a bit unsure in terms of final numbers we were anticipating up to 50,000 plus in the space – and we were right."

Surrounded by shops, cafes, offices, banks and flats, that space was Plaza Felipe II. Situated on Avenida Felipe II, a dedicated public space since 1985, it is home to 'El Dolmen de Dalí' – a giant stone monument dedicated to science and technology that was designed by the legendary Catalan artist Salvador Dalí.

Built from granite, the stone dolmen rises 43 feet tall and is formed by an oval-shaped natural rock placed horizontally on three carved granite pillars. Placed in front of it is a bronze figure of Isaac Newton, holding a pendulum while standing upon a polished black granite pedestal.

On 1 June 2019, that monument on Plaza Felipe II – aka Salvador Dali Square – provided the striking backdrop for one of the biggest street parties Madrid has ever seen.

The BOSS Session scenes at Plaza Felipe II on the day of the game were nothing short of astonishing. An estimated 50,000-60,000 Liverpool supporters engulfed the square and surrounding areas – draping flags and banners from every vantage point – to be part of an unforgettable pre-match party that went viral on social media as the crowds stretched back as far as the eye could see.

Ben Burke brought the Istanbul vibes with a burning *Ring of Fire*. John Power had *Poor Scouser Tommy* and *Fields of Anfield Road* resonating around the square. And his performance of *You'll Never Walk Alone* was a goosebumps moment.

Liverpool legend John Barnes took to the stage and sang, performing *The Anfield Rap* in full. The lads from The Anfield Wrap did their bit to keep the crowd entertained with a mixture of chat and bangers, while Chelcee Grimes finished her set with *One Kiss*, a song those in Kiev a year earlier had taken to their hearts when Dua Lipa performed it before kick-off in the NSC Olimpiyskiy.

As mid-afternoon edged towards early evening, Molyneux went through his repertoire. Where else would you hear John Lennon's *Imagine* followed by the Bobby Firmino song as flags waved and red smoke poured into the sky above?

The final hour of the tumultuous six-hour extravaganza featured Webster at his string-twanging, foot-stomping, crowd-enthralling best. "Do us a favour, clap yer hands to this," he said before belting out Peter Gabriel's *Solsbury Hill* as a banner held aloft in front of him quoted the lyrics 'grab your things I've come to take you home' alongside a Liver Bird with the handle of the European Cup in its mouth.

"You don't know how good it feels to see 50,000 people singing 'Liverpool' in front of you," he shouted into the microphone.

"It's the best thing in the world'."

Along the edges and at the back of Plaza Felipe II, countless locals came and went, taking pictures and videos of the incredible scenes. Many watched from their office and flat windows. "A lot of the police were taking photos," added Cassidy. "They were going: 'Wow!' They hadn't seen anything like it before."

Quite what the Madrileños [Madrid's equivalent of Scousers] made of thousands of Liverpool supporters singing 'Saturday night and I like the way you move, Divock Origi' while bouncing up and down on the spot is anyone's guess, but it's not something they see every day.

The ABBA-inspired 'Sad-i-o, Mane! Running down the wing, Mane! Hear the Kopites sing, Mane! We're all bouncing in Madrid' stuck in many-a-head, but perhaps the most iconic moment of all was when Webster sang: "He's our centre half, he's our number four. Watch him defend, and we watch him score. He'll pass the ball, calm as you like, he's Virgil van Dijk, he's Virgil van Dijk."

The sea of red responded by collectively bouncing underneath a smoke-filled crimson sky like waves crashing towards the shore. And as Webster strummed away on the stage with the crowd eating out of the palm of his hand and singing van Dijk's name, the backdrop of Dali's monument made it look like a weird mix of Glastonbury and Stonehenge with a sunny city-centre stage.

Elsewhere in Madrid, at Liverpool's team hotel, van Dijk was preparing for the Champions League final. He clearly couldn't be at Plaza Felipe II, but he was well aware of what was happening as footage of the Red hordes singing his name went viral with over 1.5 millions views on YouTube alone.

"What a song, what a video actually," he later told *goal.com*. "A couple of my family members were in that crowd at the time and I saw the video before pre-match − or after pre-match − of the final.

"Normally we sleep, but I couldn't sleep anymore. I was so

excited, I wanted to just go out there. I don't have that too much, but I was just ready to go. I wanted to go out there, get the trophy and party with them as well. I'm very proud to get that song and that video definitely gives me the chills."

A rousing rendition of *Allez Allez Allez* ended A BOSS Session that will be recalled through the ages and later that year the first-ever fan park in Doha for the FIFA Club World Cup was based around more BOSS sessions with travelling Kopites seeing The Lightning Seeds the headline act.

Then in 2022, when Liverpool headed to Paris for the Champions League final, came another sea of BOSS Session red at Cours de Vincennes. Who'd have thought such iconic scenes could emerge from a £1 fanzine first published in 2007?

"From a BOSS point of view I like to think we've helped a little to bridge the gap between Liverpool FC supporters in different countries," said Nicholson. "I'm not taking any credit for that – I'm just one of the organisers in the background whereas Jamie, Kieran and others are at the forefront of all – but we've seen the proof of it.

"For me, the most enjoyable events we do will always be in District. We started all this just to get our mates together in Liverpool after a match and there's still something really nice about that."

Men of bronze

FOR years there was just one statue at Anfield and it commemorated Bill Shankly, arms aloft and scarf around neck, situated outside the Spion Kop since 1997. In more recent times, though, there have been two evocative additions to the stadium's sculptural landscape – dedicated to Liverpool FC's founding father and another of its greatest managers.

December 2018 saw the official unveiling of a bronze bust of John Houlding on 96 Avenue, now 97 Avenue, near to the Anfield Forever stones. The bust and its base stand just under seven feet tall and it was created by Tom Murphy, the local sculptor behind the Shankly statue, as part of the club's 125th anniversary celebrations.

There was no 97 Avenue all those years ago, of course. No Paisley Square nor massive Main Stand. In late 1892, according to an Ordnance Survey map of the time, there was practically nothing on that side of the playing field formerly belonging to Everton FC, not until you got to Lothair Road and the ladder of terrace streets running north west between Rockfield Road and Anfield Road.

That's how it was in John Houlding's day. And in 2018, amid the landscaped public domain outside the modern stadium, this is where the monument to Houlding, portrayed in his mayoral finery, was erected.

"We didn't have any symbol at Anfield that was a representation of our founder that our supporters could see and touch and reflect upon," said then Reds chief-executive Peter Moore. "One hundred and twenty-five years is a long time and it was all started by this man – without him, football on Merseyside certainly wouldn't be what it is today. I hope our supporters take the time to go and visit as he looks proudly upon our Main Stand."

As every Reds (and Blues) fan knows, Houlding officially formed Liverpool Football Club on 3 June 1892 following a dispute with Everton who played at Anfield, the ground he owned. The Toffees left and Houlding recruited players for a new team to play here – and LFC was born. He was subsequently appointed Lord Mayor of Liverpool in 1897.

"There are very few pictures of him in existence so I did a lot of research around the style of dress that would have been worn at the time," revealed sculptor Murphy. "I was also lucky enough to be able to visit the Town Hall to understand the detail of the mayoral chain which can be seen around his neck. He was a really interesting person to work on and completely different from the Shankly statue."

Still standing at the opposite corner of the present stadium is the house in which Houlding once lived – a red-and-cream-bricked mansion at no73 Anfield Road and otherwise known as Stanley House. He'd progressed from working as a drayman delivering beer at Clarkson's Brewery in Soho Street, in the city's Islington district, to owning his own brewery in Everton's Tynemouth Street.

'Houlding's Sparkling Ales' were the tipple of choice in late Victorian Liverpool, and using profits from the brewery he set up home at Stanley House with his wife Jane and children Alice and William. With a garden and steepled tower overlooking (the then six-year-old) Stanley Park, it gave him the perfect base from which to keep an eye on the city's footballing affairs.

A little over two years after the Houlding bronze was installed, just 50 or so yards away, a footballing work of art was revealed to the world. A statue for Bob Paisley had felt long overdue by general consent, despite the presence of the Paisley Gateway on Walton Breck Road with its bronze plaques either side of the gates showing a sculpture of Bob in relief and a roll-call of his honours. But no one could have foreseen something as brilliantly original as what now appeared on Paisley Square (naturally), having been unveiled in late January 2020 by members of Bob's family and relatives of the late, great Emlyn Hughes, ahead of Liverpool's Premier League home game against Southampton.

Standing 8ft tall and designed to sit at the right height to enable supporters to take selfies alongside, it was the realisation in bronze of a real, dramatic moment from LFC history captured by a photographer over half-a-century ago. The outcome of the game in question is incidental: Liverpool 1 Tottenham Hotspur 1, on Monday 29 April 1968; centre-forward Tony Hateley on target for the hosts and Jimmy Greaves scoring for the visitors, as manager Bill Shankly embarked upon building his second great team in red.

Bob Paisley, then aged 49, was Shankly's first-team coach. He'd already been with Liverpool for almost 30 years. Emlyn, the injured player on Paisley's shoulders, blood streaming from a gash in his knee, was a 20-year-old left-half. Twelve months a Liverpool player, and a future European Cup-lifting captain, he epitomised the next generation's raw gladiatorial ethic.

The moment has echoes of a wounded soldier being rescued from the frontline by a brave comrade. But Bob, strong, selfless and ever the pragmatist, would say he was just doing his job: get the casualty off the pitch quickly and safely, get him treated, get the team going again.

The previous January, in 2019, the 100th anniversary of Paisley's birth had been marked on the front cover of LFC's official matchday programme (for the visit of Crystal Palace) with a vintage photo of Bob the player, taking a throw-in with one of those hefty old 'case-balls'.

Subsequent commemorations of his life and legacy included main club sponsor Standard Chartered producing a film series in which current and former Reds stars presented a gift to a computer-generated Paisley whose voice had been recreated using smart technology. The 2019/20 kit also paid homage to Liverpool FC's most successful manager and ultimate one-club man, with his signature featuring on the inside-neck of every jersey.

Indeed it was Standard Chartered which had commissioned the statue to mark its own ten-year relationship with the Reds, and Peter Moore revealed how it came about: "I was chatting one day about the football club with a friend of mine, Emma Rodgers, herself a hugely talented sculptor. I've always had this photo of Bob in his physio, trainer days, carrying Emlyn Hughes off the pitch. It's the first minute of the second half and you can see that Emlyn is not only bleeding from the knees but he's done some damage to his hand.

"I've always loved this photograph and I showed it to Emma and thought nothing of it. Then she asked me a few days later to send her the digital version, which I did, and next thing I get a call from her saying can I come down to a city-centre foundry, Castle Fine Arts, to meet somebody and see something.

"So I go down there and meet Andy Edwards, an incredibly talented sculptor. He did the Beatles statues on the waterfront, and the two 'Christmas Truce' soldiers in the 'Bombed Out Church'. And he showed me this maquette that he'd speculatively developed, based on the photo, a scale-model of what the statue would be – and it took my breath away.

"It's everything that I think we owe Bob Paisley as a football club. We have the Paisley Gates, we have Paisley Square, but fans will tell you they're always a little disappointed that we never had a Paisley statue, given what this man has done for this football club as a player, as a trainer, as a manager.

"Our great partners at Standard Chartered, who have been doing a lot to honour Bob this year, said, 'We're in – we love the idea of having something that is a permanent legacy to this incredible man's work'. So they funded the statue."

Potteries-born Andy, who previously worked upon a triple-figured statue of Stoke City legend Stanley Matthews, called it "an amazing image that takes football statuary to a different level." He'd read up on the subject to refresh his memory of Paisley and Hughes "and the characters they were. I started thinking about the enormity of this job, how significant it is and what it represents, and I felt a lot of pride as I put the first clay on. The anniversary is an historic occasion, there are people who don't know that much about Bob Paisley, so there's a huge responsibility to not only get the detail authentic, but to get the spirit and the feel because you're telling a story – it's kind of like 3D journalism."

The maquette which Andy presented to Peter Moore was one-fifth scale – "big enough to show the detail that will appear at full-size but also small enough to be able to hold in your hand and move around to see how the whole thing is going to work when it's seen from 50 yards away. The main thing is to get the proportions right. If you've got a hand that's too small, or a head that's too big, people are going to spot it straight away. It has to be true to a figure carrying a 15-stone footballer on his back."

Working alongside Andy was the foundry's managing-director Chris Butler, who explained how the creative process was a combination of individual talent and state-of-the-art technology: "I hadn't seen this picture before and what's great is that it shows a different side of football. These days if something like this happened during a match there would be hundreds of pictures of it, you could go online and find every angle you could possibly want. But as far as we know this is the only photograph of that moment. Andy made the model from that one photo, which is quite a skill in itself.

"We mapped out the model five times bigger and once we had the accurate internal structure, as well as the creases and folds of the clothing, we could cover the frame with clay and Andy could come and start work. We made a silicon-rubber and fibreglass mould over the whole surface then divided it into sections to be cast in their individual pieces. Of course that means there are seams, and our work then is to make it look like you don't know how it's been made."

Chris and the team most certainly succeeded. Another former skipper, Phil Thompson, who played under Bob Paisley and alongside Emlyn, vouched for that: "The likeness is astonishing – everybody who comes to Anfield will be thrilled to see it. I joined Liverpool in 1969, so this moment is from the year before, and it epitomises everything about the club in that era.

"Nowadays you see medics, stretchers, everything, but this was Bob as the humble 'sponge man', as they used to call them, because he was the physio as well as a coach. He did all of these roles."

Inscribed on the base of the statue is a famous Paisley quote: "This club has been my life. I'd go out and sweep the street and be proud to do it for Liverpool FC, if they asked me to." The same words appeared on the cover of the Liverpool v Southampton matchday programme on Saturday 1 February 2020, along with the original photo of Paisley and Hughes.

At the time of the unveiling, Liverpool were reigning European champions, newly-crowned FIFA World Club Cup winners, and 19 points clear at the top of the Premier League. By the end of the week they'd beaten Southampton 4-0 and held the biggest lead by any team at the end of a matchday in English top-flight history, having earned 100 points from the last 102 available to them, winning 33 of their last 34 matches.

Bob Paisley would have been very, very proud.

All the singing ladies

LIVERPOOL FC Women enjoyed a fine 2021/22 season as the Reds regained their place among the top-flight of the English game.

The club had felt hard done by when relegated in 2019/20 after a points-per-game criteria was applied to decide the FA Women's Super League season once the COVID-19 pandemic brought the campaign to an early end. Although Liverpool propped up the league at the time they still had several home games to play, some of which were against the teams immediately above them.

Following a largely disappointing first season in the second tier, the Reds brought back Matt Beard as manager in the summer of 2021. Beard had been responsible for leading Liverpool to back-to-back FA Women's Super League titles in 2013 and 2014 and he quickly assembled a squad to challenge for the one promotion berth in the FA Women's Championship.

Despite an opening day defeat at home to London City Lionesses, the Reds bounced back quickly and went undefeated in their next 19 league matches [a Championship record], winning 15 of them to secure the title and promotion with two games to spare.

There were some record breakers along the way too. Goalkeeper Rachael Laws broke her own club record for clean sheets in a league campaign, registering 13 by the end of the season to comfortably pass the nine she had kept during 2020/21.

At the other end of the field, local lass Ashley Hodson became the Reds' record appearance holder when she passed former captain Gemma Bonner's tally of 115. By the end of 2021/22 the winger, who hails from St Helens, had 132 Liverpool games to her name.

There was also a proud moment for the Scouser in the team, midfielder Missy Bo Kearns, who became Liverpool FC Women's youngest starting captain of the professional era. Kearns, from Allerton, was aged 20 years, 217 days when she led the Reds out for a Continental Cup win over Blackburn Rovers in November 2021, surpassing Gemma Bonner's previous record of 21 years, 247 days.

Along the way the Reds received tremendous vocal support at home and away. The backing was regularly referenced throughout the campaign by management and players alike with away games at places as far afield as Blackburn Rovers, Sheffield United, Durham, Crystal Palace, London City Lionesses, Charlton Athletic and the title-clinching fixture at Bristol City taking on the same feel as matches at Prenton Park due to the noisy backing from the travelling Reds.

A particular feature was the singing of songs for the team and individual players which had dated back to Beard's first spell at the helm. That was in no small part down to the efforts of lifelong Liverpudlian Stephen Nelson who puts together the tunes which have proved huge hits with fellow supporters and players alike.

Stephen grew up in West Derby in close proximity to Melwood and was bitten by the Liverpool bug from an early age.

"My Dad latched on to Bill Shankly during the club's days in the Second Division and went regularly during the promotion season of 1961/62 when Kevin Lewis' goals against Southampton helped the team back into Division One," he told the official *Liverpool FC Magazine*. "I grew up in a semi which looked straight into Melwood. During the holidays, my brother and I would go and get autographs at the training ground and chat to the players. In fact, my brother once shot Bill Shankly with his water pistol!"

Stephen's fascination with music was another early interest. His love of The Beatles inspired him to write his own music and, being a follower of LFC, he contributed to various fans' songs over the years.

"In the 1990s I started thinking we should have a song for Steve McManaman," he recalls. "He was our most gifted player of that era but the only song for him was that daft Muppets one. I felt he needed one with more gravitas and came up with one to the tune of *Fields of Athenry*. Of course, the Fields of Anfield Road is now a regular at matches," said Stephen, who was actually named after one of the men name-checked in that song, Steve Heighway.

Stephen had been to watch the Liverpool FC Women's team during the 1990s but had stopped going before the team's move to Widnes in 2013.

"When the club really got behind the team again following the launch of the FA WSL, I decided I would give it another go and I'm really pleased I did.

"My first thoughts on going to Widnes were that there were groups of supporters in little bubbles but they weren't connected somehow and hadn't really been introduced to like-minded people. Although there were bits of singing it was all rather tuneless. I had a think about what songs would translate.

"During that first title-winning season of 2013, the team had a motto; 'Together We Are Limitless'. I wrote a little tune which we called Old Widnes Way with the chorus ending 'Together We Are Tuneless'. It seemed popular and, gradually, the fans started to become a bit more connected."

Two examples of songs which became big favourites with the players themselves were those in tribute to Dutch duo Mandy van den Berg and Shanice van den Sanden in 2016.

"When we signed Mandy, I saw a video the team put out on Twitter of players holding roses to celebrate Valentine's Day. The sight of Mandy van den Berg holding a red rose made me think of 'Love is in the Air' and so that's how that one came about.

"I had also thought about a song to the tune of the Corvettes' *Mr Sandman* but was told it would be too complicated. I wasn't having it! I came up with some lyrics and in the end I just sang it and it was a brilliant coming together of things. Shanice ended up getting the only goal of the game in the opening league fixture against Birmingham so that one really stuck well!"

Another former favourite was that dedicated to Scottish playmaker Caroline Weir to the tune of *Mull of Kintyre*. Caroline was a confirmed fan of her song, saying: "I really liked it. It was very clever."

During the 2021/22 promotion-winning season, Ashley Hodson continued to be regaled with her song of 'Ashley Hodson, yeah, yeah, yeah!' to the tune of The Beatles' *She Loves You*, while captain Niamh Fahey had her own special tribute. The Republic of Ireland ace, who won her 100th cap for her country in February 2022, has a little ditty to the tune of *C'est La Vie* by Irish girl group B*Witched, which goes: 'She is red, she is green, number five in our team, in midfield or back three, Niamh Fahey'.

Even Scouse playmaker Missy Bo Kearns got in on the act, penning a tribute to team-mate Jade Bailey to the tune of Creedence Clearwater Revival's *Bad Moon Rising* - the tune Kopites have adapted for Diogo Jota.

Meanwhile, Belgian winger Yana Daniels acquired the tune formerly sung on the Kop in tribute to winger Maxi Rodriguez. To the tune of Buddy Holly's *Heartbeat*, it goes, 'Yana, oh Yana Daniels, run down the wing for me; do, do, do, do, do; do, do, do, do, do; do, do, do, do, do; do, do, do, do, do'.

"It's unreal really," she says. "When you grow up as a little kid, you would never think supporters would actually sing a song about you, especially at a club like Liverpool. To be fair, all of the songs that they've made for everyone are class and it does bring a smile to everyone's faces.

"We talk about it a lot after the games, saying 'Oh, did you hear that one? That one was good.' They have a big input on our performances and they just keep us pushing, which is really good and exciting. At the away games, it has felt like they've all been there too so a big thank you to them."

You can check out all the songs at *2gethertuneless.co.uk* and here's hoping fans of Liverpool FC Women have plenty more to sing about in the future!

Shanice Van De Sanden (to the tune of *Mr Sandman*)
Oh Van De Sanden
Plays like a dream
Ask FC Twente or Heerenveen
Now she's number 11 in out team
Oh Van De Sanden
Plays like a dream

Rachael Laws (to the tune of *We Love You Liverpool, We Do*)
We've got a Geordie goalie and Rachael is her name
There's no finer sweeper keeper than Lawsy in the game
She won the league with Matt Beard so Vicky brought her back
She's big and brave to make the saves then start our next attack
We love you Lawsy we do, we love you Lawsy we do
We love you Lawsy we do, Oh Lawsy we love you

Missy Bo Kearns (to the tune of *Let It Snow*)
She's our local midfield maestro
And her passes are so delightful

Everyone wants to know
Missy Bo, Missy Bo, Missy Bo

Jade Bailey (by Missy Bo Kearns, to the tune of *Bad Moon Rising*)
We've got a bad girl called Jade Bailey
She wears the Reds' number eight
She's from Walthamstow don't you know
Better than Stevie, I'd say so
Oh her name is Jade Bailey

Allez, Allez Allez (to the tune of *L'estate sta finendo* by Righeira)
From Durham down to Bristol
Chichester or Staines
We've travelled all the country
For our red women's games
Two times we've won the title
Been to Europe too
We are loyal supporters
And we come from Liverpool
Allez, allez, allez
Allez, allez, allez
Allez, allez, allez
Allez! Allez! Allez!

128/130

Where the art is

IF there'd been a book like this to celebrate Liverpool FC's 100th anniversary back in 1992, ending with a chapter looking ahead to the next 30 years, what would the authors have written about Anfield?

They might have guessed that the stadium would evolve with awesome redeveloped stands, although the concept of digital match tickets would have raised a few eyebrows. And surely they'd have taken great delight in the emergence of a new generation of Kopites with their own distinctive culture; chants going viral, singalongs in pre-match venues around the ground; colourful flags and banners for a new era; smoky red flares (strictly prohibited, mind) and lamppost-climbing fanaticism on the streets to welcome the team bus before really big fixtures; and mighty murals inspired by a love for LFC.

It's been all about the street-art in recent years, not just at home but as far afield as Africa and America. In May 2018, towards the end of Mo Salah's record-breaking debut season, the forward's image appeared on the wall of a cafe in downtown Cairo – he is of course a national hero in Egypt and the artwork formed part of a project honouring the country's most iconic figures. The cafe-owner revealed: "It's become very popular. Everyone takes pictures of it – foreigners, Egyptians. So many people come to see it that I've even had to turn people away – I tell them Salah is asleep, he's having a rest!"

Over in New York City a huge mural adorned the side of a brick building in Times Square. It showed Mo's head and shoulders with colourful patterns, along with miniature versions of him playing, in his hair and beard. American artist Brandan 'Bmike' Odums created it for the sports website *Bleacher Report*, as part of a celebration of World Cup stars, and on a flying visit to the city Salah tweeted a selfie with it behind him.

By then he'd become the inspiration for street-art back home, too. There was an 'Ode to Mo' near Church Street in Liverpool's shopping district, made by poet Musa Okwonga and local street-artist and Reds fan Guy McKinley, to coincide with the 2018 Champions League final. Another Mo Salah mural, created by artist John Culshaw who you can read about later, went up opposite the King Harry pub on Anfield Road in March 2022.

Street-art has been around for a while. Utilising techniques such as spray-painting and stencilling, and originating from the late 1970s graffiti scene in New York (one of its pioneers, Keith Haring, was recently the subject of a retrospective at Tate Liverpool), it's been described as a city's outdoor museum. Banksy is the most famous current exponent.

National Geographic magazine comments: "While it is easy, upon coming across a beautiful work of art on a city's wall, to simply snap a photo, upload it to Instagram and move on, the best street-art merits spending a few moments to think about what it wants to say."

Back in Liverpool in the summer of 2017, artist Paul Curtis created a striking image of Liver Bird wings in Jamaica Street, in the city's cutting-edge Baltic Triangle neighbourhood. People flocked to be photographed 'wearing' the wings and it quickly became one of the most Instagram-able places in town.

In December 2018 it was joined by a mural of Jürgen Klopp in nearby Jordan Street, the work of graffiti-artist Akse over the course of one weekend, while another of the Reds boss emerged on the wall of an Anfield bar, Klopp's Boot Room in Houlding Street. This one was made by John Culshaw, a self-taught street-artist who lost his arm in a childhood accident. "It was a pleasure to work on Klopp because I am a huge LFC fan," John told the *Liverpool Echo*. "I would say he is our best manager since Bill Shankly. I obviously want him to stay at the club for as long as possible and this mural is a personal tribute to him from me."

Previously, John had created an artwork featuring Steven Gerrard and Everton legend Peter Reid, for a barbershop in Huyton near where the pair grew up. "I later received a nice message from Steven on Instagram which I really appreciated."

In 2019 when the Reds won their sixth European Cup, a bar in Concert Square commemorated the triumph with a mural of Mo, Virgil van Dijk and skipper Jordan Henderson lifting the Champions League trophy in Madrid. Later that year another of John's creations appeared at the back of The Park pub on Walton Breck Road, right opposite the ground: Bill Shankly holding a red scarf aloft emblazoned with the pub's name, helping to celebrate the 60th year since the great Scot's appointment at Anfield.

But it was the Trent Alexander-Arnold mural on Sybil Road, just off Anfield Road, that really caught the eye, unveiled the day before the 2019/20 season's opening Premier League match against Norwich City and visited by the man himself. On the night that he'd helped his boyhood heroes to clinch the Champions League, Trent was asked what it meant to join the greats who'd won the trophy before him. "It's hard to think of myself as a legend," he said. "I'm just a normal lad from Liverpool, whose dream has just come true."

That quote formed the basis of the artwork, created by Akse in association with The Anfield Wrap podcast team. It also highlighted the work of Fans Supporting Foodbanks, an organisation of whom Trent is a great supporter and whose co-founder Ian Byrne said: "As someone who lives in the next street, it's brought something unique to Anfield. Well done to all involved as we are very proud of this 'boss' piece of art and of Trent, a great role-model to the kids in our community."

The Reds right-back added: "It's not just the picture – it's important that it has that message there. It shows the fans that it's only a few metres down the road, so it will just raise a bit more awareness for it and they can give back whenever they can. The main message that kids should be picking up from me and my story is that anything is possible, anything can happen. I was once that kid in a Gerrard or Carragher shirt. They were the players that made me feel as though anything could happen."

A spokesman for The Anfield Wrap said: "We're really proud of the mural. We've worked so hard on it and we hope people enjoy celebrating the local lad living all of our dreams with us."

Sybil Road now features a treble of murals. Opposite Trent is Reds skipper Jordan Henderson holding aloft the Premier League trophy, created by MurWalls and commissioned by Redmen TV to celebrate LFC's 2020 title success. And next to it is a mural in honour of 1965 FA Cup final goalscorers Ian St John and Roger Hunt, again by MurWalls. The Saint signed it in November 2020 and the passing of both legends in recent times has made the mural even more evocative.

More recently, Reds legend Steven Gerrard and double European Cup-winner Alan Kennedy were the subjects of MurWalls' latest LFC artwork on Anfield's Dinorwic Road, with the latter giving his approval in person. They also created the mural of legendary goalkeeper Ray Clemence on Wylva Road, officially unveiled by his daughter Sarah plus grandchildren Harry, Lilly, Freddie and Claudia in October 2020 a month before he passed away, plus one of boyhood Blue-turned-Reds star Jamie Carragher in honour of his 23 Foundation (which has raised almost £3 million for local causes since 2009) on Bootle's Marsh Lane. In May 2022, MurWalls unveiled a superb Ian Rush mural opposite Anfield.

Also during season 2021/22 a mural dedicated to Hillsborough campaigner Anne Williams – mum of Kevin, one of our 97 – was unveiled on Sunbury Road in Anfield. Again this was the work of Paul Curtis: "Anne is someone that the city can be proud of. She's the right sort of person to have a mural, to have a tribute to her."

If ever this book is revised and updated in another three decades' time, it would be wonderful to see all this street-art still in situ, with who-knows-what new additions by the year 2052.

129/130

Warm welcomes

WHEN Brendan Rodgers' Liverpool put themselves in the mix for the Premier League title in 2013/14, Reds fans responded with their usual tremendous backing.

However, the past decade or so has seen that fervent support manifest itself in a new way with supporters lining the streets around Anfield to welcome the team bus ahead of certain games.

It all started in January 2010 when Rafael Benitez's Liverpool entertained Tottenham in a midweek Premier League fixture.

Two goals from Dirk Kuyt gave the Reds an important 2-0 victory and the team were clearly spurred on by their vocal twelfth man.

The *Liverpool Echo* reported: "From the moment the team coach trundled into Anfield Road it was evident that team and fans would be as one. Crowds gathered on each side of the pavement to form a guard of honour, with huge banners fluttering in the night breeze and the words on the one nearest to the Shankly Gates said it all – 'Scouse Solidarity'."

Ahead of the home game against Sunderland in late March 2014, fans' group Spion Kop 1906 helped to mobilise another strong show of support via a call out on social media.

Kopites lined the streets to welcome the team coach into the stadium with a colourful display and they repeated the scene ahead of the Manchester City fixture two-and-a-half weeks later.

After the Sunderland match, a 2-1 win, manager Rodgers saluted the efforts of the fans: "Our game started on the coach on the way in here," he told reporters afterwards. "It filled me with great pride being the manager of the club. As we were driving in, to get that support and then have that in the stadium – the supporters really lifted us and they got us over the line."

The Anfield fixture against Manchester City brought a similar welcome for the team and, again, there was a winning ending as Liverpool recorded a thrilling 3-2 victory, Philippe Coutinho striking the clincher, to stay top of the table.

A spokesman from Spion Kop 1906 told *Liverpool FC magazine*: "For the City game we met on Anfield Road at the King Harry pub to welcome the coach in again before getting in the ground early to get all the flags sorted. The most important thing that day was that it was the 25th anniversary of Hillsborough and we had a design planned that was on display. Every year we use the game nearest to 15 April as a Hillsborough display. This was no different and was the centre of attention on The Kop alongside all our other flags and banners.

"The idea [behind welcoming the team for the Sunderland fixture] was that we'd previously had three away games and with it being a midweek match we wanted to generate an atmosphere around the ground as we knew a win would fire us back to the top of the league. A few years earlier, fans lined the streets before the Spurs game to get behind the team and the manager and it inspired us to win 2-0. We wanted to do something similar and create an atmosphere to get the players ready for the game. I'd like to think it worked as we got the three points and the atmosphere in and around the ground was better. It got a bit tense during the game, but overall it was job done."

The spokesman also explained that plenty of planning goes into the striking banners.

"If we are doing a long banner, then that is started a few weeks in advance. We either pass the image to a designer who creates it for us or we all meet up and paint it together. A lot of work and thought goes into the designs. It is a group effort which we are all a part of. We've been doing this for years and it is always nice to hear positive and good feedback from players and other fans. We don't do it for praise, we do it to generate an atmosphere in the ground and to make The Kop unique to anything else in this country."

Taking inspiration from those memorable days during the 2013/14 title run-in, fans repeated the dose in 2016 when Liverpool, now under the management of Jürgen Klopp, came up against their boss's former club Borussia Dortmund in the quarter-final of the Europa League.

With the approach to the ground a sea of red and a cauldron of noise, vast numbers of supporters lined the pavements to give a vocal reception to the team coach.

The scenes were captured on mobile phones by players of both teams and again proved to be the catalyst for a memorable Liverpool win as Klopp's side came from 3-1 down on the night to win 4-3 to go through to the semi-final 5-4 on aggregate and spark scenes of great celebration.

In the last four of the competition, the Reds came up against Villarreal and trailed 1-0 from the first leg in Spain.

Videos of the team's welcome to Anfield were posted on the *Daily Mirror* website with an accompanying article saying: "Fans of some clubs think Liverpool supporters make too much of the 'special European nights' at Anfield.

"The atmosphere's not THAT good," these angry fans say. "We make just as much noise at (insert name of football ground here)." Well, we have bad news for these annoyed rival fans. The clip suggests a European night at Liverpool is indeed pretty special.

"The video shows the welcome the Liverpool team bus got as it arrived at Anfield. And the reception the coach receives is mental. There are fans everywhere, surrounded by flags, red smoke and lots and lots of noise. Goodness knows how the Liverpool players sitting inside the bus felt seeing this. Our best guess: they arrived at the stadium ready to run through a brick wall for their supporters.

"Jürgen Klopp's side were treated to the kind of welcome usually reserved for cup-winning teams as Kopites produced a cascade of sound and colour that almost had the vehicle rocking as it passed the King Harry pub just outside the ground. As well as flags flying and deafening chants from the assembled throngs of crowds, flares were set off in what was a passion cauldron of an atmosphere – outside the stadium."

Inside Anfield the atmosphere was just as charged and the Reds rewarded their special supporters' extraordinary encouragement with a fine 3-0 victory to reach another European final.

In season 2017/18 Anfield Road was again packed to welcome the coaches ahead of Champions League knock-out games against Manchester City and AS Roma. Unacceptably, some missiles were thrown and damaged the Manchester City team coach – behaviour that was rightly condemned by Jürgen Klopp and the club – but there was a fantastic show of support again for the Roma semi-final despite the coaches arriving in the pouring rain.

The following season the Anfield Road pavements were full of excited supporters again ahead of Liverpool's Champions League quarter-final and semi-finals against Bayern Munich and Barcelona, adding to the anticipation and sense of atmosphere.

While a combination of the COVID-19 pandemic and the redevelopment work on the new Anfield Road stand have changed the landscape somewhat since, when the big games come around there is nowhere in English football that the players receive a warmer welcome before they arrive at a stadium than at Anfield with Liverpool fans again out in force before the 2022 Champions League semi-final against Villarreal and final Premier League encounter of an epic campaign against Wolves.

130/130

Journey Hunters

AT the start of the 2021/22 season, a campaign when crowds returned to watch football matches after 18 months of the beautiful game being mostly played behind closed doors, Jürgen Klopp took the opportunity to address Liverpool FC supporters in his programme notes before the first home game of the season against Burnley.

In doing so, he coined a new phrase to describe what those who passionately follow the Reds are – journey hunters.

"I make no promises on what we will achieve, where we will

finish or what we might win," wrote Klopp. "But I can make a full commitment that we go with all we have and we go for everything.

"We have the players, staff and club atmosphere to go for it all. We have the power and belief to make this season very special.

"But what makes this place special is the appreciation of the journey. A friend of mine who is closer to the fan culture than I could ever profess to be, said to me that people support Liverpool not because they are glory hunters but because they are journey hunters. I love this sentiment.

"Our 2021/22 journey is underway and we should enjoy every second of it. Not because we know we will have success or we expect it – but because we chase it together, as a collective."

When you think how season 2021/22 unfolded, his words couldn't have been more prophetic. His team went for everything with all their might to put themselves in a position that no Liverpool team had ever done so before.

Klopp's Redmen went into late May 2022 as Carabao Cup winners, FA Cup winners, Champions League finalists and in a two-way fight for the Premier League title with Manchester City. Never before had any English team remained in contention to win all four trophies so deep into the season. Never before had a manager led a club to the Champions League, FA Cup and League Cup finals during the same season. And new club records for the most wins and most goals scored during a single season were also set.

Alas, an unprecedented quadruple couldn't quite be achieved. The Reds missed out on the Premier League title by one point and lost the Champions League final to Real Madrid in Paris by one goal, ending the season with two pieces of silverware.

You can't get much closer to winning all four competitions and irrespective of how the season concluded, the way Liverpool supporters embraced the journey was nothing short of magnificent.

Following your team in four competitions, domestically and abroad, is an expensive way of life for match-going Reds. Watching every Liverpool match is also challenging for supporters who pay for TV subscriptions or live in countries in different time zones. We all have to make sacrifices to follow our team. Yet whether it was in person inside stadiums or at home, in pubs, cafes or online, Klopp's team were backed to the hilt and the players appreciated it.

"Our fans were incredible at Wembley," said Andy Robertson after Liverpool beat Manchester City 3-2 in the FA Cup semi-final. "We were actually talking about the fans on the morning of the game. From our point of view it is amazing to play in all of these cup competitions, but for the fans it is so exciting but also pretty expensive.

"But our away ends are always packed and look how many fans came down to Wembley despite there being no trains and things like that. We'll never, ever take that for granted. We appreciate their support so much and how much time they put into watching us."

New songs - such as the brilliant 'Jürgen said to me you know we'll win the Premier League, you know he said so, I'm in love with him and I feel fine' tribute to the Liverpool manager - emerged, as did new banners and flags, such as IMAGINE BEING US.

In every way possible, Liverpool supporters embraced being journey hunters and it was a subject that Klopp revisited in his matchday programme notes ahead of the home game against Watford in April 2022.

"During the international break, I had the opportunity to think back to the start of the season and some of the thoughts and hopes we shared," he wrote. "One of those was arriving into the situation we find ourselves in now. A situation packed with opportunity.

"That's what we've given ourselves. A real chance. And that's fantastic.

"I'm pretty sure it was the start of the campaign when I wrote about a comment I'd heard from a supporter which I really liked. It was that the phrase 'glory hunter' can often be tagged to those drawn to following certain clubs. The point was with Liverpool it's different. It's not 'glory hunting', it's 'journey hunting'. And I think this sentiment matters more today than at any point.

"It is about the journey and we are on it. This shouldn't be twisted to suggest a specific destination either – I don't mean a specific target.

"Let's get the perspective right here. We are in three competitions right now. I'm not a person who understands betting so I'm not sure what the odds are, but I doubt very much we are favourites in any? I'm sure we are not rank outsiders either, but for certain not an outright frontrunner. That's cool.

"Also, it doesn't matter. Because it's the journey that will decide, not anyone's expectation or formula. I'm not sure if I have ever been the leader of a team who at the start of a competition was outright favourite to win it, but equally I couldn't care less. This fact has never made me fight harder to win. It wouldn't make me fight less, if the other way around.

"Being journey hunters brings its own energy. It means you get to enjoy the moment and be in every moment. Being able to embrace the thrill of the journey and realise it's where fulfilment comes, really matters. In my time at this football club I think we have done this so well as a collective. No entitlement ever. We fight so hard together, give so much together because we recognise how difficult it is to achieve these special moments.

"I'm buzzing to be back at Anfield, with a full house of supporters who are here for the journey and not just the destination. It's why this stadium is always full of energy."

I'm so glad that Jürgen is a Red, I'm so glad he delivered what he said. Thanks to our manager, his staff and an incredible group of players, journey hunting in season 2021/22 was unlike any other experience in 130 years of Liverpool Football Club. And with the Liverpool manager signing a new contract until 2026, LFC's journey under Jürgen Klopp is far from over...

Bibliography

Books

Ansnes, Ragnhild Lund. *Liverpool Captains: A Journey of Leadership from the Pitch*, De Coubertin Books, 2016

Baldursson, Arnie & Magnusson, Gudmundur. *The Liverpool Encyclopedia*, De Coubertin Books, 2013

Baldursson, Arnie & Clemente, Carl with Moran, Paul. *Mr Liverpool: Ronnie Moran*, Trinity Mirror Sport Media, 2017

Bellamy, Craig, *Goodfella: My Autobiography*, Trinity Mirror Sport Media, 2014

Busby, Matt. *My Story*, Souvenir Press, 1957

Case, Jimmy. *Hard Case: The Autobiography of Jimmy Case*, John Blake Publishing, 2014

Cocker, Mark & Mabey, Richard. *Birds Britannica*, Chatto & Windus, 2005

Crilly, Peter. *Tops of the Kop*, Trinity Mirror Sport Media, 2007

Cruyff, Johan. *My Turn: The Autobiography*, Macmillan, 2016

Dalglish, Kenny. *My Autobiography*, Hodder & Stoughton, 1996

Dalglish, Kenny. *My Life (My Scrapbook)*, Trinity Mirror Sport Media, 2013

Dalglish, Kenny. *My Liverpool Home*, Hodder & Stoughton, 2010

Dudek, Jerzy. *A Big Pole In Our Goal*, Trinity Mirror Sport Media, 2016

Enfield, William. *History of Liverpool*, London, 1774

Evans, Tony. *I Don't Know What It Is But I Love It: Liverpool's Unforgettable 1983-84 Season*, Penguin Viking, 2014

Gerrard, Steven. *Steven Gerrard: My Story*, Penguin, 2015

Gerrard, Steven. *Steven Gerrard: My Captain's Book*, Trinity Mirror Sport Media, 2008

Hale, Steve and Ponting, Ivan with Small, Steve. *Liverpool in Europe*, Carlton, 2001

Hamann, Dietmar. *The Didi Man: My Love Affair With Liverpool*, Headline, 2013

Hansen, Alan. *A Matter of Opinion*, Bantam Press, 2010

Herbert, Ian. *Quiet Genius: Bob Paisley, British Football's Greatest Manager*, Bloomsbury, 2017

Hughes, Simon. *Ring of Fire: Liverpool into the 21st Century*, Bantam Press, 2016

Jack, David. *Matt Busby: My Story*, Souvenir Press, 1957

Keith, John. *Billy Liddell – The Man Who Carried The Kop*, Robson Books, 2003

Lees, Dr Andrew & Kennedy, Ray. *Ray of Hope: The Ray Kennedy Story*, Pelham Books, 1993

McDermott, Terry. *Terry Mac: Living For The Moment*, Trinity Mirror Sport Media, 2017

McLoughlin, Chris. *Shankly: The Lost Diary*, Trinity Mirror Sport Media, 2013

McLoughlin, Chris. *Oh...I am a Liverpudlian and I come from the Spion Kop*, Trinity Mirror Sport Media, 2004

Milner, James. *Ask A Footballer*, Quercus, 2019

Nemmer, Mona. *A Taste Of The Liverpool Way*, Reach Sport, 2021

Nicol, Steve. *5 League Titles and a Packet of Crisps*, Trinity Mirror Sport Media, 2016

Platt, Mark and Hughes, William. *This Is Anfield*, Carlton, 2015

Rush, Ian. *My Scrapbook*, Trinity Mirror Sport Media, 2013

Shankly, Bill. *Shankly*, Mayflower Books, 1977

Shaw, Gary and Platt, Mark. *At The End Of The Storm*, self-published, 2009

Smith, Tommy. *Anfield Iron: The Autobiography*, Bantam Press, 2008

St John, Ian. *The Saint*, Hodder & Stoughton, 2006

Thompson, Andrew and Hale, Steve. *This Is Anfield*, Genesis Publications, 2002

Toshack, John. *Gosh It's Tosh*, Gerald Duckworth & Co Ltd, 1976

Trinity Mirror Sport Media. *Liverpool FC Family Tree*, Trinity Mirror Sport Media, 2011

Walsh, Paul. *Walshy – My Autobiography: Wouldn't It Be Good*, Trinity Mirror Sport Media, 2015

Williams, John. *Red Men – Liverpool Football Club: The Biography*, Mainstream, 2010

Newspapers
Bild
Blackburn Standard
Blackpool Gazette and Herald, Fylde News and Advertiser
Burton Chronicle
Daily Express
Daily Mirror
Derby Daily Telegraph
Football Echo
KOP
Lancashire Evening Post
Liverpool Daily Post
Liverpool Echo
Liverpool Review
Manchester Evening News
New York Press
New York Times
Sheffield Daily Telegraph
Sheffield Evening Telegraph
Somerset Standard
The Guardian
The Independent
The Times

Magazines
LFC Weekly
Liverpool FC magazine
National Geographic
The Kop Magazine

Periodicals
Joint Everton FC and Liverpool FC matchday programme
Liverpool FC matchday programme

Websites
bbc.co.uk/sport
bleacherreport.com
goal.com
lfchistory.net
lfcwsc.co.uk
liverpoolfc.com
playupliverpool.com
theunitedpages.com
thisisanfield.com
shankly.com
wikipedia.org
2gethertuneless.co.uk

TV/video
BBC The Premier League Show
BBC Women's Football Show
'Ee-ey-Addio' documentary, LFCTV
Official Liverpool FC History DVD
Panorama, BBC
Pathe News
'Pride in the Shirt' documentary, LFCTV

Radio
Radio Five Live

Social Media
Twitter
YouTube

Database/Stats
Liverpool FC Official Archives
City of Liverpool Central Library Record Office
Club statisticians Ged Rea and Dave Ball

L.F.C.
130 YEARS